Praise for *Just Like Us*

"Meticulously observant."

—The New Yorker

"Thorpe personalizes an often generalized problem, and delves into questions of opportunity and identity to examine the 'intersection between the terrible mystery of our being' and the 'inevitably flawed fashion' in which we govern ourselves."

—The Atlantic

"Through the lives of four fascinating young women, Thorpe creates not only a moving examination of a complicated American issue but a well-told, inspirational story as well."

—Kirkus Reviews

"Through the girls' heart-tugging struggles, Thorpe puts a human face on a frequently obtuse conversation, and in so doing takes us far beyond the political rhetoric."

—O, The Oprah Magazine

"With striking candor, Thorpe chronicles the girls' lives over four years. . . . She personalizes the ongoing debate over immigration."

—Publishers Weekly

"Verdict: Thorpe's work raises hundreds of questions and will be a good choice for book clubs and readers interested in narrative nonfiction. An excellent, in-depth study of immigration policies gone amok."

—Library Journal

"*Just Like Us* is an accomplished book that should be added to the short list of essential works of journalism investigating the lives of underclass people in America, such as Adrian Nicole LeBlanc's *Random Family*, Alex Kotlowitz's *There Are No Children Here*, and the Pulitzer Prize–winning reporting of Katherine Boo."

—New West

JUST LIKE US

THE TRUE STORY OF FOUR MEXICAN GIRLS
COMING OF AGE IN AMERICA

HELEN THORPE

SCRIBNER
NEW YORK   LONDON   TORONTO   SYDNEY

Scribner
A Division of Simon & Schuster, Inc.
1230 Avenue of the Americas
New York, NY 10020

First Scribner trade paperback edition May 2011

SCRIBNER and design are registered trademarks of The Gale Group, Inc., used
under license by Simon & Schuster, Inc., the publisher of this work.

For information about special discounts for bulk purchases,
please contact Simon & Schuster Special Sales at 1-866-506-1949 or
business@simonandschuster.com.

The Simon & Schuster Speakers Bureau can bring authors to your
live event. For more information or to book an event, contact
the Simon & Schuster Speakers Bureau at 1-866-248-3049 or
visit our website at www.simonspeakers.com.

Designed by Carla Jayne Jones

Manufactured in the United States of America

7   9   10   8   6

Library of Congress Control Number: 2009022722

ISBN 978-1-4165-3893-6
ISBN 978-1-4165-3898-1 (pbk)
ISBN 978-1-4391-6625-3 (ebook)

FOR TEDDY

CONTENTS

CONTENTS

JUST LIKE US

INTRODUCTION

A few years ago, I had the honor of meeting four young women who were going to high school in Denver, Colorado. They had been friends since middle school; by the time I met them, they knew almost everything about one another. All four came from families who had emigrated from Mexico, and each had at least one parent who had crossed the border without a legal entry visa. The girls inherited various standings: one was born a U.S. citizen, one became a legal resident, and two lacked documents. And under current law the two without papers had no way to acquire legal status, for their parents had brought them into this country without obtaining permission from the federal government, rendering them ineligible for residency or citizenship as long as they remained on U.S. soil. They were armed to brave adulthood in different ways, and as they passed the milestones of their youth, their legal status began to affect how they saw one another. I thought the story of their interconnected relationships illuminated the vagaries of current immigration law. Also, since they were about to leave the safety of high school for an uncertain future, I wanted to know what would happen to them.

The question of what it was like for the girls to come of age in an adopted homeland intrigued me because I thought I shared something in common with them. Both of my parents were born and raised in Ireland and immigrated to England in search of work. I was born in London in 1965 and a year later we immigrated to the United States, which gave me an odd sense of dual identity. I was from another place, yet it didn't feel that way most of the time, as the only country I really knew was this one. At the same time, I did not feel 100 percent American, either. I grew up carrying a green card until I was twenty-one and became a naturalized citizen. By then I had learned how to hold fealty to two places: I had grown up making transatlantic telephone calls to faraway relatives, mailing overseas packages on the holidays, and traveling to see my Irish cousins every other summer. When I was in high school, I had to explain what *freshman* and *sophomore* meant to my mother, because she had never heard those words before. But of course I had no idea what it was like to be labeled an illegal alien. I didn't know what it was like to translate for a parent, or to purchase fake documents, or to hide the truth about my identity. I was drawn to the four girls because we had something in common and we had nothing in common, because they had been assigned a position at the bottom of society and I had gained a spot at the top. I wanted to know if they were anything like the person I had been at their age and what kind of relationship they had with America.

After I had been following the girls for more than a year, fate drew my family into the immigration debate in a shocking and personal way. John Hickenlooper, then the mayor of Denver and presently the governor of Colorado—to whom I am married—became engulfed in a local political scandal, after an immigrant who lacked legal status committed a shocking murder in our hometown. I had been working as a journalist for fifteen years when I met John and was used to operating independently and without obvious conflicts of interest; suddenly there was no way for me to write about the girls without addressing a crime that affected my own spouse. In the process, I also came to know and care about relatives of the murder victim, whose lives had been shattered by the actions of an illegal immigrant. I had imagined that the girls and I would stay sequestered in the part of town where they had spent their formative years—that we would remain in the barrio—but we did not. Instead, a suburban family suffered the worst kind of loss, my own family became embroiled in controversy, the political world became obsessed with immigrants, and the undocumented students I knew took to the streets. Fortune handed me a messy braid of narratives, spliced together by bizarre connections. In the end, though, this is what immigration is like: inherently messy. The issue bleeds. And we are all implicated.

I'm not sure if the girls expected something in return for the hours we spent together. I made it clear on several occasions that I could not give them financial assistance, but sometimes I wondered if they expected some other, less tangible form of aid. Eventually, I came to see that the girls craved legitimacy, and I suspect they found it in some roundabout way by spending time with me. When I asked them about their lives, it might have seemed to them as though Denver itself was interested in who they were—given the position my husband occupied in the city's hierarchy—and if that was the case, then I suppose our conversations may have provided them with a sense of being recognized, a sense of being seen as important.

For my part, I have to say that it was often a relief to step into their world. The girls served as an antidote to everything else that was happening in my life. When I wasn't with them, I socialized with people who belonged to exclusive clubs and wore gowns to charity balls and hired private chefs for their dinner parties—which wasn't what I was used to. The girls kept me from becoming overwhelmed by high society. Their families reminded me of my own, despite our many differences, and being with them kept me in touch with my origins. The girls also helped me hold on to my youth: As I spent time in their company, I learned how to send text messages and started dressing less conservatively and relived my girlhood relationships. In the neighborhoods where the girls lived, few people had expectations of the mayor's wife, and I was free to be myself. Overall, I am certain that I got at least as much from the girls as any one of the girls may have gotten from me. And probably much more.

Many people in this book entered the country illegally, and to protect them from any repercussions, I have changed their names. I have also changed the names of all the students mentioned in these pages, whether or not they have legal status, and the names of certain adults. In addition, I have changed key details about several of the main characters, out of concern that they might suffer retribution if they are publicly identified or that identifying them might in turn identify others who are vulnerable. Otherwise, to the best of my knowledge, everything that follows is true.

PART I

INSTANTANEOUS RATE OF CHANGE

I

PROM NIGHT

Three-quarters of the way through her final year of high school, Marisela Benavídez ran into a problem. Her father wanted to attend her senior prom. Marisela went to an inner-city public school in Denver, Colorado, that I will call Theodore Roosevelt High School. On Friday, April 23, 2004, twenty-four hours before the prom, she took a break from arguing with her father to appear in the school's annual dance recital. Halfway through the performance, Marisela breezed into the auditorium looking like a Vegas showgirl. She wore tight black satin trousers, a see-through white shirt, a revealing black camisole, copious amounts of makeup, and a liberal application of silver body glitter. Her hair was a froth of curls. It was intermission, and Marisela had come in search of her friends, still wearing her dance costume. As soon as she appeared in the audience, a group of peers moved into orbit around her—in their galaxy, she had the gravitational pull of a large star. One of the girls asked about Marisela's ongoing negotiations with her conservative Mexican father.

"I don't know what to do!" cried Marisela. "He still says he's going to come!"

For several years, Marisela and her parents had been warring over the pace at which she was growing up and the extent of her Americanization. Marisela was a straight-A student—AP chemistry, AP calculus, AP literature, Chicano studies, sociology, and dance—who also liked to party. She divided her time equally between boys and books. The question of whether she would be allowed to go to the prom without her father marked the latest in a series of battles over how much freedom she should be allowed. As usual, Marisela was using the conflict to entertain her peers. Her best friend stood beside her. Yadira Vargas and Marisela Benavídez were wearing exactly the same attire but remained a study in opposites. Marisela was dark-skinned and had a round face and a full figure. She wore twice as much makeup as anybody else in her circle, and her shoulder-length hair changed color often. At the moment, it was auburn, but the month before it had been brown with gold streaks, which had highlighted the unusual gold tint of her eyes. This was not their natural color—she wore gold contact lenses to enhance her appearance. And yet, in spite of all this artifice, Marisela's features constantly betrayed her emotions. In contrast, Yadira was slender, had lighter skin, wore modest amounts of makeup, always kept her long black hair its natural color, and never gave away anything important with her facial expressions. While Marisela was loud and boisterous, Yadira made such a small emotional footprint that, were it not for her striking coltish figure, it might be possible to forget she was present at all. Right now she remained quiet as Marisela announced her woes with abandon.

"I'm getting cramps—right before prom!" Marisela told us.

Despite their differences, the two girls had become close because they both faced the prospect of graduating from high school without legal status or a legitimate Social Security number, their main concern for months until they got distracted with the prom. Now all that mattered was what color dresses to wear, how to fix their hair, and what to say to Marisela's father. They settled on getting ready at Marisela's apartment. It would take about five hours, they calculated, and they were going out to dinner before the prom, so they planned to start primping at noon the next day.

Recently Marisela and her family had moved to Lakewood, a suburb west of Denver where rents were cheaper. At twelve on Saturday—the day of the prom—I pulled up at their new apartment complex. It consisted of a vast warren of boxy cinder-block structures, all painted light green. The complex had the air of a place that had seen many tenants come and go, and the dilapidated cars in the parking lot suggested that their owners did not have a lot of money. A concrete walkway led to the ground-floor apartment where Marisela's family now lived. Outside, I found her father, Fabián, with her mother, Josefa, and their younger daughter, Rosalinda. Fabián worked for a janitorial company called National Maintenance, waxing the floors of commercial properties at night, and Josefa worked for a maid service, cleaning houses. Josefa was a pretty thirty-four-year-old woman with a round face and full figure like Marisela. While Josefa had a warm, jolly manner, Fabián looked more severe. He was forty-two, and had high cheekbones, a long nose framed by grooved lines, and a goatee. At the moment, his face wore a forbidding expression. Fabián was mercurial—he could be gregarious, but he could also fly into a fury without warning. Now he seemed preoccupied with thoughts of what Marisela might be up to this evening, as she had been behaving secretively. Fabián was almost as Mexican as he had been when he first came to the United States, but his daughter was a hybrid—someone he could not fully understand. Fabián explained in Spanish that Marisela wasn't at home; she had gone to pick up several friends. Then two roly-poly boys emerged from the apartment, and Fabián's mood lightened. He grabbed one of the boys and began tickling him furiously.

"This is Rafael, my youngest son," he said proudly in Spanish. "He's the fattest in our family, too!"

Fabián pointed to the older boy, Nestor. "He is just like Marisela—straight A's."

"All of our children are good students," interjected Josefa, also in Spanish.

"That's right," echoed Fabián. "They all get good grades."

Fabián and Josefa spoke almost no English, and my Spanish was scant, but whenever we failed to understand each other, the boys would translate for us. We expressed wonder at the idea that Marisela and her friends planned to spend five hours getting dressed. What were they going to do for that copious amount of time?

"Dad says that Marisela puts on so much makeup, she looks like a clown!" Nestor hooted.

Josefa called Marisela to check on her progress. "*Cinco minutos,*" she reported.

"*Quieres agua?*" Fabián asked.

I accepted a glass of water and Fabián joined me. He had recently stopped drinking alcohol and his body had started aching as a result. He had been much happier when he drank, but admitted that he could not do so in moderation and had sometimes consumed up to thirty beers a day. Drinking helped him sleep during the day, enabling him to work nights. But Fabián could no longer afford to court oblivion so assiduously—not when his older daughter was challenging his authority.

"*El carro!*" shouted Rafael, announcing the arrival of Marisela's car. "They're here!"

We all stared as Marisela, Yadira, and two friends walked up the concrete walkway carrying gowns, shoe boxes, suitcases, and bags filled with makeup. Marisela and Yadira belonged to a close-knit foursome along with two other girls who had similar backgrounds, and one of them, Clara Luz, had opted to dress at Marisela's house, too. The fourth girl, Elissa Ramírez, was going to meet them later at Cinzetti's, the Italian restaurant where they were having dinner. Meanwhile, a friend named Annalisa had tagged along to get ready at Marisela's, even though she was not part of the foursome.

The girls marched into the apartment and through the living room to Marisela's bedroom. Frilly curtains framed the windows and a shag carpet covered the floor. On the walls were two portraits of Marisela: the first showed her in a vampy pose, wearing a red strapless dress, while the second caught her looking pensive, holding her chin in her hand—the sexpot and the thinker. Her sister Rosalinda pointed to the photographs and said breathlessly, "Everybody thinks she should be a model!"

Eight of us crowded into the bedroom: the four high school seniors, Marisela's mother, Rosalinda, me, and a teenager wearing a pair of striped flannel pajamas who had shown up unexpectedly. She turned out to live next door. Marisela turned on the TV to a Spanish-language game show, which everyone ignored, and Yadira carefully unpacked her suitcase. It contained silver jewelry, three different curling irons, her gown, which was navy blue with swirly silver lines on it, and a black sweater with a faux fur collar. Yadira carefully hung up her clothes to make sure they didn't get wrinkled. The other girls unpacked in a more helter-skelter fashion, and within minutes, Marisela's bed was covered in hair ties, bobby pins, body glitter, cosmetics, bags of cotton balls, shoes, purses, and brand-new costume jewelry still pinned to white cardboard backing.

Yadira's cell phone rang. "I just wanted to tell you that we got a boutonniere for you," she said. There was a pause. "It's like a corsage, but for guys," she explained. Her boyfriend, Juan, was a junior at a different high school. Juan spent his free time fixing up cars or driving them around. He aspired to become an auto mechanic, although like his girlfriend he did not possess legal status or a legitimate Social Security number. Nor did the boy who Marisela had invited to the prom. A few weeks ago, she had started dating a tall, attractive sophomore at Roosevelt High, but their relationship seemed highly flexible, as she had invited a former boyfriend, Fernando, to be her date instead. She considered Fernando the love of her life, much to the dismay of her parents. Marisela had started dating Fernando two years prior; they had met at a Mexican nightclub in Denver. (Although she was under-age, Marisela had no difficulty getting into clubs with a fake Mexican driver's license that added three years to her age.) Marisela had dated Fernando until he moved to Arizona to work in construction. The major drama of the past few weeks had been the question of whether Fernando and Marisela could achieve their hoped-for reunion, given certain logistical challenges. The first difficulty was the matter of how Fernando would travel from Arizona to Colorado that day. He had to work the day before, and could not fly from Phoenix to Denver, as he lacked the identification needed to board an airplane. Therefore Fernando had set out by car that morning at four A.M. to make the 930-mile journey in time to join them for dinner.

The second difficulty was what to tell Marisela's parents, who had forbidden her to see Fernando ever again. Both Fabián and Josefa had grown up in small towns in rural Mexico. They disapproved of Marisela's freewheeling American lifestyle, and Fernando struck them as the type to lead their rebellious daughter further astray. Marisela had lied and told her parents she was going to the prom with a young man named Vicente, who had promised to pose with her for a formal photograph to bolster her story. Her parents were suspicious, however, which was why her father thought she needed a chaperone. For days, Marisela had been trying to convince Fabián that parents didn't go to proms in America, but Fabián found her claim highly questionable.

As soon as Marisela's mother left the bedroom, Clara asked for an update on Fernando's progress. Marisela disclosed the latest drama: Eight hours after he'd left Phoenix, Fernando's car had broken down, leaving him marooned somewhere on the side of Interstate 25. He had convinced two friends from Denver to pick him up, and the rescue mission was now in progress, but Marisela did not know when he would arrive.

"Maybe he'll be fat and ugly!" said Clara gleefully.

"I haven't seen him in six months. Who knows?" replied Marisela with equanimity.

Marisela was waiting for a professional hairdresser, and offered to help the other girls arrange their hair until the stylist, Yolanda, arrived. Clara wanted to leave her hair down, but Marisela pronounced this idea unacceptable. Both Clara and Yadira agreed to let the Benavídez girls put up their hair in twisties, which involved parting their hair in a checkerboard pattern, pulling each square into a small ponytail, and inverting the ponytails. Clara sat cross-legged on the floor before Rosalinda, and Yadira sat before Marisela. Marisela's big-toothed comb proved unwieldy, however, so she decided to use a pen. "I won't write on you, I promise," she told Yadira. "Oh, never mind! I'm writing on you already."

Then she announced to the room, "We should have bought more hair spray, you guys."

"I have hair spray," said Clara.

"I have hair spray, too," said Yadira.

Yadira wondered out loud if the twisties were going to give her a headache.

"Just sit down and have the boy rub your head," suggested the girl in pajamas.

Yadira said she was hungry, and Clara said she was, too, but Marisela decided that nobody could eat. Then Yadira said she was bored, and Marisela told her that she was complaining too much. Clara scrunched up her face in pain as Rosalinda began inverting her ponytails. Yadira pronounced that she did not like her twisties, and Marisela began using a skinny curling iron on her hair instead. "*Oye!* You are burning me!" Yadira protested.

Unconcerned, Marisela applied a cloud of hair spray and unrolled one perfect ringlet, immobilized in a tight coil.

"Look! *Todo así,*" urged Marisela.

"Do all my hair like that? It's going to take forever!" objected Yadira, who had slipped into a black mood.

I began to appreciate why this might take some time.

"Okay, I am getting dizzy," conceded Marisela. "I need food, too."

Marisela left and returned with a bag of *pan dulce*—white cake with shockingly bright pink icing.

"Yolanda is making me nervous because she's not here yet. What can I do? Do you want me to do your makeup, Clara?"

Clara, who almost never wore makeup, seemed alarmed. "Um, you could do my nails," she said.

"What? You don't like the way I do my makeup?" cried Marisela. "I wasn't going to do it like mine!"

Yadira pulled her hair into a ponytail, swathed herself in a furious cloud of hair spray, then took the ponytail down.

"I hate hair," she pronounced.

"You're lost, huh?" said Marisela's little sister sympathetically.

"Yeah," said Yadira miserably, picking up the *pan dulce*. "I think I'll just eat."

At last Yolanda arrived. She was a large woman in stretchy pants and a striped T-shirt. After Marisela selected an image of a smiling model with straight hair and a wild topknot of curls from one of the magazines that Yolanda had brought, the stylist set to work. Yolanda pulled mousse through Marisela's hair and cordoned off a section of it. Stiff with mousse, the topknot stuck straight up in the air. The hairdresser plugged in a fat curling iron with bristles that blew hot air from its vents. With this tool, she started curling Marisela's topknot, but then Yolanda got some of Marisela's hair stuck in the bristles and spent several minutes yanking it out. The topknot looked worse than ever.

To make conversation, Yolanda asked what Marisela was planning to do after she graduated from high school. The hairdresser must have expected to hear that Marisela was going to work or to marry, as that would have been typical for a student from Roosevelt, but instead Marisela told Yolanda that she was waiting to hear back from the University of Denver, a private institution with a high-caliber faculty.

"Oh, yeah?" Yolanda asked, obviously surprised.

"Yeah," said Marisela, with pride.

"Waiting to hear—when?"

"Next week. I'm nervous."

The possibility of going to the University of Denver had just come up, and Marisela viewed it as her only chance to get a college degree. If she had possessed legal status, she would have been able to afford community college, but the state of Colorado classified immigrants who lacked documents as international students, which meant they did not qualify for in-state tuition. Because she did not have a legitimate Social Security number, Marisela also did not qualify for a Pell grant, financial aid, or many private scholarships. The unspoken question hanging over the girls at the moment was whether Marisela was about to be left behind. Clara and Elissa both had legitimate Social Security numbers, and each of them had received substantial offers of financial aid. Meanwhile, in a surprising twist, Yadira had secured a private benefactor. Only Marisela still had no idea how she would pay for higher education—unless she won a private scholarship to the University of Denver. Her only other hope was that some government body might act in time to help her. Members of the state legislature had been debating what to do with undocumented students since the beginning of the calendar year, and members of the U.S. Congress had been discussing the subject, too, but so far neither group of officials had taken any action.

College-bound students were likely to lead stable, middle-class lives, while students who went no further than Roosevelt were likely to live in rental houses and do menial work. Which kind of life was Marisela going to lead? She had one foot in the orderly world of Advanced Placement classes and one foot in the precarious world of her parents. Meanwhile, watching Marisela encounter so many difficulties had unnerved the other girls, who were used to considering her an expert on matters they considered important, such as math, boys, and grooming.

Now Rosalinda handed Clara a mirror to show her the twisties.

"I'm done," Clara declared.

"Clara, come here," ordered Marisela. "It's too simple."

"I'm simple! Let me be simple!"

"Okay, do your makeup," Marisela conceded.

Clara began to apply blush, but Marisela said she should apply foundation first. Clara picked up a small black compact.

"Is that powder?" Marisela asked. The compact contained powder in a shade that matched Clara's fair skin. "Oh, yes," commented Marisela. "White, *white* powder." She wiped a streak onto her face, where it stood out like flour. "Look!" she giggled.

Irene Chávez arrived, bearing boutonnieres and corsages. Irene, who served as a mentor to the girls, had fine brown hair and merry brown eyes. Although many people mistook her for Latina, she was actually Anglo—her maiden name was McKenna—but during the 1960s and 1970s Irene had participated in the women's movement, the antiwar movement, the civil rights movement, and the Chicano movement. She had met Justino Chávez while they were both serving on a volunteer committee to support the United Farm Workers of America. Irene and Justino remained active in various political causes, and when the girls were in their sophomore year of high school, the couple had recruited them to help stop a political initiative that would have banned bilingual education as it was being practiced in Colorado. Halfway through Yadira's senior year of high school, her family had abruptly decided to relocate to California, and at that point Yadira had moved in with Irene and Justino. Now Irene had bought each of the girls a corsage and a matching boutonniere, anticipating that their own parents would not know enough about American culture to supply these accessories.

"Okay, these have to go in the fridge," Irene pronounced and bustled off.

Clara pulled a long black dress dotted with tiny red roses out of Marisela's closet, where she had hung it up earlier.

"Where did you get that dress?" Marisela asked in Spanish.

"JCPenney," Clara replied.

Marisela reached out to examine the price tag, and saw it had cost $150.

"*Ciento cincuenta!*" she exclaimed. "*Por qué?*"

"Because it's one of a kind."

"So is mine!"

"Are you *sure*?" taunted Clara. "Wait till you get there."

"I'm sure! Wait till *you* get there!"

When Irene returned, Marisela asked to borrow her cell phone so that she could call Fernando, saying dramatically that she couldn't use her own phone, because her parents might check to see what phone numbers she had dialed. Irene was older than Marisela's mother, but her relationship with the girls was part guardian angel, part older sister, and she happily gave Marisela her cell phone.

"It's so romantic!" cried Irene. "He's on a mission to take her to the prom. It's like a *novela*!"

Fernando didn't answer.

"I'm wearing too much makeup," Clara worried, scrutinizing her face in the mirror.

"Let me see," ordered Marisela. "No, you're not. Put *blanco* here." She pointed to Clara's brow bone.

"*Blanco?*" questioned Clara.

"*O algo,*" said Marisela, with a wave of her hand. Or something.

Clara decided to consult Yolanda, who was, after all, a professional.

"*Qué color?*" she asked Yolanda, holding up her black and red gown.

"*Azul,*" said Yolanda decisively.

"*Azul,*" repeated Clara doubtfully. "Okay, Marisela, do you have blue?"

Marisela pointed to a large black leather case. Inside, Clara beheld various shelves of eye shadow, grouped by color—there were eight different varieties of blue.

Soon Marisela had a flourish of perfect curls on top of her head, held in place with silver and paste clips. She inspected Yolanda's work in a hand mirror.

"*Sí! Me gusta!*" she pronounced enthusiastically.

Yolanda methodically applied hair spray to Marisela's elaborate coiffure, continuing long past the point that seemed healthy. Marisela left to show her mother, and after a moment we heard howls of laughter from the next room. When Marisela came back, she explained Nestor was entertaining the rest of the family by joking that he wanted to get ready for the prom, too, and had just announced that he needed to borrow some of his sister's fancy undergarments. "My brother wants to come in and look for a bra," she said wearily.

Then Clara accidentally sprayed everybody with deodorant. She had intended to aim for her underarm, but had pointed the aerosol can in the wrong direction. We all turned in her direction.

"Whew!" said Irene.

"I feel watched!" yelped Clara, one arm still pointing at the ceiling.

In a surprising move, Clara had applied dark pink eye shadow, along with brown lipstick, and now looked vaguely punkish.

Marisela borrowed Irene's phone again and this time she reached Fernando. "He's only half an hour away!" she reported. Marisela disappeared into the bathroom to put on her gown, and came back a vision in clingy aqua. The dress was backless, and from behind she appeared half naked. Too preoccupied to enjoy the impression that she made, however, Marisela knelt down and spoke urgently to Clara. Apparently Fabián and Josefa wanted to speak with Marisela's friend, who went to church faithfully and never frequented nightclubs. Adults viewed her as utterly reliable.

"They're going to interrogate you!" warned Marisela. "You have to talk to them—but you can't tell them anything!"

"What do I say?" asked Clara fearfully.

Marisela instructed Clara to confirm that Vicente was Marisela's date. Clara should also say that in America it was not customary for fathers to accompany their daughters to the prom.

"They want to go with me!" Marisela moaned to Irene.

"I want to go, too, but I'm restraining myself," Irene replied nonchalantly.

"You guys, we only have one hour left!" warned Yadira, waving a mascara wand around.

Yolanda began to apply Marisela's makeup. In a few minutes, Marisela wore a little blush, a lot of lip gloss, and vast oceans of blue eye shadow. She wondered out loud if her father would approve. "It's always too much for him," Marisela said with a sigh.

Yadira hadn't begun to dress, but her head was now covered in perfect, shiny ringlets.

"Your hair looks great, Yadira!" complimented Marisela.

"See, none of those twisties or anything," replied her best friend.

Clara came back and flashed Marisela an okay sign. It seemed that she had survived the interrogation without disclosing any secrets. Marisela waltzed into the living room and pirouetted before Fabián and Josefa, who sat on the sofa looking dazed by their daughter's transformation, while soccer players stormed unnoticed across the television screen. The few strings holding Marisela's dress in place seemed barely adequate to the job of keeping it on her body. "Okay, *Papí*?" she asked. Fabián wore his forbidding expression, but nodded silently. Back in the bedroom, Yolanda began spraying silver body glitter all over Marisela. Then Clara, who typically dressed like a tomboy, appeared shyly in her dress, which had a halter-style neckline and a hem that came up over one knee. She had traveled farther than the rest from her usual self—we were catching a glimpse of some future, grown-up Clara, in her elegant attire and strange makeup.

Yadira pointed to the large gold crucifix that her friend always wore.

"I don't take it off," said Clara firmly.

Marisela handed her fake ID over to Clara, saying sotto voce that her parents would probably search her purse, although they did nothing of the kind. When Yadira put on her slim navy sheath, she looked even more willowy than usual. She wore silver sandals and her toenails were painted silver and her eyes gleamed with silver shadow—she had become a silver and blue sylph. Marisela was spraying Yadira with body glitter when their dates arrived. The young men trooped into the apartment wearing ill-fitting tuxedos and foolish expressions. They nodded affably to Marisela's parents and tried not to stare too much at the girls.

"Oh, the flowers, the flowers!" cried Irene, running to the kitchen.

Fabián manned a Polaroid. He took a shot of Marisela alone, a shot of Marisela with the boys, a shot of Marisela with me, a shot of Marisela with Irene, and a shot of all the girls. Soon every member of Marisela's family was waving a damp Polaroid around in the air. Then one of the boys, oblivious to the danger they were in, asked casually if Fernando had made it yet. Marisela hissed at him to *shut up, shut up,* then called out loudly, "I just need to brush my teeth!"

"I just have to do my hair!" squeaked Nestor in a falsetto.

Rafael translated this for his father, who howled.

"You guys!" chastised Marisela.

As Marisela brushed her teeth, her brothers performed a wild pantomime of spraying themselves all over for the benefit of the crowd. They were still horsing around when she returned. *"Vámonos!"* cried Marisela. And she slipped away to meet her real date. The seniors gabbed excitedly as they strolled down the concrete walkway toward their cars, a bright cavalcade of unexpected glamour passing through the dreary courtyard. The adults who were being left behind spilled out to witness their eye-catching departure. Josefa called out to her daughter in Spanish to lift up her dress, which was dragging on the ground, and Marisela heeded her mother's advice, but did not look back. In the end, Fabián's threats of chaperoning proved empty. Once he had been able to keep his daughter safe within his orbit, but now she had traveled beyond his control, and maybe that was what all the fuss had been about.

Fernando was waiting for Marisela at Cinzetti's, just as attractive as ever. He had brought along the two friends who had rescued him on I-25, and Marisela immediately invited them to come to the prom, too, pointing out that neither Clara nor Annalisa had dates. After consuming large plates of pasta, everybody squeezed into several cars and drove in a caravan to the prom. It took place at a rented social hall, where a DJ played both hip-hop and *reggaetón,* the fast-paced music from Puerto Rico. Marisela objected that the DJ didn't play enough Mexican music—she would have preferred to hear *música norteña, ranchera,* or *cumbia*—but she spent a lot of time on the dance floor anyway. As the evening progressed, one of Fernando's friends fell for Clara, looking lovely in her black dress with the red roses on it, but she spurned his advances and he left early. Meanwhile, Yadira and Juan were like an island unto themselves. Fernando had such a good time with Marisela, he asked if she would be his girlfriend again. She declined, however, unwilling to go that far in defying her parents' wishes.

All the girls who had gotten ready at Marisela's plus their friend Elissa eventually made it back to the apartment in Lakewood somewhere around four in the morning. Then they started drinking—christening the special commemorative glasses inscribed with the date of their prom—and fixed a late-night snack. Just as the sun started to come up, they all piled into Marisela's big double bed together, having abandoned their dates to spend the night with one another.

The four girls had forged their bonds from myriad nights like this—from years of secrets, squabbles, and private jokes, years of out-maneuvering their Mexican parents, years of figuring out adulthood and America, which for them often seemed like one and the same thing. Now they wondered whether their friendship would survive the changes that loomed before them. The prom had served as a temporary distraction, but once it was over they became preoccupied again with the issue that had concerned them for more than a year: All four of the girls shared the same kind of dreams about the future, yet only two of them appeared to have a clear path forward. Yadira had figured out an interim solution to the problem of growing up without legal status, but Marisela had not yet arrived at a solution of any kind. Now no major event stood between the girls and the moment when they would graduate from high school, in exactly one month's time. At that point, Marisela would have to solve the question of how to create a meaningful life in the United States without a green card or Social Security number. She still had no answer for this riddle, and because she was the kind of student who was accustomed to having the right answers all the time, being without a response to a query of such vast proportions filled her with unease. Being a teenager, she worried about this predicament primarily in terms of what it would mean for her socially, because she would have to watch her three closest friends achieve a type of success that appeared to be out of her reach. And Marisela had good reason to fear that she might lose her friends in the process, for the subject of college had already caused the four girls to suffer their first major rift.

2

QUESTION MARK

I first met Marisela, Yadira, Clara, and Elissa two-thirds of the way through their senior year of high school, when the saga of how their immigration status was affecting their relationships was beginning to unfold. It was early in March 2004—almost two months before the senior prom—and the girls had been at odds with one another all winter. A friend of a friend had introduced me to Elissa, who arranged for all of us to have lunch at a chain restaurant the girls frequented called the Old Country Buffet, in a suburb on the west side of the metro area. The four girls were standing together outside the restaurant when I pulled up. Looking them over, I could not discern who had documents and who did not, although I knew the group was bifurcated along lines of legal standing. Elissa had shoulder-length medium-brown hair, an athletic build, and a scattering of freckles across her nose. She had won several leadership awards in high school, as well as two varsity letters (soccer and swimming), and she was the kind of person who applied lessons from the playing field to life. If the four girls had been a sports team, Elissa would have been their captain. Clara was wearing blue jeans, sneakers, a T-shirt, a sweat jacket, and the gold crucifix that she never took off. Her plain attire made me think of her as boyish, though I soon learned that she was also the sensitive one—the person who cried most easily, the friend who saw everybody else's side. Marisela was the dramatic one, the girl who experimented with everything first; her clothing was flashy and she had on a lot of makeup—foundation, blush, mascara, eyeliner, and eye shadow in three different shades of brown. Meeting Yadira for the first time, I was startled by her figure, for she was as skinny as a runway model. It was hard to get a sense of her personality, given her reserve, but she had dressed boldly in tight jeans with pegged legs, a belt with silver chains hanging from it, and a tiny T-shirt that revealed her flat midriff.

All four girls had grown up on the west side of Denver, a part of town that has traditionally been home to many Latinos. Denver is a city of half a million people located on the edge of the Great Plains, hard beside the Rocky Mountains; those spectacular peaks dominate the city's skyline. When residents of the city are lost, they typically orient themselves by noting that the mountains lie to the west. The city's downtown area is all modern glass and steel skyscrapers, and the historic lower downtown area features old redbrick warehouses. Coors Field, Invesco Field at Mile High, and the Pepsi Center are centrally located, since Denver is a sports town. No matter what time of year it is, people are always rooting for at least one of the city's eight professional sports teams: the Avalanche, the Broncos, the Crush, the Mammoth, the Nuggets, the Outlaws, the Rapids, or the Rockies. Surrounding this urban core are a series of leafy, kid-strewn neighborhoods that fall within the city limits. Another two million people live in suburban communities that ring the city and, generally speaking, these suburbs have tended to be less ethnically diverse and more politically conservative than the city itself, although lately that has been changing, as more people of color have started to move to the outskirts of the metro area, where the cost of living can be cheaper.

In recent decades, Colorado has become a magnet for both retirees and immigrants, making the state a prime example of how much the United States has changed from a demographic point of view. During the 1990s, local newspapers began calling Denver the "baby boomer capital," because it had the highest percentage of baby boomers in the United States. Meanwhile, from 1990 to 2000 the number of foreign-born people living in Denver tripled. Recognizing that Denver had become a major hub for newly arrived immigrants, the Brookings Institution designated it a gateway city. Denver currently has a huge Mexican population, the largest Mongolian enclave in the United States, and sizable Russian, Polish, Ethiopian, Lebanese, Cambodian, Chinese, Eastern Indian, Filipino, Hmong, Japanese, Korean, Laotian, Pacific Islander, Thai, and Vietnamese communities. One-quarter of the students enrolled in the city's public schools are categorized as English Language Learners, because that is not their native tongue.

Inside the Old Country Buffet, the clientele fell into two categories: aging white people and young Latinos. The four girls and I sat down at a long table at the other end of which sat an elderly couple. Within a short time, Yadira identified herself as one of the students who didn't have legal status, and Marisela soon volunteered that she didn't, either. The two undocumented girls and I occupied the same position within our respective families: We were the oldest children, the ones who had been born somewhere else before our parents settled here.

The four girls explained that they had met in eighth grade, back when they were awkward adolescents at an urban middle school in Denver. Marisela had befriended Elissa in an English-speaking class, while Yadira had become close with Clara in a class taught in Spanish. Those were the original pairings back when they'd been aligned according to disposition. Marisela and Elissa were the outgoing ones, while Clara and Yadira were introverted. By the time the four girls started their freshman year at Roosevelt High, they had become inseparable. They slept over at one another's houses, went to parties together, took the same courses. All four spoke English fluently by this point, even though they spoke Spanish at home; among themselves, they switched back and forth. They were oblivious to the differences in their immigration status since it did not affect them in any tangible way during the early years of their friendship.

Back in those days, Clara had lacked legal status, too. Clara could not recall precisely when she learned that two of her friends were growing up without documents—she just remembered that in middle school they were all "on the same level." When she was seven, Clara had crawled under the wire fence that separated the town of Nogales, Sonora, from the town of Nogales, Arizona, with her mother and three siblings. She had no concept of what it meant to be an illegal immigrant at the time; the main thing on her mind was that now she would get to live with her father. Carlos Luz worked at a meatpacking plant in Colorado, and by that point he had obtained a green card, having successfully applied for amnesty when the U.S. Congress passed the Immigration Reform and Control Act of 1986. It took six years for Clara and her siblings to acquire legal residence. During that time, an unscrupulous attorney stole several thousand dollars of their father's money, and he had to start saving all over again. They were lucky, however, because federal law prohibits granting legal status to anybody who has entered the country illegally; as it happened, Clara, her siblings, and their mother were fortunate enough to apply for citizenship during a time when this prohibition was temporarily lifted for close relatives of legal residents of the United States, thanks to a family reunification program that no longer exists. Clara acquired both a green card and a genuine Social Security number right before her sophomore year of high school, just in time to become eligible for all kinds of funding for college.

Meanwhile, Elissa had acquired U.S. citizenship at birth, even though her parents were living in the border town of Ciudad Juárez, Chihuahua, at the time. Her mother had walked across the border and delivered Elissa in a clinic in El Paso, Texas, because she wanted her child to have an American birth certificate. After Elissa turned three, her family moved to California and then to Colorado. While Elissa's father got a green card, her mother worked without papers for several years before gaining legal status. As a result, Elissa felt as though her heritage was indistinguishable from Yadira's and Marisela's. "I was born in the United States, but I'm Mexican inside, you know?" she explained. It was not yet clear to her how divisive the matter of her privilege would prove to be.

Not surprisingly, the four girls hailed from the three states in Mexico that send the largest number of people to Colorado. Elissa is from Chihuahua, which sends more immigrants to Colorado than any other state in Mexico, while Clara is from Zacatecas, which sends the second greatest number of immigrants. Durango, where both Yadira and Marisela were born, ranks third on the list of Mexican states that send people to Colorado. Only the two girls with legal status returned to Mexico during school breaks. Yadira and Marisela were unable to visit their birthplace for fear of not being able to return to the United States. Consequently, the two who legally qualified as Americans knew more about Mexico than did the two Mexican nationals, which all four girls considered a great irony.

The four girls had grown up believing they were equals. They had held on to this belief until their junior year of high school, when they became old enough to drive. Marisela and Yadira were among the first undocumented immigrants to come of age in Colorado after the state legislature had passed a law called the Colorado Secure and Verifiable Identity Document Act, which made it impossible for them to obtain legitimate Colorado driver's licenses. (Fabián and Josefa had been able to procure driver's licenses when they first moved to the state, but under the new law they would not be able to renew them.) "When I was growing up I didn't really think about it," Marisela said of her illegal status. "It hit me when I wanted to get a driver's license, and I couldn't. So I started driving with a Mexican driver's license—a fake. And that's when I realized how I was going to grow up—doing everything the wrong way."

The girls needed driver's licenses for all kinds of reasons. Yadira found it impossible to get into nightclubs without identification, for example. Marisela purchased fake IDs that would get her into clubs, but couldn't get a permit to park her car in the lot at Roosevelt High because she needed a valid U.S. driver's license to get the permit. Clara flew with other classmates to Washington, D.C., but neither of the undocumented girls could go on the trip because they lacked the necessary ID to board the airplane. Once Yadira even tried to rent a movie from Blockbuster, but was unable to when the store clerk asked to see a license. The two undocumented girls could open checking accounts, but nobody would take their checks since neither could show proof of identity—nor could they apply to get credit cards.

The slow accumulation of ordinary things that they could not do became painful for the girls who lacked legal status to endure, especially given that their legal friends were able to accomplish basic tasks without difficulties. But nothing was more painful than the subject of college, which had also come up during their junior year. "The teachers say: 'Everybody can go to college! Everybody can do it, no matter what!'" Yadira recounted. "And it's hard, because I can't just raise my hand and say, 'Well, miss, I don't have my papers.' It's not clear who you can trust."

When the subject of college first arose, Yadira and Marisela had been confused about whether they qualified for aid, because their teachers kept telling them they looked like strong candidates for public dollars. In search of answers, the two undocumented students had gone to Roosevelt High's post-secondary options office, where they had confided in a warmhearted secretary named Aurora Valdez. "I remember going in there and trying to get information about different colleges," Marisela recalled. "And she asked me if I had done my FAFSA. So I asked her what that was. She explained that it was the financial aid form you have to fill out. The first thing she asked me was if I remembered my Social Security number. And I said, 'Oh, I don't have one.' So that's when she started explaining to me what I had. She talked a lot about community college. And she talked about sponsors. She even talked about going to the different *panaderías* on Thirty-second Street and asking people to donate, like, a pair of boots, or a belt, and we could hold a raffle."

One day, Yadira had been using one of the computers in the post-secondary options office to type up a homework assignment when a recruiter for the University of Colorado walked in.

"What's your name?" he asked.

Yadira answered.

"What's your ACT score?"

"Twenty-three."

That put her around the 70th percentile in terms of her national ranking, which was quite high for a student from Roosevelt. Because bilingual students often tested lower than their peers on standardized exams, the recruiter pressed for more information.

"What classes are you taking?"

Yadira recited her course list and grade point average, which was 5.2 because of all her Advanced Placement classes. The recruiter dug out his business card, and started extolling the virtues of the University of Colorado. For somebody like her, he said, the university would be happy to waive the application fee.

"So, have you filled out your FAFSA yet?" he asked.

"No," said Yadira.

Usually she let it go at that, but there was something about the recruiter's jolly demeanor that made her want to see what would happen if she said more.

"Actually, I've got a problem," Yadira told the recruiter.

"What is it?" he wanted to know.

"Well, it's a really big problem," Yadira said.

"What?"

"I don't have papers."

The recruiter seemed at a loss. "Well, you could apply as an international student," he finally offered. "We can't waive your application fee, of course, and we don't guarantee you any scholarships. But you could still try." To Yadira, who was ashamed of her liability, the encounter left her feeling as though she had been examined and found wanting. Meanwhile, other recruiters told Clara and Elissa that they qualified for financial aid, federal Pell grants, and private scholarships. It was excruciating for Marisela and Yadira to watch the two girls with legal status reap rewards that were unavailable to them, even though they had all achieved the same level of academic success.

Matters had come to a head after all four girls had qualified to compete for a prestigious scholarship from the Daniels Fund. The late Bill Daniels had made billions in the cable industry, and his foundation awarded full-ride scholarships to high school graduates in the states of Colorado, New Mexico, Utah, and Wyoming. At a presentation about the program, Marisela and Yadira persuaded a friend to ask whether undocumented students could apply, and a representative from the Daniels Fund mistakenly replied that they could, although the board of the organization had decided not to give money to students who could not show proof of legal status anymore. All four girls were selected to participate in the competition, and Marisela and Yadira set their hearts on winning a scholarship from the Daniels Fund, which appeared to be their best shot at going to a top-notch college. For the rest of junior year, Yadira, Marisela, Clara, and Elissa had slogged through the extensive requirements, writing multiple drafts of college essays, filling out application forms, and attending seminars on how to manage their time.

Between their junior and senior years of high school, the Daniels Fund had sent participants to spend a week in a college dorm so they could experience the college lifestyle. Marisela spent a week at the Colorado School of Mines, because of her love of math, while Yadira went to the University of Colorado at Boulder. Sleeping in a dorm and eating in a dining hall and walking to class made the possibility of college seem almost within reach. Shortly after they returned to high school to begin their senior year, however, a rumor swept through Roosevelt that all the illegal kids were getting kicked out of the Daniels Fund program. At the program's next meeting, Yadira and Marisela learned that the rumor was basically true: Anybody who did not have a Social Security number would not be eligible for money.

The two girls had spent fall of senior year angry at the universe. It was hard for Marisela and Yadira to see why they should labor over their homework if they were just going to end up working at McDonald's. The two girls started cutting school, "ditching" all the time. Marisela slid into trouble with ease, but Yadira found the experience profoundly disorienting. "Probably my lowest point was when I stopped going to school for a week," she remembered. "My grades dropped so low—I had never gotten grades like that. I came back to class and I didn't even know what was going on. I felt so disorganized, and I'm always organized. Part of me was saying, 'You have to go to class! What if there's still a chance?' Then the other part of me was saying, 'Screw it. There's not a chance. You've kept your grades up for nothing. Just have fun now.'"

At that point, Elissa went into sports captain mode. She pestered Yadira and Marisela about the importance of staying in school and badgered them about finishing their college applications. So what if they were not being handed full tuition? Plenty of people put themselves through community college. Elissa persuaded the two girls to finish high school, but her lectures also drove Marisela and Yadira away, because they felt as though Elissa could not imagine what it was like to be them. After Clara and Elissa began hearing back from institutions that wanted to give them financial aid, they noticed how their good tidings made the two undocumented girls visibly uncomfortable. Clara and Elissa started hiding their news, which further alienated Yadira and Marisela. Eventually it just became easier for the foursome to split up along lines of immigration status. As we sat in the Old Country Buffet, Marisela pointed at her two documented friends. "I would hear them talking about college, and I'm like, 'Agh!'" she said. "I felt left out. I knew they weren't doing it on purpose, but I could see a line there separating us. It feels like we have our hands tied. Everybody else is going ahead, and we're just watching them."

During the height of their estrangement, Yadira and Marisela had joked about forming a club to address their isolation, which they wanted to call "Girls Like Us." To them, the way things were playing out did not seem fair. All four girls had at least one parent who had entered the country illegally, and they had all grown up exactly the same way. They ate the same food, and they listened to the same music. "We were all the same," Yadira pointed out. "We had the same type of parents, the same type of living. I was mad that they had their papers and we didn't, when in fact we were the same. Like, what did I do wrong?" Yadira and Marisela thought Clara and Elissa were just like them.

The bitterness had lasted for months. Eventually, however, the four girls had simply missed one another too much, and held a series of meetings to air out their grievances. At the point when I met them, the reunion was still in a tentative phase, and it was not clear if it would hold, particularly as new developments kept testing their reconciliation. Before we left the Old Country Buffet, the girls agreed that I could accompany them to their classes at Roosevelt High, a redbrick fortress at the heart of the city, and I soon had the chance to witness several of these tense moments in person. Later it occurred to me that while the girls had been wary when I had first started asking questions, their secrets had soon tumbled out. In retrospect it seemed as though I had gained their trust rather easily, which made me feel protective of the girls—they were vulnerable, particularly the pair who lacked legal status, and the world was not always a kind place.

At 7:15 one morning, two weeks after I had first met with the girls, I pushed through the swinging doors that led into the front lobby of Roosevelt. A river of students rushed around me, as a short Latina woman wearing an orange safety vest called out to those who forgot to flash their school identification cards. "IDs! IDs! IDs!" bellowed the guard cheerfully. "*Adelante! Adelante!*" Roosevelt was not one of the city's top-performing schools: Less than one-quarter of all freshmen scored proficiently in reading on state exams, and less than 5 percent scored proficiently in math. To an outsider, the school appeared homogeneous—85 percent of its students were Latino—but tension often flared between English and Spanish speakers. Undocumented students were typically discreet about their situation, yet somehow other Spanish-speaking students learned who among them lacked legal status, in the way that high school students have always mysteriously apprehended one another's secrets. The ranks of undocumented students at Roosevelt included key players on the girls' and the boys' soccer teams, a track star, several members of the National Honors Society, a couple of thespians in the drama club, and many participants in ROTC. I had arranged to meet the girls in the lobby, yet they were nowhere in sight.

After a few minutes, Clara pushed through the swinging doors wearing blue jeans, with her dark hair done in a thick braid. She was carrying a large yellow backpack. "Marisela is probably going to be late," she said. "She usually doesn't make it to first period on time."

We walked to her locker, and Elissa found us there. The two girls took AP chemistry during first period, along with Marisela. By the time the bell rang, thirteen students had made it to class (one Anglo, one African American, and eleven Latinos), but Marisela's chair remained empty. The teacher announced that he wanted the students to identify unknown solutions by observing their reactions with known solutions. "Okay, I'm waking up," Elissa said dryly. The girls put on safety goggles

and black plastic aprons. For the next forty minutes, they mixed different chemical solutions together and wrote down what they observed.
Marisela never made it to class.

When the bell rang, Elissa went to see Miss Valdez in the school's
post-secondary options office, a small room covered in felt pennants.
There were pennants for the University of Colorado, Colorado College, Regis University, the University of Northern Colorado, Fort Lewis
College, Colorado State University, the Community College of Denver,
Adams State, Metro State, Red Rocks Community College, and the
University of Denver. Magazine racks were filled with college leaflets
grouped by state. Miss Valdez was not an official counselor, but she
devoted herself to the students, so all four girls viewed the secretary
as the best source of information on their future. Elissa pulled out a
manila folder. She had questions about a letter she had just received
from Regis University, a highly regarded Catholic institution in Denver
that had promised her a partial scholarship.

"It says here that if my course work is not done in four years, I can
complete it at no additional cost," Elissa pointed out. "Is that true?"

"I would assume so," said Miss Valdez. "It's in writing. You hold on
to that letter—it's gold."

Elissa said she wanted to go to Regis, but it would depend on
whether she could secure additional money. If not, she would go to a
less prestigious school.

"Did you apply for the Daniels? Is that kind of the big factor?" Miss
Valdez wanted to know.

"Yeah," said Elissa.

Miss Valdez took note of Elissa's sense of urgency. "You are in that
mode, Elissa, I can see," the secretary counseled. "Just wait. And don't
let money be the only factor, because if you are not happy, you're going
to want to move."

The sounds of a distant mariachi band drifted in from the hall—
an accordion, several guitars, and voices in harmony. Later we heard
over the loudspeaker: "Good morning, Pilgrims. Today is Monday,
March 22, and these are your announcements, in English first. Over
the weekend, five of your fellow students were in a car accident. All
were injured, but they're going to be fine. We would appreciate your
thoughts and prayers. Miss Brown baked some cookies and took them
over on behalf of all of us. Congratulations to the drill team and the

color guard for the trophies they won. Additionally, tomorrow morning, the army will be here to evaluate our ROTC program. The military spends quite a bit of money in this school, and they want to make sure their money is well spent. Don't forget, seniors, that this Friday are your cap-and-gown photographs." Then the announcements were repeated in Spanish.

Elissa had AP calculus with Clara and Marisela at 11:20 A.M. "You can sit here, because Marisela isn't here today," Elissa told me, pointing to the desk next to hers.

"Marisela is here," another student piped up. "I just saw her."

"She wasn't here for first period," Elissa objected.

"No, Marisela is here today," the other student insisted.

Two minutes after the bell rang, Marisela burst into the classroom. She pulled a desk close to us and whispered in Spanish that she had overslept.

"That's no excuse!" Clara replied tartly in English.

Marisela said her grandparents were visiting at the moment, forcing her to sleep on the couch. Her mother was supposed to wake her up at 5:30 A.M. but had not woken her up until seven. Still, Marisela had taken the time to look sexy. She was wearing black platform shoes, tight black trousers with pink pinstripes, a black lace top with spaghetti straps, six gold rings—three on each hand—and a gold necklace. She had curled her medium-length hair and then secured the curls on the top of her head with multiple bobby pins. Bill Paul, who taught AP calculus, wrote an integral on the board and demonstrated a shortcut that told whether the integral converged. The shortcut was called the p-series. The teacher had barely finished writing the result on the board when Marisela interrupted him.

"Wait, I have a question!" she called out. "Can you do that p-thing when you have a polynomial on the top?"

"Yes, you can," he told her.

Marisela's irrepressible curiosity amused Bill Paul. He had demonstrated the use of the p-series using a relatively simple equation, and she was worried about whether she could use the same tool to analyze a more complicated problem. The teacher wrote more integrals on the blackboard and asked the class to divide up into pairs and apply the p-series to each. Marisela pulled her desk close to a tall, big-boned student named Miguel.

"Okay, so which one diverges?" Marisela asked out loud.

She conducted a running monologue about infinity and convergence as Miguel listened obligingly. They finished before anybody else.

Once Elissa had solved the problems, she turned her attention back to Marisela's failure to show up for first period.

"Why can't you wake yourself up?" asked Elissa.

"I slept in the living room!" Marisela protested. "I didn't have a clock!"

"Let's focus here, guys," Bill Paul admonished as he wrote another problem on the board.

The girls worked assiduously until they figured out the answer to the teacher's next question. Then Marisela took out a compact and began applying coffee-colored face powder. Clara asked about an assignment for another class, which led Elissa to pull out a book entitled *Literature*. Bill Paul was explaining that they would be taking practice tests all week to prepare for the upcoming AP exam, when he noticed what Marisela and Elissa were doing. "Hey, guys—hey, girls, could you put that away until lunch?"

They put away the makeup and literature book.

"*Gracias,*" said the teacher.

"*De nada,*" said Marisela in a saucy voice.

Clara poked Marisela with a pen to keep her in line.

"*Cómo se dice* 'derivative' in Spanish?" asked their teacher.

"*Derivado,*" replied Elissa.

The teacher wrote the following on the blackboard:

AP TEST
    1. Finance and functions
    2. Derivatives
    3. Sketching graphs

"Do you guys remember points of inflection?" he asked. "Does that ring a bell?"

Groans from the class.

    4. Optimization and related rates
    5. Integration

"I like integration," Marisela observed.

"Sort of . . ." Clara appended.

"Mr. Paul!" Marisela called out. "Are related rates the same as growth and decay problems?"

He explained that they were not exactly the same thing, although they both had to do with the rate at which things change. He added that it was a good question.

    6. Applications of integration
    7. Logarithms

"When are we taking this test?" asked Elissa as the list grew.

"Tomorrow," said Bill Paul.

"We're taking this test *tomorrow*?" shrieked Elissa.

"It doesn't count," explained Marisela, who had managed to pay attention while applying her makeup.

Paul wrote a complicated equation on the board. Marisela jiggled her feet, Elissa put her head down on her desk, and Clara leaned back so far that she slanted.

"Does that converge or diverge?" the teacher asked.

"It diverges," Marisela answered.

"How about this?"

"It diverges, too," volunteered Marisela.

It seemed hard for Marisela to get herself to school, but once she was there, she lit up the classroom. When the bell rang, Yadira hovered at the door, waiting. The two undocumented girls typically spent their lunch hour together.

"Should we go to McDonald's or Wendy's?" Marisela asked.

McDonald's, Yadira decided. They went in the worn bronze truck Marisela shared with her parents. A crucifix, a pine tree air freshener, and a collection of Mardi Gras beads dangled from the rearview mirror. On the way, the two girls talked about what they had done over the previous weekend. Marisela had gone dancing in a Mexican nightclub, while Yadira had gone to see in *The Passion of the Christ*.

"We're suffering from senioritis," Marisela announced.

After lunch, the girls returned to Roosevelt for their last class, AP literature. They were studying concrete poetry, in which words or phrases are written in a shape that illuminates a poem's theme. Miss Brown gave them Dylan Thomas's "Vision and Prayer," which has stanzas in

the shape of diamonds, as an example. Then she had them write an
original concrete poem. When Miss Brown asked for volunteers to read
their poem out loud, Marisela raised her hand.

She read:

> *I'm confused.*
>> *Am I going*
>>> *to college?*
>>>> *Should I obey*
>>>> *my parents?*
>>> *I can't find*
>>> *my identity.*
>> *I am confused,*
>> *I am lost.*
>
> *I am a*
> *teenager.*

"Beautiful!" exclaimed Miss Brown. "Wonderful! Is that your shape
poem?"

"It's in the shape of a question mark," Marisela replied, holding the
piece of paper up for her teacher. "I don't know if you can see it."

Miss Brown beamed at her.

3

INSTANTANEOUS RATE OF CHANGE

" **I** remember clearly how it was when I jumped the border,"
Marisela told me once, after we had known each other for some
time. "Laying in the back of the truck—laying like I was sleeping—and
trying not to make any noise. There were piles of people all around me,
and I didn't know who they were, and I didn't know where my mom
was." She recalled driving through a desert of white sand, and thinking
that if she got out of the truck and stepped onto the sand, she would
sink. Marisela was seven at the time, and it was her second illegal entry
into the United States. She was three years old the first time she crossed
the border but had no memory of that previous journey.

Marisela was born in Durango in 1986, when her father was
twenty-four and her mother was sixteen. By that point, Fabián had
already worked in various parts of the United States, but had returned
to Mexico and was driving a delivery truck for the Lala milk company.
Eleven months after Marisela was born, Fabián decided to go back
to the United States, but only for as long as it took to save up money
to build a house. In California, Fabián found work as a janitor cleaning stores at night, and supplemented his income by working as a day
laborer. However, as he freely confessed, he spent much of what he
earned in dance halls and on beer.

Despite his intention to return to Mexico, Fabián was hoping to
legalize his status in the United States, which would have made it easier
to secure other employment, but he never managed to make his way
through the bureaucratic maze of the Immigration and Naturalization
Service. He did try. Fabián first attempted to apply for citizenship under
the Immigration Reform and Control Act—a law known to policymak-
ers as IRCA, though Mexicans just called it *la amnistía*. The law levied
penalties against employers who knowingly hired illegal aliens, and it
also provided a path to legal residency for about three million immi-

grants who had entered the country without the proper documentation. IRCA gave priority to workers who held agricultural jobs. Though Fabián had heard of people who could sell him false documents asserting he worked in the fields, he didn't have enough money to buy them. Instead, he asked the owner of the janitorial service to vouch for him. His employer's letter was written in English, however, and Fabián never knew what it said. When he presented it to the authorities at the Immigration and Naturalization Service office in Fresno, they scoffed at the letter and told him that he wasn't eligible for amnesty.

During the years he spent away from his wife and child, Fabián regularly sent them money and told Josefa to begin construction on their house, but he never managed to amass the funds they needed to complete the project. When Marisela turned three, Fabián abandoned the idea of building a home in Mexico, and decided that his wife and daughter should join him in the United States. He returned to Durango so he could help them make the journey. It was January 1990 when they walked through the Sierra de Juárez mountains of Baja California, south of San Diego County. A cold rain started to fall at 6 P.M., and as the night drew on, the temperature plummeted. Marisela caught a chill in the rain, and shivered violently. Once they were on the American side, hiding under a freeway, her skin turned blue and she wouldn't answer her mother. The *coyote* they had hired to guide them kept hissing at them to hide because he had seen Border Patrol agents, and Fabián and Josefa hid in the culvert for as long as they could bear. Finally Fabián told Josefa that he feared their daughter was going to die. He stepped out of the culvert and started yelling to attract the attention of somebody who might provide medical attention, but there was no one. Then the *coyote* took them to San Ysidro, California, in southern San Diego County. They stayed in a hotel room for one day and night, after which they piled into the back of a van with more than a dozen other immigrants, and drove until they reached Los Angeles. Fabián held Marisela in his arms for the entire journey, because he feared she would be crushed if he put her down.

Friends in Mexico had told Josefa that the United States was *un lugar de hermosura*—a place of beauty—and she was devastated to discover that it was not, at least judging by the rough neighborhood in Canoga Park, on the outskirts of Los Angeles, where they stayed with some of her relatives. Fabián intended to find a place of his own in

Bakersfield, California, where he had a cousin, but one Saturday morning he fell off the roof of a house he was painting and broke his right arm badly. He couldn't work for several months, and Josefa had to find a job cleaning houses for $120 a week. After he was better, Fabián took a bus to Bakersfield that was boarded by federal authorities and he was deported. Josefa had to borrow $300 to pay another *coyote*, and more than a month passed before Fabián returned.

Eventually Fabián and Josefa did find an apartment in Bakersfield. Rent was $380 a month, and Fabián secured another job doing janitorial work that paid him $1,000 a month. They were supposed to savor their arrival in the promised land now, but instead, Fabián and Josefa grew increasingly disillusioned. They worked too hard and earned too little, their apartment was shabby, and violence surrounded them. One day, Josefa walked to the corner store to buy some groceries, only to get trapped inside when gang members started shooting at one another outside the store's entrance. Meanwhile, Fabián hired an immigration attorney for $350, who told him to present certain paperwork to the INS and assured him he was a solid candidate for citizenship, but after Fabián appeared at the INS office in Fresno, an official there advised him otherwise and said he should sue his attorney for fraud. At that point, Fabián decided to stop wasting his money and ceased his attempts to become legal. Overall, the United States struck Fabián and Josefa as a cruel and an unwelcoming place, and they became sorely nostalgic. They wanted to go home. Two years after their epic journey north, they decided to return to Durango.

Each time the Benavídez family changed countries, they welcomed a new child. In 1991, Josefa gave birth to Marisela's brother Nestor in California, making him an American citizen. Josefa was pregnant again when the family decided to return to Durango, where Rosalinda was born, just like her older sister. When the local economy soured, the family decided to make their second journey to the United States. Fabián came over first so he could secure a job, and one of Josefa's cousins who had legal papers brought baby Rosalinda over using a common ruse: The cousin flashed her own infant's American birth certificate at authorities while passing off Rosalinda as her child. Meanwhile, Josefa, Marisela, and Nestor crossed over with a *coyote*. Just as they were approaching a freeway on the American side, a Border Patrol vehicle appeared, and the *coyote* yelled for everybody to run. Josefa grabbed Nestor, another adult grabbed Marisela, and everyone ran pell-mell until they found hiding spots. After the searchlights stopped casting about, they emerged and clambered into the back of a waiting pickup truck, where seven-year-old Marisela pretended to sleep while uncertain where her mother was in the vehicle. The baby of the family, Rafael, arrived in Bakersfield in 1995—an American citizen, just like his older brother. Among her own siblings, in other words, Marisela found herself part of another foursome that was bifurcated by legal status. As they grew older, the Benavídez children became conscious of their alternating nationalities (Mexican, American, Mexican, American), especially after the two girls experienced limitations that the two boys did not. "All the benefits, it was the guys," Marisela told me. "If we got the flu, we just had to take care of it at home, but they could go to the hospital because they had Medicaid."

Once they were back in California, Fabián and Josefa hoped to find a safer environment in which to raise their four children. Then one of Josefa's cousins told them about National Maintenance, a janitorial service that was hiring in Denver, Colorado. In 1996, when Marisela was ten years old, her parents decided to move to Denver, chasing the American dream they felt had eluded them thus far in Bakersfield. The Benavídez family noted that Colorado had the same arid plains, immense mountains, and dramatic thunderstorms as they remembered from Durango, which made them feel at home. Initially, the family of six shared a rental house with two other families, and later shared another rental house with one family. After Josefa found a job cleaning a Michaels arts and crafts store, the family was able to rent an apartment on their own, located on the west side of Denver, where they lived until Marisela's sophomore year of high school, at which time her father purchased a house on the north side of town, in a neighborhood that had once sheltered many Italian immigrants. Despite it being a dilapidated structure, Fabián felt proud to own his own home.

Back in California, Marisela had taken classes in Spanish, but in Colorado, she took classes in English. Teachers often praised her intelligence. Josefa, who had never learned to read or write, marveled at her daughter's precocity. Her parents had taken her out of school after second grade. Above all, Josefa wanted her children to graduate from high school so they would not have to do the kind of work she did. She told me, "I want my children always to be behind a desk."

Marisela routinely earned high grades, even after she started working full-time as a clerk at a local supermarket chain called King Soopers. She got the job during her freshman year at Roosevelt; she was only thirteen but lied and told the manager she was eighteen. Her parents purchased a fake Social Security card and fake alien registration card for her for $80 on the black market. The numbers on the cards were made up. Marisela paid state and federal taxes, even though she would never collect Social Security payments—she was padding the fund for America's legal retirees. For most of her high school career, Marisela went to school from 7:30 A.M. until 2:45 P.M., frenziedly changed clothes in the girls' lavatory, and then checked groceries from 3 P.M. until 11 P.M. She did her homework when she was on break, and gave most of the money she earned to her parents to help pay the family's bills. Still, Marisela managed to earn straight A's. Her friends nicknamed her Superwoman.

Much to the alarm of Fabián and Josefa, once Marisela started going to high school, she also began to enjoy an active social life. Her first cousin, Román Ortega, was four years older, and they began going to nightclubs together when Marisela was fourteen or fifteen. She looked a lot older than she actually was, and the fake Mexican driver's license that she purchased got her into the city's Mexican clubs. Fabián and Josefa tried to curb their elder daughter's love of nightlife, but found they could not, as Marisela would lie or sneak out of the house. Once she was riding as a passenger in a car driven by a friend who got into a fender bender, and when a police officer asked to see their identification, Marisela handed over her Mexican license. "He knew right away it was fake," she told me. "But he didn't do anything. He just punched a hole in it so that I wouldn't be able to use it anymore. It still works in some clubs, though."

Marisela's boundless curiosity extended to all aspects of life, and she soon forged ahead of her peers in the sexual arena. She lost her virginity during sophomore year, after her first boyfriend pressured her to have sex. Afterward, a friend of Marisela's called on the telephone, worried that she might be pregnant, and Marisela told her about the morning-after pill and other precautions. When Marisela hung up the phone, she walked out into the living room and found her parents in a state of hysteria. "You're not even married!" wailed Josefa. "My little girl!" howled Fabián. Somebody had picked up an extension and listened to everything she'd said. Fabián believed things would have been different in Mexico, and that America was ruining his daughter.

During her time at Roosevelt, Marisela slept with several different boyfriends. Meanwhile, her closest friends remained far more cautious about sex. Over the same four-year period, both Yadira and Elissa were involved in only one serious relationship apiece, and as far as I could ascertain both practiced abstinence. Clara eschewed relationships entirely and never so much as kissed a boy. When I asked Marisela about her experiences in this realm, she said somewhat breezily, "Oh, I've been very open about my sexuality." There was bravado in her voice, but there was also a touch of uncertainty, as if she feared being judged. It was probably that combination of fearlessness, pride, and insecurity that led her to have more romantic adventures than her peers. Marisela always said she was having a good time, but to me it seemed as though she kept throwing herself headlong into harm's way and didn't yet know how to protect herself.

After they learned Marisela was sexually active, Fabián and Josefa began to feud with their daughter over how much makeup she could wear, how revealing her clothes could be, and whether she could date certain boys. Pulled in one direction by the nightclub scene and pulled in the opposite direction by her parents, Marisela started to come apart. On one occasion, she tried to take her own life by swallowing a large quantity of Tylenol, and managed to ingest enough pills to require a short stay in the hospital. Marisela told only a handful of her closest friends about the suicide attempt, and refused to discuss the subject with me. What her friends remembered most vividly about the incident was walking into the hospital room and seeing Marisela wearing a paper gown and no makeup. They had gotten used to seeing her features enhanced by blush and kohl, and found it unnerving to see her looking so naked.

By senior year, Marisela had gained a lot of perspective on the ongoing struggles she had with her parents, and the central drama of her life became the matter of how to deal with the end of high school. At the end of March, one week after she had read her question mark poem aloud, I arranged to meet her in the lobby of Roosevelt High. Dozens of other students rushed through the swinging front doors, flashing their IDs, but there was no sign of Marisela. Finally, Elissa pushed through the doors wearing a striped T-shirt and cargo pants. "Marisela moved this weekend; she's probably going to be late," she announced. "She lives farther away now." I knew that Marisela admired her father for becoming a homeowner, and I had not heard of the family's plans to relocate; the decision seemed to have come about abruptly. I wondered what had precipitated it. Elissa and I found Clara in the AP chemistry classroom buried in a novel. Clara put down her book to reminisce about a church retreat.

"Oh! Did I tell you I got an interview with Daniels?" Elissa interjected. "Clara did, too."

Both documented girls had just reached the final phase of the Daniels Fund competition. I wondered how these tidings would affect Marisela and Yadira.

After chemistry, I found Marisela in the hallway, wearing stretchy pants that looked like blue jeans but were actually made of spandex and a blue-and-white-checked blouse and white tennis shoes. Her eye shadow was a matching shade of blue, and she had ratted her hair into a messy bouffant, making her look like a 1950s housewife gone wild.

"We moved to Lakewood," she announced. "The drive took forty-five minutes. I had to take my little brother to his middle school first."

The family had just relocated to the green warren of cinder-block buildings over in the nearby suburb, where the girls would soon congregate to get ready for their senior prom. I asked what had prompted the move.

"We had to give our house back to the bank," she said. "So now we are in an apartment. But it's nice—it's nicer than the house was."

Fabián later explained that right after he had purchased the house, he had discovered that the electricity didn't work properly and the basement periodically flooded. Meanwhile, the mortgage payments had been steep—$1,300 each month—and Fabián had fretted continuously that bank officials might repossess the home if they discovered he was illegal (he had left the Social Security box blank on the papers he had signed for the loan). After Fabián had taken out a second mortgage so he could make essential repairs, he had kept $15,000 in cash in the house, as he did not have a bank account. A relative of Josefa's had stolen the cash. Fabián and Josefa were able to recover only $7,000.

Right around the same time, Fabián's father died, and Fabián had taken time off work to travel to Mexico for the funeral. His return trip took far longer than anticipated. The *coyote* kept him waiting in a safe house in Ciudad Juárez for weeks, until he finally crossed back over curled up in a box hanging between the tires of a passenger bus. He could hardly breathe. Fabián resumed his job as a janitor, but by that point the family's finances were in a bad state, and he had to use the $7,000 left over from his second mortgage to make payments on his first mortgage. Most recently, the family's garage had burned down, and at that point Fabián had decided not to invest any more money in the property. Instead, he had found the three-bedroom apartment in Lakewood, which cost only $800 a month to rent. The saga was not unusual at Roosevelt High—most of Marisela's classmates moved a lot. In her senior class, only one-third of the students had been enrolled at Roosevelt for three consecutive years. Simply staying at the same school from freshman to senior year represented an unusual accomplishment.

When I met her in the hallway, Marisela was on her way to Chicano Studies. In that class, she sat down beside León, a burly guy with whom she was friends. Marisela rummaged around in her capacious purse, pulled out a bottle of saline solution, and fished a contact lens out of her eye. Without the gold contact lenses, her eyes were chocolate brown. Noticing that Yadira was absent, Marisela cried: "I miss her quietness!" The class discussed family values, and fell into a heated debate about abortion. When another individual observed that infants were precious, Marisela responded: "You don't just have to think about how pretty the baby is; you have to think about its future. What if you can't offer them anything?" On the way to her next class, Marisela passed a tall student with a flattop and reached out to pinch his cheek. This was Gabriel, the sophomore she had recently started dating. When I asked if the relationship was serious, Marisela laughed and said she liked younger men.

While flirting with Gabriel, Marisela radiated confidence, but this attribute faded from her countenance later in the day as she listened to her fellow seniors recount their latest triumphs regarding college. One such conversation took place that afternoon, after Marisela's sociology class broke into small groups to discuss prejudice. Marisela and two other students chose to examine the tensions between U.S.-born and

Mexican-born students at Roosevelt, whom they referred to respectively as Chicanos and *mexicanos*. None of the students at Roosevelt High called themselves Hispanic, a label used mainly by outsiders. "Latino" was an umbrella term that encompassed virtually the entire student body, and it wasn't useful in terms of allowing them to distinguish themselves from one another. Some students came from families who had settled in Colorado before the *Mayflower* had even set sail, and they occasionally used the term "Spanish," but most students identified themselves as *mexicanos* or Chicanos. Since the 1960s, activists had used the term Chicano to signify participation in a civil rights movement, but at Roosevelt it was typically used to claim native-born status. Chicanos often resented the immigrants who had moved into their neighborhoods and spoke a different language; they sometimes made fun of Spanish-speakers by calling them *ched* or *cheddar,* a derogatory term derived from *ranchera,* the country-style ballad favored by many *mexicanos*. Marisela was intimately familiar with the divisions at Roosevelt, and often felt caught in the middle. Her achievements were too great for her to fit in with the majority of the school's *mexicano* students, yet she did not identify with Chicanos, either. "Ever since I've been here, I haven't felt American as much—I mean, not all the way," she told me later. "I always stand out: the color of my skin, my accent, my background. But in my family, I stand out, too. I speak Spanish, but not as well as they do. That's the hardest part. You don't know who you are. You don't know where you belong."

After Marisela finished writing up a report about their discussion of prejudice at Roosevelt, which was due before the end of class, her classmate Daniela mentioned that she had just gone to an interview at the University of Denver.

"What did you wear?" asked Marisela.

"Jeans," said Daniela, a Chicana student.

"Jeans!"

"And a blouse. But I got in."

"You got in? With money?" Marisela asked.

"Yeah."

"How much?"

"I think, like, $7,000."

"I'd like to go to the University of Colorado," Marisela said with a sigh.

"Did they accept you?" Daniela asked.

"Oh, I didn't apply," said Marisela in an offhand tone. "The deadline was really early."

Actually, she hadn't applied because she didn't qualify for in-state tuition, but Marisela did not want to reveal this to a Chicana. Daniela indicated that she knew about the early deadline.

"You got accepted there, too?" asked Marisela.

"Uh-huh," said Daniela.

Afterward, as we walked downstairs to her calculus class, I asked Marisela if it had been hard to listen to Daniela talk about the prestigious schools that had accepted her.

"Yeah, but I'm used to it," she said stoically.

Then I mentioned that Clara and Elissa had gotten interviews with the Daniels Fund.

"Oh, I would be preparing for that right now!" cried Marisela, with obvious regret.

When we walked into calculus class, however, Marisela greeted Clara and Elissa warmly, as if nothing was wrong. She mentioned that she had taken her little brother to his school that morning, before driving to Roosevelt.

"Oh, is this referring to your lateness?" Elissa said pointedly.

Marisela ignored this remark. "You guys, on Saturday I'm going to have a sleepover at my house," she announced. "Can you come?"

"What for?" asked Elissa.

"For inaugurating the apartment!"

The girls settled into their seats and pulled out their calculus textbooks. On the blackboard, Bill Paul wrote:

Instantaneous Rate of Change
Slope of Tangent Line

Then he wrote a problem that he wanted the students to solve. The class was silent as everybody bent down to work on the equation. Marisela got the right answer first.

"I need a Spanish-speaking person," the teacher announced. "Who wants to be the Spanish-speaking person who gets the extra bonus point?"

"Me!" called Elissa.

"Me!" called Marisela.

"Me!" called Clara.

All three girls thrust their hands in the air. Nobody else volunteered.

"I think I saw Elissa's hand first," said Bill Paul.

He had to call a parent who spoke only Spanish, and needed an interpreter. The teacher dialed a phone number and handed the receiver to Elissa. When Elissa returned to her seat, Marisela asked about the Daniels Fund interview. Elissa pulled out the letter she had received and showed it to Marisela.

"I'm so happy for us," said Elissa.

"Me too," said Marisela gamely.

Clara pulled a different letter out of her backpack. She ran her finger down the piece of paper with her brow furrowed.

"At Colorado College, tuition is $38,324," Clara announced. "Guess how much I got?"

"Like, the whole thing," Marisela ventured.

"That's right."

"*Oh, my God!*" Marisela screamed. "Congratulations! I have to run out the door! I think I just swallowed my gum!"

Clara giggled uncontrollably as Marisela bolted out of the classroom.

"What's going on?" Bill Paul demanded.

"She got a full ride to CC!" Marisela cried from the doorway. "That's why I was almost choking!"

Bill Paul turned to Clara.

"You got a free ride to Colorado College?" he marveled. "All right!"

The bell rang. Marisela had done a seamless job of acting. She had been funny; she had been gracious. Inside, however, the familiar sensation of watching Clara and Elissa move forward with their lives as she remained stuck in place left her feeling terribly alone. Marisela had a hard time staving off a dark hopelessness. Where would she find the time to sort everything out? Senior year was rapidly unspooling; all her friends knew where they were going to college already. Intellectually, she understood that it was not her fault that she did not have a Social Security number and could not figure out how to pay for a college education, but she considered herself the culprit regardless. She felt it was her fault that she could not keep up with her peers. Ashamed of her unworthiness, she buried her emotions as deeply as she could. She didn't want her friends to know what she was experiencing, because she feared they would look down on her. While Marisela kept her mounting unease almost entirely hidden, it remained discernible to those who knew her well, for in the weeks to come there was an increasingly brittle quality to her cheerfulness, an escalating theatricality about her enthusiasm.

4

RISE AND FALL

Precisely when Marisela and Yadira were approaching adulthood, a lot of people who lived in Colorado were simultaneously growing impatient with the large number of immigrants moving into the state. Colorado served as home base for many social conservatives, including one of the country's most outspoken opponents of illegal immigration, U.S. Congressman Tom Tancredo. He represented the sixth congressional district, a sprawling territory of tract homes located south of Denver. Tancredo's district stretched across Douglas, Elbert, Arapahoe, Jefferson, and Park counties—places that had seen astronomical growth in recent years. During the 1990s, Douglas had been the fastest-growing county in the entire United States. The voters who had moved into the 6th Congressional District had turned Colorado's politics upside down—they were neither rural nor urban, but rather quintessentially suburban in their outlook. Tancredo himself lived in a suburb called Littleton, which was only half an hour's drive from Denver's west side, but the two neighborhoods might as well have been separated by an ocean, so great was the cultural divide. Throughout the past decade, as the superheated American economy had pulled in hundreds of thousands of immigrants every year, many of the people who lived in the 6th Congressional District had become concerned that the arrival of so many poor newcomers was having a negative impact on their own wages. Tancredo wanted to seal the border with Mexico, and deport everyone like Josefa and Fabián. After I started spending time with Marisela, I came to see that it was impossible to understand her family properly without also considering the views of Congressman Tancredo. They were opposite sides of the same coin, sparring partners in the same debate.

One night, after I had already gotten to know the girls and their families quite well, I went to hear the congressman speak at the Tat-

tered Cover Book Store in Highlands Ranch, one of the many suburban communities that he represented. Tancredo was a stocky,
broad-shouldered man, with salt-and-pepper hair, large brown eyes,
and an expressive face. He had drawn a big turnout, despite inclement
weather, and appeared delighted with the crowd. Tancredo had just
written a book called *In Mortal Danger: The Battle for America's Border and Security,* in which he laid out the dire threats he believed were
destroying Western civilization, one of which was illegal immigration.
Previously, Tancredo had come across as intemperate—once he had
caused an international media incident by suggesting that it might be
a good idea for the United States to bomb Mecca—but at the moment
he was positioning himself as the sober-minded savior of American
culture. The congressman was considering whether he might seek the
Republican party's nomination for president in 2008. He did not think
he could win, but he thought he might be able to steer the debate
toward the issues he cared about so passionately.

Now Tancredo stood at a podium in the middle of the bookstore,
facing the crowd. "Do you think our country is under attack?" he
asked. "Do you think we do face something deadly?"

"That's right!" called out a member of the audience.

"Islamo-fascism is the enemy," Tancredo pronounced.

"That's right!"

Tancredo segued from the militarization of Islam to immigration,
deftly tying the two issues together. "One of the most amazing things
about America is that so many different people have come here," he
said. "But they need to come as Americans first. Is it not important to
first have something that holds us together? And if language is a key
part of that, then I am unabashedly in favor of having English as our
national language." The intersection of education and foreign-born students was of particular interest to Tancredo, who had begun his career
as a teacher in Colorado's Jefferson County school system, where he
had watched with growing ire as elements of what he called "multi-
culturalism" crept into the curriculum. As he saw it, American public
schools were supposed to teach children about American culture—not
the cultures of other countries. In 1976, Tancredo was elected to the
Colorado House of Representatives, where he attempted unsuccessfully
to eliminate taxpayer funds for bilingual education in the state. In 1998,
he gained a seat in the U.S. House of Representatives, after campaigning

primarily on the issue of immigration. Soon after he was elected to Congress, Tancredo started the Immigration Reform Caucus, which began with only sixteen members; most everybody else in D.C. saw Tancredo's fixation on immigration as a little peculiar. And then a catastrophic series of events transformed the immigration debate forever.

Marisela and Yadira had just begun their sophomore year at Roosevelt High when nineteen men from Saudi Arabia, Egypt, and the United Arab Emirates—all of whom had entered the United States using nonimmigrant travel visas—hijacked four jetliners and flew them at various targets including the World Trade Center buildings. After the September 11 terrorist attacks, Tancredo appeared on hundreds of conservative talk radio shows and television programs, arguing that America needed to close its borders and cleanse itself of foreign influences. He mastered e-mail and the Internet, too, earning the distinction of becoming the first member of Congress to embrace blogging, which suited his acerbic sense of humor. "Is it just me or does anyone else find it amazing that our government can track a cow born in Canada almost three years ago, right to the stall where she sleeps in the state of Washington," Tancredo wrote in his blog, shortly after a case of mad cow disease was discovered in the United States. "Also they track her calves to their stalls. But they are unable to locate 11 million illegal aliens wandering around our country."

One year after the terrorist attacks, construction workers who were remodeling Tancredo's house contacted the *Denver Post* to complain about the congressman's hypocrisy. At the same time that he was taking to the airwaves to rail about illegal immigration, he was also using workers who lacked proper documentation to turn his basement into a high-tech getaway complete with a 102-inch television set. ("We have friends over and I have now shown *Pearl Harbor* about six times," Tancredo told the *Rocky Mountain News*. "But I mainly just show the attack scene because the sound is so good.") Tancredo responded to the charges by saying that the construction workers were not his employees; they worked for his contractor, Creative Drywall Design of Denver, and he had no control over how that company ran its business.

While the story amused Tancredo's critics, it did not impede his growing influence. To the alarm of people like Irene and Justino Chávez, the politically active couple who had befriended the girls during Colorado's battles over bilingual education, the congressman from

Littleton helped transform his home state into a superheated environment, a place where the national arguments over immigration raged even more intensely. Tancredo did not believe in providing aid to students who lacked legal status. He thought they should be deported, along with their parents. In fall 2002, just as the girls were starting their junior year at Roosevelt, an undocumented student named Jesús Apodaca described his predicament to the *Denver Post*. Jesús was one year ahead of Marisela and Yadira in his schooling, and like them, he had achieved top marks, in his case at Aurora Central High School, in the nearby suburb of Aurora, Colorado. He wanted to go to college, but did not qualify for public aid, in-state tuition, or most private scholarships. As soon as Congressman Tancredo read the story about Jesús, he called up the local office of the Immigration and Naturalization Service to ask what the organization did about an illegal immigrant who chose to identify himself publicly on the front page of the local newspaper. Were they going to deport the student and his family? Television trucks were parked outside of the Apodaca home, reporters called the family's home incessantly, and ugly things were written about them on the Internet.

The Apodacas subsequently moved to a different part of the metro area and got an unlisted phone number. In the meantime, however, a private benefactor stepped forward and offered to pay Jesús's tuition at the University of Colorado at Boulder. Later, this benefactor withdrew his support, and Governor Bill Owens, a conservative Republican who nevertheless sympathized with Jesús's desire to continue his education, quietly called up one of his biggest donors to ask if this businessman would take responsibility for the undocumented student's college tuition. The Republican businessman agreed, and Jesús continued to pursue a degree in engineering, albeit at a different university. The businessman found this experience unexpectedly moving, and within a short period of time he was also sponsoring the education of several other individuals who lacked legal status at a variety of public and private institutions around Colorado.

Meanwhile, Tancredo told the *Post* that he thought Jesús Apodaca was brazen. To the congressman, the idea that illegal aliens could openly discuss their status without suffering consequences seemed proof of how far American culture had strayed from the rule of law. The *Post* editorialized that it was unheard of for an elected official to go after an individual family in this fashion, and suggested that Tancredo's actions "smack[ed] of bullying," but Tancredo's many followers saw things differently. These social conservatives were tired of politicians who looked the other way on immigration. They admired Tancredo's gusto, his nerve. To them, he was fearless; other politicians appeared paralyzed by political correctness, but Tancredo bucked convention. Tancredo's followers loved him for his adamant opposition to the dilution of American culture, and cheered him for pointing out that an illegal family now felt comfortable enough to disclose its status on the front page of the local paper.

Several months after Tancredo singled out Jesús Apodaca, my husband, John Hickenlooper, announced that he wanted to run for mayor of Denver. Almost a dozen candidates jumped into the race, which would be decided in an election held in spring 2003, and the chances of John winning seemed unlikely. He was a rookie politician, straight out of the business community. A former geologist, he had been laid off when the price of oil collapsed during the 1980s, and had used his severance pay to start the Wynkoop Brewing Company, which for a while became the largest brewpub in the world in terms of barrels of beer sold annually. By the time he began campaigning, John owned eight restaurants, was serving on twelve nonprofit boards and committees, and had more than one thousand people in his address book. He was a fiscally conservative Democrat, and his acquaintances ranged from stalwart Republicans to liberal idealists such as Irene Chávez, whom he had befriended at an event for a local left-leaning nonprofit. Their meeting had been a classic demonstration of John's belief that political differences should not matter. Irene had walked up to him and stuck out her hand.

"Hi, I'm Irene Chávez, and I'm a socialist," she said.

"Nice to meet you," he replied, without missing a beat. "I'm John Hickenlooper, and I'm a capitalist."

"Really?" asked Irene, with horror.

"Yes!" said John unabashedly. "But I'm so glad that we're working together!"

During the mayoral race, John positioned himself as the best candidate to guide the city during financially challenging times. Scrimping was a family tradition—John could remember his mother washing pieces of used tin foil and taping them onto the refrigerator to dry. He came from solid Puritan stock. One of his maternal relatives had signed the Declaration of Independence, while another was widely credited with having drafted various segments of the U.S. Constitution, including its famous preamble ("We the people of the United States, in order to form a more perfect union . . ."). On his father's side, John is related to both a Civil War general from Ohio and a former Republican senator from Iowa. More to the point, John himself is as good at pinching a penny as any of his Puritan ancestors. After we married, I got into trouble for all kinds of wasteful habits, such as using the clothes dryer. ("We live in Colorado! You can dry clothes with the air!") While he was running for office, John predicted correctly that the next mayor would have to close an unforeseen budget gap of huge proportions, and endeared himself to voters with ads that spoofed his legendary frugality. One showed him buying a used suit at a thrift store, and riding off on a scooter to save gas.

Immigration came up several times during the race. Early on, after John gave a speech on economic development to the local Rotary Club, which met at the Wynkoop Brewing Company, a member of the audience asked John for his position on the subject. "Every small business I know has a number of people whose first language is Spanish," he told the crowd. "And they are among the hardest working and best employees." He thought that the country should secure its borders, and then adopt a viable guest-worker program. Later, the *Denver Post* published a story reporting that the various restaurants owned by the Wynkoop Brewing Company employed a total of eighty people whose Social Security numbers did not match their names. Twelve mismatches seemed to be the result of typographical errors, but sixty-eight employees appeared to lack valid documents. John explained that the restaurant company asked for Social Security numbers from every person it hired, and when it was notified that a number did not match a name, it asked the employee in question for a Social Security number once more, as the federal government advised. The very same letters that notified the company about mismatches also instructed that firing the individuals could violate federal labor law, because mismatches occurred for all kinds of reasons (people got married and changed their names, people accidentally reversed digits in their Social Security numbers, employers made clerical errors). The *Post* noted that it often took as long as a year or two for the federal government to respond after the company submitted an employee's information. "That leaves open the possibility that Hickenlooper's eight Colorado restaurants and bars unknowingly hired illegal immigrants, a common problem in the restaurant industry," the *Post* reported. "The way Hickenlooper's businesses have dealt with the federal notification clearly follows the law."

John's advisers thought he got off easy. It was hard to name his sin precisely, and the *Post* never got it quite right, but if I were going to be so disloyal as to take a stab at it, I would say that John was guilty of avoidance. Arguably, he should have known the uncomfortable truth—that some of his Spanish-speaking employees lacked legal status—but it was convenient not to examine the matter too closely. As long as he didn't really know one way or the other, he could claim innocence. Thousands of business owners in the region behaved the same way, and in certain industries—restaurants, landscaping, construction—such hiring practices were more the rule than the exception.

John won in a landslide. He immediately put his restaurants into a trust, hoping to ensure that they would never again become a subject of controversy. During his first year in office, he also resolved a $70 million budget gap without significant layoffs, and amended the city's charter so that he could offer incentives to workers. In fall 2003, John flew to Washington to meet with various federal officials, as well as lawmakers who represented the metro area. In the course of making these calls, he paid a visit to Congressman Tancredo, which was when the two men had their first argument. I got to hear both of them describe the conversation, as John came home and told me about it, while Tancredo recounted it on talk radio. In the meeting, Tancredo objected to what he called Denver's sanctuary city policy regarding illegal immigrants. When John responded that there was no policy offering sanctuary, Tancredo countered by asking why the city's police officers did not arrest every illegal immigrant who they came across. Tancredo also took issue with the fact that a previous mayor had authorized city officials to accept an identity card issued by the Mexican consulate. "I told him that this was something I was very concerned about—Denver being a sanctuary city—and also agreeing to accept the matricula consular card for proof of ID," Tancredo remembered on KHOW, a local talk radio station. The identity card from the Mexican consulate was controversial because immigrants who could not obtain official documents from any American branch of government often used it, and Tancredo wanted the new mayor to reverse his predecessor's stance.

John believed that rounding up immigrants who didn't have the legal right to be here was the job of the federal government. Asking the city's police department to take on the task would divert police officers from their core mission—keeping the city's residents safe from violent crime. Local police had no jurisdiction to enforce federal immigration laws, and if they locked up every undocumented worker who committed minor infractions of state and local laws, then they would soon run out of jail cells. There was also the delicate matter of trust. The city's detectives would have a harder time solving crimes if everybody in the immigrant community feared being turned over to federal authorities. John told Tancredo it would be irresponsible to divert police manpower away from solving murders, rapes, and assaults to rounding up people who were guilty of nailing down roof shingles without a Social Security number. He added that jailing illegal immigrants who had not committed violent crimes on the city's dime would drive up the cost of local law enforcement. He agreed there was a problem, but thought the federal government should resolve the matter. The city couldn't afford to.

John next ran into the immigration issue inside one of the city's public schools. Less than half of the Latino students who entered the Denver public school system left with a diploma, and African American students fared almost as poorly. Civic leaders were struggling to address the glaring achievement gap between white students and students of color, and soon after he was elected, John had begun raising money for a private fund to assist any graduate of Denver public schools who needed money to go to college, with the aim of persuading more students to stay in school. He had yet to find enough money for the entire district, and was not ready to announce the idea. In January 2004, however, Superintendent Jerry Wartgow asked the new mayor to speak at a pep rally at Denver's struggling Cole Middle School. Cole ranked as the worst middle school in Colorado, and its principal had organized a tutoring campaign to help the students improve their performance. At the pep rally, John bounded onto the stage—a tall, skinny guy with a mop of light-brown hair and a perpetually boyish look—and said that he wanted the students to believe in themselves. On the spur of the moment, he added that if the students stayed in school, he would find a way to pay for their college educations. "I guarantee we will find the resources and you will go to college," he told the assembly. "If you go to college, you can do anything you want."

Afterward, a reporter from the *Rocky Mountain News* asked to hear more about John's scholarship plan. "We're trying to get it to a full-blown plan whereby it would not just be limited to Cole," he told the reporter. "At this point, we're not discussing the details until we have them all in place." The following day, the *News* splashed the story of the mayor's pledge on its front page: A PROMISE OF COLLEGE. Several days later, John's office started getting questions about whether undocumented students were going to be included. It would cost more to send these students to college, because they weren't eligible for Pell grants, and as it turned out, undocumented students were not distributed evenly throughout the district—they were concentrated in the poorest schools. School district officials believed that Cole had a disproportionate number of them. "Do you know how many undocumented kids there are at Cole?" John asked me. "It's incredible! They think it might be as much as one-third of the school!"

Federal law mandated that public schools serve all children, regardless of immigration status, and the school district did not inquire about the possession of documents, for fear of scaring students who lacked them away. Instead, the district based its estimate on a variety of factors, such as the number of students who spoke Spanish. John wondered if their numbers were inflated. Either way, it was clear that there were more children without legal status at Cole than he had realized. "If the number of undocumented kids is really that high, then I don't know how we can fund them," he said to me. "Our scholarship was only supposed to kick in after public funding. If these kids don't qualify for Pell grants, then they would need many thousands of dollars more than the legal kids." Yet how could he announce that he would not provide scholarships to one-third of Cole, and then expect the school to ace the state exams?

The media caught wind of the snafu several weeks later, when Cole students held a press conference. Students were writing down on pledge cards where they wanted to go to college, and signing the cards with a promise to stay in school. One of the students asked Dr. María Guajardo, the director of the mayor's Office for Education and Children, whether undocumented students would receive money.

"My concern is not to ask if they are undocumented or not," replied Dr. Guajardo.

Reporters called the mayor's office for further clarification.

"All of these issues will be addressed when the specifics are worked out," pronounced John's spokeswoman, Lindy Eichenbaum Lent. In other words, she didn't have an answer, either.

I began spending time with Marisela and Yadira at Roosevelt High while John was grappling with the question of how to provide scholarships to everybody at Cole, and in the months that followed we had many conversations about undocumented students. While I took care not to introduce John to the girls from Roosevelt for fear of embroiling him in some sort of political flap, I did tell him stories about their lives. In the process, I typically tried to weigh whether it was fair for the two girls without legal status to be denied opportunities that were being offered to their peers. John thought about the matter differently. He asked what dollars were being spent on undocumented students, and how much they were going to give back. He wanted to know if they represented a good investment, and how society would reap its returns. He wanted to do the math. John knew that immigrants contributed to the local economy by providing low-wage labor and paying various types of taxes. Most immigrants paid property tax, either indirectly as renters or directly as homeowners, and many also paid income tax; meanwhile, everybody in Denver was subject to the local sales tax, which was the city's primary source of revenue. However, John also wondered if immigrants who lacked legal documents used social services in a way that was more costly than the average citizen. Over at Denver Health, the city's public hospital, the number of uninsured patients had swelled to record proportions. Federal law required Denver Health to treat anybody who faced a life-threatening situation, regardless of ability to pay or citizenship status, but immigrants who couldn't obtain any other form of health care often came to the emergency room with trivial complaints, and it was hard for doctors and nurses to turn them away. Apparently the hospital became more stringent during the city's budget crisis. When Marisela went to Denver Health to seek treatment for the flu that spring, she was outraged when a hospital worker asked her for $100 and her Social Security number—something that she said had never happened during previous visits. Marisela departed without seeing a doctor. When I told this story to John, he said it was appropriate that the hospital staff had prevented Marisela from using the ER as a neighborhood clinic. He did not think the doctors at Denver Health should refuse care in a true emergency—

in fact, he increased the city's spending on emergency health care during his time in office—but he was glad to hear that the hospital's gatekeepers were taking a tougher stance in terms of giving away care to people who were basically healthy.

After his initial dustup with Tom Tancredo, John had several more interesting encounters with the congressman from Littleton, but I did not meet Tancredo myself until around the time he published *In Mortal Danger*. Then we discussed his boyhood in North Denver, and I learned that the congressman had grown up in a small brick house located only a few blocks away from the home that Marisela's family had owned. During Tancredo's childhood, the city's north side had been flooded with recently arrived immigrants from Italy, including all four of his grandparents. At one point the congressman startled me by referring to his old stomping grounds as "Tancredoland," since I thought of the area as belonging to Marisela. Eventually I came to see that the congressman meant that for him the streets of North Denver remained saturated with memories of his extended family, even though many of his relatives were now dead and their places were being taken by people from Mexico.

Tancredo fascinated me because he possessed an immigrant's heritage and yet he stood for closing our borders. At the Tattered Cover Book Store, Tancredo expounded on the idea that illegal immigration constituted a national security risk. "The border is controlled by the drug cartels," he told his listeners. "And in a recent report for the first time the government admits that we have arrested people in this country belonging to Hezbollah who came across the southern border. People say no, no, no—terrorists don't enter the country that way. Of course they do! It's the easiest way in, especially if you want to stay under the radar!" My gaze wandered as he spoke, and I noticed that Tancredo was standing in front of a section on world history. Above his head was *An Irish History of Civilization*; at his elbow was *The Sack of Rome*; at his hip was *The Rise and Fall of the Third Reich*, which had a large swastika on its cover. I pondered whether this could be a coincidence; some of the bookstore's employees had been upset when they'd heard Tancredo was coming to speak, and I wondered if one of them had arranged for Tancredo to stand beside this classic summary of the ascent of Adolf Hitler. Liberals in Colorado liked to cheer themselves up by calling Tancredo a modern-day Nazi, but after spending time in his company, I did not think he could be so easily dismissed. His critics failed to acknowledge the congressman's considerable charm.

"I was the subject of a *Saturday Night Live* spoof recently," Tancredo told the crowd. "They had somebody playing Anderson Cooper, somebody playing me, and somebody playing Vicente Fox. It was totally unfair—*totally* unfair. The guy playing me looked like me, and the guy playing Vicente Fox looked like Antonio Banderas!"

The crowd hooted. Then the congressman grew sober. He brought up NAFTA and CAFTA, the trade agreements that were transforming the economic relationships between this country and its neighbors. "You know what, guys? Do you know why they're not called treaties? Do you know why they're called agreements?" he asked. "They meet all five criteria of being a treaty, but they aren't called that. A treaty needs to be ratified by two-thirds of the Senate, and they can't do it. They don't have the votes. Therefore, they are not called treaties; they are called agreements."

"That's insanity!" called out a member of the audience.

"That's *politics*," replied Tancredo.

And politics was always on the horizon, whenever I spent time with Marisela and Yadira. The furor over immigration occupied a hulking presence in the emotional geography of the two girls, much in the way that the Rocky Mountains dominated the physical landscape. Other teenagers did not follow the intricate twists and turns of bills as they moved through the state legislature, nor repeat remarks made by members of the U.S. House of Representatives, but Marisela and Yadira did. As locals used the snowcapped mountains to orient themselves in space, the two girls without legal status used the fiery political debate to orient themselves with respect to the idea of America. Was the country going to embrace or reject them? The answer wasn't clear yet, and consequently they assumed a cautious stance toward this place their parents had chosen. The two girls kept hoping that elected officials would accept their presence before they finished high school—in time to resolve their dilemma about paying for college—but of course Tancredo wanted to make sure this did not happen.

5

LIFE'S MIGHTY QUESTION

In the middle of April, two weeks after Marisela almost choked on her gum during calculus, I arrived at Roosevelt High to spend the day with Yadira Vargas. Marisela's best friend had come to school early and was waiting for me in the lobby, wearing hip-hugger jeans, a baby-blue hooded sweat jacket, and light blue sneakers. The lenses of her small rectangular glasses were also tinted blue, and her shiny, straight dark hair was pulled up into a high ponytail. She could have stepped out of the pages of *Seventeen*.

On the way to algebra class ("I was in chemistry, but a teacher told me that four years of math was better for college"), Yadira caught me up on what had happened since my last visit to Roosevelt. At the end of the previous week, she had stopped by the post-secondary options office with Clara, when a student had shouted that he had won a Daniels Fund scholarship. To learn whether she had won a scholarship, too, Clara needed to check with Miss Fracasso, the teacher who was delivering the news. She had not wanted to go by herself and had begged Yadira to accompany her. When Miss Fracasso had smiled broadly at Clara, indicating that she had also been selected for this honor, Clara had thrown her arms around Yadira, ecstatic that she could go to any college she liked. In that instant, Yadira had realized that if she had been able to stay in the Daniels Fund program, she probably would have won a scholarship, too, since her grades were even higher than Clara's. It was like living through what might have been. Then Yadira had learned that Elissa had won a Daniels scholarship as well, and it had taken her all weekend to recover her equilibrium.

In algebra class, Yadira pulled out her textbook, a calculator, and a hot-pink day planner. I never saw Marisela write down a single homework assignment, but Yadira mapped out her life with care in the pink planner. When the teacher asked the students to take out their homework, Yadira obediently put hers onto her desk; not many other students appeared to have completed the assignment. Then the teacher said the word *asymptote,* and the class erupted into hoots and whistles, while Yadira ignored the commotion. As the teacher put a transparency about functions onto an overhead projector, Yadira told me: "I heard back from Colorado College. They accepted me, but they didn't offer me any money. So it's like, if you have $37,000 lying around, you can come here." She tried to say this in an offhand way, but did not quite manage to do so. She figured that Colorado College was not courting her because of her immigration status. Why else would they give a full ride to Clara and nothing to her?

"I have my Whittier scholarship letter here," Yadira announced in a brighter tone.

The letter referred to a partial scholarship that Yadira had just acquired with the help of Irene and Justino Chávez. Back in the fall, after she had learned that she could not compete for money from the Daniels Fund, Yadira's stony silence had become so absolute that Irene Chávez had peppered her with questions to find out what was wrong. When Yadira finally explained, Irene and Justino advised her to go to the media. They knew it was a risky strategy, given the unwelcome attention that Jesús Apodaca had drawn, but they introduced Yadira to a writer for the *Denver Post* who agreed not to publish her real name. In the newspaper column that followed, the writer described Yadira's plight and advocated for the passage of the Development, Relief and Education for Alien Minors Act, or DREAM Act. Senators Orrin Hatch and Richard Durbin had introduced this piece of federal legislation, which had created the prospect of a national resolution to the girls' predicament. "Each year, about fifty thousand undocumented immigrants graduate from high school in the United States," Hatch said in a speech to the Senate Committee on the Judiciary. "Most of them came to this country with their parents as small children and have been raised here just like their U.S. citizen classmates. Many of them view themselves as Americans and are loyal to our country." Hatch pointed out that the students had not made the decision to enter the United States the wrong way, yet could not work legally, and were effectively barred from higher education. "We have a choice either to keep these talented young people underground or give them a chance to contribute to the United States."

Coached by Irene Chávez, Yadira and Marisela had spent hours lobbying elected officials to support the DREAM Act. The only problem was that Hatch had squared off against cultural conservatives in his own party—voters in neighborhoods like Highlands Ranch considered the DREAM Act a ludicrous example of bleeding-heart liberalism—and the opponents of illegal immigration lobbied against the measure as ferociously as the students and their allies lobbied for it.

Meanwhile, a reader called the *Denver Post* and said she could not get the story about the undocumented student out of her mind. Cynthia Poundstone was not wealthy, but she knew how to raise money, as she had been active in various civic causes. That winter, Poundstone contacted Irene Chávez and offered to raise enough money to pay for Yadira's education at her alma mater, Whittier College, a private liberal arts institution located in Whittier, California. Poundstone was serving on the college's board of trustees. Yadira had never heard of Whittier, and she thought the idea of a stranger raising tens of thousands of dollars for her sounded farfetched, but she saw no other options.

Yadira soon discovered that her benefactor needed tutoring in the reality of life without documents. First Poundstone suggested they fly to California to tour Whittier, and Yadira explained that she didn't have a form of identification that would allow her to board an airplane. Then Poundstone suggested they take the bus, and Yadira described the federal searches for illegal immigrants on all major bus routes. In the end, Yadira had applied to Whittier without setting foot on the campus. Two weeks before I accompanied her to algebra class, Yadira had learned that she had been accepted. Now she pulled a green folder out of her backpack. Written on the front in embossed silver script was a stanza from "To a Maiden," by John Greenleaf Whittier, a Quaker abolitionist:

> *Early hath Life's mighty question*
> *Thrilled within thy heart of youth,*
> *With a deep and strong beseeching:*
> *What and where is Truth?*

Inside the folder was a letter from Kieron Miller, the director of admission at Whittier.

Dear Yadira,

I am pleased to inform you that you have achieved the highest academic honor possible for new students at Whittier College, namely designation as a John Greenleaf Whittier scholar. You have been selected to receive the John Greenleaf Whittier scholarship valued at $12,000 for the 2004–2005 academic year.

The scholarship is awarded to students whose outstanding academic performance and personal qualifications place them at the top of the entering class. It is renewable for four years if you have maintained a 3.0 grade point average and full-time enrollment and stayed in good standing at Whittier.

If you want additional need-based aid, contact an admissions counselor as soon as possible.

When the letter had arrived, Yadira had showed it to Irene Chávez, who immediately did as it suggested—she called to ask for more money. After Irene got off the phone, the John Greenleaf Whittier scholarship had been increased to $14,000, and the school had agreed to give Yadira an additional $8,000 in aid designated for international students. This brought the total amount of money that Whittier was offering to $22,000, and Yadira needed only another $10,000 to go. By the point when Yadira showed me her letter, Poundstone had organized a series of house parties for upper-middle-class women who might donate, and was predicting that she would soon raise the rest of the money.

After algebra class, Yadira wanted to stop by her locker. On her way there, she pulled out a Whittier key chain. "Look, they gave me this," she said proudly. "They've given me lots of stuff: a shirt, a hat, two pens." Sharing the news about Whittier with Marisela had been awkward. "It almost made me feel bad that I have this advantage over her," Yadira said as she twirled the dial on her locker. "That's why I haven't told her about the rest of the money—she knows about my $12,000 scholarship, but when I found out it was really $14,000 and then I got another $8,000, too, I didn't tell her. I didn't want to make her feel worse." Now Yadira was keeping things from Marisela, just as Clara and Elissa had done. "The reason that she and I got so close was that we had that in common," Yadira said, taking off her jacket. "Now I've got money, and she doesn't, and I'm almost sure I'm going to make it—and that built a wall right there."

Yadira hung up the jacket in her locker. Underneath, she was wearing a sleeveless white tank top that said "U.S.A." in red, white, and blue letters. I found this incongruous, but she did not. Her parents had brought her to this country before she could make an internal record of their actions, leaving her with the recollections of a native-born American, despite her lack of legal status. Her mother, Alma Sandoval, had grown up in a small *colonia* in Durango. While still a teenager, Alma had married Mario Vargas, a rough man from a neighboring *colonia*. Yadira had been born eight and a half months later. Shortly after his daughter's birth, Mario had left for Glendale, California, where he had worked as a cook at Clancy's Crab Broiler, according to Alma.

Mario soon obtained a green card, after Congress passed the Immigration Reform and Control Act of 1986. Even though he had never picked fruit or vegetables, he filled out paperwork claiming that he had worked in the fields, and bought a fraudulent letter on the black market to back up his story. Several of Alma's brothers were working in California at the time, as was her father, and in 1989, she decided to move there, too. After Mario paid them a visit, Alma and Yadira traveled with him as far as Tijuana, where Mario left them with relatives, promising to send money so they could continue their journey. Five months later, Alma grew impatient, and crossed the border with a legal friend. They drove through a checkpoint with Alma sitting in the front seat of the car, holding Yadira on her lap; a Border Patrol agent waved them through after glancing at the driver's documents.

Yadira's earliest memories started in Glendale, where she had shared a house with her parents and her father's siblings—her *tías* and *tíos*. She possessed no memories of her native country. This came to disturb her later, when she began grappling with the thorny question of her identity. How could she call herself Mexican when she did not retain a single impression of the country of her birth? The entire sum of her subjective experiences had taken place here in the States, but the official world insisted that what mattered more was the illegal act that had occurred before her own sense of beginning.

While living in Glendale, California, Alma and Mario had two more children—Yadira's sisters, Zulema and Laura, both of whom entered the world as citizens of the United States. Then Mario started spending a lot of time in Tijuana. A family friend eventually informed Alma that Mario had a new girlfriend and was dividing his time between the two women. He left for good when Yadira was seven. She did not retain many memories of the man who had sired her, although her mother always said she looked exactly like him; he had been tall and slender, too.

Alma had submitted an application for citizenship based on her relationship with Mario, but once he abandoned the family the application became void. Yadira's mother did not speak English, had no Social Security number, and had never held a job in the United States. For several years, she provided for her children solely with the welfare checks she collected for Zulema and Laura—benefits to which Alma's two younger children were legally entitled, thanks to their U.S. citizenship. Then Alma's mother moved to California and began watching the children, which enabled Alma to get a job as a sales clerk at a flea market. The family who owned the market paid Alma $30 a day in cash, off the books. Her meager salary never quite covered the family's expenses, so they moved whenever they could not pay the rent. As a result, Yadira went to five different elementary schools. "I never had a stable life," she told me.

When Yadira was eight years old, a major earthquake rocked the apartment building in which her family was living. Suddenly everything was getting tossed around, and they had to run outside in their pajamas. Inspectors declared the building unsafe. Alma had scraped up to buy used furniture—a sofa bed, refrigerator, and television set—all lost. For a brief period, Yadira and her family lived in a homeless shelter. "It was at this point that I gained an incredible thirst for stability, and for what people would consider a 'normal life,'" Yadira later wrote in an essay.

The family moved out of the homeless shelter with help from the Federal Emergency Management Administration, which paid for Alma and the girls to stay in a hotel, and then subsidized the rent on a split-level duplex for a period of time. (Occasionally, FEMA gives aid to undocumented immigrants, if they have children who are citizens.) The duplex was far nicer than the other places where they had lived, and Yadira remembered it with awe. "It was a really pretty apartment," she told me. "It had a living room, a dining room, a big kitchen, and two floors, with the bedrooms upstairs. It was very, very cool. It was like 'Wow!' for us."

While they were living in the duplex, Alma's brother brought over a friend, Jesús, who was also from Durango. Both men were working in the kitchen of a Holiday Inn Hotel at the time. Alma recognized Jesús instantly; they had once been sweethearts. When Alma was sixteen, they had talked of marriage, but later the couple had quarreled and Jesús had left for California without saying good-bye. Within a few days of their unexpected reunion, Jesús called and asked Alma out to dinner. She told him that he would have to take her three daughters, too. "If you invite one of us, you invite us all," she announced. Jesús said that would be fine. He knew her husband had left her thanks to the grapevine that knit together people from Durango who lived in the United States. Jesús took Alma and the girls out to a Mexican restaurant in Pasadena, and later Alma remembered the evening as one of the most special moments of her life.

The family's fortunes stabilized after Jesús joined the household. He received a promotion—from dishwasher to cook—and was making $7.50 an hour. Jesús had applied for legal residency, but his application had been denied, and instead he used a fake Social Security card that bore his real name and a made-up number. When Yadira was twelve, her mother gave birth to Jesús's son, Raúl. Like Laura and Zulema, he was born in the United States, making Yadira the only child in the family who had failed to acquire legal status in this country at birth. "My brother would cough a couple of times, and there they would go off to the doctor again!" she said. "But I'm having a fever, and we don't go."

Yadira was thirteen when Jesús and Alma decided to move to Colorado, in search of a lower cost of living. Jesús got a job as a cook at a Hops Restaurant Bar and Brewery on the outskirts of Denver, then found more lucrative work laying sewer pipes to all the new homes that were springing up around the metro area. He started out making $12 an hour and earned steady raises until he was making $16 an hour. Meanwhile, Alma bought a fake Social Security card on the black market using a made-up number and began busing tables at La Loma, a Mexican restaurant on the northwest side of the city. She was paid $5.10 an hour, then $5.75. After a few months, Alma left to work briefly as a sales clerk, and then found a job sorting through used clothing at a Goodwill Industries in the metro area. Alma set aside items that were stained or ripped, separated men's things from women's and children's, and then grouped similar apparel together—all the dresses belonged in one place, all the blouses in another. She started out making $6.50 an hour, and throughout several years her hourly wage increased to $8 an hour. She was not surprised to see the quantities of clothing that Americans gave away, as the Goodwill managers explained about the tax credits that donors received in exchange for giving to the charity. She was amazed by the brand names that came across the sorting table—Calvin Klein, Donna Karan, Victoria's Secret—and by the cash she found in the pockets of items. Alma frequently discovered crumpled-up tens and twenties, and once stumbled across one hundred dollars in a jacket. For a long time, Alma kept expecting people to come back, looking for those missing dollars, but they never did. Apparently Americans had so much money, they did not notice when they misplaced significant sums.

In Denver, Yadira started the eighth grade. She soon met Clara, then Elissa and Marisela, but she shared nothing of the difficulties she had experienced with her new friends. It wasn't her nature to give much away. "I don't show strong emotions," she told me. "If I'm extremely sad, I don't cry. It's hard for me to do that." Her friends observed Yadira's meticulous ways—the cleanliness of her clothes, the neatness of her handwriting—and assumed she must be leading a secure and orderly life. During a sleepover, Elissa said that she envied Yadira's perfect existence, and Yadira was so taken aback that she lay in the dark without speaking. She realized afterward that she would have to admit to her friends how imperfect her life was if she wanted them to know her. In high school, Yadira began to open up. Clara, Elissa, and Marisela were the first people in the world in whom she ever confided. Never before had Yadira gone to school with the same students for long enough to build such trust.

During her junior year of high school, Yadira started having difficulties at home after Jesús became overly protective of his tall, striking stepdaughter. "He wouldn't let me go out," Yadira recollected. "He wouldn't let me talk on the phone. I didn't understand why." Alma and Jesús began to fight a lot—Alma could be stubborn, and Jesús had a bad temper. Sometimes they fought over Yadira. Yadira met Juan the summer between her junior and senior years, after Irene Chávez recruited the young man to work on one of her projects, and Yadira's relationship with her stepfather deteriorated. Jesús forbade Yadira to see Juan, and when she continued to do so over his objections, Jesús started following them around in a way that seemed menacing. Yadira ran away from home, staying overnight with Julio, another friend from high school. After that, Jesús told Yadira that he understood she was getting older, and things were better for a while, but in a few months, Jesús started following Yadira again. This time she ran away to Marisela's. Marisela wondered if Jesús was attracted to Yadira himself, but Yadira never spoke of anything of the sort with her friends. When I asked if Jesús had ever sexually abused her, Yadira said he hadn't—he had just driven her crazy with his desire to keep her confined.

Halfway through Yadira's senior year, during a slump in the local economy (the cause of the city's budget crisis), Yadira's parents decided to move back to California. Jesús could no longer support a family of five by laying down pipe, because rents had increased while his salary had remained the same. Alma told Irene Chávez about the impending move shortly before the Christmas holidays. At the time, Yadira had just met Cynthia Poundstone and was in the middle of applying to Whittier, and Irene worried that if Yadira moved, she would never complete the application. California granted in-state tuition to undocumented students, but only if a student had gone to high school in that state for at least three years; Yadira would not qualify. That was when Irene and Justino Chávez had invited Yadira to live with them. Jesús thought it was a terrible idea, but Alma decided her daughter could stay behind. Once Alma had been denied an opportunity to continue her education, back in her hometown of Dolores Hidalgo, when a wealthy cousin of her mother's had offered to pay the tuition that her school began charging after sixth grade, but her mother had declined out of pride. Afterward, Alma had left school and spent her days at home, helping to raise her younger siblings. Later she worked in the fields, harvesting potatoes and picking apples. She had never forgiven her mother for refusing the offer of tuition. Alma was not going to deprive her daughter of a chance to go to college.

Irene and Justino Chávez lived in a handsome two-story brick house on the northwest side of Denver, on the edge of the once Italian neighborhood where Tancredo had been raised. When Yadira moved into their spacious bungalow, she was used to living with more people in much less square footage, and she began hoarding familiar Mexican snacks in her bedroom to make herself feel more at home. Irene often discussed things that Yadira considered taboo, such as her inner state of mind. Yadira's family never discussed such ambiguous matters. Irene even asked Yadira point-blank if she was having sex with Juan. When Yadira replied truthfully that she remained a virgin, Irene startled her by delivering an explicit lecture about birth control and sexually transmitted diseases anyway, just in case. "Irene, she likes to communicate," Yadira told me. "If something is wrong, she wants to sit down and talk about it. She and her daughters talk on the phone all the time. I hear them, and it's so easy for them. Me and my mom—we are close, but we don't talk like that. At first Irene thought we were really weird, because we didn't communicate how we were feeling. Irene would always ask, 'How are you? How was your day?' My mom would never ask me that. That's why I don't talk to my mom so much, now that she's in California. I want to tell her that I love her and I miss her, but she would say, 'What's wrong?'"

At the same time, Yadira was now sharing a house with two adults who knew more than anyone else in Colorado about the obstacles undocumented students face. Public schools across the country were required to serve all children, regardless of immigration status, because of a 1982 U.S. Supreme Court decision in a case called *Plyler v. Doe*. Coincidentally, Irene and Justino Chávez had been living in Houston, Texas, when the various lawsuits that became part of *Plyler* had started unfolding in courtrooms around that state. Texas had revised its educational statutes to say that it would no longer reimburse local school districts for the education of children who could not prove their right to live here—local districts could ban children without legal status from public schools or charge their families tuition. Several parties had challenged the constitutionality of the revised statute, and a judicial panel had consolidated most of the lawsuits into a single action that was going to be heard in federal court in Houston. Along with other community leaders, Justino Chávez formed La Coalición para los Derechos de Niños Indocumentados (the Coalition for the Rights of Undocumented Children) to drum up public support for the affected children, and the group packed the courtroom with demonstrators. The emotional climax of the trial came when attorneys representing the children in question put a nine-year-old witness named Gabriela on the stand. She testified that she wished to go to school just like her eight-year-old brother, who had been born in this country. Attorneys representing the state of Texas countered by saying that educating children such as Gabriela cost the state as much as $1.65 billion per year.

When U.S. District Court Judge Woodrow Seals ruled in favor of the undocumented schoolchildren, the state of Texas appealed his decision, setting in motion a chain of events that brought the case to the Supreme Court. In 1982, the Supreme Court justices decided, in a deeply divided 5-to-4 ruling, that Seals had been correct—all children growing up in this country had a constitutional right to attend public schools. It was the first time the court found that the Fourteenth Amendment's guarantee of equal protection should extend to anyone, citizen or stranger, who lived within the country's boundaries. "The illegal aliens who are plaintiffs in these cases challenging the statute may claim the benefit of the Equal Protection Clause, which provides that no State shall 'deny to any person within its jurisdiction the equal protection of the laws,'" wrote Justice William J. Brennan Jr., in the majority opinion. "Whatever his status under the immigration laws, an alien is a 'person' in any ordinary sense of that term."

On this matter, the justices were unanimous. The justices split over the extent to which public education was a right that merited equal protection. The Supreme Court had already ruled that education was not a fundamental right (like free speech or the right to bear arms), and so the strictest level of equal protection scrutiny did not apply. Justice Brennan argued for applying the middle standard of scrutiny, and four other justices—Marshall, Blackmun, Powell, and Stevens—agreed with Brennan. "The deprivation of public education is not like the deprivation of some other governmental benefit," wrote Brennan. "Public education has a pivotal role in maintaining the fabric of our society and in sustaining our political and cultural heritage; the deprivation of education takes an inestimable toll on the social, economic, intellectual, and psychological well-being of the individual, and poses an obstacle to individual achievement." If Texas wanted to deny one group of children access to public education, then it had to show the act of discrimination was justified by serving some substantial state interest, under the middle level of equal protection scrutiny. Texas had claimed that its actions would help curb illegal immigration, but Brennan rejected this idea. "The dominant incentive for illegal entry into the State of Texas is the availability of employment; few if any illegal immigrants come to this country, or presumably to the State of Texas, in order to avail themselves of a free education." Texas had also suggested it cost more to educate children who didn't have legal status, but Brennan pointed out that speaking a foreign language, not lack of citizenship, made children costly. Undocumented children were "basically indistinguishable" from documented children who lived in Spanish-speaking households, in terms of expense. "It is difficult to understand precisely what the state hopes to achieve by promoting the creation and perpetuation of a subclass of illiterates within our boundaries, surely adding to the problems and costs of unemployment, welfare, and crime," added Brennan. "It is thus clear that whatever savings might be achieved by denying these children an education, they are wholly insubstantial in light of the costs involved to these children, the state, and the nation."

Chief Justice Warren E. Burger wrote a stinging dissent, and was joined by Justices White, Rehnquist, and O'Connor. "Were it our business to set the nation's social policy, I would agree without hesitation that it is senseless for an enlightened society to deprive any children— including illegal aliens—of an elementary education," wrote Burger. But it was not, he argued; the court was wrongly assuming a policymaking role. Burger thought education should not be distinguished from other government services, and merited the lowest level of equal protection scrutiny. The only issue should be whether the distinctions Texas had made between groups of people were rational, in Burger's opinion, and he considered it so to distinguish between people who were lawfully present and people who were not. "By definition, illegal aliens have no right whatever to be here, and the state may reasonably, and constitutionally, elect not to provide them with government services at the expense of those who are lawfully in the state."

Yadira and Marisela had not yet been born when Justices Brennan and Burger wrote their opposing opinions in *Plyler v. Doe*. Yadira and her mother had driven through the border checkpoint in Tijuana seven years after the historic decision took place, and by the time Marisela had huddled in the back of a pickup truck, uncertain of where her mother was in the vehicle, eleven years had passed. Irene and Justino Chávez sometimes marveled to think that events they had witnessed in Houston two decades ago could now be influencing the lives of students growing up in Denver. Justino had never dared to envision so lofty a goal, back when he was organizing the Coalición; the thought of shaping national policy had never entered his mind. It was the state of Texas that had chosen to pursue the matter all the way to the Supreme Court, and thus granted every undocumented child in the United States the newly created right to a public school education. Justino had just thought that all the kids in his neighborhood belonged in school.

After hanging up her jacket, Yadira closed up her locker and made her way toward the classroom where she had Chicano studies. Marisela found us in the crowded hallway.

"I made it on time today!" she announced.

The gold streaks were gone, and her hair now had a reddish sheen. In Chicano studies, the girls read a news report about a student protest at Denver's Abraham Lincoln High School. Marisela, Yadira, and León pulled their desks together to discuss the material.

"What happened at Lincoln?" asked Yadira, uncertainly.

"They found out it was an inferior education, so they walked out," León told her.

"How did they find out?" Marisela wanted to know.

"They went to a white school."

"Oh!" Marisela and Yadira said in unison.

"Kind of like what we did," added Marisela.

The girls had once taken an illuminating field trip to Cherry Creek High School, an affluent suburban facility located in Tom Tancredo's congressional district. They had discovered that Cherry Creek was like a mirror image of Roosevelt: The suburban high school was 85 percent Anglo, while theirs was 85 percent Latino. Only ten miles separated the two schools, yet Roosevelt served a far greater number of poor students with fewer resources. In previous years, busing and white flight had caused enrollment to plunge in Denver, and afterward the city school district's pension obligations had ballooned, creating a financial disaster. Meanwhile, the suburban school district of Cherry Creek had enjoyed the opposite situation—increased enrollment and lower pension obligations. The affluence of Cherry Creek had stunned the students of Roosevelt. The athletic facilities looked like something out of a magazine; the textbooks were brand-new and there were enough of them to go around; the computer labs contained dozens of machines. In Chicano studies, as soon as Marisela read about students taking to the streets, she wanted to stir things up, too.

"We should walk out, you guys!" she urged.

"What for?" León wanted to know. "You have to walk out for a reason."

"Well, why did those kids walk out?"

"They had demands. You have to have demands."

"Oh," said Marisela. Her fiery desire to strike dampened, and she turned her attention back to other matters, such as whether Yadira wanted to come over that weekend.

"You can spend the night," Marisela offered.

"I don't know," said Yadira, uncertain.

"If you *want*!"

They often fenced this way: Marisela made demands, and Yadira refused to acquiesce. Yadira had a tensile strength that I found surprising. Now she pulled out the green folder with the silver writing on it, and peeked inside.

"What is that, your diploma?" Marisela teased.

Yadira showed her the letter.

Marisela studied it. "You have to maintain a 3.0! Is it a hard school?"

"She can do it," said León.

"Did you tell your mom?" Marisela asked.

"Yeah," said Yadira. "She was like 'Oh my God!'"

"I can't have lunch with you today because I have some business to take care of," Marisela announced mysteriously.

Her friends stared. Marisela flashed them a huge grin.

"I'm having lunch with Gabriel," she clarified.

"Oh! An executive session!" ribbed León.

"*Suave!*" said Marisela, using Mexican slang for *cool*.

The bell rang. It was time for dance class, which Yadira and Marisela both took. The dance studio had three walls made of cinder block that all featured large mirrors, and one folding wall that separated it from the rest of the gym. Donna Marie Valentino, the school's dance instructor, strode in wearing a pink leotard, black sweatpants, and black dance shoes. Yadira and Marisela sat cross-legged on the floor, along with two dozen other Latinas and one African American. One Latina was wearing a pair of navy sweatpants that said BAD GIRL down her left leg, while another had on gray sweats that said CHEER! across her backside. The school's AP classes were filled with native English speakers, and dance class was the only time that Marisela and Yadira mixed with students from the English Language Acquisition program. As usual, the *mexicanas* had segregated themselves on the opposite side of the studio from the Chicanas. Yadira and Marisela had to explain this to me later, however, for I couldn't tell the difference between the two groups. The two friends chose to sit with the *mexicanas*, as if their loyalties were secure, but in truth they shared more classes with the Chicanas, and were not entirely accepted by either group.

Just as Donna Marie Valentino was calling the class to order, Elissa appeared at the door and said Marisela had to come to the post-secondary options office. Valentino distributed handouts, and Yadira took two copies of everything—one for herself, the other for Marisela. Later this week, the school's dancers were going to perform a showcase in the school auditorium, and now the students broke up into small groups to practice their routines. While BAD GIRL set up a boom box out in the hallway, Marisela returned and pulled Yadira aside. "Guess what?" she cried. "I just got into Metro! The woman said that because of my GPA and my class rank, they would accept me!" Metropolitan State College of Denver was a public institution with a reputation for providing a solid education to poor students at a lower cost than other four-year institutions in Colorado. Marisela's manner shifted. "It's going to be out-of-state tuition though," she added.

"How much is out-of-state tuition?" Yadira asked.

"Nine thousand dollars," said Marisela glumly.

If she had been classified as a Colorado resident, her tuition would have been $3,370, but instead it was going to be $9,570. Marisela's father earned $22,000 a year, and paid $12,000 in rent and utility bills annually; he spent the rest of his income on groceries and clothing. He didn't have an extra $9,000 to spare. BAD GIRL turned on a song by the Kumbia Kings called *"Mi Gente,"* and the girls lined up in front of a display case, using its glass front as a mirror. Beneath their reflections, I could see dusty trophies, old team photographs, and an orange T-shirt that said PILGRIMS. It seemed odd that a school full of *mexicanos* and Chicanos would call themselves Pilgrims, but I suppose that was another group of people who had left a homeland in search of opportunity. As the girls danced, I studied the pictures of the bygone athletes. During the 1940s and 1950s, everyone appeared to be Caucasian, then came a period of flux during the 1970s and 1980s. By the 1990s, almost every-one appeared to be Latino. The shift had happened so quickly.

The Kumbia Kings sang:

Sufro, siento, rio, lloro,
callo, grito, con toda mi gente.
Sufro, siento, rio, lloro,
callo, grito, porque no me entienden.

I suffer, I feel, I laugh, I cry,
I am silent, I shout, with all my people.
I suffer, I feel, I laugh, I cry,
I am silent, I shout, because they don't understand me.

After dance class, Yadira and I went out for lunch at a nearby café, where we bumped into Mr. Baker, a French teacher at Roosevelt.

"Yadira!" Mr. Baker called out. "I have lunch here every day! It's a great place. Hey, did you get the Daniels scholarship?"

Yadira looked at him with a poker face.

"No," she said. "I wasn't participating in that."

Mr. Baker seemed nonplussed.

"No?" he said uncertainly. "How about Clara?"

"Yes, she got it. And Elissa, too. But not Marisela."

Mr. Baker nodded, looking confused. After he left, Yadira said with exasperation, "He knows that I don't have papers, because I told him a while ago, but he always forgets. He knows about Marisela, too." After a moment, however, Yadira forgave the French teacher for his absentmindedness. "He really, really likes Marisela," she added, her face softening. "He told her something inspiring. He told her, 'Marisela, you are going to succeed, and it is going to feel so much better for you than it does for other people, because you are going to have to struggle more.' And it's true. We are going to succeed, and it is going to feel better than it would for somebody who has had everything handed to them."

6

AMERICAN WOMAN

Three days later, I returned to Roosevelt High and found the two girls without legal status in a state of greatly heightened animation. Hope had arrived unexpectedly in the form of Cezar Mesquita, the director of diversity enrollment for the University of Denver. The University of Denver was a private school with excellent faculty and a prestigious reputation. It was not known for the diversity of its student body, and to address that situation university officials had been pursuing enterprising students from local inner-city high schools. The university had developed a particularly close relationship with Roosevelt, and last week a recruiter had sought out Marisela, Yadira, Clara, and Elissa after reading about their accomplishments in the local paper, where they had been featured in a story about student leadership. In the process, the girls had learned that the admissions office was still considering applications on a case-by-case basis, and that university officials knew of a Republican businessman who sponsored immigrant students. This businessman was now paying for the education of more than a dozen bright students who lacked Social Security numbers, including Jesús Apodaca, at a number of colleges around the state. In the past few days, Yadira and Marisela had completed applications to the University of Denver (Elissa had not applied because she wanted to go to Regis and Clara had already applied to DU), and had gone to the campus for hastily arranged interviews. Now Mesquita wanted to meet with Marisela and Yadira in the post-secondary options office at Roosevelt, to discuss the donor who helped immigrant students.

The two girls had dressed up for the occasion in black slacks and fancy blouses. This had been Irene's idea; she had wanted the girls to make a good impression. She didn't want them to look like they'd come straight from the barrio. Irene had instructed Marisela to go easy on the makeup and not to rat her hair ("Sleek, Marisela! Sleek!"), and she had taken Yadira shopping at the Gap for a new suit. Meanwhile, Clara had informed Mesquita that she had won a scholarship from the Daniels Fund, which suggested that she might not need the support of the Republican donor, but Mesquita still wanted to recruit her. He had arranged to meet with Clara after he spoke with Marisela and Yadira.

Coincidentally, Elissa was sitting at a computer in the post-secondary options office when Yadira and Marisela arrived. She was working with a fellow soccer player named Estela, who had asked for help with a paper on *Lord of the Flies*. Both Elissa and Estela were wearing orange sweat suits, because they had a soccer game that afternoon, and both had pulled their hair back into ponytails. No casual observer would have been able to see any difference between the pair; the fact that Estela lacked papers just like Yadira and Marisela was something Estela preferred to keep to herself. She was hoping to go to community college if her family could raise the money for out-of-state tuition.

Marisela and Yadira sat down at a table facing Mesquita, who was tall and burly, and had an easygoing manner. "Basically, the two of you are nominated for this very, very good scholarship," he told them. "It is an outside donor who gives the money. And the two of you, along with Clara as well, are in the running." Mesquita explained that the donor was out of the country at the moment, and might not be able to make a decision for several weeks. "I know you are both considering other schools, but I strongly encourage you to wait a little bit longer," Mesquita said. "If you do get this scholarship, you won't have to worry about anything. I know this makes you very nervous, but just hang in there."

"Who else is being considered?" Yadira asked.

"You both, and Clara, and also a student from Manual High School. Basically, the four of you are in the running."

"So how many students will get the scholarship?" Yadira wanted to know.

"At least two."

Marisela groaned.

"I know, I know. She's shaking over here!" said Mesquita. "Somebody give her some juice!"

While Marisela's emotional state was easy to read, Yadira wore a tight, closed expression.

"You're not mad at me, are you, Yadira?" asked Mesquita playfully.

Yadira shook her head, embarrassed.

Clara arrived in blue jeans and a green sweater. She had less at stake, and appeared more at ease. Before Mesquita could begin talking with Clara, however, Marisela asked for his advice about filling out a financial aid form from the University of Denver.

"It asks for a Social Security number, or a passport number, and there is a box that asks whether you are a permanent resident or not."

"Do you have any of those numbers?" asked Mesquita.

Marisela shook her head.

"Did you check the box saying you are a resident?"

Marisela shook her head again. She knew that some undocumented students lied about their status—even going so far as to write down a fake Social Security number—but she had been honest. She pushed the half-completed form over to Mesquita, so he could see for himself.

"Okay, you are all right then," he said.

Mesquita told the girls he would let them know the instant he had any news.

"Do you check your e-mail regularly?" he asked.

"Not regularly," said Marisela. "But I could start to. But—did I get accepted into DU?"

"I don't know yet," said Mesquita.

"Because Miss Valdez said you sent an e-mail saying we were both accepted into DU."

"No. Not me," said Mesquita. "Let me look into it."

"*Miss Valdez!*" yelled Marisela.

Mesquita held up his hand. "You have an incredible résumé, and your interview went very, very well, so don't worry about it."

"Maybe it wasn't you, maybe it was someone else!"

"Don't be nervous," Mesquita counseled. "I know. I know. But it is an exciting time—very exciting."

The girls left the meeting in a dither. To Yadira, the University of Denver seemed much more attractive than a school she had never visited. Her stepfather had worked on a construction project on the DU campus, and she had seen the beautifully manicured grounds. "I want to stay here, because all my friends are here," Yadira told me. "And because I've visited DU, it's easier to imagine going there." For Marisela, it seemed like a reprieve—one last chance to go to college. Applying also gave her the opportunity to consult with her friends about a pres-

tigious school, which made her feel once more their equal. She asked
Clara to proofread her essay, and consulted her about which teacher
should fill out the college's teacher recommendation form. Clara told
her to ask Miss Brown, from AP literature.

"She loves you," Clara said.

"Oh, yeah, she had a dream about me once!" remembered
Marisela.

Marisela said she didn't know why, but she had a good feeling
about DU.

Initially, the girls had little time to fret about hearing back from
Mesquita. Their meeting with him had taken place on the Thursday
morning before the school's annual dance showcase and their senior
prom. On Friday evening, when the dance showcase was supposed to
begin, a late spring blizzard tumbled down from the Rocky Mountains,
and people arrived at Roosevelt shaking off the snow. The school's
principal greeted parents and students in the lobby. Inside the auditorium, I took a seat next to Irene and Justino Chávez. Nobody from
Yadira's family was present, nor anybody from Marisela's. Marisela's
father was getting ready to go to work, while her mother was making
dinner for her siblings; Yadira's mother was still in California. Irene
and Justino were the closest thing to parents that either of the girls had
in the auditorium.

The lights went down and Marisela stepped out from behind the
curtains, along with her dance instructor, Donna Marie Valentino. Valentino was wearing normal street clothes, but Marisela looked like a
sexy character in a superhero comic book. Her audacious bell-bottoms
and matching tank top were made of skintight, electric-blue spandex.
The fabric had a metallic sheen, which made her glisten every time she
moved, and her skin was covered in body glitter.

"Good evening!" Valentino called out to the half-filled auditorium.

"Buenas noches!" Marisela translated.

Valentino listed the different types of dance traditions from which
her students had drawn their routines (modern dance, hip-hop, fla-
menco, *cumbia*) and Marisela repeated the instructor's words in Spanish. Together, the teacher and her star pupil explained that the opening
number was called "American Woman." Seconds later, an ear-splitting
thunderclap broke over us—the guitar riff that introduces Lenny Kravitz's cover of that song (originally written and recorded by The Guess

Who, a Canadian band). The curtains parted to reveal three dozen young women arrayed in the same form-hugging outfit Marisela was wearing. One-third of them wore a shade of electric blue identical to Marisela's, another third wore scarlet, and the final third wore silver. They executed staccato hip-hop moves in time to the music.

American woman, said get away
American woman, listen what I say

Midway through the song, the dancers left their own color groups to form a human flag. Over in one of the stripes, I spotted Yadira, looking otherworldly in silver, with an *I Dream of Jeannie*–style ponytail sprouting from the crown of her head.

I don't need your war machines!
I don't need your ghetto scenes!

As the song reached its finale, the girls returned to their original color groups and bowed. The audience broke into furious applause. The next time we saw Marisela, she had put on another outfit, and during the second half of the show she changed again into tight black satin pants and a long-sleeved purple blouse. Yadira wore the same black satin trousers and a red blouse. They performed with several other girls to *"Mi Gente"* ("My People"), the song by the Kumbia Kings. Before their rehearsals, the girls had never heard of Lenny Kravitz, but they were intimately familiar with everything by the Kumbia Kings, a group that was founded by A. B. Quintanilla III, the older brother of the late Tejana rock star Selena. *Cumbia* and *ranchera* or *norteño* songs were what the girls listened to at home and what they heard when they went to clubs. Now the girls swiveled their hips while twirling their hands in the air in a way that made the top halves of their bodies seem disconnected from their bottom halves. In Yadira's case, this was emphasized by the fact that on her face she wore a prim expression at odds with the sultry, come-hither movements. Then, as if she couldn't help herself, she broke into an immense grin. Yadira didn't allow herself to smile often, because she had not been able to see a dentist regularly as a child, and she was embarrassed about the state of her teeth. They had brown stains on them, and had grown in crooked. If Yadira let herself smile, it was a special occasion. At the end of the dance, Marisela spun Yadira around in a traditional *cumbia* move, then bent her down in a dip. They froze, with Yadira's ponytail spilling across the floorboards.

"Wow!" exclaimed Irene. "Yadira really came to life during that one!"

The dance captured something essential about the last year and a half, a tumultuous time when Yadira and Marisela had repeatedly prevented each other from falling. The girls desperately wanted to figure out how to become American women, yet they were so firmly rooted in the world of *"Mi Gente."*

As soon as the major distractions of the dance showcase and the senior prom had passed, Marisela and Yadira grew increasingly nervous. Days passed with no word from Mesquita. After a week, both girls went to see Miss Valdez in the post-secondary options office, but she had no news. Later that day, Yadira and Marisela were supposed to perform their dance routines again downtown, and after they boarded the bus that was waiting in the school's parking lot, Marisela urged they call the DU admissions office. Yadira gave her the number for the woman who ran the university's international admissions department. This woman told Marisela that she had some bad news: The donor had not elected to sponsor her. The university could give Marisela $10,000 in aid designated for international students, but a year's tuition cost four times that amount, and she would have to come up with the other $30,000 on her own.

Stunned, Marisela gave the phone to Yadira, and watched her friend's face as she spoke to the woman. Yadira looked back at Marisela the whole time.

"You got it, huh?" Marisela said, after Yadira hung up the phone.

"Yeah," Yadira replied, her eyes all watery.

Yadira did not know whether she was crying out of happiness at her good fortune or unhappiness at Marisela's bad luck. Marisela felt numb but managed to give Yadira a hug. It was hard for them to talk to each other for the rest of the day. Marisela moved through her dance steps automatically, spinning when she was supposed to spin, and catching Yadira when she dipped, but inside she had turned to ice. After they returned to Roosevelt, Marisela surprised herself by snapping at a girl who said she was sorry—somehow the news had spread already. Marisela felt exposed; she had been compared to her best friend and judged to be worth less. Too upset to stay in school, Marisela tried to leave, but in the parking lot, her truck wouldn't start. She called her mother, and as soon as Josefa arrived, Marisela broke down.

"Qué pasó? Qué pasó?" Josefa kept asking, but Marisela was crying too hard to get the words out. Finally she managed to say that she hadn't won the scholarship.

"No te preocupes, mija," Josefa said, crying, too. Don't worry, my child. *"Guardaré suficiente dinero para escuela de belleza."* I'll save enough money for beauty school.

"Ay, Mamá," replied Marisela.

What else could she say? Marisela knew that Josefa considered beauty school a significant accomplishment, and did not want to hurt her mother's feelings by pointing out that she considered trade school beneath her. She never brought up the scholarship again. When she returned to school, Marisela acted as though she had no concerns. Secretly, she was acutely disappointed in herself for being incapable of conquering her illegitimacy, when Yadira had overcome the same impediment, but Marisela hid her self-doubt, because she was tired of being at odds with her friends. She played the party girl, talking about clubs and nightlife and anything except what would happen after June. Irene Chávez and Aurora Valdez saw right through her act, and worried about Marisela's volatile nature. Aurora Valdez told Irene that Marisela was the most sensitive of the foursome. Irene agreed—Marisela was the toughest and yet the most sensitive one. They hoped she didn't try to hurt herself again.

Marisela dropped the false cheeriness when she got home, where she was listless and spent hours in her bedroom under the framed photographs of her dual attributes. Sometimes she did her homework, but often did not bother. She would mostly talk on the phone, or just sit around. One day, while cleaning her room, she came across two bags of material that she'd collected from the colleges that had once wanted to recruit her. She sat down and went through the glossy brochures. At first, she made sarcastic comments to herself as she read the pamphlets, but then she became unbearably sad. She lay down on her bed, thinking about all of those gorgeous college campuses. She envisioned what her life was going to be like without a college degree, and saw bad things coming: working at King Soopers forever, or marrying young, just to get out of the house. She felt certain that she would disappoint her parents. "I mean, they work at maintenance jobs," she told me. "I've seen how many hours a week they work, and how they still struggle. My dad, ever since he got here, that's all he's done—he cleans stores in the night. I didn't want to do that. And I didn't want him to see me like that. Because I know that even though he does that kind of a job, he doesn't want me there. He doesn't want any of his children there."

7

SYMPATHY

As the school year drew to a close, the single remaining hope that Marisela cherished was the possibility that either federal or state lawmakers might act to help undocumented students by the time she graduated high school. While the federal government had taken no action on the DREAM Act since last fall, the state legislature had been actively debating what to do with students like Marisela all that spring. A number of other states had already acted to offer in-state tuition to undocumented students: Texas, California, New York, Utah, Illinois, Kansas, Oklahoma, New Mexico, and Washington. The girls were praying that Colorado would follow suit. It did not seem likely, as legislation that would have made in-state tuition available to them had already failed to pass, but state lawmakers had taken up the question again halfway through the girls' senior year, when two different bills on the subject had been admitted into the legislature. For months, news about the progress of these measures had filled local newspapers and Spanish-language radio stations. Marisela had followed every feint and jab in the convoluted debate, her sense of optimism rising and falling in concert with the progression of the bills.

Back at the beginning of the legislative cycle, I had gone over to the gold-domed statehouse in Denver to watch the pro-immigrant and anti-immigrant forces square off before the House Education Committee. Both bills on the subject—one that would grant in-state tuition to undocumented students, and one that would expressly deny it—had come before the committee on the same day. Republican Ted Harvey, who wanted Colorado to prohibit students who couldn't show proof of legal status from qualifying for in-state tuition, spoke first. He represented the suburb of Highlands Ranch, and was a social conservative in the mold of Tom Tancredo, his U.S. congressman. "Right now, in Colorado, there is nothing in statute that prohibits giving in-state tuition to individuals who are here in the country without having their full and total immigration status legal, the way it needs to be," said Representative Harvey.

A long list of people had signed up to testify against Harvey's bill, including Justino Chávez. First a teacher from Greeley, Colorado—the center of the state's meatpacking industry—told lawmakers that Colorado's schools were experiencing an epidemic of undocumented students. "These are students that want to go to college, that want to live the American dream, that want to succeed," the teacher said. "Now we're telling them they can get K–12 education, but they can't get a driver's license, they can't get medical insurance, and they can't get a Social Security number. They can't go to college, and they can't get a good job. So what hope do we leave them? Is it any wonder that we have a high rate of incarcerating these youth, or that we have a high dropout rate?"

Nancy Spence, the chair of the Education Committee, was a moderate Republican who represented the wealthy suburb of Greenwood Village. Previously, she had spent thirteen years on the board of the Cherry Creek School District, the affluent school system that had shocked Yadira and Marisela with its amenities. Spence did not see eye to eye with liberals who wanted to give public subsidies to illegal immigrants—her official motto was "Individual liberty, personal responsibility, and limited government." Later, she interrupted the testimony of another witness who reiterated that blocking access to higher education made students more likely to drop out. "Well, I feel compelled to make a statement," Spence interjected. "Don't they just have a sense of pride and accomplishment? Getting through high school—and if that is all they have the possibility of doing—I would think that a child, a student would have a sense of inner accomplishment and doing their best. Wouldn't it be worthwhile simply to finish high school and get good grades?"

Justino Chávez took the microphone next. He had the high cheekbones and almond-shaped eyes of his Indian ancestors, and wore his long hair in a braid down his back. When people first met Chávez they sometimes assumed that he'd been born in Mexico because he spoke with a slight accent, but he had actually been born in San Jose, California, and had grown up on both sides of the border. His father was a migrant farmworker from Jalisco who had traveled to the United States periodically to pick cucumbers and tomatoes. As a teenager, Justino had worked alongside of his father during school breaks, picking onions, carrots, strawberries, apples, peaches, apricots, cantaloupe, and watermelon. He had something to say on the subject of whether illegal aliens lacked pride. "They know they could get a high school diploma, but their education dead-ends at grade twelve, and they have to go get those low-paying menial jobs anyway, and they have a family in need," he responded. "So they make a choice: I can stay at the same school for two or three more years and still be guaranteed only a minimum-wage job, or I can do the best for my family and my siblings and go out there and join the workforce, even though I'm not going to get a high school diploma. I'll go out there and dig ditches, I'll go out there and cut lawns, I'll go out there and wash dishes, and do the best for my family that I can. That's why they drop out. It's not because they don't have pride. They do have pride. And they have a sense of family, and they have a sense of priorities."

After more testimony, Spence called for a vote on Harvey's anti-tuition bill. By a 6-to-5 vote, it squeaked out of the committee. Democrat Val Vigil's pro-tuition bill was up next, and it was referred back to the Finance Committee, where it was postponed indefinitely. Meanwhile, Harvey's anti-tuition bill gained a place on the calendar to be heard by the legislature as a whole. This created hysteria in the undocumented community. "I have to pull my application from community college, because the Harvey bill passed!" Marisela told me at one point, shortly after this development. "They're going to take all those applications with blanks in the Social Security box, and they're going to investigate them!" Her statement was riddled with misunderstandings—the Harvey bill had not yet passed, and as far as I could tell nobody was investigating college applications in which the Social Security boxes had been left blank—but Marisela's hazy sense of what was going on was typical of students in her situation.

In March, while Marisela was still waiting to hear whether she had been accepted at Metro, the Harvey bill had come up for discussion on the floor of the state senate. At first its prospects looked good, as Republicans held a slim majority, and John Andrews, the president of the senate, was cosponsoring the bill. He represented Centennial, Colorado—another suburban district in the metro area—and plugged the bill as a reasonable one, given that the state's higher education institutions were under tremendous financial pressure. Several Republican colleagues spoke in support of the bill, and at first it appeared likely to pass in its original form, but then Democratic state senator Paula Sandoval introduced a surprise amendment. Sandoval represented northwest Denver, including the neighborhood in which Fabián and Josefa had purchased their home. Her amendment called for the state to deny in-state tuition to undocumented students *unless* they had graduated from a high school in Colorado after attending school in the state for at least three years—that is, those students *would* qualify for in-state tuition. Sandoval observed that all immigrants paid sales tax and most paid other taxes as well. "In some ways what we are saying is that it is okay for people to come to this country, and it's okay for them to clean the universities, to plow the fields, to harvest the crops, and to work in our restaurants, but when it comes to enjoying the fruits of those labors, what we're saying then is, 'Hey, you're not invited to sit at the table for dinner,'" she said. "So I would ask support of this amendment. Thank you."

Senator Andrews rose to argue against the proposal. "The effect of this amendment would be to make separate immigration policy for the state of Colorado," he objected. Andrews added that the amendment would privilege residents of Colorado who didn't have legal status over residents of other states who did. "The effect of the amendment would be a slap in the face to students who are making sacrifices from other states, that we would suddenly be excusing a category of students [here] from making, because there is a sympathy toward them. It is a sympathy we all share, but certainly not good public policy, and we need to say no to this amendment."

Senator Abel Tapia, a Democrat who represented the heavily Latino city of Pueblo, Colorado, one hundred miles to the south of Denver, countered by pointing out that the amended bill would affect only "the cream of the crop of the children of these immigrant workers." They were smart kids who could contribute to society, he argued. "If we're really truly concerned about illegal immigrants coming into the country, we should go after the people who employ them. We should go after their parents. But to hurt the children, and not allow them to make a success of their lives and become U.S. citizens, tax-paying, high-producing citizens, I think is a shame."

Andrews stepped forward again. "Senator Tapia, an eighteen-year-old high school graduate is not a child," he countered. "An eighteen-year-old high school graduate is an adult, in law and in fact. . . . It is simply not the responsibility of the taxpayer to provide for these young adults who are not in this country in compliance with the law."

Senator Ken Gordon, another member of the Denver delegation, reminded his colleagues about the other waves of immigrants who had come to the United States. "This is an immigrant country," said Gordon. "My grandparents came here from Russia, they were persecuted there as Jews, and my uncles went to the University of Michigan undergraduate school. They both became doctors, and they had long medical careers. They were children of immigrants. It is so shortsighted to say, 'Let's not spend a little bit of money on kids, not give them an education, not let them become doctors, or people that might invent something that is helpful to the country. Let's let them have menial jobs.'"

Senator Jim Dyer, a Republican from fast-growing Arapahoe County, stood to respond. "Senator Gordon, there are probably a billion perfectly deserving young people in the world who would like to come to the United States and come to Colorado and partake of an education that the taxpayers subsidize," said Dyer. "That is the criteria: 'Because we have nice deserving people and we are punishing children.' That's an emotional plea, and I reject that out of hand. The hard fact of the matter is that we are asking Colorado taxpayers to subsidize the children of people who are not here 'without documents,' they are here illegally."

Gordon replied heatedly that the immigrants Dyer spoke of *were* Colorado taxpayers. "The state doesn't say, 'We're not going to accept taxes from them because they are illegal!'" he fumed.

Senator Sandoval intervened. "Well, let's get away from the emotional arguments just for a moment," she said. "Let's talk about some hard data. A 1999 Rand study has shown that a thirty-year-old Mexican immigrant woman who has graduated from college will pay $5,300 more in taxes and cost $3,900 less in criminal justice and welfare expenses each year than if she had dropped out of high school."

The amendment was put to a vote. When the chair asked all those in favor to rise, in a surprising twist, two moderate Republicans stood with the Democrats. The chair pounded his gavel. "The amendment is adopted," he announced. And then the amended bill passed unanimously. Even those who opposed the change did not vote against the amended measure, for doing so would have doomed the original bill, which they planned to resurrect. When the *Rocky Mountain News* asked Representative Harvey if the change was acceptable to him, he replied: "Absolutely not. I will be asking for a conference committee and I will ask that the Senate amendment come off." Yet news of Senator Sandoval's accomplishment raced through the city's immigrant community, where undocumented students latched onto the idea that they might become eligible for in-state tuition that year. Marisela, who had vehemently opposed the old Harvey bill, became an avid proponent of the new version; particularly after she heard back from Metro, she spent hours on the telephone lobbying elected officials to support the measure as amended, because it would have drastically reduced her tuition bill at the public institution.

Marisela's vision of a legislative solution to her problems soon proved unrealistic, however, as the Harvey bill languished. Throughout the month of April, Representative Harvey struggled in vain to strip off Sandoval's amendment, and as he failed to do so the measure was repeatedly laid over, until it was finally deemed lost when the session ended in May. Marisela had been born in 1986, the same year that the federal government of the United States passed the Immigration Reform and Control Act—the last massive legalization of workers who had entered this country without authorization—and it did not seem like a coincidence that the Colorado state legislature found itself wrestling with the question of undocumented students just as she was coming of age. Marisela represented the vanguard of immigrant children who had grown up in the United States since the IRCA. The federal government of the United States had done nothing significant to address illegal immigration since Marisela had been born, other than to pass several measures making it easier to deport immigrants who committed crimes while they were living in the United States. Federal law required that undocumented children be treated equally through twelfth grade, but after that nobody seemed to know what to do with them. Individual states were left to figure out whether they wanted to treat the students as lawbreakers or potentially productive members of society. Colorado's elected officials had tried to grapple with this conundrum, but after months of debate, they had chosen to do nothing. The matter of children growing up here without legal status was simply too confounding. Now all the talk had come to nothing, high school was going to end in a matter of weeks, and Marisela still could not figure out how to pay for college.

8

CRASH TEST DUMMY

At the beginning of May, the girls began practicing the speeches they planned to deliver at their graduation ceremony, which would take place at the end of the month. In the interim, Yadira grew distraught over the question of where to go to college. After speaking further with officials at the University of Denver, Irene Chávez discovered that Marisela was next in line for a scholarship from the Republican businessman, meaning that if Yadira declined his offer, then Marisela could go to DU. But Cynthia Poundstone had not yet raised all the money Yadira needed for Whittier, and it was hard for her to imagine giving up a certain slot at DU, a school she knew well, for an uncertain slot at Whittier, a school she had never seen. At the same time, she could not bear the idea of being personally responsible for blocking Marisela's access to higher education. Yadira spent hours on the telephone with her friends, dissecting the dilemma, and became increasingly hysterical.

Irene Chávez felt frustrated by the timing of it all. High school was almost over, and college would begin in a couple of months. How could they raise an additional $30,000 for Marisela? Irene called anybody who might be able to help—the admissions office at the University of Denver, supporters of immigrant rights, an oilman who had promised to send an entire middle school to college after being inspired by the pledge that John Hickenlooper had made at Cole. She even called me, but I had to tell her that ethically I could not give money to Marisela if I was planning to write about her life, although I did provide the names of several other people who might help. Finally, Irene remembered that Yadira had two benefactors, and Marisela had none. Why couldn't Yadira persuade one of her supporters to help Marisela? When Yadira telephoned Cynthia Poundstone with this request, it seemed to take an eternity to get the idea across, but finally Poundstone grasped that

Yadira had too much money, and her friend had too little. Poundstone mulled whether the money she had raised for Yadira could be given to Marisela, and said she needed to speak with the donors she had assembled so far. In a few days, Poundstone called to say these individuals wanted to meet Marisela, but thought it would be fine to give her the money. Of course, the partial scholarship that Whittier had offered to Yadira could not be used at any other school, which meant that all Poundstone had to offer was the $10,000 she had pledged to raise personally. Marisela already had $10,000 from DU, which brought them to $20,000—half of what DU required. Soon Irene squeezed another $10,000 out of a variety of individuals and organizations, bringing the total to $30,000. Surely they could raise the last $10,000 that Marisela needed, Irene thought.

On the second weekend in May, Marisela was giving Yadira a ride home in her bronze truck when Irene called. "I need to talk to you," Irene told Marisela. "Can you come in for a moment when you drop Yadira off?"

"Irene wants to talk to me!" Marisela said to Yadira. "What is it about?"

"I think it's about school," Yadira said in a casual tone.

When they pulled up at Irene's house, Marisela jogged up the steps. Irene ushered the girls into the living room, where she announced that Cynthia Poundstone had agreed to help Marisela. Then Irene explained how they could patch together the money that Marisela needed for the University of Denver. Irene expected Marisela to be overjoyed, but instead the news struck her as implausible. By that point, she had been hoping for and despairing of a chance to go to college for months, and she didn't want to suffer another disappointment. Marisela steeled herself against the possibility that this, too, might prove a mirage. "What are the chances that it would happen?" she wondered later. "Especially to a good college. I felt like that wasn't for me—it wasn't meant for me. I wasn't good enough."

That weekend, Yadira decided to accept the Republican businessman's offer of a scholarship, and go to the University of Denver. At the beginning of the following week, I returned to Roosevelt in the middle of the day, just as Marisela was fetching Yadira from one of her classes. Marisela had told Yadira that she needed to come to a meeting with the principal. In the lobby of the school, however, they encountered a woman wearing a Papa John's delivery uniform, holding several boxes of pizza.

"Are you Yadira Vargas?" the woman asked.

"Yes," Yadira confirmed.

"You have to pay for all these pizzas."

"Not me!"

"Oh, yes. Somebody called from the main office and said you would pay for them. You are Yadira Vargas, aren't you?"

"Right, but I didn't order any pizza!" Yadira insisted. "I have to go back to class!"

The woman from Papa John's opened up the top box of pizza and revealed a $1,000 check. Yadira had been selected to be a Papa John's scholar, because of her academic performance, her community involvement, the strength of her character, and the obstacles that she had overcome. A dozen friends who had been hiding in the school's conference room nearby threw open the door and yelled, "Surprise!" Then they had a pizza party. Yadira sat halfway down the long table, looking like a flower child in a lacy black camisole and velvet hip-huggers. All her friends were crowded around the conference table, and several adults—Irene Chávez, Aurora Valdez, and Maya Rodríguez, a financial aid counselor—soon joined them.

"Congratulations!" I said to Yadira. Then I told Marisela, "Congratulations to you, too!"

"What for?" Marisela asked, looking puzzled.

"I heard you're going to DU!"

Marisela shrugged and gave a wan half-smile. "Maybe," she said.

The students started passing around yearbooks. As they wrote interminable messages to one another, I leafed through a stray yearbook looking for the girls' senior portraits—there they were, memorialized in all their unfinished glory.

"Hey, everybody!" Elissa announced. "I am planning a graduation party, and you are all invited to come!"

After half an hour, Miss Valdez kicked them out, saying that another group had booked the conference room.

"I registered for classes at Regis the other day," Elissa said as she packed up her things. "It was scary. I don't wanna go there anymore! It's such a big place. I'm worried about what it's going to be like. Going from *this* to *that* is going to be very hard."

Elissa had just turned down the Daniels Fund scholarship, after receiving an even better offer from the Bill and Melinda Gates Foundation. Two days later, I found her in the school's lobby in an entirely different mood. "I slept last night!" she announced. "For the first time in ages, I have no worries—I even rented two videos!" She was on her way to graduation rehearsal, and I tagged along. The gym's orange bleachers had been folded up to make room for all the seniors, who were sitting in rows of metal chairs, yammering. They were restless, ready for summer, and hard to control. Half a dozen weary-looking teachers stood on the sidelines, looking eager for a vacation themselves.

At the microphone, an earnest young man from a local nonprofit tried to quell the chatter. "What we're going to be doing is registering to vote," he called out. "Politicians ignore many people like you because you don't vote. We want to register over one thousand students in Denver Public Schools. We want to send a message to politicians in Colorado that they have to care about students like you. We only need the last four digits of your Social Security number. If you don't know that, then put down your driver's license number. You only need one of the two."

A student sitting toward the back raised her hand.

"Yes," the speaker said.

"What if you are not a citizen?" she asked.

"If you're not a U.S. citizen, then you can't fill this out, okay?"

Somebody shouted, "Ha!"

The front row was reserved for students who had made it into the National Honor Society. I found Marisela there, wearing a black tank top, pink jeans, and lots of makeup.

"This is so sad!" she said, happily, of high school coming to an end.

Farther down in the front row, Yadira had on a T-shirt with a row of dancing teddy bears on it, while nearby Clara sucked on a green lollipop.

"I'm going to cry any second!" Clara announced, beaming.

They were the survivors. When the girls had arrived in this building, there had been more than 600 students in their freshman class; now only 235 seniors were preparing to graduate. Nobody at Denver Public Schools could say exactly what had happened to the other four hundred students who had once gone to Roosevelt High. They had moved away, dropped out, gone missing. The gym's loudspeakers crackled and the drone of the daily announcements brought the rehearsal to a halt. Members of the school band tuned their instruments as a lone basketball player shot hoops, his shoes chirping on the shiny floor. When the announcements finally ended, Tom McIntyre, the teacher in charge of the rehearsal, reminded everyone that the actual graduation would take place in ten days, over at the Buell Theatre, in the Denver Center for the Performing Arts. McIntyre went over how the students should walk, sit, and behave. The seniors horsed around as they practiced, while glum-faced junior escorts tried to keep them in line. Donna Marie Valentino strode through the gym with her springy dancer's walk, and soon we heard the dim throb of rap music emanating from the dance studio. Then the band struck up a march, drowning out the noise.

"Okay!" bellowed Mr. McIntyre. "When the music stops! That's your cue to sit down!"

The band ceased to play, and the entire graduating class sat down with one immense shuffling sound.

"Guys, that looked great!" Mr. McIntyre said excitedly. "Honest to God, that looked really good! Now, the two people doing the welcome, I need you to come forward."

Marisela and Daniela—the Chicana who had gotten into so many top colleges—stepped up to the microphone together.

"Yeah!" a student called out. "Go, Marisela!"

Daniela welcomed all the parents who were not in the gym, and Marisela repeated her welcome in Spanish. Next came the National Anthem. Yadira and another Chicana student introduced Principal Amy Harrigan; a white-haired male faculty member stood in for her. The school's salutatorian, Dave Thomas, one of the few Anglos at Roosevelt, announced that his speech was entitled "Most Eligible Bachelor." Catcalls ricocheted off the gym walls and several seniors emitted war whoops. The faux principal quickly cut off the salutatorian and introduced the valedictorian, Cristián Gonzáles, a Chicano who seemed painfully shy. "Um, how are you doing?" he asked timorously. "Can you hear me okay?"

"*Sexy!*" a female student thundered back.

Elissa and another Chicana student delivered the closing remarks, again in two languages. After a speech-writing competition, the Roosevelt High faculty had selected Marisela, Yadira, and Elissa to represent the Mexican students in the school by delivering speeches in Spanish, while their English-speaking counterparts were representing the Chicano, Anglo, and African American students. Clara had not submitted a speech, as she was certain she would cry.

At the end of the rehearsal, Mr. McIntyre released the boisterous seniors to go to a formal lunch with Principal Harrigan at a downtown hotel. In the banquet hall, Marisela, Yadira, Elissa, and Clara sat down together at one table, along with Estela, Annalisa, and the girl whose sweatpants had said BAD GIRL. Then León and his friends crowded in, too. León, who did not have papers, was planning to go to Metro State—he had received a partial scholarship from a nonprofit that gave to undocumented students, and planned to work while he went to college. Estela and BAD GIRL both lacked documents, too; unexpectedly, Estela had won an athletic scholarship to a four-year university, but BAD GIRL had not found a way to pay for college. Meanwhile, Annalisa did have papers but had opted not to go to college. Instead, she was going to work full-time to help her family pay the bills.

Harrigan walked up to the podium at the front of the room. "There are a lot of kids who didn't graduate from Roosevelt High, so I want you to realize how special you are, and how talented you are," she told the students. "You are going to be successful. In order to do that, you need to continue your education—whether through college or through other means. It is very, very important, because life is tough out there. Enjoy your success."

The girls ignored the other speakers until Aurora Valdez took the microphone. The secretary on whom they had relied so much told the students that she loved them, and wanted them to stay in touch.

"Oh!" said Elissa.

"Don't cry!" Yadira instructed.

But Clara was already weeping, and so was Marisela.

Their real graduation exercises were held on a brilliant Sunday at the end of May, in Denver's vast performing arts complex, at the same time as the matinee shows. Elderly Anglo men and women in elegant attire streamed into the complex to catch the shows being performed in the other theaters, while alongside them residents of the other Denver—middle-aged men in Wrangler jeans whose skin had been burned the color of coffee, accompanied by women in tight-fitting cocktail dresses with their hair teased up high—streamed into the Buell. Family members of Roosevelt students filled every section of that theater, from the orchestra to the rafters. The same parents who had worked through soccer games and dance performances arrived en masse with babies and toddlers and nieces and nephews to witness the sight of their children receiving diplomas. Elissa's mother brought her siblings and cousins, while Clara's entire extended family showed up, and most of Marisela's clan, too. Only Yadira had no blood relatives inside the Buell, although Irene and Justino Chávez came in their place.

The junior escorts, now wearing white tuxedos with orange bow ties, showed members of the school board to their seats. After the Roosevelt High teachers filed in, the band broke into "Pomp and Circumstance," which even the *mexicanos* in the audience recognized as the sound of high school graduation in America. The crowd let out a roar, and kept whooping and stomping while the seniors, wearing orange gowns and mortarboards, marched proudly onto the stage. Suddenly, the band stopped, and the entire senior class swished into their seats in perfect unison. Somewhere, Mr. McIntyre said a silent hallelujah.

All four of the girls sat in the front row, which was reserved for honors students. Once again, they appeared equal in their success, as though the differences in their immigration status had been erased. Elissa looked like she was struggling to keep her emotions in check, while Marisela wore a blasé expression, and Yadira couldn't keep from smiling. I thought I saw Clara crying, although she later claimed her eyes had been dry. Right on cue, Marisela and Daniela walked up to the microphone together. Daniela said nobody on the stage could remember a time before cable television, and Marisela added that many of the students had encountered obstacles in their lives, but these travails had only strengthened them. Four students in ROTC uniforms led the audience in the Pledge of Allegiance, and then the crowd belted out the National Anthem. As school board officials handed out diplomas, family members rushed the stage with cameras.

"Graduates!" Amy Harrigan pronounced. "You may now switch your tassel from the right to the left!"

The stage blossomed orange as students hurled their mortarboards into the air.

"Whoops!" laughed Harrigan.

Originally, the girls' graduation party had been Elissa's idea, but after much deliberation she had decided the celebration should take place in Clara's backyard, because it was bigger. When Yadira had called to give me the address, she had mentioned being "stressed" by the party planning. When I asked why, she said, "Oh—money. There's not enough money. There's never enough money." Clara lived on Umatilla Street, a scruffy road where beat-up cars sat in front of tired-looking houses, immediately behind the city's gleaming new football stadium. The Luz family, which was made up of six people, lived in a two-bedroom house made of red brick, with black iron bars guarding the windows. Clara's father had bought the modest structure and had never missed a mortgage payment. Yadira answered Clara's front door in a black tube top and a floor-length skirt with huge crimson flowers on it, with her black hair falling loose to her waist. She looked like a Hawaiian dancer. Yadira cautioned me to tiptoe past the sheet that hung over the entrance to the dining room, which had been converted into a makeshift bedroom, as Clara's father was sleeping in there. He had quit his job at the meatpacking plant several years ago, and now spent his nights cleaning casinos in the former gold-mining towns of Black Hawk and Cripple Creek.

In the Luzes' small kitchen, Clara's mother stood at the electric range, stirring an enormous pan of beans. Bernadina Luz was dressed in a simple black T-shirt and long black skirt, and she greeted me in Spanish. She worked as a housekeeper at the Westin Hotel in downtown Denver. Elissa's mother, Ana Ramírez, had come straight from the office, and now stood at the counter peeling avocados. She looked smart in a forest green suit, her hair in a perfect pageboy. Elissa's mother said hello in English. She had a desk job and looked American, yet she seemed at ease in the Luzes' kitchen—in a rare feat for an immigrant parent, she had mastered two worlds.

A short flight of stairs led from the kitchen to Clara's backyard. It was deep, and at the far end, two old cars stood rusting in the grass. A large tree shaded most of the yard, and folding tables had been placed under its branches. All four of the girls were wearing party finery—Elissa had donned a printed silk dress and had put her hair in a twist, and even Clara was wearing an off-the-shoulder black chiffon dress. Marisela looked the most va-va-voom, in a red halter dress with a plunging neckline. I found the contrast between the elegance of the girls' attire and the squalor of their surroundings almost painful.

The girls hurried from the kitchen to the yard, ferrying bowls of chips, salsa, tortillas, chicken, tamales, and enchiladas. No alcohol was served. Elissa introduced me to her boyfriend, Juan, who had braces and a polite, unassuming manner. He was a freshman at Metro, where he was studying computer technology. He seemed pliable, and I wondered how he was faring in a relationship with the strong-willed Elissa. Then Clara introduced me to her older brother, who had just completed his freshman year at the University of Northern Colorado. Once again, Yadira was the only one present without family. Her surrogate family had made it, however—Irene and Justino Chávez were sitting at a table with Aurora Valdez and Maya Rodríguez from Roosevelt High. Justino had on a purple union T-shirt that said JUSTICE FOR JANITORS. That was the name of a recent labor campaign in which the Service Employees International Union had set out to organize the two thousand workers who cleaned Denver's downtown office towers at night. The union had signed up 90 percent of the workers, even though most of them lacked legal status, and had staged demonstrations until the city's twelve largest cleaning contractors had agreed to better pay and more benefits. It was labor's first success at organizing undocumented workers anywhere in the United States, and had become a national model.

As I sat down beside Justino, Irene mentioned that Yadira's mother had just decided to move back to Colorado.

"Why are they moving again?" I asked.

"Same reason they left," she said. "They just can't make it."

In California, Jesús had found construction work, but for only $9 an hour. Alma had landed a job as a hotel housekeeper for $7 an hour, which had bolstered the family's income, yet rents had jumped in California, and so had other costs. They couldn't make ends meet. Jesús was planning to return first, and then Alma and the children would follow. Alma had just called the Goodwill store where she had formerly worked to make sure she could get her old job back.

Clara's backyard filled with other students and their supporters. Cezar Mesquita from the University of Denver arrived with his son, Diego, who was two years old. Then Mr. Baker, the girls' French teacher, appeared bearing a bouquet of pink roses, as if he had anticipated the girls' sentiments about the occasion. Practically everybody who had helped the girls get this far was present. When their mothers emerged from the kitchen, figures loosened by age and childbirth, the older women looked careworn beside their vivid daughters. They had made so many sacrifices. A soft breeze moved through the yard and everything turned golden as the sun slipped down toward the rusted cars. When Marisela swung by our table, Irene consulted with Mesquita on a matter that had just come up.

"Cezar, speak from your heart," Irene said. "Should Marisela and Yadira live together next year, or should they share dorm rooms with other people and branch out a little?"

"Together!" Mesquita replied. "Together, together, together! That support they can give each other is going to be big."

Irene looked taken aback.

Mesquita turned to Marisela. "What do you want to do?"

"I want to live with Yadira."

"How does she feel?"

"Oh, she feels the same way."

"Really?" Mesquita asked. "Then why is she shaking her head at me right now?"

Marisela whirled around, but Yadira was nowhere in sight. Mesquita giggled.

"Just joking. I got you, though."

Irene said she was helping the girls find a writing tutor for the summer. Yadira had a vast vocabulary and an easy, fluid style, but the other girls lagged behind her in their writing abilities. Mesquita thought that a tutor was a terrific idea. "At DU, we have no remedial classes in writing," he said. "It's sink or swim." Nearby, Clara and Yadira vied for attention from Mesquita's son, Diego, while Marisela picked up somebody else's baby. It seemed like a snapshot of what might have been—if they hadn't stayed in school, if they hadn't found college tuition. They knew so many girls who became mothers before they turned twenty.

Elissa said I should come inside to see their piñata. The misshapen creation was lying down on a bed, a discernibly female figure with an unfortunately square torso. The girls had drawn sketchy features onto her papier-mâché face, and tucked her brown yarn hair under a black mortarboard. She clutched a rolled-up diploma, and sported a backpack that I recognized as Elissa's. The doll was as much a blend of two cultures as they were, but far less attractive.

"Nice job," I offered gamely.

"We've been working on her all week!" Elissa announced.

In the kitchen, Yadira hefted an enormous pan of refried beans, calling back over her shoulder to Marisela that she should flip the tortillas. Their male friends stood around, watching the activity. Aside from their boyfriends, the girls were closest to Julio, a burly guy with pale skin and a sincere manner. They always seemed to turn to Julio whenever they needed assistance; it was to his house that Yadira had fled when she first ran away from home. I suspected that he was in love with one of the girls, but did not know which. Now I asked Julio what he was doing next, assuming that he was going to college, as he had papers. Julio explained sheepishly that he had not earned enough credits to graduate. He added that he was returning to Roosevelt High in the fall, however. "The girls persuaded me," he said. "I wasn't going to go back, but they talked me into it."

"What do you guys think of the piñata?" I asked.

"She looks pregnant!" cracked León.

Her makers erupted in a chorus of protest. The girls ransacked Clara's meager makeup supplies to beautify the unfortunate-looking dummy. Then Clara's older brother and Elissa's boyfriend hoisted it up over a tree branch, but the papier-mâché graduate was so heavy that the branch bowed down too low. Marisela jumped on a chair and rearranged the doll to sit higher in the tree, but in the process she accidentally knocked the doll's head askew.

"It looks like we are hanging her!" objected Yadira.

The boys took down the doll, fixed her head, and hoisted her aloft again. Clara found an old broom handle, while her youngest sister ran inside for a blindfold. Maya Rodríguez spun the piñata until it twirled like a top, and Elissa swung wildly at the doll, as Clara's older brother raised and lowered it with the rope. "Adelante!" people shouted. "A la izquierda! A la derecha!" To the left! To the right! Then Elissa gave a great whack, and the doll's head flew off. Marisela tossed it to the kids, who ransacked the head for candy. Clara was wearing high heels, which she wasn't accustomed to, and after Elissa spun her around, she started wobbling and leaping like a drunken ballerina. Elissa blindfolded Marisela next.

"Don't tie it too tight, because of my contacts," Marisela instructed.

Elissa spun her around.

"Oh, no, I just ate!" Marisela cried.

Marisela cavorted blindly, then whacked the doll's legs off. Small children flailed at the doll without wearing the blindfold, but the graduate remained impervious to their gentle assaults.

"She's a crash test dummy!" Mesquita yelled.

"She's made of concrete!" hollered Justino.

Then Marisela's sister, Rosalinda, put on the blindfold. Rosalinda, a star athlete, connected almost immediately and did not stop swinging until an arm flew off and the torso smashed to the ground. It was all over then. Elissa and Marisela hurled candy at the party guests, while little kids dashed in, making pockets out of their T-shirts. Clara emerged from the melee sucking candy powder from a straw, and Marisela savored a lollipop. The high school graduates devoured the candy with as much greed as the younger children. They were still kids at heart.

The sky deepened until it was hard to see people's faces. The girls brought out a boom box to play *norteño* music, the polkas that still bore the influence of the German immigrants who had once settled along the country's southern border. Elissa shimmied enticingly as Juan held her stiffly apart from himself, while Elissa's mother danced with Maya Rodríguez. Marisela twirled seductively with another boy as Julio looked on. Against the backdrop of rusting cars and chain-link fencing, the girls looked like migrating birds that had been blown off course. Their fancy attire said that they dreamed of transcendence, of jobs that paid real money, of lives that mattered. If only one of them had dressed up, she would have looked foolish, but all of them had done so, validating one another's ambitions. They had banded together against the pull of this street, stubborn weeds determined to flower.

Elissa had left an old photo album on one of the tables. While the girls danced, Aurora Valdez leafed through it. She laughed when she saw the students at twelve and thirteen, all gawky and awkward. "They've been friends for so long," she murmured.

The girls were still dancing when I left. Out in front of the house, every detail of Umatilla Street had been thrown into sharp relief by the fierce white glare from Invesco Field, even though it was still several months before football season. The stadium's spotlights must have been illuminating some civic function, but soon enough the rest of Denver would become preoccupied with the Broncos again. Few of the city's sports fans knew much about life on Umatilla Street, even though the struggle taking place there fell within the arc of the football stadium's blaze. It was an old struggle, the newcomer's struggle for betterment, but when immigrants had last come in such large numbers, there had been no such thing as Social Security, no easy way to categorize people as legal or illegal, documented or undocumented. It was a struggle in which much would be gained and much would be lost. When Clara returned here after her first year of college, how would Umatilla Street appear to her?

Maybe only Aurora Valdez, who had watched so many other students come and go, recognized the loss as it was happening. A moment, an era, was passing, and what the girls were leaving behind was irretrievable. What I could not see, as I drove away, was that I was leaving something behind, too—a time when this story seemed straightforward, a time when I felt uncompromised. Politics was going to rob me of the capacity to see myself purely as a journalist, standing at a safe remove from my subjects. And it would relieve the city's residents of some of their cherished illusions—the idea that their popular mayor was infallible, the sense that casual violence did not occur in Denver, the belief that all immigrants were good. As I look back on that evening, I think of it as a resonant hour in the years when we were all more innocent, and what strikes me now is our naïveté.

PART II

MANY DWELLING PLACES

I

LIAR, LIAR, LIAR

During the summer between high school and college, Yadira, Marisela, and Clara walked the city streets and buttonholed Latinos about voting. John Kerry was vying to unseat George Bush in the 2004 presidential election, and Colorado appeared up for grabs. In large part this was because of a U.S. Senate race in which state attorney general Ken Salazar was running neck and neck with beer baron Pete Coors. Salazar was a cautious fifth-generation Coloradan with deep roots in the San Luis Valley and strong ties in Denver, Colorado's two largest strongholds of Democratic votes. However, Coors had deeper pockets and close to 100 percent name recognition, and had sewed up the Republicans. Meanwhile, he and Salazar were splitting the independents, now one-third of the state's voters. The entire election would depend on who turned out. All summer, Yadira, Clara, and Marisela scoured Latino neighborhoods, registering new voters. Often, people would ask if they were registered, and when this happened, Clara said truthfully that she wasn't allowed to vote because she was not yet a full-fledged citizen, while Yadira and Marisela dissembled. "I just say I'm not eighteen yet, and they believe me, because I don't look like I'm eighteen," Yadira said one afternoon, as she sat with Clara in Rosalinda's, a popular Mexican restaurant. Both girls had spent the morning talking with potential voters at a bus stop at Fourteenth and California. The temperature had spiked into the nineties, and they now sagged over their lemonades. Yadira had registered sixteen people in four hours, but Clara had registered only one person. "Everybody else I spoke to was either registered already or was a felon," Clara explained. "One guy I spoke to was a Vietnam vet, and he went on a tirade."

"A lot of people get mad at me," Yadira reported. "They say, 'I don't want to register! I don't want to vote! I don't like this government at all!' I'm, like, I'm just doing my job here."

The organization that had hired the three girls was paying Yadira and Marisela through a convoluted scheme. Yadira shared a job with Julio, their friend from Roosevelt, while Marisela partnered with Clara. The arrangement functioned like this: Both Clara and Marisela worked for half a day, and then Clara submitted paperwork as if she had completed a full day's work. After she got her paycheck, Clara gave Marisela half her earnings. Yadira and Julio split their job in the same fashion.

As the weeks slipped by, the color of Yadira's skin deepened to chestnut and Marisela's to chocolate. Clara's fair skin never browned like theirs—she just turned more golden. Halfway through the summer, the girls started joking about how poorly they were going to fit in at the almost entirely all-white University of Denver. "Look at us!" Clara said on another scorching afternoon, as the girls took respite in the cool of the Denver Public Library. "Yadira thinks our new nicknames should be 'Dark,' 'Darker,' and 'Darkest'!"

At the beginning of July, Yadira applied for an identity card from the Mexican consulate. Elissa, who was working as an assistant in the marketing department of a local film society that summer, accompanied her on this mission. At the consulate, an official gave Yadira a form written entirely in Spanish. She puzzled over the questions, one of which asked for the *población* where she had been born. Elissa decided the word meant *population,* and told Yadira to write down the number of people who lived in the city of Durango. In search of this figure, Yadira consulted the woman at the front desk, who explained that in this context *población* meant "town" or "city." She just needed to say she had been born in Durango, Durango. The form also required the applicant to list an address in Mexico, but Yadira had none to supply, having left the country as a toddler, so she put down the address of one of Elissa's aunts. Clearly, she did not fit the profile of the person the Mexican consulate expected to serve. The experience left Yadira feeling as though there was no term for what she was, nor a bureaucracy that could recognize her. She realized then it wasn't only legal identification she lacked—on a more profound level, she was missing any official acknowledgment of her existence.

Marisela did not struggle in the same way over her place in the universe, perhaps because she could remember the journey she had made to the States, or perhaps because her flamboyant personality garnered other forms of acknowledgment. Once that summer, Marisela mentioned that she could not check out a book from the library, because the librarians would not issue her a card since they did not recognize her fake Mexican driver's license as a legitimate form of identification. At the same time, she also made it clear that she was suffering more from renewed friction with her parents than from any failure by local bureaucracies to recognize her. The trouble had begun after Marisela told Fabián and Josefa that she planned to live on campus in the fall, which her parents felt was a bad idea. "I had to sit down with them and explain, this is a good opportunity, detail by detail," Marisela said. "We've had lots of arguments. They feel like I don't want to be part of the family anymore, but that's not how it is."

Then National Maintenance cut Fabián's pay from $1,050 every two weeks to $760. The company also shrank the size of the cleaning crew he ran from four workers to two, yet expected them to accomplish the same amount of work. Disgusted, Fabián quit. A close friend in North Carolina encouraged him to move there, saying that he could earn $13.50 an hour framing houses. Fabián decided to drive to North Carolina to investigate the situation; he planned to send for his wife and children once he got settled. Now he instructed Marisela to change colleges. She should pursue her education in North Carolina, he thought, where the rest of the family was going to live. Marisela tried to explain that college was different from high school—she couldn't just go somewhere else at the last minute. "They thought that I could just transfer to any other school," she said. "It was really hard for them to think about leaving me in Colorado all alone. They were worried about the decisions I would make. They envisioned me out on the street, living out of control."

As Fabián and Josefa prepared to move once more, Marisela loosened the bonds between them to secure for herself a less transient lifestyle. Ultimately, I got a long voice mail from her in which she discussed another matter, and then casually added in a tired voice that I should call her back at a different number, because she had moved out of her parents' house. She was living with an ex-boyfriend until school started. "I've been getting more independent, and they don't like it," she said when we spoke again. "At first, I would cry myself to sleep; I thought I couldn't stand it. But now I'm relieved. I have more freedom. I'm better able to concentrate."

Soon afterward, I returned to the apartment in Lakewood to see

Josefa. "She hasn't slept here at the house for two weeks!" exclaimed Marisela's mother. "I'm afraid that she is sleeping with a boyfriend! And the problem is she likes Mexican boys. All the Mexicans, they just want to have a woman in the house—they want someone to clean and cook and do the laundry. I'm so worried, because I'm afraid that she won't finish anything. She won't have a career, or a degree, or anything. And I don't want her to live the way that I live." Josefa said she had told all of this to Marisela, and her daughter had replied, "Don't worry, *Mamá*, I want to be somebody." Josefa bemoaned that her children continually did things she would not have permitted, and then told her about them afterward. She had raised them in a country where people talked about freedom all the time, and they had turned out defiant. "The thing that I am worried about is that she is going to live at the university. She told me, '*Mamá*, I have to take my car.' And I think, in the evenings, she is going to leave the university. To go where? I don't know."

While stormy weather was taking over the Benavídez household, dark clouds were massing on the political horizon, too. At the end of July, I drove to North High, another inner-city school in Denver, to attend a forum on immigration sponsored by First Data Corporation. First Data owned the largest ATM network in the United States, and it was also the parent company of Western Union, the largest money transfer business in the world. Throughout the previous year, workers had wired more than $150 billion around the globe in the form of remittances—money that sojourning workers sent back to their countries of origin—and 14 percent of that sum had gone via Western Union. With a market capitalization of $38.5 billion, First Data was one of the largest companies operating in the state of Colorado.

Its headquarters were located in Greenwood Village, an affluent suburb to the south of Denver represented by Congressman Tom Tancredo. Back in June, Tancredo had announced that he wanted to tax remittances, after reading a report that stated workers in the United States sent $30 billion annually to Latin America. The congressman had not discussed his idea with executives of First Data, even though the company was one of the biggest employers in his district. Congressman Tancredo did not know that First Data was based in his district. "We weren't aware," Tancredo's spokesman told the *Rocky Mountain News*. "But that wouldn't have changed his mind."

"Shame on him if he didn't know," railed Fred Niehaus, senior vice president for public affairs at First Data, in the *News*. "The fact that they have no idea that our world headquarters and thousands of our employees are located in his district is really troubling."

Within a few weeks, Tancredo changed his stance to advocate reducing U.S. foreign aid to countries that received remittances. "We wanted to do something," his spokesman told the *News*. "We've decided that maybe taxing people is not the way to go. The more we looked at remittances, we realized that at least it was getting money to people who need it. It's their governments that aren't doing anything about illegal immigration."

"It appears to me he's trying to get over a big oops," responded Niehaus. "That doesn't cut it. This guy is off in left field, and we're tired of his antics, tired of his games."

First Data announced publicly that they didn't believe Tancredo was the right person to represent their interests anymore. Local political circles buzzed about the feud between the congressman and the colossus, as the company started a political action committee and made a $2,000 contribution to Joanna Conti, a chemical engineer who was challenging Tancredo for his seat. Conti argued that the country as a whole and her congressional district in particular were headed in the wrong direction, but she was running as a Democrat in a district where Republican voters outnumbered Democrats two to one. And when Conti suggested that her opponent's views on immigration did not dovetail with the opinions of his suburban constituents, Tancredo begged to differ. "Anyone who says that immigration is not a factor and not an issue in the 6th Congressional District is truly out of touch," Tancredo told the *Denver Post*.

Now First Data was hosting a series of forums on immigration across the country in cities such as Chicago and Los Angeles. On July 22, one of these forums took place in the auditorium of North High, in the formerly Italian neighborhood where Tancredo had grown up. I recognized many elected officials, activists, and business leaders in the crowd. Down in the front row, Charlie Fote, the chief executive officer of First Data—another grandson of Italian immigrants—sat near Juan Marcos Gutiérrez González, the Mexican Consul General for the Rocky Mountain region. On the stage, six speakers sat behind a table. First Data had not invited Tancredo to join the panel, nor had it included Dick Lamm, a prominent Democrat who had served three terms as governor of Colorado and now opposed illegal immigration. Instead, First Data had selected a slate of entirely pro-immigrant speakers, all of whom were Latino.

"Aren't you going to say the Pledge of Allegiance?" yelled a heckler at the start of the program.

Startled, the panelists rose to recite the Pledge. From that point on, they were repeatedly interrupted.

"This panel has been stacked!" bellowed a lean man with a shock of white hair. "There is no diversity on this stage!"

The man with the white hair was Mike McGarry, a former Vietnam War protester who now helped run the Colorado Alliance for Immigration Reform. CAIR was part of a loosely linked network of organizations around the United States that opposed immigration at current levels. McGarry subsequently told me that he had called First Data before the event to ask if a representative from CAIR could be part of the panel, but First Data had chosen not to include anyone from the group, so CAIR had packed the audience. The speakers on the stage battled to be heard over their derisive catcalls, boos, and shouts.

Midway through the evening, Thomas Sáenz, the vice president of litigation for the Mexican American Legal Defense and Educational Fund, said he had led the opposition to California's Proposition 187, a ballot initiative that sought to prevent illegal immigrants from obtaining access to social services, health care, and public education. "We challenged that law and proved that it was unconstitutional and inconsistent with national values," he said.

In the back of the room, an attractive woman wearing a red V-neck sweater stood up. *"Liar! Liar! Liar!"* she hollered. News reports later identified her as Terry Graham, a member of CAIR from Boulder, Colorado. Sáenz tried to go on, but Graham kept yelling.

"Ma'am! Ma'am!" Sáenz shouted fruitlessly. He resorted to stabbing his finger in Graham's direction. "I was involved in the case!" he roared. "Every single federal judge, five federal judges who heard the case, understood that it was inconsistent with federal law! And if you understood, you would know that the proponents of Proposition 187 acknowledged that it was unconstitutional!"

"Liar! Liar! Liar!" chanted Graham.

"That's the truth!" bellowed Sáenz. "You may be unhappy with that, but that's the truth!"

"Liar! Liar! Liar!"

"I will not let you or anyone else tear up the Constitution of the United States!"

Graham subsided, and Sáenz resumed a normal tone of voice. He said there were four elements to comprehensive reform, and was about to list them, when another panelist jumped to his feet. Sáenz looked aghast. In the back of the auditorium, Terry Graham was grappling with a squarely built Latina woman; I saw the Latina woman grab Graham by the hair, and then Graham hit the floor. Two police officers broke up the catfight and escorted Graham's assailant out of the auditorium. Local newspapers subsequently reported that Julissa Molina Soto was a Mexican immigrant with a green card. When the forum ended, I walked out of the auditorium with an unsettled feeling; it had been a raw, confrontational evening. In the school's front lobby, I bumped into Consul General Juan Marcos Gutiérrez González, who had been speaking with Molina Soto. He looked morose.

"It could be bad for her," said the consul general. "She's not a citizen yet, and this could mean she loses her chance."

"What was she thinking?" I asked.

"I don't know what she was thinking," he said ruefully. "It reflects badly on all of us. It's very unfortunate that she couldn't control her temper."

(Later Molina Soto was charged with criminal assault, although a jury would find her not guilty.)

Over the consul general's shoulder, I caught sight of Yadira and Clara, who had come to see the forum. I introduced the two girls to Gutiérrez González, explaining that they had graduated from Roosevelt High and were about to begin classes at the University of Denver. His face brightened. The consul general bowed slightly to each of the girls, and shook their hands with precise formality.

"You are doing a great honor to your community!" he said warmly.

Pleased and mortified, the girls were suddenly too shy to make any response. The diplomat put them at ease by asking about their grades at Roosevelt, and their responses were sufficiently impressive to elicit another flurry of compliments from Gutiérrez González. As he spoke, Yadira became even more quiet, and Clara turned faintly pink. After such an ugly evening, it was a refreshingly innocent moment, and it was also revealing. Even in the midst of a crisis, Gutiérrez González had paused to appreciate what these two young girls had accomplished: The diplomat knew what sort of challenges they faced, and he wanted to let them know that their accomplishments mattered—to him, and to their entire community. He wished them luck in college.

2

BREAKING IN

One week before college classes began, the University of Denver held a special orientation for students who had received full scholarships. Almost all the recipients were minorities from low-income families who had graduated from inner-city high schools. Now they were expected to function in an environment where most of their peers were going to be better off, suburban, and white. DU enjoyed a reputation for academic excellence, which the scholarship students found intimidating. The place had even been nicknamed the Harvard of the West—although the average combined SAT scores of its students were around 1200, and DU's top administrators considered their true competitors to be schools like Boston University, Southern Methodist, and Tufts. Perhaps the university's most famous alumna was Condoleezza Rice, who was serving as national security adviser to President George W. Bush at the time (later she would become his secretary of state).

I found Clara, Marisela, and Yadira on campus shortly after the meeting for scholarship students ended. It had been a relief for them to discover that there were other students of color in the incoming freshman class. Marisela had even recognized a friend from middle school who had come to her *quinceañera*. Although classes didn't start for another week, the girls wanted to see their dorm, and after much searching, they finally located the building—a two-story brick structure called Johnson-McFarlane Hall. Unfortunately, the doors were locked. Marisela pointed to windows hidden behind dense shrubbery. "Hey!" she exclaimed. "Are those the dorm rooms? Let's peek in!" She dove into the shrubbery, calling back, "I don't know if this is legal!"

Yadira and Clara exchanged looks, and then clambered into the bushes. They couldn't wait to glimpse their future, either. What they saw was dispiriting, however—tiny, drab rooms filled with dressers, desks, and bed frames.

"Oh!" said Yadira. "They're ugly!"

This was the general consensus.

"You guys, we look so dark, the security guards are going to think we're trying to break in!" cried Marisela.

This struck Yadira and Clara as hysterically funny. The joke named their predicament: They were entering the white world, and they had not decided whether they were entitled to be there or whether they were intruders. The three girls lolled on the grass outside their dorm, speculating about college. Marisela and Yadira had secured a room together, while Clara was going to live with a student from Hawaii named Alison. She had e-mailed that she was into punk music and black clothing, which had alarmed Clara; she was hoping that Alison didn't find her nerdy. Clara had spent more than an hour composing a two-line response that basically said she was looking forward to meeting her new roommate.

"Is she on scholarship?" Yadira asked. "Because if not, then she is rich. That's what I would want to know."

"I don't know," said Clara.

"I bet she's rich if she lives in Hawaii," offered Marisela.

The three girls decided to make a trip to Office Depot. They pushed one cart up and down the aisles of the megastore, scrutinizing prices. Nothing went into the cart unless it was marked down or bargain-sized; when they bought pens, they selected a value pack to divide among themselves. They found lined paper on sale, and plain black scissors that cost half as much as the brightly colored pairs. Yadira could not resist pink plastic folders, but pointed out that they cost the same as the ones she had priced at Target. Cynthia Poundstone and her friends had purchased an IBM laptop for Marisela and another for Yadira, but the two girls hadn't been able to get the machines to function, and had concluded that they didn't have any software. They walked over to the computer aisle to look at Windows XP. It cost $299.

"Three hundred dollars!" yelped Marisela.

One of them ventured it might be possible to buy the software for less from the University of Denver, and they left the Windows XP behind. Over the next several days, e-mails about the missing software flew back and forth between the girls and their donors, becoming increasingly hysterical, until finally a friend of Poundstone's wrote, "Calm down, everybody!" She had checked, and the laptops did have

Windows XP installed—the girls just needed to buy Office Pro. It was available from the university for $99.

Orientation week: much socializing, many meetings, little sleep. Clara stayed up all night talking to Alison, who turned out to be of Japanese and Korean descent, from a middle-class background, and not at all snobby. Yadira and Marisela transformed their room into a cozy haven. They made up their beds with matching pink and blue bedding, and piled them high with stuffed animals. They covered their bulletin boards with photographs of their lives at Roosevelt. Yadira did not mind when Marisela took up more than her share of the wall space. "She has a Mexican flag, and she said, 'Where should we hang this?'" Yadira observed. "We decided to hang it in the middle of the room. But if it had been another person she was living with, she would have had to get a smaller flag—'cause it's, like, *big*."

Each of the girls signed up to take four classes that fall. They all took English literature and a seminar on political activism. Marisela also signed up for calculus and sociology, while Yadira took the same sociology class and a second-year Spanish class (she had placed out of first-year Spanish), and Clara took calculus with Marisela and Spanish with Yadira. When Yadira got an 89 on her first paper in English literature, she was elated: "Missed the A by one point!" she wrote in a cheerful e-mail. Marisela was shocked to receive a D, though. She had written her essay on the DREAM Act, and assumed that her professor had not agreed with her point of view, but learned otherwise when she made an appointment to discuss her grade. "It was a lot of making transitions between paragraphs and staying on topic," said Marisela. "And making the whole paper connect to the thesis statement. That should have been stuff that I learned in high school." Marisela had strong analytical skills and an aptitude for math, as well as a keen interest in social issues, but she had to struggle to produce papers that her college professors would deem adequate. In the end, she earned a B after she rewrote the paper.

Clara landed a coveted work-study job with flexible hours at the Center for Multicultural Excellence. Yadira and Marisela met the income qualification for work-study, yet they could not obtain a job from the university without legitimate Social Security numbers. Yadira opted not to work—her scholarship covered all her expenses—while Marisela found a job clerking at a liquor store. She did her homework in between taking care of customers. The immigrant who owned the store knew that Marisela had given him a made-up Social Security number, but he hired her anyway as he was sympathetic to her plight. Plus, it was hard to find someone who was willing to work at night, as the store had been robbed two times already. Between their jobs and their classes and their family commitments, none of them had much time to spare for Elissa, who was having a lonely start over at Regis. She told the three other girls that she hadn't made any new friends at all.

Meanwhile, thanks to Marisela's splashy personality, the dorm room that she shared with Yadira soon became a hub of social activity. One evening that fall, while I was hanging out in their room, three different visitors dropped by within half an hour. Among them was Clara's roommate Alison, who had cropped hair and a sweet smile at odds with her doom-and-gloom attire. Another visitor, Luke Harrigan, was a business major from Las Vegas, Nevada. Given his conservative beliefs, Luke did not fit in well with some of the liberal-minded students at the college, but he had taken a shine to the girls from Roosevelt. By the third or fourth week of school, he had adopted Marisela and Yadira as his constant companions. Like many students at DU, Luke loved to ski, and after the first big snowfall of the year, he headed up to the mountains. None of the girls from Roosevelt had ever been skiing before, even though they had grown up within sight of the snow-capped Rockies; skiing cost too much money. Luke's family had a lot of money—they lived in a house worth $1.5 million, he told the girls. "And we don't even own a house!" marveled Yadira.

Clara kept a picture pinned to her bulletin board that showed her sitting on the back steps of her house on Umatilla Street, holding her little sister in her lap. One day, she said to Luke, "Look, there's my little sister."

Luke peered at the photograph. "Is that your house?" he asked with surprise.

"Yes, that's my house," said Clara defensively. "What's wrong with it?"

"You have bars on your windows!" Luke marveled.

Clara didn't know how to explain Umatilla Street to someone like Luke, so she changed the subject. "We feel like this with all the kids here," Yadira said afterward. "We can't explain ourselves." As the quarter slipped by, the girls gradually developed a sense of being viewed as curiosities. "I'm sitting in class, and then they start asking me questions and make me the center of attention, like I'm doing a talk show or something," Marisela said. "Sometimes I feel like they see me as something strange—something that they've never seen before. It's like we're teaching them. And then you're always scared that they're not going to accept you." Meanwhile, in the dining hall, every server was an immigrant from Latin America, and so were all of the university's janitors. The girls made a point of addressing these employees in Spanish, since the service workers reminded them of their parents, and soon the servers in the dining hall began greeting the girls like family whenever they arrived for a meal. Clearly the sight of *mexicanas* mixing with the Anglo students made the kitchen staff proud. Occasionally, Anglo students mistook the girls for service workers. Once Marisela went to the dining hall wearing sweatpants and a T-shirt, rather than her usual flashy attire, and was standing on one side of the salad bar when a well-meaning underclassman on the other side looked at her across the lettuce, and said, "Thanks for making this food!"

Both Marisela and Yadira derived comfort from living with somebody else who understood what it was like to go from a high school like Roosevelt to a college like DU. "If your help had not continued after I received my [other] scholarship, my best friend, Marisela, would not be here with me, and I would not be sharing my room with her," Yadira wrote in an e-mail to Cynthia Poundstone. "Having my friends with me is really helpful in those moments of 'It's too hard, I don't know if I can do it.'" When the two roommates experienced difficulties, it was usually because Marisela overstepped a boundary—her clothes ended up on Yadira's side of the room, she played her *norteño* music too loud, or she stayed up too late. Marisela could sleep through a storm, but Yadira woke up if she heard a creak. Sometimes Yadira slid into a state of silent resentment, and then it was hard for Marisela to discern how she had transgressed. Initially, however, their bond trumped any other concerns. Yadira and Marisela had told trusted friends about their lack of legal status back in high school, but at the University of Denver, the two girls told their secret to nobody. They didn't feel safe disclosing it to friends or faculty, for fear the news would spread. "You wouldn't reveal such a thing to an outsider," Yadira said. "A lot of it is the safety issue. You never really know if that person is sensitive, or whether they'll tell other people or not. And I fear being looked down on—people looking at me like I'm truly different."

At Roosevelt, other students had known to steer clear of matters related to immigration status, such as why a peer might lack a certain document. This was not the case at the University of Denver, where classmates asked Marisela and Yadira uncomfortable questions all the time; other freshmen wanted to know why they didn't qualify for work-study, why they didn't have Colorado driver's licenses, why they didn't travel to Mexico. Keeping mum was hard for Marisela, especially once she befriended Alison. "We tell her intimate stuff—stuff we would tell each other," Marisela said. "It feels weird that she doesn't know our whole story. I've been really close to telling her, but I'm not really secure yet. So I'm still saying little things that are not true." Marisela did not worry that Alison might reject her; rather, she wasn't sure if Alison would be sufficiently discreet. "I think I'm scared that in some way without her wanting to, it would come up in other conversations. We have classes together and I'm scared that it would come up in a conversation about immigration or something like that. It would make me uncomfortable if a lot of people knew, because then I would be viewed as a special person. And I'm pretty sure that if it got to the wrong ears, they would try to do something—like set me up."

As it happened, Luke held strong opinions on the subject of immigration. The girls did not realize how conservative he was until the eve of the 2004 presidential election, when all conversation turned to politics. Marisela began to apprehend the scope of their differences when Luke told her he was supporting George W. Bush. "Why? He's just giving all these tax breaks to rich people!" she objected.

"He's doing a really good job of protecting our country," Luke told her. "He's doing a really good job with the war."

Luke added that the United States would be better off if somebody could stop illegal immigrants from pouring across the southern border. "That's why a lot of people in this country are poor," Luke said, according to Marisela. "They come here and take our jobs. The government should secure the borders and block any new people from coming here. And the people who are here should make an effort to get legalized."

"Don't you know how hard it is to get papers?" Marisela demanded.

"No," said Luke.

"It takes about twenty years, and it costs a lot of money!" Marisela spluttered. "You have to pay all these lawyers!"

"Well, if they really want to be here, they should do it."

From that point forward, Luke engaged the girls in a running argument on the subject. Yadira always kept her temper, but often Marisela could not check hers. "I have to say it in a 'they' form, so Luke doesn't know that I'm talking about me, too," she told me. "But I raise my voice because—the comments he makes!" Marisela began to question whether she wanted to remain friends with Luke, given the polarity of their views, but then she got the flu and he stopped by to take her temperature. "He's not racist, he's just anti-immigrant—or anti-people-without-papers," Marisela concluded. "At some points, I have gotten mad at him, but we like each other for our personalities."

When Luke asked directly about their status, the two girls lied and said they had green cards. Yadira did not have a hard time maintaining this fiction—she could have been a sphinx, she said so little. Marisela, on the other hand, found it hard to remember to watch what she said in front of Luke. "I don't think about things before I say them, and I mess up really easily," she confessed. One evening, Yadira and Luke were studying in Clara's room when Marisela burst through the door with news. She had been talking to a student at Roosevelt who was thinking about DU, and he had mentioned that he knew she had made it into college without papers. When Marisela had asked how he knew this, he had said her former AP English teacher had told him.

"Do you know what Ms. Brown is saying?" Marisela announced now. "She's telling people that I don't have papers!"

Luke looked at Marisela with an odd expression. "You don't have papers?" he asked.

"Of course I have papers!" fudged Marisela. "I just haven't become a full citizen yet. But I don't want her saying that kind of stuff—what if people think that I'm illegal or something?"

Afterward, the girls dissected the incident and concluded that Luke had not caught on. The slip unnerved Yadira, though, who was counting on Marisela not to betray either one of them. Sometimes the girls contemplated what would happen if they told Luke the truth. "I don't know what he would do, because we're really, really close," Marisela said. "He's always in my room, and I'm always in his room. I don't know how he would change. We're thinking of telling him, just to see."

One evening, however, Clara conducted an impromptu test, after Luke said he believed the immigration system worked well, according to the girls. He thought immigrants who remained illegal had adopted that life of their own free will. Clara took the opposite point of view—she thought the system was broken. Luke scoffed at this.

"What if I had come over here illegally?" Clara asked him. "What if I didn't have papers? What would you think of me then?"

"Well, then I couldn't trust you," Luke said, according to Clara's recollection. "I wouldn't want to be your friend."

"Why not?" Clara asked in surprise.

"Because you would have lied to me. You said you were a resident, and it wasn't true. But you must have papers, because you couldn't be in college if you didn't."

"Well, what if I crossed the border illegally when I was a child, and then got papers while I was living in this country?"

"Then you're still to blame, because you knew what you were doing."

"What if I was little and I didn't understand the consequences, and my parents didn't ask me, and I didn't have a choice?"

"Well, how old were you?"

"Oh, I don't know—three, seven, somewhere along those lines."

"I guess in that case, you didn't know, and it is your parents' fault."

"They were just trying to give me a better life!"

"It is wrong. If you break the law, then you break the law. That's all there is to it."

Previously, Yadira had assumed that if she revealed her true identity, Luke might modify his beliefs. Now she concluded that she could never tell Luke the truth. Yet she continued to spend hours in his company. That fall, Luke began taking Yadira and Clara to ice hockey games. The University of Denver Pioneers had won back-to-back championships and were the most popular athletes on campus. Sitting in the stands, cheering for the Pioneers, Yadira had the sense of being just another student, of being normal. That was part of Luke's appeal—he represented the average student at DU, and if Yadira had to hide things to win his acceptance, it was a tax she was willing to pay.

As long as she remained in the present, Yadira could hold on to this sense of belonging. The problem was life after graduation. Yadira hadn't settled on a major yet, but hoped to become a teacher. Clara wanted to become a psychologist or a social worker. Marisela seemed to adopt new career plans almost as frequently as she changed the color of her hair, and some of these plans seemed wildly improbable. One day, when we were talking about the future, Marisela said, "I don't know what is waiting for me. It all seems very, very blurry. I have goals, but I don't have ways to get there."

"What are your goals?" I asked.

"I want to be a homicide detective," she said. "I want to get a major in criminology, and then work with the CIA or the FBI."

"The CIA or the FBI? Aren't they a little bit like the INS?"*

"I'm intrigued by criminal behavior, I guess," said Marisela blithely. "I just like the psychology behind it. I don't know how I'll work with the INS, but hopefully they won't come after me."

"And how did you get interested in criminology?"

"I don't know, from watching too many *FBI Files* on the Discovery Channel."

Their longtime mentors Irene and Justino Chávez frequently talked with the two girls who lacked documents about how they might acquire them, but the girls did not appear to have any viable options. Neither of them had a legal parent who could serve as a sponsor, and both girls lacked entry visas. After Yadira's mother, Alma, returned from California, Irene and Justino held a meeting with an immigration attorney to see what they could do to rectify Yadira's status, but the attorney just shook his head. Alma and Yadira could apply for citizenship, but he

---

* By "INS," I was referring to the Immigration and Naturalization Service, the arm of the United States Department of Justice dedicated to enforcing the nation's immigration laws. Technically, however, the INS had ceased to exist by this point. In 2003, after the creation of the Department of Homeland Security, many of the INS's functions—such as the determination of permanent residence, naturalization, and asylum—were taken over by a new organization, the Bureau of Citizenship and Immigration Services (BCIS), and then this entity was shortly renamed the U.S. Citizenship and Immigration Services (USCIS). In the meantime, the investigative and enforcement duties of the INS were combined with aspects of the Customs Service to form the newly created U.S. Immigration and Customs Enforcement (ICE). Needless to say, this was all quite confusing, and afterward many people referred interchangeably to the INS or ICE when talking about the federal government's efforts to enforce immigration laws, while forgetting about USCIS entirely.

thought it would be a waste of time and money, and could even jeopardize their safety by informing officials of their whereabouts. Because they had entered the country illegally, they were prohibited from being granted legal status, he explained; any application they submitted would be pointless, given that they could not provide valid entry visas. Even if they were to disregard the attorney's advice and apply, due to the backlog of applications piled up in Washington, it would take years for their case to be considered. There was simply no way for Yadira to gain legal status by the time she graduated from college.

For a while, Yadira toyed with the idea of marrying Julio, her friend from high school who had papers, although her boyfriend Juan did not approve of this idea. "Marriage is sacred to him," Yadira explained. "It feels weird for him to have me marry somebody else—even if it's a pretend marriage. It conflicts with his beliefs." Then Irene did some research and explained to Yadira that gaining legal status through marriage was not possible for somebody like her, unless she was willing to return to her country of origin; currently federal law required immigrants to prove they had entered the country legally before they could obtain a green card by virtue of marriage. For several years, the government had allowed exceptions to this rule (which was how Clara, her siblings, and their mother had gained legal status), but at this point anybody who lacked an entry visa had to return to their home country and apply for residency through an American consulate there—and individuals who had lived in the United States in violation of its laws were often denied residency, even if they were married to a U.S. citizen. Yadira gave up on the scheme. As the two girls became more wrapped up in college, both of them began putting off the question of how to solve their problem. When they envisioned the future, they had the hazy sense that they would acquire citizenship by some means, even though they could not say how. Washington became the focus of their vague hopes: Maybe Congress would pass some sort of comprehensive immigration reform, or a version of the DREAM Act that might provide them with a path to citizenship.

"I think we will become citizens someday," said Marisela optimistically. "I think eventually we will."

"Yeah, someday we will," echoed Yadira.

"What if you don't?" I asked.

"If we don't, that's going to be a humongous obstacle," Yadira said.

"Even if I have the potential to be the best teacher ever, without a Social Security number, I could never teach. So if we don't manage to become legal, then we would have gone to school for nothing."

"How do you live with that possibility?" I asked.

"I try not to think about it," Yadira said. "I refuse to even consider the possibility of it."

"Me, too," said Marisela. "I just avoid it."

"Is it, like, you've made it into college, and you just want to put this off until you are seniors?"

"Yeah," said Marisela sheepishly. "I know that's a bad thing to do, but that's what I want to do. I want to just enjoy the college life, the college experience."

"When I think about it, it just ruins everything," added Yadira. "I just wish we had, like, magic or something, and it would come. I know that won't happen, though. Always, at the back of my mind, I'm thinking, 'I have to do something, time is flying.' I don't know what, but I will do something."

3

THREE TENS AND A NINE

In November, toward the end of their first quarter, the wealthy Republican donor who had given Yadira a scholarship threw a dinner party for the students he was supporting in the Onyx Room at the Brown Palace, one of Denver's finest hotels. Gold wallpaper glinted in the light from crystal chandeliers, while painted cherubs gamboled on the ceiling. Linen tablecloths, ornate silverware, and fancy glasses adorned the tables. Various dignitaries of higher education were present, including the vice chancellor and assistant vice chancellor for enrollment from the University of Denver. I joined Yadira at a table with her mother, Alma, and her grandfather, Tomás. Alma was an attractive, middle-aged woman who had Yadira's clear skin and pretty features, though her figure was plump rather than slender. Tomás was lean and wiry, with an alert expression on his square face, a silver moustache, and silver hair. He had been working in the United States for more than fifty years, originally as a bracero, most recently as a busboy. He and Alma looked stunned by the finery.

The Republican donor's wife came over and sat down with us. She possessed an enviably slim figure and an ash-blonde bob. I knew her slightly, as we attended many of the same civic functions, and introduced her to Yadira. Like most people in her upper-class world, the donor's wife appeared to have had little exposure to this side of Denver, but she gamely dove into conversation with Tomás, describing a recent trip to India. "There were far fewer beggars this time," she said brightly. "There were more people who wanted to sell handicrafts. I thought that was terrific!"

Yadira's grandfather smiled politely but said nothing in reply.

Marjorie Smith, the director of international admissions at the University of Denver, told Yadira's mother that she must be very proud of her daughter. Alma looked apologetic.

"*No hablo inglés,*" she replied.

"She doesn't speak English," translated Yadira. "Neither does my grandfather."

The donor's wife looked nonplussed. "Oh, dear! I was nattering away, and nobody said anything!" she fretted. She was an elegant woman, but the gulf between America's social classes had grown too large for her to bridge with her customary ease. Yadira offered to translate, and finally everybody managed to converse. The donor's wife asked Alma when she had moved to the United States. They shied away from tricky subjects, such as the matter of how the family had crossed the border. The conversation felt like a chess game—one had to be careful where to put the pieces. After a while, though, everyone loosened up, and by the time dessert came, we had achieved a sense of shared conviviality.

The Republican donor got up to say a few words. He asked all the parents and grandparents in the room to stand up. Tomás and Alma got to their feet, clutching their linen napkins.

"I know you are terribly proud of your children," the donor told them. "But you need to be thanked for raising such wonderful children. And we see that."

Jesús Apodaca interrupted the donor to say that their parents couldn't understand him, and offered to translate.

"Oh!" said the donor. "Oh! Good! Help me out."

Jesús, a rangy young man with pale skin and a thick shock of dark hair, shyly repeated the donor's words in Spanish.

Then the donor turned his attention to the students.

"You are energetic and courageous," he told them. "You are bringing an academic success and energy to your schools that is extremely valuable. And so it has been a privilege for all of us—for me personally—to organize this program, and to be a part of it. As far as I can tell, it is going well. Is anybody failing?" Laughter. "No? Good! So that concludes my remarks."

Marjorie Smith turned to Yadira. "I hope you'll consider studying abroad," she urged. "It's a wonderful experience."

Yadira stared at Smith without replying.

"You'll have to get her a passport first," I interjected.

"Oh, my goodness!" Smith said. "I didn't even think about that!"

It was hard to keep in mind the limitations that Yadira faced, for the image that she presented was so far from the stereotype of the illegal alien—an illiterate manual laborer. At the University of Denver, all students were expected to study abroad at some point during their four years (there was even a scholarship fund for those who could not afford the expenses)—and recently another faculty member had pressed Yadira about where she planned to go. "Well, I don't think I'll do it this year; I'm not ready," Yadira had hedged. She worried that she had made a bad impression. "I guess to her it seemed like I didn't really care, because she was, like, 'You should really consider it, it is a great opportunity,'" Yadira told me. "And of course I want to go, because it *is* a great opportunity, and I've never been anywhere at all."

Yadira tried to be realistic. If an opportunity was not available to her, then she did not let herself dream about it. Marisela, on the other hand, talked endlessly about somehow going abroad, and fixed on the notion of studying in Azerbaijan. "I saw it on a brochure," she explained. "So it stuck to me. Plus, the name is kind of weird." Clara and Yadira didn't want to tell Marisela that it would be impossible, given the heightened security measures adopted by American airports. "She talks about how maybe she could get a student permit or visa," Clara said. "With the college thing, she didn't give up, and she was able to go in the end. Maybe she can work out some special thing here, too. I don't want to crush her feelings by telling her she can't. Maybe she can—the possibility is just very small."

Meanwhile, Clara signed up to go on a field trip to Mexico, as I learned when I returned to the campus in the middle of November, one week after the dinner at the Brown Palace Hotel. I found all three girls studying for their final exams in Marisela and Yadira's room. Marisela was sitting on her bed, surrounded by textbooks and pillows. Yadira was studying at her desk, and Clara was on the floor. Their exams fell right before Thanksgiving, and the girls had off the entire month of December. They couldn't believe that finals loomed—the first quarter had flashed by. The girls were accustomed to earning top grades, and agonized about whether this would continue; Marisela was also vexed about her family. In North Carolina, Fabián had found a job framing houses, but for only $8.50 an hour. The pay wasn't what he had hoped for, and there was a lot of static on the Spanish-language radio stations. North Carolina was not the paradise he had envisioned.

Next he had driven to Arizona, where his cousin Kiko lived. Kiko made more money than anybody Fabián knew, because he worked as a *coyote*. In the past, Kiko had helped immigrants cross the border illegally, but now he ferried them from Phoenix to other cities around the United States. (Once, when I had asked how much Kiko earned, Fabián had rolled his eyes and said: "A *lot*! A lot of money!") In Phoenix, Fabián had found a two-bedroom apartment for $500 a month, and had secured a job with a different branch of National Maintenance. It paid $1,200 a month. Then he sent for Josefa, who found a janitorial job as well. Marisela's sister and two brothers transferred into a school in Phoenix that went from kindergarten through eighth grade. The only problem was that when they arrived they found Arizona engulfed in a fiery debate about illegal immigration, thanks to a ballot initiative that would ban government services to anyone who lacked documents. The Federation for American Immigration Reform poured hundreds of thousands of dollars into passing the measure. "If it's passed, it would be a launching pad for similar initiatives in other states," Ira Mehlman, the media director of FAIR, said to the *San Diego Union Tribune*. Senator John McCain argued against the proposal, saying that the immigration issue required a national solution.

Just a few weeks before I dropped by the dorm room, however, 56 percent of the voters in Arizona had cast their ballots for Proposition 200. Marisela had been so upset that she had forgotten to speak about the measure as if it would affect *other* immigrants in front of Luke. Only when he asked why her family was in danger did Marisela realize she had slipped up again. "Oh, 'cause they're Hispanic, too, people might think they are undocumented," she had scrambled to say, aghast at her own indiscretion. Now she cried, "Even if my brothers are sick, my mom can't take them to the hospital! They are legal, but she can't go, because if the hospital realizes that she's illegal, then they'll turn her in!"

Conversation turned to the upcoming winter break. Yadira and Clara were spending it in Denver—Clara was going back to Umatilla Street, while Yadira was going to join Alma, Jesús, and her siblings in a new apartment on Mississippi Avenue, across the street from the Salon Ocampo, a popular Mexican social club. Marisela had not seen her parents or siblings since their move to Phoenix and was eager to be reunited with her family, but wondered how to make the trip safely.

"Are you going to drive?" I asked.

"No, I think I'm going to take the bus," she said, making a face. "I'm really worried, though—what if they have agents waiting in the bus station in Phoenix? I guess I'll just show them my DU ID, and say that I forgot my driver's license. One of my friends told me that if I dress all preppy, then it will be fine."

"What will you wear?" I asked.

"Oh, you know, I'll put in my colored contacts and wear my Tommy Hil clothes," Marisela replied.

"Tommy Hilfiger?"

"Yeah. Sporty clothes. Something an American would wear."

I paused to appreciate the fact that Tommy Hilfiger sportswear could be used to foil federal agents.

"Anyway, if they do deport me, I have an uncle who is a *coyote*," added Marisela, "so I could just come right back. But I don't want to have to do that—I've heard it's really hard."

"Last night, I drank one of those energy drinks at around eleven o'clock," Clara announced. "I had to do something so I decided to go to the gym, but it was closed. I ended up just running around campus."

The girls discussed their love lives. Yadira remained devoted to Juan, while Marisela was between boyfriends, and Clara had developed a crush on an Anglo student who needed help with his Spanish homework. "I love white boys," she said. "Nerdy white boys—they are the best." Clara reported that her crush was also going on the field trip to Mexico.

"We're not going to be able to go," Marisela said ruefully.

There was a knock on the door. It was Alison—and so the girls abruptly changed the topic.

In the end, Marisela did not take the bus to Phoenix, as her parents decided it was too risky. Instead, Josefa drove nine hundred miles to pick up her daughter, and then nine hundred miles back to Arizona. I flew there to visit Marisela in the middle of December. The Benavídez family now lived in an apartment on North Twenty-third Street, an industrial area full of warehouses and the noise of vehicles in motion. Planes whined overhead as they flew in and out of Sky Harbor International Airport; heavy traffic thundered up and down Interstate 10. On my way there, I had driven past a collection of tiny shanties made of corrugated tin. The building where the Benavídez family lived was formerly a motel, and at least it looked structurally sound. When I knocked on their door, Marisela greeted me with a wan smile. She was the only one at home, as her mother had taken her siblings to school and her father was at work. She wore no makeup; gone was her normal vivacity. In Arizona, Marisela was living a ghost's life, dispirited by her surroundings. She had negotiated the transition into college successfully—it was the transition back home that she had not been able to manage. The apartment consisted of two small bedrooms and one main room that functioned as a kitchen, dining room, and living room. Marisela's brothers shared one bedroom, while Marisela slept in the second with Josefa; Fabián took his turn in the same bed after his wife and daughter rose. Marisela's sister sometimes slept with her brothers, and sometimes at the home of a relative. In the room that Marisela shared with her mother and father, clothes spilled out of a bright red duffel bag. Three weeks after her arrival, she still had not unpacked.

"You can't wait to get back to school, huh," I said.

"Yeah," said Marisela. "When I came here, at first, the lifestyle they are living, it was a total shock. I guess I adjusted very quickly to the college life. My parents are very stressed out about money. I had forgotten what that was like. Every time I would call, they said they were doing fine, but when I got here I realized they weren't. I knew things were bad, but I didn't realize they were this bad."

Marisela feared that by pursuing a college degree, she was leaving her family behind. She hadn't thought this way in Denver, but in Phoenix she could not avoid seeing how she was becoming unlike her mother and father. "Seeing my parents struggle, while I'm over there in a good place, getting educated—sometimes I feel guilty," she said. "I feel like they deserved a good education, too, and for some reason they didn't get it. I'm living in luxury compared to them. I could be doing other things to help them pay the bills—I used to help them so much. I feel like I'm not part of the family anymore."

Sometimes Marisela went to work with her mother to bring in extra income. "I feel invisible when I'm cleaning," she said. "No one pays attention to you—the managers just do their own business. Being in college, I feel important, but when I'm there cleaning, it's like someone is stepping on me. The managers talk to me like I'm stupid. They're like, '*Entiendes?*' I'm like, 'Yes, sir, I know.' It's just a different life. It's people treating you like you're dumb. It doesn't even cross their heads that I could be going to one of the top universities." She had not told her bosses that she was a college student, and nursed a hidden satisfaction at allowing them to feel superior. With a spark of her old defiance, she said, "It proves that even though I'm going to school, I'm still doing a job they won't do. I still haven't lost my humbleness."

When she had graduated from Roosevelt, Marisela's self-esteem had been at a low ebb. Over the past several months, she had felt her confidence rise, but in Phoenix, it sank again. She thought maybe she should drop out. It seemed impossible to return to that other life, that other identity. Then one weekend she went to the public library and logged onto the Internet and discovered her grades: In her first quarter, she had received three A's and one B plus. She screamed out loud in her excitement. Her father asked why she was making such a fuss, and Marisela listed her grades, but Fabián only looked bewildered. Then she translated the grades into Mexican terms: "I got three tens and a nine!"

"You always get tens," Fabián replied. "What's the big deal?"

Marisela's brother Nestor intervened, explaining that it was easy to get an A in high school, but much harder to earn such a good grade at a college like the University of Denver. Throughout the next few days, in text messages and e-mails, Marisela shared her news with Clara, Yadira, and Elissa, with whom the girls at DU now resumed contact, as they were all on break and had time to spare. It came as no surprise to the others to learn of Marisela's high marks. Back in high school, Clara and Elissa had garnered the greatest number of scholarships and Yadira had acquired the most benefactors, but the girls themselves had considered this unjust because they believed the smartest of them all to be Marisela. In their first quarter, both Clara and Yadira had done well: They had each gotten two A's and two B's. Over at Regis, Elissa had earned two A's, two B's, and one B plus. But Marisela—the one who almost hadn't made it into college—she had done the best of all.

4

BAD PAPERS

In January, Marisela increased the time she spent at the liquor store each week to twenty hours, so she could send money to her parents. Throughout the winter quarter, she gave them about $600. She also took four classes, which was almost too much to juggle. Yet after winter quarter ended, she learned that she had scored straight A's. The chancellor of the university posted her name on a list of excellent students in a glass case outside of his office. Marisela was now spending less time with Luke, which came as a relief, given her propensity to divulge critical information. Instead, she began to surround herself with students of color. Most of them had gone to public high schools with significant numbers of Latino students, and several were immigrants themselves. One, Zahra, had been born in Somalia and lived in a refugee camp in Kenya for several years before moving to Denver. Another, Matías, had been born in Mexico and grown up in Denver. So had his friend Rosalba, who struggled harder than any other freshman they knew, because she was raising a baby as well as going to school full-time and working part-time. Soon Marisela was inviting these students over at all hours—even if Yadira was studying. Marisela's circle of friends kept growing larger, and the bigger it grew, the more disruption Yadira had to endure. At the same time, Yadira recognized that with these other students, she could be more free. They were acquainted with the reality of illegal immigration, and if somebody couldn't get a work-study job, they did not ask why.

Over at Regis, Elissa was miserable. She still had not made any new friends. She tried reaching out to Clara several times during the winter quarter, but Clara was busy and slow to respond. Now Elissa accused Clara of not having enough time to be her friend anymore. The two girls were still sorting things out when Marisela introduced Clara to Matías's high school friend Jaime, who was a freshman at Regis. Clara immediately called Elissa. "Here! Talk to this guy!" she ordered. "He goes to Regis!" Elissa later described her friendship with Jaime as the one thing that made her freshman year bearable. Soon Elissa and Jaime began visiting their old friends at the University of Denver on a regular basis, and the four girls began spending significant amounts of time together again, just like they had done in high school. The original alliances now reasserted themselves: While Yadira and Clara often chose to hole up with their books, Marisela and Elissa frequently stayed out until the early morning hours at various campus parties.

Although Marisela hardly saw Luke at all anymore, Yadira and Clara ate dinner with him almost every night. By the time spring quarter began, Clara and Yadira were straddling two worlds. They spent most of their time with Luke and his friends, who were all Anglo and upper-middle-class. At the same time, they also got to know Marisela's new companions Matías, Rosalba, Zahra, and Jaime, as well as another Latino student named Alfonso. "There are no white people in this group," Yadira observed. "And most of them are immigrants, too. It's not completely new to them." Back in the fall, Clara, Yadira, and Marisela had started calling themselves "the Brownies," as an in-joke about being students of color at a predominantly white school, and they still referred to themselves this way if they wanted to name their trio, but both Yadira and Clara had lighter skin than Marisela, and it was easier for them to mix with white students. Being able to blend in—at least part of the time—was important to them. Clara told me that she was determined to have a normal experience during freshman year, "not a brown one, if you know what I mean."

In the spring quarter, Yadira's favorite class was an urban studies course called Urban Education. Her professor, Nicholas Cutforth, who had emigrated from London, England, made clear that he valued her gritty background. When the subject of bilingual education arose, he asked her opinion, as she was the only student in the class who had gone through such a program. Yadira felt flattered by his attention, but she also felt singled out. As part of her course work, she wrote about her mentoring of Ángel, a middle school student who had moved to Denver from Mexico City. He had been living in the United States for four years and was still learning English. Once, Yadira had asked if he had papers, and Ángel had whispered, "Don't tell anybody—no, I don't." Despite the fact that it might have encouraged Ángel, Yadira had not revealed that she shared his predicament. "I didn't tell him in case he told other people," she told me afterward. "It could get to the wrong ears." When Yadira gave an oral presentation about Ángel in Urban Education, she told the other college students that he had moved here from Mexico and was taking classes in Spanish, but omitted his illegal entry. Then Professor Cutforth asked if Ángel possessed documents. Ashamed of her own illegitimacy, fearful of betraying Ángel's, and worried that she might somehow give herself away at the same time, Yadira nonetheless followed her strongest instinct, which was to please her instructor, and confessed the truth about Ángel. As she did, her face grew hot, as if she had inadvertently given away something critical about herself, and she sat down in a state of turmoil. "I was not prepared for that at all," she said later.

As the school year progressed, tension mounted between Yadira and Marisela. One night, the two of them went out dancing, along with Clara and Annalisa, their old friend from Roosevelt High, who was now working full-time as a food server at a local franchise of Sonic, "America's Drive-In." Marisela picked up Annalisa at her house, and Annalisa was depending upon Marisela for a ride home. After dancing, however, the girls went to a friend's house, and as it grew late Marisela persuaded Annalisa to spend the night in their dorm. Annalisa agreed, on the condition that Marisela take her to work at five o'clock in the morning, and Marisela promised to get her to Sonic on time.

Then a friend called Marisela and invited her to another party. Afterward, Marisela maintained that she had invited the other girls along, but they declined to go, saying the other scene was too *charro* for them—too country, too rough. Yadira said that Marisela left with no explanation, leaving the rest of them stranded. When hours passed and Marisela did not return, Yadira and Clara grew worried. By dawn, she was still missing. When Marisela finally surfaced the following afternoon, she was bewildered to discover that Yadira wasn't speaking to her and Clara was almost as chilly. Belatedly, Marisela explained that she had never made it to the second party—en route, a police car had turned on its lights and pulled her over. Marisela had imagined winding up in the detention center for illegal immigrants in Aurora, Colorado. When the police officer asked to see her license, she assumed her most polite manner and explained that she was a student at the University of Denver, and handed over her student ID. She confessed that she did not have a Colorado driver's license, however, at which point the officer impounded the vehicle. The sky had begun to lighten by the time she located a friend with a legitimate driver's license who could help her get the truck back.

Yet nothing Marisela said could melt Yadira's icy demeanor. As far as Yadira was concerned, her roommate's disappearance and her failure to follow through on her promise to Annalisa were just the latest examples of a chronic problem. "Marisela didn't call us until that afternoon," Yadira told me in a curt voice. "That was an example of her irresponsibility again. She failed us again. It goes all the way back to high school. Marisela has always had unhealthy things that she does, and Clara and I have always supported her, and given her advice. When we started college, she didn't stop. She still had all these problems. She has problems with her family, with the way she treats herself, with her love relationships. Because I was living with her—I'm the kind of person where if you are having a bad day, the energy transmits. Therefore, I have a bad day, too. I decided to distance myself from her for my own health. We got sick of her not dealing with her issues."

Marisela expected the conflict would resolve itself. Instead, it grew only bigger. First Matías criticized Yadira for being inflexible, and Yadira got angry with Matías. Pretty soon Clara wasn't getting along with Alison, either, after her roommate stuck up for Marisela. Even Elissa and Jaime, over at Regis, were drawn into the mess. Only Luke sided with Yadira and Clara. Everybody was confused by how the matter had grown so large, but nobody seemed capable of making it smaller. Tired of getting the cold shoulder in her own room, Marisela started sleeping at her cousin's house. "I couldn't take it anymore," she said.

Irene Chávez speculated that the real issue was race. Irene thought Yadira and Clara were trying to fit in with white students at the University of Denver, while Marisela was too dark-skinned and too Mexican to follow suit. "Supposedly the fight happened when Marisela forgot to pick up Annalisa, but that's not what it's really about," said Irene. "They are trying to assimilate, and Marisela can't."

Shortly before spring break, Clara and Yadira proposed reorganizing their living situations. Clara and Yadira wanted to live together, and suggested that Alison would make a better roommate for Marisela. To make things easier on her former best friend, Yadira offered to move out of their room, although this meant Alison would have to change rooms, too. Alison had already arranged to live with Marisela during sophomore year, but she didn't see why she had to change rooms now, when she hadn't done anything wrong. Paralysis set in. One evening, Luke, Clara, and Yadira were studying in Yadira's room when Marisela returned and started playing *ranchera* music loudly. Luke objected, pointing out that he was trying to read. Marisela told him that he couldn't object, as it wasn't his room. Later, Marisela stepped into the hallway to speak to some friends, and accidentally locked herself out. Nobody would let her back in. "This is so childish!" yelled Marisela. "Open up the door!"

"I can't! It's not my room!" Clara yelled back.

"What is going on with you guys?" demanded Alfonso.

Yadira opened up the door. "Nothing."

"Why don't you just change rooms?" he asked.

"Okay." She shrugged.

"Fine! Let's move right now!" exclaimed Clara.

And they did. None of the girls wanted to bother packing, so they just carried armfuls of clothes down the hallway. The boys carried Yadira's dresser into Clara's room, and Alison's dresser into Marisela's. Then Yadira declared that Alison's mattress was too soft, so they started hauling mattresses around, too. Disturbed by the chaos, their resident adviser emerged from her room.

"What's going on?" she demanded.

"We're switching rooms!" Marisela offered brightly.

"You can't do that without permission."

"No, you don't understand—we *really* need to change rooms."

"I can't let you do that. You can sleep in separate rooms, but I can't let you move your stuff."

"All right," said Marisela sweetly. "No problem."

They stealthily completed the move later that night. In the weeks that followed, relations between the two pairs of girls worsened, as they began a campaign of petty slights. Alison left behind papers, and Yadira threw them out; Yadira asked Alison for her key, and Alison refused to give it to her; Marisela failed to give Yadira phone messages. At the same time, each pair of girls found the new living arrangements to be a relief. Clara and Yadira created a zone of peace and quiet, while the other twosome flourished in a louder fashion. "Me and Alison are just crazy," said Marisela. "It is, like, if you have the music on, I don't care.

If my music is on, you don't care. You can go to sleep whenever you want, and if you leave the light on, it's okay. We are the wild ones."

In April, Josefa and Fabián returned to Colorado. They left Arizona because they felt oppressed by the political climate and they did not want to live so far from Marisela. Josefa also wanted to move back because her nephew, Román Ortega, whom Josefa had helped to raise since he was a small boy, had been accused of participating in the gang rape of a fifteen-year-old girl. Josefa believed her nephew to be innocent, and she wanted to be in the courtroom when his trial began in June. Marisela's parents found a small two-bedroom apartment in Thornton, a suburb north of Denver, for $655 per month. With only a few months left in the school year, Marisela's siblings started over again in new classrooms at various schools in the metro area. Josefa began cleaning a King Soopers grocery store in the suburb of Arvada, while Fabián cleaned a different King Soopers in Aurora. After several raises, he worked up to a salary of $1,000 every two weeks—almost the same amount of money he'd been earning several years earlier, before National Maintenance had slashed his pay. Marisela spent any free time visiting her parents and siblings in Thornton.

Meanwhile, Luke practically moved into the room that Yadira shared with Clara. The two girls dedicated a corner of the room to him, where they amassed a collection of Luke's belongings: his textbooks, shoes, and a hot pot that he used to cook instant noodles. Clara and Luke now began a flirtation that never quite blossomed into full romance. Once they were standing in line for a party that had an entrance fee, and Luke offered to pay for Clara's ticket; the boy she had asked to accompany her looked confused. He said, "Wait, are you two together?" This question hung over their relationship. At the same time, small things reminded the girls of their fundamental differences with Luke. One time he dropped by as Yadira was painting her nails, and she asked him to help. He did a messy job, however, and Yadira complained about his handiwork.

"Why don't you just go to the salon?" Luke told her.

"Are you crazy?" she said. "I can't pay to get my nails done professionally!"

"Why not?" he asked, mystified. "All my friends back home used to do it."

When I asked Yadira if she felt close to Luke, she hedged. "It depends on how you define *close*," she said. "I define *close* as 'okay to tell all about my life.' I can't do that with Luke. I do spend most of my time with him, but I don't define our relationship as close." And so, at the beginning of May, Yadira had nobody to turn to except Clara when she learned that her world was falling apart.

The bad news came in a cell phone call from her mother, who was crying so much that Yadira had a hard time understanding her. Finally Alma made clear she was in jail, and then the call abruptly ended. Yadira did not know where her mother was being detained, which law enforcement agency had picked her up, or whether her mother was being charged with a crime. Yadira's sense of impotence grew as she realized how many critical details she lacked. She left repeated messages on her mother's cell phone, but Alma never called back. Yadira missed her first class of the day—a sociology course called Women and Violence—while trying to locate Alma. Family and friends called the federal detention center in Aurora, but the personnel said they were not holding a woman by that name. It was as if Alma had vanished.

At dinner that evening, Luke noticed that Yadira was morose, but she told him only that she was feeling poorly. For the rest of the week, Clara kept Luke at bay by saying that Yadira needed to rest, and indeed she spent most of the time curled up in bed. Irene Chávez finally located Alma at the Denver County Jail on Smith Road. It was the local police that had arrested her, not federal immigration authorities. At Alma's arraignment, the Denver District Attorney's Office charged her with "criminal impersonation," a felony. For the past several years, Yadira's mother had been using a stolen identity to work. When the judge asked Alma if she had any children, Alma listed only her legal offspring, and never mentioned Yadira. Irene figured that Alma did not want to create problems for her undocumented daughter, but I was struck by the way that Yadira never seemed to exist in the eyes of officialdom, and wondered what it cost Alma emotionally not to name her firstborn. The judge set bail at $5,000.

After Alma was arraigned, Jesús called Yadira and told her that he was struggling to care for the children. He asked her to move back in, so that she could tend to her siblings. He figured she would still have plenty of time for college. Yadira stalled, saying she couldn't return until the following weekend, and then called Irene Chávez for advice. Irene said her job was to finish college. She had to go to every class, write each of her papers, take all her final exams. Her siblings were resilient, Irene maintained; Yadira should stay where she was. Jesús erupted when Yadira refused to comply with his wishes. "He got so mad, he told me not to come home at all," Yadira told me. "He kicked me out of the house. He said I didn't care about what was happening. Then he kept calling to harass me. I wouldn't answer the phone, but he left messages. 'If you don't come home right now, I'll do something bad that you'll regret!'"

The last weeks of school passed in a dismal blur. Yadira was split in two—she could not integrate what was happening in her family with what was expected of her on campus. Her mother's arrest left her half illegal immigrant and half college student, not fully one thing or another. The only person she knew who could understand was Marisela. When Yadira's uncle told her they needed to find a bail bondsman who would not require a Social Security number, Yadira walked down the hallway of Johnson-McFarlane and knocked on the door of the room she had once occupied, where she found her old roommate lying down.

"I need to talk to you," Yadira said.

"What's up?" asked Marisela, surprised.

"My mom just got arrested."

Marisela gave her the name and number of the bail bondsman that her cousin had once used. As Clara said later, "I guess in those circumstances you can't really turn anybody away." The following week, when I stopped by the dorm to see Yadira, I found her in her usual stylish attire, looking as young and carefree as ever, but on second glance she possessed a new air of weary maturity, as though recent events had jolted her soul into growing up faster than usual. Final exams were one week away. Taking a break from their studies, Clara and Yadira decided to have dinner at a Middle Eastern restaurant they had recently discovered.

"It must be crazy at home," I said as we left the dorm.

"Yeah," said Yadira, sadly. "That house does not function without her."

Her aunt and uncle had recently moved into the same apartment building, however, and her grandfather was visiting from Mexico. All these relatives plus a few more had assembled to discuss raising the $5,000 bail. The entire family could not scrape up that much money between them. Jesús said he would borrow some cash from his brothers, but nobody could agree on what Alma should do next. If they found the bond money, should she face the charges? Or should she flee? Jesús had a cousin who worked as a paralegal at a law firm, and he said that if Alma stood trial, she would serve time in jail. Complicating matters, Yadira revealed that Alma had just conceived another child, and was now three months pregnant. Everybody in the family believed that if she had the baby in jail, then the child would be taken from her, as Jesús could not step forward to claim the infant, given that he didn't have legitimate documents. Most of all, Yadira wanted her mother to be safe, and hoped she would flee to Mexico—even though that could mean they might not be able to see each other again. At least for now, Alma remained close by, even if Yadira could not visit her at the jail because she did not possess the right kind of identification.

"It's an amazing twist, isn't it?" Yadira said with her new world-weariness. "Our stories had seemed like they were going to have a happy ending—we had made it into college, and everything was going to be all right. But then something like this happens. It's a real awakening. I haven't thought about anything like this in a serious way for a long time. Now I realize that it's always hanging over us."

Marisela joined us halfway through the meal. Her hair was red again, with gold highlights. She struggled with the unfamiliar menu.

"I've never been here before—I don't know what to eat!"

"The chicken is good," said Yadira. "Here, have a bite of mine."

It had been a long time since I had seen Yadira make such a friendly gesture to Marisela. I thought it was a good thing that Yadira had been able to initiate this thaw, as in the months to come it seemed likely she would need friends, particularly those with whom she could discuss what was happening in her family.

5

TALK RADIO

On the second Sunday in May 2005, John and I woke to the ringing of the phone in our hotel room. It was six days after Alma's arrest, and we were in Chicago, Illinois. John had flown there for a meeting of the U.S. Conference of Mayors, and I had tagged along so that we could celebrate Mother's Day together. For the last several months, John had been busy campaigning to persuade the city's voters to spend $378 million on a new jail, because the old facility at Smith Road was dangerously overcrowded—men were sleeping on the gymnasium floor—and he believed it was time for the city to invest in a new building. It was a tough sell, however, and he had been slogging hard to get the initiative passed. We were looking forward to spending a weekend away.

When I picked up the phone, however, Sarah Kendall, John's deputy chief of staff, apologized for calling so early. "We need to reach the mayor," she said.

It was clear there was some kind of emergency. After he got off the phone, John said back in Denver two police officers had been shot. One had been wearing a bulletproof vest, and it was clear he would survive, but the other had no vest on and had died. John had to call his widow. This was not how any of us had planned to spend Mother's Day. For a brief moment, I felt sorry for myself; then I thought of the police officer's widow, and felt ashamed of my self-absorption. For the rest of her life, she was going to mark this holiday as the morning when her husband did not come home.

We boarded the next flight to Denver. Throughout the next few days, details trickled in: Both officers had been shot in the back, and neither had drawn his weapon. They had been manning the door of a popular Mexican social club, Salon Ocampo, where a Latino family had been celebrating the baptism of an infant. A young man had left the party and then tried to return, but could not produce a written invitation. The banquet hall was overcrowded, and the police officers had refused him entry. When the guest grew belligerent, one of the officers had escorted him out, and apparently the officer had grabbed the young man by the neck. The police suspected that the party guest had returned with a weapon, looking for payback.

On Tuesday morning, John's cell phone buzzed shortly after 7 A.M. It was his chief of staff, Michael Bennet. I asked if I should get John out of the shower.

"Well, there's a possibility that this guy who shot the cops worked at the Cherry Cricket," Bennet said. "I'm hoping this turns out to be nothing more than a crazy rumor."

The Cherry Cricket is a dive bar and burger joint located in the upscale Cherry Creek shopping district. It advertises itself with a wacky neon sign at odds with the otherwise posh surroundings. Sports fans camp out at the bar while their wives browse in expensive boutiques, then families with young children arrive for dinner, and later the college kids show up. The Wynkoop Brewing Company had bought the Cherry Cricket in 1998, five years before John took office, and it was the single most profitable restaurant in the company that he and his partners owned. I got John out of the shower.

By Tuesday evening, the police confirmed they were looking for an alleged perpetrator by the name of Raúl Gómez García, whom the Cherry Cricket had employed for the last ten months, first as a dishwasher and then as a busboy. Hired after John's interest in the restaurants had been placed into the trust, Gómez García had presented a Social Security card and a resident alien card to the restaurant's manager, but the police had determined those documents were false. The *Rocky Mountain News* quoted Lee Driscoll, the chief executive officer of Wynkoop Holdings, as saying the restaurant company had received a letter from the Social Security Administration two months earlier, alerting the company to the fact that Gómez García's name and Social Security number did not match. The same letter had warned the restaurant company not to fire Gómez García, and the company had taken no action. The following day's newspapers splashed a grainy picture of Gómez García across their pages, taken from the restaurant company's copies of his forged documents. He had a shaved head, a pencil moustache, and a big jaw. The mayor had employed an illegal alien who had killed a cop.

The Denver Police Department typically struggled to solve crimes that occurred in the Mexican community, due to the language barrier and the cultural chasm and the complicated nature of trust, but in the case of their hunt for the killer of Detective Donnie Young, the department's homicide detectives had gotten their big break early. In the hours immediately following Young's murder, residents of the city had inundated the police department with phone calls. Most wanted to express their condolences or their outrage, but one caller had information. The caller said the man who had shot the two officers was romantically involved with a young woman named Sandra Rivas, who had recently delivered a baby over at Denver Health. A limited number of people had given birth at the city-run hospital within the past month, and it possessed records on all of them; detectives pressed the hospital to divulge the names, but the hospital refused, citing patient confidentiality. The police had to obtain a subpoena to prise the information out of the medical institution. Sandra Rivas and Raúl Gómez García had named their newborn daughter Stacy, and unlike her parents, she was born an American citizen. The police learned her father's name from Stacy's birth certificate.

Within twenty-four hours of the shootings, the police were knocking at the door of the Rivas family's home, where Sandra lived with her parents and her siblings. At first Sandra denied knowing anything about the murder of a police officer, but eventually she told the police that her boyfriend had confessed. Detectives found Jaime Arana del Ángel, a close friend of Gómez García, living with the Rivas family, too. It was common for poor Mexican families to take in boarders, because they helped pay the rent, and one year earlier, both Gómez García and Arana del Ángel had moved with the Rivas family from Los Angeles to Denver. Arana del Ángel informed the police that Gómez García had fled to Los Angeles. He knew this because Gómez García did not know how to read or write and had asked his friend to show him the way. After the murder, Arana del Ángel had driven in his own car, with Gómez García following in his white Neon, across Colorado almost to Utah. Then Arana del Ángel had purchased a road map for his friend and pointed out the best route to Los Angeles, where Gómez García had family.

Among the police officers who flew from Denver to Los Angeles on the next available flight were Martin Vigil and Teresa García.

Vigil, the lead investigator on the case, was an experienced homicide detective who sported colorful bow ties. Teresa García was a rookie in terms of murder—the police brass had asked her to join the homicide unit immediately after Donnie Young was killed. She spoke fluent Spanish, a skill that nobody else in the homicide unit possessed, and she knew scores of people in the immigrant community. García herself had been born in Mexico. While she was a child, her family had crossed the border illegally, and initially she grew up without a Social Security number, although while she was in high school García had acquired a green card.

In Los Angeles, the homicide detectives found Gómez García's white Neon abandoned on a street in South Central L.A., with the laminated road map that Arana del Ángel had bought inside of it, but no clue as to Gómez García's whereabouts. By now, three days had elapsed since the murder, and the detectives knew that the longer their suspect eluded them, the less likely they were to make an arrest. When they interrogated Gómez García's mother, she said that her son had caught a bus to Mexico, although the detectives later came to suspect that one of Gómez García's uncles might have driven him to Tijuana. The fugitive probably crossed over the United States–Mexico border on the evening of May 11 or the morning of May 12—four days after the murder.

Meanwhile, back in Denver, the political maelstrom had begun. Several days earlier, Congressman Tom Tancredo had asked my husband to explain why Gómez García's immigration status had not been investigated previously. According to the local newspapers, during the year that he'd spent in Denver, police officers had issued three traffic tickets to Gómez García: one for speeding, one for running a red light, and one for "infractions following an accident." He had presented a valid Mexican driver's license in each instance, but no proof of insurance. Once again, Tancredo accused the Denver police department of having a sanctuary policy. He called it unconscionable that Gómez García had had three prior run-ins with the police yet had been released on each occasion. "Mayor Hickenlooper's refusal to reverse Denver's failed and illegal sanctuary policy is dangerous to all Coloradans," declared the congressman.

"Congressman Tancredo appears to misunderstand the law and the facts in this instance," fired back city attorney Cole Finegan, in the *Denver Post*. Foreign driver's licenses were an acceptable form of identification according to state law, Finegan observed; local police could not detain individuals merely for being from another country. Other Colorado law enforcement officials told the papers they typically contacted immigration authorities only in serious cases such as felony investigations, just like Denver. "We can't prove whether they are illegal or not. We don't know if they're [in the United States] on a visa or something," Colorado state trooper Eric Wynn told the *Post*. Meanwhile, federal immigration officials said they focused on keeping undocumented workers out of high-security jobs in airports, nuclear power plants, and military installations—not neighborhood restaurants. "We are prioritizing our resources, just like everyone else," said Immigration and Customs Enforcement spokesman Carl Rusnok.

During this time, I did not see either Marisela or Yadira, since the spring quarter was drawing to a close, and they were consumed with their final papers and exams. Irene Chávez had been calling almost daily with updates on Alma's situation, however, and as soon as the murder occurred, she observed that Gómez García's crime was going to make matters much, much worse for Alma—and for every immigrant who was living in Colorado. This was an opinion shared by many people. On the day that Tancredo called for John to explain why Gómez García had not been arrested previously, John and I had to go to a fund-raiser for a local charity, where an immigration attorney brought up our tie to the Cherry Cricket.

"Of all the gin joints," said John, in a tone beyond rueful.

He had spoken to Kelly Young, the police officer's widow, on the phone before the department's homicide detectives had named their suspect. Later that week, we were going to meet her for the first time. It was shocking to learn that we had a personal connection to her tragedy, and both of us felt ashamed about the circumstances of our bond. At the party, our hostess tried to steer the conversation away from the treacherous subject of the Cherry Cricket by predicting that critics of illegal immigration would use the murder to deport those immigrants who couldn't prove their legal status.

"They don't know what they're talking about," scoffed the immigration attorney. "The cost would be astronomical."

"What are there, about three hundred thousand illegal immigrants living in Colorado?" said John, doing the math. "Let's say one hundred thousand of them live in the metro area. If we stopped twenty percent of them for traffic violations in five years' time, and then put them through the proper deportation process—because we have something called due process in this country—let's see, if it cost $5,000 per case, times twenty thousand individuals, that would be about $100 million."

John enjoyed astronomical approval ratings, and *Time* magazine had just named him one of the five best big-city mayors in America. The fatal shooting of Detective Young was the first occasion when his political rivals spotted an Achilles' heel. The political drubbing continued the next morning at five, on KHOW, "Denver's Talk Station." John stood in our kitchen in his bathrobe, fielding questions over the phone from radio host Peter Boyles.

"Your Honor, thanks for coming on the show!" Boyles started off.

"I'm glad to be here," John said gamely.

"Like so many people, I have some questions. But just—your thoughts this morning?"

"Well, I'm not sure, that's the toughest question of all, because there are no thoughts that are satisfactory. I think that when something like this happens, to a family and to a community, the hardest thing is that words don't have any relevance. Certainly our thoughts and prayers are with the Young family and with Officer Bishop and his family as he recovers. You know—it's unspeakable."

"Let's begin. Do you have any plans to reverse sanctuary city status in Denver?"

John said there was no such thing, and Boyles insisted there was. Or else why hadn't Gómez García been arrested during one of the routine traffic stops?

"I will tell you, in terms of traffic stops, if we arrested every person who didn't have their ID or their valid driver's license and brought them in, we would need a jail three or four times the size of the one we just voted on last week," John shot back.

Boyles tried a new line of attack. "At the Cherry Cricket, does the buck stop with you?"

"Well, for the record, no one called me from the restaurant, and I haven't talked with Lee Driscoll about restaurant affairs for a year and a half. So what identification he uses, how he runs the restaurant, that buck doesn't stop here. That's the whole reason we set up the trust."*

Peter Boyles kept John on the ropes for a few more minutes, and then John turned things around. "I think that the challenge here is not to get too caught up in this stuff and make sure that we catch the guy," he said. "The other thing is, here's this guy, and he's working—and I don't think that it matters in what restaurant—but he's working in a restaurant for ten months, beside other people. You know, restaurants are very close-knit. Restaurants function very much like families. And all of a sudden it turns out that someone in your family is capable of—and again, right now, this is conjecture, no one has been found guilty—but we have an alleged perpetrator of something that is bestial, inconceivable. It was an execution—cold-blooded murder. And I think that is chilling to think that you could have been working next to someone and relying on someone who is capable of that, and you have no idea."

"Ann Rule's great book *The Stranger Beside Me* is a classic story," Boyles replied enthusiastically. "Ann Rule worked next to Ted Bundy on a hotline as a volunteer while Ted Bundy was going to law school. And she knew him and worked with him every night, talked with him, had coffee with him. It's a remarkable book."

They had found common ground. Boyles became more solicitous, and wished the police luck. "God bless, Mayor Hickenlooper, thank you very much," he said. As soon as John was off the air, however, Boyles added: "No matter what you hear, Denver *is* a sanctuary city." Later, he spoke with Congressman Tancredo, who insisted once more the city did have such a policy. "It definitely preceded Hickenlooper, but he knows about it," asserted the congressman. He and Boyles kicked this idea around for a while, insinuating that John must be lying. Then Boyles moved on to the subject of Gómez García's child. "Front page of the *Rocky Mountain News* this morning has this young woman,

---

* Within a short period of time, the Wynkoop Brewing Company would announce that it was now verifying the Social Security numbers of all prospective employees, to make sure it no longer hired anybody whose name and number did not match. Lee Driscoll estimated the new practices cost the company about $1,000 a week, because it was hard to keep the kitchens fully staffed and the company had to pay additional overtime.

Sandra Rivas, she's eighteen, and she has a three-week-old daughter, the baby of the guy that's on the run for killing the cop," said Boyles. "That's the anchor baby, right?"

"Yeah, that's right," agreed Tancredo.

"That baby now—"

"—will be given citizenship status," finished Tancredo.

Boyles ventured that Rivas was most likely here without legal status herself.

"If she is illegal, she probably will not be asked to leave the country, because she's got this baby that is an American citizen," said Tancredo. "We tell the INS all the time: 'So what?' The baby may be an anchor; deport the mother, the baby will go with the mother. But they don't."

The Denver city attorney fired back later on the *Caplis & Silverman* show, which aired on the same station. "This has been an enormous distraction," said Finegan. "What we're focused on in the city is trying to find the person that killed Detective Young and who wounded Detective Bishop, and Congressman Tancredo, frankly, by injecting himself into this situation has complicated it and has been a distracting factor. And I think he's let politics get in the way of us trying to find the person who killed a police officer."

He reminded listeners that state law deemed a foreign driver's license a legitimate form of identification. "People get pulled over all the time, and they simply are issued tickets, and they go on. And there are a lot of reasons for that. One is, for example, some guy flies here from Germany to visit Colorado. He wants to go skiing. He gets a car at DIA, he rents the car, he's on his way to Vail, hopefully he's going to spend hundreds of dollars to boost the economy. And he gets a speeding ticket on Peña Boulevard. We pull him over, and he has a German driver's license. If it's a valid driver's license, we just issue a ticket."

Caplis and Silverman brought Tancredo back on to respond. "Congressman, was it inappropriate for you to raise these issues at this time when Denver and the nation are searching for this cop killer?" asked Caplis.

"It seems to me that it is exactly the time to talk about the fact that we have these problems," Tancredo replied. "How many people have to die? Other people throughout this country have suffered as a result of the kind of policies that both Denver and many other cities have in place. Because there are illegal immigrants here in the country, and in

these localities, their presence becomes known to the local law enforcement agencies, but nothing is done beyond that."

Silverman interrupted to say that they'd just heard from the police
department. He read from a statement: "'Denver's policies comport
with federal law, and do not prevent Denver law enforcement officers
from cooperating with federal officials on immigration matters. There
are no executive orders, regulations, or ordinances that establish a
sanctuary policy in Denver. Congressman Tom Tancredo's statements
are inaccurate.'"

"Now," Caplis continued, "Cole Finegan said, 'We do it the way
that almost every other city does it.' Can you point to examples of
major cities that do it right in your judgment?"

"Well, I can tell you about a place that I just came from not too
long ago," Tancredo said. "It's called New Ipswich, New Hampshire.
The police chief there, when he comes across people, he takes them
into custody and charges them with trespassing, as a matter of fact. He
then calls the INS. Now, admittedly, the first time he did it, they didn't
come out. But after he sent out a little press release, showing all these
undocumented immigrants, illegal immigrants, illegal aliens, showing
them walking away because ICE wouldn't come and get them—you
know what happened? The next time that he collected a bunch of illegal immigrants—about twenty illegals, in his city—twenty minutes
later, ICE was there and picked them up, because of course it got some
attention."

Technically, New Ipswich doesn't meet the definition of a major city.
According to the U.S. Census Bureau, only 4,289 people live there (and
within a few months time, a district judge would rule that a local police
department could not use trespassing laws to usurp the federal government's authority on immigration matters, ending the practice in New
Ipswich), but neither of the radio hosts objected to the comparison.
Later they invited former governor Dick Lamm onto the show. Lamm
now served as the codirector of the Center for Public Policy and Contemporary Issues at the University of Denver, and in recent years he had
become the most vocal Democratic critic of illegal immigration. In an
era of global warming, Lamm argued, elected officials could not allow
unlimited numbers of people to come to the United States, struggle,
prosper, and buy SUVs. "I think that there is a massive movement of
illegal aliens, and I think that the mayor and almost all of the establish-

ment in Denver have turned their back on it," Lamm said on *Caplis &
Silverman*. He alleged that employers considered illegal immigration
"the greatest thing since slavery." Later he added, "I think we've got a
good mayor—but I think he's turned his back on any kind of interest in
enforcing the immigration laws."

"Why, Governor? What do you think is driving this politically?"
Caplis asked.

"Well, you know, his wife wrote a big article in *Westword* about how
we should give college tuition—we should pay for college tuition—for
illegal aliens," Lamm responded. He said John and I were "just good-
hearted liberal people who think that we're all God's children—which
we are—and that we should know no [borders]—I guess that illegal
immigration is tolerated and encouraged."

Actually, I did not believe that illegal immigration should be encouraged. I thought that the phenomenon damaged this country, not to
mention those people who entered it the wrong way. If spending time
with Yadira and Marisela had taught me anything, it had shown me
that their opportunities were curtailed by their lack of documents—
their inability to obtain legal status perpetually threatened to stunt their
potential. Now that the political climate was darkening, their futures
looked even more precarious. But the idea that I was somehow the driving force behind the phenomenon of illegal immigration in Colorado
seemed to appeal to the talk radio types. Later, Peter Boyles asked John
if he thought I should be allowed to continue to write about immigration, as if by doing so I might somehow exacerbate the problem.

"If you think I can control my wife, you might give me some more
advice!" John replied.

"I can't," Boyles said. "My wife loves you."

And it was in the midst of all this kind of chatter that we went to
Donnie Young's funeral, which carried the emotional force of a tornado
or a raging fire, and made all the political back-and-forth seem incon-
sequential.

6

MANY DWELLING PLACES

John knew many police officers, because he had hired them to work off-duty at the Wynkoop Brewing Company back when he was in the bar business, but the guys in his security detail were the first I came to know as friends. On Friday, May 13, 2005, when John picked me up on his way to Donnie Young's funeral, Ken Overman was driving the car. I knew Kenny as a mild-mannered guy who put up with John's assiduous backseat driving with admirable restraint. Later I learned that Overman had been one of the first responders on the scene at the Columbine High School massacre, but he never spoke of anything like that with us. He just talked about his impending retirement. All the officers in John's security detail became part of our extended family—dapper Reuben Gomez, who left the SWAT team to join the detail; curmudgeonly Bobby Bogans, the Vietnam vet; quiet Mike Taylor, who loved to ski. Eventually, Kevin Kreuzer joined the detail, too. Kreuzer was the first police officer to be shot after John was elected, and they had met while Kreuzer was in the hospital, recuperating from his wounds. They shared a fondness for practical jokes. One evening, after Kreuzer accompanied us to a gala at the Denver Art Museum, he got on the police radio and spoke at length to the entire department about the quality of the lobster mousse being served. Dispatch got so mad they turned off his radio broadcast.

As Overman drove us to the funeral, I said, "Kenny, I don't think I've seen you since all this happened."

"Oh, I said to the guys, 'Of all the restaurants in the city, for him to work in one of John's places—it's unbelievable,'" replied the officer.

We commented upon the amount of devastation that one nineteen-year-old had caused. Gómez García had torn apart Donnie Young's family, and rendered his own infant daughter effectively fatherless. Meanwhile, local businesses had begun firing workers who could not produce legitimate Social Security numbers.

"This thing has just blown up." Overman predicted, "A lot of folks are going to lose their jobs over this."

John spent the car ride on the phone, calling his big donors, trying to amass a $100,000 reward for Gómez García's capture. After tracking their suspect to Los Angeles, the police had lost his trail. Every second mattered now, and the only thing John could think of to do that might help was to raise money. Then Governor Owens called: The president of Mexico was scheduled to visit Colorado in four weeks, and the governor didn't like the timing. John called the Mexican consul general.

"Juan Marcos, I know you still want your president to come, but after the shooting of this police officer, I think you're better off waiting. He could have several thousand people protesting him, and that could be very embarrassing for everybody.

"Exactly. If at all possible, push it off."

Overman parked in an alley. The Cathedral Basilica of the Immaculate Conception could hold one thousand people, but three thousand mourners had shown up, and every available parking space was taken. Directly in front of the cathedral, we encountered several hundred uniformed police officers, immobile and silent, standing in rows. I found walking this gauntlet, immediately on the heels of the latest news, to be excruciating. In theory, we were all on the same side, but I suspected most of them didn't see it that way. Even before the news of Gómez García's employment at the Cricket, many of the police department's rank and file had viewed John critically. Weeks before he took office, a white police officer had shot and killed a mentally challenged sixteen-year-old African American boy who had been threatening his mother with a kitchen knife. In one of his first acts as mayor, John had suspended the officer for ten months, despite the fact that his police chief had recommended only twenty days. "Chickenlooper!" uniformed police officers had chanted during a protest outside of the City and County Building. Then John had asked the police union to make concessions during the budget crisis, and launched a reform of the department that involved hiring a civilian police monitor. Now this. Outside of the cathedral, a huge television screen displayed an image of Donnie Young in his navy blue uniform, smiling broadly. He had dark hair, brown eyes, and a jovial look. Chief Whitman stood on the steps of the cathedral.

"I'm just waiting to greet the family," he said.

"I'll wait with you," offered John.

I wasn't sure where I belonged.

"I'll have somebody show you to your seat," Chief Whitman suggested. He turned to another officer. "This is Mrs. Hickenlooper. Will you take her inside?"

The officer steered me through the crowd and over to an attendant. "This is Mrs. Hickenlooper, could you show her to her seat?"

It did not occur to me to point out that this was not my name—today, I had no other role. The trip to the pew took a remarkably long time. I walked past row upon row of official blue, under soaring ribs of stone, and my footsteps echoed loudly in the vast, chilly silence. In the pew labeled "Mayor's Office," press secretary Lindy Eichenbaum Lent, chief of staff Michael Bennet, and city attorney Cole Finegan were waiting, along with a man I did not recognize. He leaned over to share that he was the new civilian police monitor. He had yet to move to Denver. "The head of the police union called and asked if I could issue some kind of statement," he whispered. "I said, 'Why don't I just come out there?'"

At the sound of camera shutters clicking, we turned around. I caught sight of Kelly Young's fiery red hair beside the silver coffin. Up in the choir loft, reporters and photographers were leaning over to record what was happening below. I used to be one of those people, I thought—above it all, removed. Kelly Young walked the length of the cathedral to the front row, her heels striking the stone floor, and it was strange to see a woman surrounded by such a large crowd look so alone. Attendants wheeled the silver casket forward and a police officer walked up to the lectern. "In My Father's house are many dwelling places," he read in a shaky voice. "If it were not so, I would have told you; for I go to prepare a place for you."

Archbishop Charles Chaput told the audience that police work was not a personal choice. The whole family sacrificed. He asked the mourners to remember that they lived in safety because of the risks that police officers took every day.

Chief Whitman walked up to the altar, tired and grim. "I know that there's one thing that all of you want to hear, and that's that we've made an arrest," he said. "Well, as of ten o'clock this morning, we haven't." Whitman talked about what kind of man Young had been: Facing an armed kidnapper, Young had rescued two victims without firing a shot.

Fellow police officer Jeff Baran remembered that he had gone out to breakfast with Young three days before the murder. Young had talked about his daughters: He had just taken thirteen-year-old Kourtney to buy a pair of new jeans, because she had outgrown the last pair already; five-year-old Kelsey had learned some new soccer moves. Baran was telling the two girls that their father's last thoughts had been of them.

From the cathedral, an endless line of police cars with their lights silently flashing followed the hearse to the grave site. We drove past people standing on the sidewalks with their hands on their hearts, under the ladders of two fire engines that had been crossed over the street in a sign of respect, by children standing at the fence of an elementary school, waving hand-lettered signs. It was only a twelve-mile journey, but so long was the funeral cortege, it took more than an hour for the last car to arrive at the graveyard. I found Kelly after the burial, standing in a circle of police officers. Her eyes were red but her bearing was firm, and she looked poised despite her obvious emotional disarray. It was a remarkable combination. Afraid she might condemn us, I felt timid about approaching, but compelled to do so. I introduced myself and tried to say how sorry I was.

"Thank you," she said, with weary grace. "Thank you for being here."

The vast choreography of the funeral swept around her, but she was utterly still, the axle at the center of all the motion. Immobile, she waited for people to greet her and she waited for people to go, waited to experience the rest of her grief. She had not yet gone to pieces nor had she pulled herself back together again—it would take several years for her to recuperate to the point where she would say that she felt ready to go out on a date. As we drove home, it was clear that everything had changed. We had been bloodied, drawn into the conflict. Kelly Young burned in my mind, an icon—of family, of safe suburban streets, of violation. All of us found ourselves in new territory, far from our point of origin. I didn't know what the rules were anymore.

7

SALON OCAMPO

O nly after the funeral did I learn that Marisela had been invited to go to the party at Salon Ocampo. Earlier that spring, she had started dating a handsome ranch hand named Ramiro. They originally met at Roosevelt High—Ramiro had been a year behind her at school until he dropped out—and then found each other again at a club called Malibu. Ramiro was working with his father on a ranch near Brighton, Colorado, keeping horses for a wealthy family. At the beginning of May, he had asked Marisela to go with him to the baptismal party. Initially, Marisela was enthusiastic, even though neither she nor Ramiro had a formal invitation. This did not bother Marisela, because her parents were friendly with the owners of Salon Ocampo, and she figured she could talk her way into the party. Uninvited guests often turned up at Mexican weddings, baptisms, and *quinceañeras*, because the food and drinks were free. It was the most economical way to have a good time.

Several of Marisela's relatives were going to the party, as well as one of her friends from Roosevelt. At the last minute, however, Ramiro casually mentioned that the person who had invited him was his ex-girlfriend Gisela. Upon hearing this news, Marisela huffily told Ramiro that he could go by himself—she wasn't going to compete for his attention. Mystified, Ramiro attempted to change his girlfriend's mind, but he could not sway Marisela, and in the end he went to Salon Ocampo alone. Marisela went to a dance club called Palladium instead. After a while, her friend from Roosevelt called to persuade her to come over to Salon Ocampo, but Marisela convinced her friend to leave the baptismal party and come to Palladium. They stayed out late dancing. Marisela enjoyed the rare circumstance of knowing that she had a boyfriend yet finding herself unencumbered by him, and did not miss Ramiro at all. "It was just us girls having a crazy time," she said afterward.

Marisela had no idea how badly the evening had gone wrong until the next morning, when in a contrite mood she called Ramiro.

"I almost got killed last night!" he told her.

"What do you mean?"

"This guy started shooting when the party was over!"

"Did he hit anybody?"

"He hit these two cops."

The story sounded far-fetched to Marisela. She assumed Ramiro was exaggerating until she saw the news on TV. Only then did she begin to appreciate the magnitude of what had happened—a man had lost his life, and the political context in which she was living had been upended. When she next saw Ramiro, she quizzed him about what had occurred at the ruined party, and Ramiro told her that in the instant when the shooting took place, he had been standing inside the bar, which had interior windows that opened onto a main hallway. At the *pop-pop-pop* sound of bullets, Ramiro had glanced up and found himself looking over the shoulder of a guy with a shaved head, straight at two police officers, just as one started to crumple. Ramiro did not know the gunman, who never turned around to face him, but when he heard later that one of the officers had died, he understood that he had witnessed a murder.

Marisela urged Ramiro to go to the police. He would not, however, because he had been arrested for driving under the influence previously, and he had neglected to show up in court. After that, he had hit another car and left the scene of the accident. The police would put him in jail, he said; they would deport him. By this time, the police had already lined up other witnesses who could be more helpful, and for many reasons the prosecutors might not have wanted to rely on Ramiro, but they surely would have preferred to make that call themselves, rather than having Ramiro make it for them. That Marisela's boyfriend had failed to report what he knew showed how easy it would have been for the case against Gómez García to founder. What if Ramiro had been the only person to see the murderer pull the trigger?

Neither Marisela nor Ramiro harbored any sympathy for Gómez García. He had fired in the direction of a crowded hall filled with families they knew well. Salon Ocampo was a touchstone for Marisela and her parents, a place where they marked important occasions, a place where they wove the fabric of their side of Denver. Marisela bumped into old boyfriends and second cousins and former neighbors whenever she went, while her parents encountered old friends from Durango. Salon Ocampo was a destination that made displaced families feel more at home. Consequently, Gómez García's actions were deeply resented by everyone who frequented the social club, because he had brought disrepute to their place of solace. Two weeks after the murder, when Marisela returned to Salon Ocampo for a *quinceañera,* she found that the crime had cast a pall over the entire hall. "People were tense," she said. "You could feel it."

At the same time, Marisela learned from Spanish-language television that Gómez García hailed from her home state. This made her feel tied to the suspected killer. She experienced an unwanted sense of kinship, as if his crime reflected badly upon her, too—upon everyone from Durango. As fate would have it, Raúl Gómez García and Marisela Benavídez were almost exactly the same age. Both of them had been born in the state of Durango within several months of each other, and each had followed the same immigrant's trajectory, moving first with older family members to California, and then to Colorado. The remarkable parallels between the pair emphasized how they represented two extremes in the debate over immigration: Raúl Gómez García had just made himself into a poster child for the critics of illegal immigrants, while Marisela Benavídez was becoming the darling of those who wanted to defend the rights of the undocumented.

After finishing her first year of college, Marisela moved back in with her parents and worked full-time to help pay the bills. She had a new job. Toward the end of the school year, she had quit her job at the liquor store and started working for an organization that fought for social justice. She was working as a community organizer for $15 an hour—more than twice what she'd earned at the liquor store. The nonprofit's director knew Marisela's true status, yet hired her anyway after she supplied the fake Social Security card that her parents had purchased for her. The nonprofit deducted the required taxes from her paycheck, just as though she were legal. Knowingly hiring an illegal immigrant put the organization in jeopardy, however, and I asked the director why he was willing to take such a risk. He said he wanted to save Marisela from the ignominy of clerking at a liquor store, and added that she was the best organizer on his staff.

For Marisela, the emotional core of that summer had little to do with work or Ramiro. Even the crime that had taken place inside of Salon Ocampo seemed peripheral to her, compared with the significance of her cousin Román's rape trial. It began in June and continued into July, and as the proceedings dragged on, Marisela became increasingly subdued. The courtroom sucked the vitality out of her just like her trip to Phoenix, leaving her deflated. Marisela worshipped Román. When he had lived with the Benavídez family, he had stood up for Marisela whenever she battled for freedom. He was the person who had introduced her to nightlife, to men, to adulthood—he had been the key to her liberty. After her suicide attempt, Román had driven to a drugstore and bought a package of hair dye, and dyed her hair himself. Then he had taken her dancing. At the darkest hour of her life, he had given her a new start, a new beginning. And so, throughout the entire court proceedings, her loyalty remained unswerving. "My cousin dresses kind of baggy, and the prosecutors are saying that he is a gang member," she said one evening, after listening to hours of testimony. "He's not part of a gang, though—none of the guys are. And when the girl testifies, it's a different story each time."

Supposedly the victim had gone to four different clubs that night. She had first encountered Román and his friends inside one club, and later crossed paths with them again at a Conoco station on Federal Boulevard. By this point she was intoxicated, and had horsed around with the four men in the gas station's convenience store. They claimed that she climbed into Román's vehicle willingly and participated in everything that happened inside of it without protest; she said she had been gang-raped. Everyone agreed that Román had not participated in any sexual activity, but he had been inside of the vehicle, which made him an accomplice, according to the prosecutors. The jury deliberated for days but could not reach a unanimous verdict, and finally the judge declared a mistrial. Román would be tried all over again in the fall.

Marisela could not believe she would have to relive the ordeal that she had just endured. In between his first and second trials, Román called her often, and she went to visit him in prison. Technically, she should not have been able to do so, but before going to Smith Road, Marisela would carefully remove her makeup, take out her gold contact lenses, and smooth her hair into a demure ponytail. Then she would smile until her dimples appeared and tell the guards that she did not have a Colorado driver's license because she was not yet eighteen.

By August, Marisela was dreading college. Going back to the University of Denver meant reentering that other world—the one where nobody had cousins like Román, the one where nobody understood her. Watching the prosecutors try to convict her cousin had left her with a grudge against the system, had allied her once more with the street. As she braced for the second trial, she identified more closely with the sunburned laborers she encountered in Mexican nightclubs than she did with her white college classmates. Meanwhile, her organizing work took her deep into the city's Mexican neighborhoods, where she kept meeting younger versions of herself. "I think it's going to be harder for me," she said before school started. "I've been talking a lot about racism, spending a lot of time with youth of color. It'll be a bigger shock to me. I feel angry."

At the end of the summer, Marisela threw herself a birthday party. She made a point of inviting Yadira, in the hope of furthering their reconciliation. Elissa teased their old friend for coming. "What are *you* doing here?" she asked. Yadira replied, "I guess somebody really wanted me to come." It was late August, and Hurricane Katrina blew into New Orleans that day, while they were singing "Happy Birthday." Afterward, Marisela conflated the memory of her birthday celebration with the televised images of black people stuck on the roofs of tenements, waving at the news helicopters to save them from the rising water. Marisela saw herself stuck on those rooftops; she identified with the residents of the overlooked slums. It was one more log on the fire of her anger, one more reason to hate the system. Román's second trial began at the end of September, and it also ended in a mistrial. He was tried for a third time that winter, and the following January another jury voted to convict. Boys from poor Latino families dropped out of school at a far greater rate than girls did, and in the course of the years that I knew her, a few of Marisela's male relatives as well as several of her boyfriends ran afoul of the legal system. Even Fabián wound up in local courts several times, albeit for driving offenses. Sometimes it almost seemed as though Marisela's extensive connections to the street put her at one or two degrees of separation from every significant interaction between the city's justice system and its Mexican community.

8

BLACK MARKET

Although it was Marisela who planned to go to Salon Ocampo on the night when the two police officers were shot, in the end it was Yadira whose life was most affected by the murder. It took time for me to understand this, because after Alma's arrest, Yadira declined to answer my phone calls or e-mails for some time. During May, I had known that she needed to focus on the final exams of her freshman year, and had not pushed her. In June, I reached out, but got no response. It was the middle of July before I finally tracked her down at the home of Irene and Justino Chávez, where she was living for the summer. Yadira apologized for being unresponsive, saying she had been overwhelmed by the confluence of her final exams and the crisis in her family.

She said that her mother had been released from jail on a Friday evening toward the end of May. Yadira's aunt had driven over with Alma to the University of Denver to pick up Yadira for the weekend. "In my family, we don't really give hugs," said Yadira. "We just looked at each other with a look that said, 'I'm glad to see you. I'm glad you're okay.'"

Alma told Yadira that at first she had been locked in a holding cell with a young woman who talked to herself. Afterward, she had moved to the county jail, where it was cold and the food was disgusting. There were thirty women on the cellblock, and she had no privacy. News of the illegal Mexican dishwasher who had shot the two police officers convinced Alma's friends and relatives that there was no longer any possibility she would be given a lenient sentence. "No matter what I do, it's going to be bad," Alma told Yadira. "If I show up in court, then I'll be taken away from all of you. And if I leave on my own, I'm still leaving you behind." If she fled to Mexico, Alma could bring her legal children with her, as they could easily return to the United States, but she would not take Yadira. Her dusty hometown was a place of dirt streets and stray dogs and hopelessness, and she did not want her oldest child to become trapped there. That weekend, Jesús lobbied for Alma to move to California. He said he would go with her, but made it clear that if Alma fled to Mexico, she would go alone—Jesús was not leaving the United States. Alma said she did not think she would be safe in California; she would always be looking over her shoulder. They had one of the worst fights of their entire marriage.

Within a few days, Alma opted to run to Mexico, at least for the summer. She decided to bring thirteen-year-old Laura and nine-year-old Raúl with her. In the fall, maybe the younger kids would start school in Durango, or maybe they would return to Colorado. Meanwhile, everybody agreed that Yadira and Zulema should remain in Denver. At fourteen, Zulema had just completed her first year at Abraham Lincoln High School, and didn't want to disrupt her schooling. Alma asked Yadira to move in with Jesús and Zulema—if the family had to be divided in two, Alma wanted each half to stay together—but Yadira refused to live with Jesús. Enraged, Jesús moved out to live elsewhere with a group of single men who were splitting the rent—a much cheaper arrangement. Zulema moved in with her aunt and uncle and their children, while Yadira made plans to spend the summer with Irene and Justino Chávez.

One week after Alma's release, she said good-bye to her two oldest daughters. On the way to the bus station, Alma cried, Zulema cried, and even Yadira broke down. Jesús did not accompany them. The family that was about to be sundered stood together beside the bus for as long as time would permit. "Okay," the driver finally said. Yadira's uncle suggested it would be easier if they drove away, but Yadira and Zulema would not go until they saw the bus vanish. Yadira's final exams began the following day. She could not remember a single thing about them, she said, but she had received three A's and one B.

Zulema was having a hard time adjusting to the new living arrangements. When she fought with her thirteen-year-old cousin, her aunt and uncle took her cousin's side; she did not have an advocate. Yadira had just taken Zulema shopping to cheer her up. The two sisters, who looked so much alike, had spent several hours in the inexpensive boutique where Yadira was now employed. Yadira had bought Zulema blouses, sweaters, and bras. She was making only $6.50 an hour— "which is very little," she observed—but received a sizable discount.

It looked as though Yadira had been augmenting her own wardrobe, too. At the moment, she was wearing a white cotton top with spaghetti straps and low-slung hip-hugger jeans. The greater the actual chaos of her life, the more carefully she arranged her appearance. This always threw me off, and I found it hard to discern what was going on inside of Yadira until I asked pointed questions—otherwise her trendy clothes made me thing that her life also must be stylish and ordered. When she had parted with Alma, Yadira had barely made up with Marisela, and was still at odds with Matías, Rosalba, Alfonso, Elissa, and Jaime. I observed that it must have been painful for her to lose her mother without the support of her friends. "I felt like I had to tell someone, but there was nobody there to tell," Yadira replied. "So I kept it inside." At the same time, her mother's departure seemed to have acted like a solvent, loosening her bitterness, softening her rigidity. Not long ago, Matías had called to make up, and she had told him about everything. Yadira seemed lighter in spirit now that she didn't have to keep her secrets quite so close.

"Oh, guess what?" she volunteered. "I just bought a fake Social Security card. Do you want to see it?"

I did. Yadira rifled through her purse and pulled out a white and blue Social Security card with a mixture of pride and chagrin. It looked like the real thing, and Yadira seemed to think it was cool to have acquired any kind of Social Security card—even a fake. Yet she also seemed ashamed of what she'd done. I asked how it had come about. She explained that when the owners of the clothing boutique had originally hired her, she had given them a made-up Social Security number, which she had concocted by taking Zulema's real Social Security number and changing one digit. She never had a problem with the fake number, but this summer a number alone was not enough: After Raúl Gómez García shot the two police officers, employers in the metro area had begun to require further proof of legality, and students who could not produce actual Social Security cards and government-issued IDs found it impossible to line up their usual summer jobs. Yadira's employers had told her she had to show them a Social Security card and an alien resident's card or driver's license.

"Juan knows these guys who make these things," Yadira told me. "He called them, and they said, 'Get Yadira to call us.'"

The two men had arrived at the Chávez house within half an hour.

They told Yadira to remove her jewelry and expose her right ear, then took her picture. She wrote down her name, nationality, and the nine-digit number she'd always used. The two men came back in one hour with her documents. She paid them $100 for the forged Social Security card and resident's alien card. When she showed the cards to Juan, he said they looked too new, and explained that she had to get them a little dirty. He rubbed the cards on the ground until they looked dog-eared. Acquiring the forged identity cards had been a rite of passage—a marker of adulthood—and seemed to give Yadira the same kind of pride that a teenager feels upon earning a real license. Yet buying fake documents was something done by illegal aliens—the very category from which she sought to escape—and I saw her purchase as a defeat for her American side. To me, the cards marked the first time I saw Yadira act like an illegal immigrant. As if she read my dismay, Yadira hastened to add: "I didn't want to do it. This was new to me. I mean, I knew how it worked—that they would come to your house. I saw it with my uncles. I saw it with my mom. I saw it when they came to Juan's house, for his mom. So it wasn't entirely new to me, but it was new for me to do it. I felt like I was forced to do it."

I'm sure she did, but I knew other people without legal status who chose never to enter this netherworld of black-market transactions. This was the darkness at the heart of illegal immigration, as far as I could tell: Otherwise good people committed crimes like buying forged Social Security cards or stolen identities. And all they wanted to do was work. Did that make the transgressors reprehensible, or was there something wrong with the law? Certainly one could not argue that such crimes were victimless. In Yadira's case, perhaps a legal resident or an American citizen might have wanted her job and had to find work elsewhere. And in Alma's case, as it turned out, there was another victim, too.

9

COMAL

During the period when prosecutors were trying Marisela's cousin for the first time up on the fourth floor of the City and County Building, I had been down in the basement, looking through old court documents, trying to learn whatever I could about the charges against Alma. With help from Jesús and Yadira, I gradually pieced together what had happened. Apparently, Alma had bought the stolen identity—an actual person's name, alien registration number, Social Security number, and Colorado driver's license number—when Yadira was a junior in high school. According to the court documents, the other woman's name was Isbel Morales. Alma bought a fake Social Security card that bore Isbel's name and Social Security number, and a fake Colorado driver's license that bore Isbel's name and license number underneath Alma's picture.

Jesús had instructed Alma to stay at Goodwill for a maximum of two years after she purchased the stolen identity. By then, the Internal Revenue Service was likely to notice that Isbel Morales was working in more than one location, he said. When they returned from California, Jesús had urged his wife not to resume her job at the sorting table, given that she had already worked there for two years under the name of Isbel Morales. Alma looked for work elsewhere, but the local economy was still sluggish, and in the end she went back to her old job—again as Morales.

As far as I knew, it was unusual for the district attorney's office to pursue a case of identity theft unless it involved a ring of people who were manufacturing false identities, or other crimes had been committed, such as fraud. Why had prosecutors targeted Alma? A police officer I consulted asked whether Alma might have taken out credit cards in Isbel's name and run up unpaid bills. "It makes a difference to me whether or not she destroyed the other woman's credit," said the officer. "If she just used the other person's name to work, that's one thing. I would do that myself, if it meant putting food on the table for my kids. But if she ruined the other woman's credit—that's something else entirely." Nobody in the police department knew the answer to this question, however, and the only way to find out for certain was to locate the real Isbel Morales. The information in the basement of City Hall mentioned the name of a detective who had worked on the case, and after obtaining Isbel's permission, that detective provided me with the crime victim's home telephone number.

"*Bueno?*" said a man's voice over the sound of children creating a ruckus.

"Oh. *Está Isbel Morales allí, por favor?*"

"*No, no está aquí.*"

Isbel's husband said that she would be home from work in a few hours. In the background, I heard the tumult of a Spanish-speaking household. It sounded far more like Alma's home than I had anticipated. When I called back, Isbel said that she would be happy to meet, but she worked full-time, went to community college at night, and was raising two children.

"Work, school, the kids—it's hard," she said.

I wrote down in my notebook: *This is a person who is playing by the rules.* Actually, Isbel's story turned out to be more complicated and more interesting than that. It took weeks for us to meet in person—by the time we did, Marisela and Yadira had already started their sophomore year of college—but we finally spoke one evening over coffee, after Isbel had finished putting in a day's work at Anthem Blue Cross and Blue Shield, where she authorized health insurance claims. She had a full figure, straight brown hair, and features that did not line up properly, giving her face a Picasso-like quality. She was wearing a large blue sweatshirt and jeans. Her only adornment was a large silver cross, and she had an attractive, girl-next-door quality that fit with her forthright personality. Isbel announced proudly that she had become a citizen of the United States just two days earlier.

"I feel much more—how should I put it—there's a freedom, you know?"

"When did you come to this country?" I asked.

"When I was eleven years old," she said. "I had no papers, of course."

Just like Yadira and Marisela, Isbel had crossed the border illegally as a child. An aunt had brought Isbel to the United States.
Her father had never involved himself in Isbel's upbringing, and her
mother had been diagnosed with a brain tumor when Isbel was a
toddler, and later treatment rendered her a permanent invalid. Until
the age of eleven, Isbel was raised by her mother's older sister in
Nuevo Laredo, on the Mexican side of the border. Then her mother's younger sister, a United States resident, brought her across the
International Bridge that spanned the Rio Grande. Coached by her
aunt, Isbel lied to the Border Patrol agents on the other side, saying
she was a legal resident who lived in Texas. "Where do you go to
school?" one agent asked. Isbel gave him the name of a school in
Laredo, and he waved her through.

Isbel enrolled in the very school that she had named, where she
took classes in Spanish for one year, and then continued her education in English. Her grandmother successfully petitioned to obtain legal
custody of Isbel, but Isbel did not have a green card or a Social Security number. Growing up without those markers of legal status compounded the sense of not belonging that haunted Isbel thanks to her
fractured childhood. The hole inside of her was impossible to fill. At
sixteen, she ran away and spent the night with a boyfriend, creating a
family scandal. Isbel moved in with her boyfriend, and soon became
pregnant. She married the baby's father, an American citizen. Isbel had
an intense personality, and because she felt insecure about the perma-
nence of her husband's loyalties, she went to extraordinary lengths to
keep him close. Once, when he wanted to go out with his friends, she
put his sneakers into the toilet bowl to keep him from leaving. He broke
her nose that time, and later he broke her jaw. Because Isbel required
medical treatment for her injuries, she soon had a thick file of hospital
records and police reports documenting the abuse. Her features did not
line up, I finally understood, because her first husband had beaten her.

Isbel's grandmother was a practical woman, and told Isbel to put
up with the beatings until she obtained a green card. "You might as
well get something out of this," her grandmother counseled. Months
passed before Isbel secured an interview with an agent at the Immigration and Naturalization Service office in San Antonio. The official letter she received said she must appear with her spouse, but
Isbel's husband refused to go. She made the trip anyway. In San

Antonio, the INS officer regarded the intense young woman sitting before him.

"Where is your husband?" he asked.

"He's not here."

"I'm sorry," he told her. "Didn't you read the letter? It says here that you have to bring your spouse with you. I can't help you unless your husband is here."

"Listen to me," Isbel Morales replied. "I'm not leaving until you give me something that allows me to work. I have a kid to raise. Are you going to raise my kid for me? Are you going to pay for his food? I'm not going to ask for food stamps. I want to work."

The INS officer asked why her husband could not support the child, and Isbel explained about the beatings. She wanted to end the marriage, but first she needed to be able to earn a living.

"Wait here," he told her. "I'm going to see if I can do something for you."

When the INS officer returned, he told Isbel that he could give her a temporary work permit. Immigration law made exceptions for individuals who suffered physical abuse at the hands of their American spouses. If she could document the abuse, she could become a full citizen. Before Isbel departed, the immigration official said one more thing: "Do people ever call you *comal*?" he asked, referring to the griddle on which Mexican women warm tortillas.

"What do you mean?"

"Because you heat up pretty quick!"

Isbel Morales stayed in touch with the INS officer, calling him up once or twice every year. He became a fixture in her life, since she viewed him as the pivot around which her fate had turned. When Isbel came of age, she obtained an alien resident card through a special petition prepared with the help of the Webb County district attorney's office, thanks to her extensive file of hospital records and police reports. Afterward, she decided she wanted to work in the criminal justice field.

Now Isbel was trying to fulfill that dream. In the evenings and on weekends, she was attending classes at the Community College of Aurora, working toward a degree that would allow her to pursue a career in law enforcement. At the moment, she was taking psychology, technical writing, and law enforcement operations classes. She wanted to become a police officer, and was trying to get in shape for the physical exam at the Denver Police Academy. "My main reason is the diverse country that we have," she explained. "A lot of people don't want to report things. There's no trust between the community and the police. That's why I want to be a police officer: I hear an accent and I say, 'Where are you from? I'm from Mexico, too. I was illegal, too. Look at me—it can be done.'"

Isbel learned that her identity had been stolen after receiving notices from the Internal Revenue Service. "The IRS sent me a letter saying that I owed money. You know how people procrastinate—I said, 'Oh, I have to pay this bill.' I never did. Then they sent me a second notice. I said, 'Okay, I'll look into this.' At the end of the letter it said something about Goodwill. So I called Goodwill, and I said, 'Hey, I got this letter, but I never worked for you guys.'" Isbel met with the local director of human resources, bringing the letters from the IRS, as well as her Colorado driver's license. It bore the same number as the license that had been presented by Goodwill's employee, but a different picture. Isbel asked if she could confront Alma, but the woman in charge of human relations suggested that it would be better if she contacted the police instead, according to Isbel. A spokeswoman for Goodwill declined to comment about the matter.

With the assistance of Goodwill, Isbel provided the Internal Revenue Service with proof that somebody had been impersonating her, and the agency said they would absolve her of responsibility for paying taxes on the income that Alma had earned, although it would take many months for the federal government to follow through on this promise. Isbel was an idealist who thought in black and white terms, not shades of gray. Her identity had always been under siege—was she Mexican or American, loved or unloved? Nobody was going to steal her hard-won American self and get away with it. From Isbel's point of view, the thief who'd stolen her identity had done wrong—period, end of story. "Most of all, my grandmother taught me I had to be law-abiding," she said. Isbel obtained an image of Alma's fake driver's license and pinned it to her bulletin board at work, next to a copy of her own. She wrote BEFORE over her own picture and AFTER over Alma's—a sick joke about being the victim of identity theft. "I was trying to make light of it because it got me down," she explained. "With work and the kids and school, I really didn't have a lot of time to be investigating something like this. Even trying to call the IRS is ridiculous—you have to be on hold for the longest time."

No bureaucracy moved fast enough for Isbel Morales, and no police investigation was sufficiently thorough. She incessantly called the detective who was working on the case. When the detective suggested that the Denver police department did not have jurisdiction because the Goodwill store was located in another political subdivision in the metro area, Isbel proved that the department did have jurisdiction because she lived in Denver, as did Alma. Then the detective suggested the department might not have enough manpower to pursue the matter right away, which only made Isbel push harder. Ultimately, she could not resist making a phone call to Alma at the Goodwill store. "I was told not to, but it's like finding out that your husband is cheating on you, and you see the other woman's phone number. I just wanted to hear her voice. I just wanted to tell her, 'What the heck is wrong with you?' I was curious. Because, you know, you're thinking: What does she look like, how does she act, how does she pronounce my name? Does she say my name with the Spanish pronunciation? Because I don't use that. I felt like she stole part of me." Actually, Isbel did not say much during the phone call. She asked if she was speaking to "Isbel Morales," and then, when Alma replied, "*Sí,*" she hung up. She could not continue because her emotions were too tangled. "I was enraged, but I also felt sad for her. I'm assuming she has kids. I was mad—yet I can't be. Even though I can't relate to her, I do have friends who are using somebody else's papers. I'm kind of in the middle. I cannot judge her. I can't decide if I hate her or love her or embrace her."

Isbel's second husband had also entered the country without the legal right to do so. She had not known that Mario was undocumented when they married; only after they were wed did he confess that his green card had been purchased on the black market. "I don't know where he got the Social Security number that he's using," Isbel said. "He says he made it up, but I'm not sure. I think it might belong to somebody who is real old, because the other day he got a membership form from the AARP in the mail." The couple lived in a home that they had purchased in Green Valley Ranch, a farflung neighborhood of Denver where houses were more affordable. It took both of their incomes to make the mortgage payments. Mario loaded and unloaded frozen meat for Shamrock Foods, a large food service conglomerate that supplied prepackaged goods to food stores and restaurants. The Arizona-based company operated a mega-warehouse in Commerce City, Colorado, an industrial area to the north of Denver. Mario had bought his green card from a coworker. Isbel's best friend, who was also undocumented, had purchased a fraudulent green card from the same colleague. Later, after this friend accidentally got pregnant, even though she was unmarried, Isbel invited her to move into the home that she and Mario shared in Green Valley Ranch. And therefore, at the very moment when she began receiving the notices from the IRS, Isbel Morales was living under the same roof as two other illegal immigrants, both of whom may have committed exactly the same crime as Alma. "I am surrounded by it," Isbel conceded. "I cannot run away from it. That's why I keep saying, 'I can't judge her.'"

Isbel's husband found it strange that his wife wanted to pursue a woman who, in his mind, was not a bad person. "He was upset," Isbel recounted. "He was all for her. It was funny to watch his reaction." Meanwhile, motivated by the experience of having someone steal her identity, Isbel decided to become a full citizen. She had possessed a green card for years, but had never taken the next step. "I was procrastinating, you know—work, school, kids, home. I had printed out the application, and had tried to fill it out, but then it got smudged and I had to start all over again. Finally this happened and I said, 'Now I am going to do it.'" She still did not know whether her credit rating had been affected—she had called the three largest credit-rating companies, but the single credit report that she'd received so far had been inconclusive. She did have a bad credit rating, but confessed that she had not always paid her bills on time, so it was difficult to say if the messy report was her own fault or someone else's. Isbel hoped the additional information she was expecting to receive in the mail might clear things up.

I did not tell Yadira anything about my conversations with Isbel Morales for several years. The subject seemed too sensitive for a very long time. When I finally revealed that I had gotten to know her mother's nemesis, and said that this woman had crossed the border illegally as a child, the news floored Yadira. She had imagined a very different foe—someone entirely unlike her. "This is so ironic," she said. "It's like a movie." I felt the same way. None of us had expected Isbel to be who she was. And the true scope of the immigration issue became clear to me only after Isbel told me about her husband and her best friend. Illegality was rampant.

10

MANHUNT

Meanwhile, during the summer between the girls' freshman and sophomore years of college, police continued to chase their elusive suspect in the murder of police officer Donnie Young. Once Gómez García had reached Tijuana in the middle of May, he had boarded an airplane bound for Durango, Durango, the capital city of his home state. He was about to turn twenty years old, a birthday he would celebrate on the run in the country of his birth. Coincidentally, Gómez García had entered Mexico just as Yadira's mother, Alma, and her stepfather, Jesús, were fighting over whether Alma should flee there, too, and as fate would have it, Alma and her two youngest children crossed the border two weeks after Gómez García caught his airplane, on a bus that was also bound for Durango. By the time Yadira's mother arrived in that city, however, Gómez García had moved on again: He headed for the tiny town of Francisco Javier Leyva, estimated population 865, where he was born. Francisco Javier Leyva sits at the foot of the Sierra Madre Occidental mountain range, and it is so remote that the bus dropped off its passengers by the side of the highway, leaving them to walk another mile and a half to their destination. Raúl Gómez García's older brother, Reyes, still lived in the tiny town. Perhaps Raúl had imagined that in this farflung village he could escape from the reality of his crime, but most of Francisco Javier's residents had family in the United States now, and by the time he arrived, everybody in his hometown knew that he had been accused of murdering a police officer.

Once Gómez García crossed the border, detectives Teresa García and Martin Vigil could no longer pursue him. They had to entrust the investigation to Mexican federal authorities, who had received word from high that this case needed to be resolved. An envoy of Denver police brass had flown to Mexico City, and was lobbying hard for a successful outcome to the case. Within days of Gómez García's arrival in Francisco Javier Leyva, two Mexican federal agents visited the town in search of their culprit; traveling with them was U.S. Marshal José Chavarría. Reyes Gómez García told the Mexican agents that his younger brother had paid him a visit, but had stayed for only two or three days. He said he did not know where his brother had gone. Chavarría and the Mexican agents backtracked to the city of Durango, where they believed that Gómez García might be hiding, but he appeared to have had no contact with any of his relatives there. It is not clear what happened next, but most likely Gómez García caught a bus to Zacatecas. One way or another, he surfaced in the state of Sinaloa, where he had a grandmother who lived in the small town of Oso Viejo. The village's roads were not paved and many homes had no running water, yet many people drove spectacular cars, such as Hummers and BMWs. The area was controlled by *narcotraficantes*. When I spoke with U.S. Marshal Chavarría, I mentioned that I had heard that he and the Mexican agents had run into a roadblock manned by the *narcotraficantes,* who were known to assassinate federal officers, yet had somehow talked their way out of the tense situation. Chavarría exhibited such discomfort that I came to suspect the two Mexican agents might have pledged to look the other way if they came across any evidence of drug trafficking in exchange for free passage to hunt down their quarry, but Chavarría denied this.

After they located Gómez García's grandmother, Chavarría and the two Mexican agents discovered to their frustration that again they lagged several steps behind their suspect. His grandmother told the federal agents that Gómez García had showed up without notice, saying he was on a vacation. She had found him sinister, with his shaved head and his tattoos. They had never met before, and she even wondered if he was truly a relative. Still, she had given him a place to sleep, and he had stayed for about a week, until he tired of the living conditions. He moved on to stay with her daughter in Culiacán, the capital of Sinaloa. The city has more than half a million residents and is located on the Pacific coast of Mexico, approximately a thousand miles south of Los Angeles. Gómez García was staying in an apartment with his aunt and her husband. When these relatives heard that two federal agents were hunting for their houseguest, they offered to turn him in. It might have been dangerous to do otherwise, because supposedly the *narcotrafi-*

cantes had put out word saying that the *americano* (for they thought of Gómez García as American, even if he didn't possess legal status in the United States) was not welcome in Sinaloa. Coached by the Mexican agents, who offered her the sum of about thirty dollars for her trouble, Gómez García's grandmother paid a visit to her daughter in Culiacán and lured her grandson out of the apartment by asking him to run an errand at a bodega. The two agents were waiting inside the corner store to arrest him.

On June 4, 2005, four weeks after Donnie Young's death, John and I were sitting in a restaurant in downtown Denver when John's cell phone rang. It was the chief of police, Gerry Whitman.

"They got him," John announced. "The Mexican government has just arrested Gómez García."

He left without eating to go to a hastily arranged press conference. It would take months for the district attorney's office to complete the extradition process, but Gómez García was coming home to face a jury in the city where he had chosen to take another man's life. During the same period, due in part to the publicity surrounding the murder of Donnie Young, Mexico would change its extradition laws to allow the return of suspects who faced life sentences elsewhere, which it had previously forbidden. I had imagined that once Gómez García was arrested, many of the political issues raised by his crime would subside, but the opposite happened. The political climate got stormier.

One week after Gómez García's arrest, Congressman Tom Tancredo traveled to New Hampshire and told a crowd of about thirty people assembled in an assisted-living facility in Nashua that he was considering running for president of the United States if no other candidate adopted a tough stance on illegal immigration. Then he sharpened his language. Some illegal aliens were coming to the States to find work, Tancredo told the elderly audience, but others were coming for blood. "They are coming to kill you, and you, and me, and my children, and my grandchildren," he said. When I read an account of Tancredo's remarks in the *Denver Post,* I found them to be so extraordinary that I had to reread the story several times. His image of a horde of murderers invading the country struck me as an outrageous instance of demagoguery.

At the end of June, Congressman Tancredo took exception to the

fact that the Denver Public Library was converting small branch operations located in heavily Latino neighborhoods into language and learning centers. The plan called for the branch operations to have more
Spanish-language books, hire bilingual librarians, and teach English.
"Denver Public Library's apparent shift toward a Spanish-language-
only library, Spanish-language book quotas, and coercion of librarians
to learn Spanish is of great concern," wrote Tancredo in a letter to the
mayor, which he released to the press.

"Because more than 20 percent of all Denver residents speak Spanish at home, the library is interested in providing additional Spanish-
language materials and services, but it is not considering any 'conversion'
plan along the lines suggested in your question," replied John in a mis-
sive that he also published. "English is and will remain the primary
language of the Denver Public Library."

That July, in the middle of the library controversy, John delivered
his second annual State of the City address in Denver's Civic Center
Park, a vast swath of formal lawns that stretches from City Hall to
the State Capitol. He had planned to bring up the thorny subject of
immigration, but his top aides urged him not to tackle it. Instead,
John's speech called for ending homelessness, finding scholarships for
the city's poorest students, passing an initiative to pay teachers more
if they raised student achievement, establishing the city as an arts
destination, strengthening the local economy, and putting more cops
on the streets. He had just finished speaking when a wiry guy with a
shock of white hair jogged toward the stage. It was Mike McGarry of
CAIR. "End the sanctuary!" McGarry hollered. "Stop the sanctuary
city!"

The elected officials froze in their chairs. John's security detail
conferred, but did nothing. "This is the United States of Mexico!"
yelled another protester. "The Mexican flag is the new flag of the
city of Denver!" A reporter for the *Rocky Mountain News,* April
Washington, rose with a weary sigh and walked over to McGarry,
who stepped aside to give her an interview. After the speech, I learned
that CAIR had sent an e-mail to its members that called for them to
show up in large numbers and disrupt John. "Question him on the
de facto sanctuary city policy that allowed Denver Policeman Don
Young to be assassinated by an illegal alien who should have been
deported the first time he was stopped for a traffic violation—an

illegal who worked at Mayor Hickenlooper's restaurant," said the e-mail. "'What about Donny Young?' 'No more sanctuary for illegal aliens!'" At first I thought the failure of most of McGarry's cohorts to appear meant that their movement lacked momentum, but I couldn't have been more wrong. They might not attend a protest against my husband, but many of McGarry's friends were as angry as he was, and they were busy writing furious letters to elected officials all over the state.

11

SOCIAL INEQUALITY

At the end of the summer, Marisela, Clara, and Yadira moved into a new brick dormitory in the center of campus to begin their sophomore year. Their old dorm had worn furniture and tired carpets, but everything in Nelson Hall looked fashionable. They lived on the fourth floor, which they accessed by a gleaming stainless steel elevator, and the doors opened onto a hallway covered in a modern-looking tan carpet with a geometric black pattern. Clara and Yadira shared a capacious double in a quiet cul-de-sac. The room even had its own bathroom. Its cinder-block walls were painted off-white, and the bed frames were unusually high, permitting the girls to stow their dressers underneath, which made the room seem bigger. They had a small fridge and a microwave in one corner, and on the bulletin boards they hung the familiar photographs of their former lives at Roosevelt High. On a whiteboard, Yadira and Clara wrote a list of things they wanted to acquire before sophomore year began.

It said:

Doorstop
Trash can
Toothbrush cup
Tapete
Towels
Food
Jabón de trastes
LATIN AMERICAN MAP

They needed to acquire these items to feel at home; the list was written primarily in English with a sprinkling of Spanish, the capital letters indicating the emotional significance of the map. It read like an accidental revelation of who they were becoming: experienced college sophomores, far more secure than the scared freshmen they had been one year before, who knew what they needed to make themselves comfortable. They still used Spanish words for certain household items because they had grown up hearing their mothers use those words, which made them hard to relinquish (*jabón de trastes* means "dish soap," and *tapete* means "little rug"). Yadira had suggested the all-important map when Clara had asked what they should hang on the walls. At college, both girls had been embarrassed to discover that they knew almost nothing about the geography of Latin America. They could locate Georgia and Ohio on a globe, but they could not point out Guanajuato or Oaxaca, and what happened below Mexico remained entirely shrouded in mystery.

I had not seen Clara for ages. She had spent most of the summer in Zacatecas. "The bus rides are so horrible," she said with a grimace. "When you're here, you want to go there, but you don't want to do the trip, and when you're there, you don't want to come back, because of the trip." She said she had recently started filling out paperwork to become a citizen of the United States. Earlier that morning, I had met Yadira at Starbucks, where she had picked the sugar topping off a muffin and left the rest untouched. Now she was sprawled on her bed, hugging a shaggy pink pillow to her chest. "These are so soft," she observed. "They were really cheap. We got them from Costco."

Yadira reported that her siblings Laura and Raúl had just returned from Mexico. Their mother had stayed behind, unable to cross the border easily due to her lack of legal status and the outstanding felony charge. Alma had given her two youngest children the choice of remaining in Durango and starting school there or returning to the United States, and both of the children had opted to return. Jesús had arranged for them to make the journey with a man he knew who lived in Aurora, Colorado. This man was not a *coyote*—he did not help immigrants cross the border without legal permission—but for a fee he would escort American children through the border checkpoints that their Mexican parents could not navigate. He also transported ordinary household goods, such as refrigerators or televisions or VCRs. When the man carried inanimate objects, he made the journey by himself, but when he transported children, his wife accompanied him to reassure parents that nothing untoward would happen.

Jesús had paid the man several hundred dollars when he had collected Laura and Raúl. Then Laura and Raúl moved back in with him, as did Zulema. Alma insisted upon this arrangement, as she wanted the family to be reunited. Marisela's mother privately expressed disapproval of Alma's decision; Josefa said a woman should never leave her children with a man who was not their biological father. Everyone in Yadira's family thought the arrangement was only temporary, however, because Alma had told them she would soon follow the children north. She now regretted her decision to flee to Mexico, as she had been unable to find work and it was hard to keep the hopelessness at bay when she was living with her mother and there was nothing to do except watch *telenovelas*. The baby she was carrying was due in November, and Alma wanted to return before the child was born. She was trying to cobble together the money for a *coyote*, but in the unsentimental calculations of the border she was an unattractive client. Pregnant women moved slowly, required extra water, and could develop medical complications. At seven months, Alma's condition was highly visible, and none of the *coyotes* she had contacted so far wanted to take her.

Yadira cherished the hope that Alma would return. Irene and Justino Chávez worried that Alma's plans were foolhardy, however; if she were to be apprehended while crossing the border, she would spend years in jail. In addition to whatever sentence she might earn as a result of the original charges, there was the additional penalty she would pay for having become a fugitive. Apart from this, Justino fretted about the idea of Alma walking across the desert during her third trimester. Still, he recognized that if she gave birth in Mexico, the child might be doomed to relive Yadira's fate. And he conceded it would not be easy to cross with a newborn or toddler. Alma's body functioned like a stopwatch, counting down the time she had left to make the journey; with every day that passed, the risks increased and her chances of success diminished, making the prospect of doing *el brinco* (literally, "the jump") increasingly treacherous.

Meanwhile, all along the border, the issue of illegal immigration had become increasingly charged. At the end of July, elected officials in Texas had introduced legislation to deputize citizens to bolster the Minutemen; in August, the governors of New Mexico and Arizona had declared states of emergency due to the degree of border traffic. During the same time frame, Congressman Tom Tancredo and other like-minded conservatives had begun lobbying for the federal government to build a fence between the United States and Mexico—a wall between Alma and Yadira. And so aside from the physical perils Alma faced, there was also the matter of how the Vargas family saga intersected with the national political drama. At the very moment when the subject of the border was becoming intensely politicized, half of the Vargas family was stuck on one side of it, and half was stuck on the other.

Yadira began classes in a fog. Once again, she divided her time between friends who knew the secrets of her life and friends who did not know. At the beginning of the school year, Yadira and Clara stayed up all night with Luke, waiting in line to buy season ice hockey passes. Students could purchase a limited number of passes for $60 apiece, and rabid fans spent the night outside in a boisterous line. Students pitched tents and unfurled sleeping bags to hold their spots, all of which the girls documented on their cell phones.

Luke lived in a suite close to Yadira and Clara, also on the fourth floor of Nelson Hall. At the other side of the building, Marisela occupied another suite with three of her new friends. Suites consisted of two double rooms connected by an adjoining bathroom; Marisela shared one of the doubles with Zahra, the student who was originally from Somalia, while Clara's former roommate Alison shared the other double with Beatriz, a Bolivian American who had grown up in Wyoming. Zahra put her bed on top of Marisela's to form a bunk, which gave their bedroom an open feeling, and they put up raucous posters on the walls. One showed a person drinking from a keg with a headline that read: "Do not disturb, blood alcohol experiment in process." This suite immediately became the locus of all social activity involving students of color in Nelson Hall. Jaime, who had transferred from Regis, lived across the hall with Matías. They frequently joined Marisela and Zahra to do homework or to revel. So did others. Elissa still came over from Regis, but now that she was a sophomore she began to forge stronger connections on her own campus, and as the school year continued her visits became infrequent. Yadira and Clara visited Marisela's room, too, although they often preferred to cloister themselves away in their quiet double instead.

The University of Denver insisted students meet a broad spectrum of requirements, including math and science courses as well as survey classes in the humanities. Generally, the girls were cautious about inviting me into their classrooms, as they didn't want my presence to alert an unfriendly professor to their status, and consequently I saw them only in settings where they were most at ease. That fall, Marisela, Yadira, and Clara assumed they would be most comfortable in Social Inequality, a required course for sociology majors, and invited me to attend the class with them. Both Marisela and Yadira were planning to declare a major in sociology, and Clara thought she might declare a minor in it. A new assistant professor, Lisa Martínez, was teaching the course. Half a dozen students of color had signed up for the class, among them Marisela's roommate Zahra. The class also included more than a dozen Anglo students, some of whom held politically conservative beliefs, which led to interesting clashes.

On the first day of class, Lisa Martínez handed out the syllabus. "Modern societies are characterized by social stratification whereby the resources of wealth, power, property, and prestige are unequally distributed among members," it declared. "The main premise of this course is that social class, power, and public policies shape every aspect of our lives, including our chances for upward mobility." Two weeks later, Martínez told the students to divide up into groups to discuss Karl Marx. She asked on what basis Marx thought resources were unequally distributed. Marisela and Clara found themselves working with a conservative white student from Texas named Sue Ellen. That day, Marisela had painted her eyes with metallic silver shadow and applied bold quantities of kohl, while her hair shone with new brassy highlights; she was wearing a black tube top with flashy red corduroy trousers. Clara appeared more wholesome in a white T-shirt, pink sweater, and blue jeans, while Sue Ellen wore a red University of Denver ice hockey sweatshirt that said PIONEERS. In previous classes, Sue Ellen had already made clear that she disagreed with Lisa Martínez's central premise—she thought people could overcome any disadvantage if they pulled hard enough on their bootstraps. Sue Ellen was a bright student who often had the right answers to questions, which appeared to irritate Marisela. She viewed everything through the prism of race these days, and was irked by those who did not.

"Marx is primarily about class," Sue Ellen announced confidently. "Resources are unequally distributed based on class."

"Race, too," objected Marisela.

"Really?" responded Sue Ellen in a skeptical tone. "Where did he say that?"

"In the part where he talks about slaves and masters," Marisela replied.

"Well, I think we are just supposed to pick the main idea, and I think that's class. Resources are unequally distributed by class."

"Actually, he talked about all three—race, class, and gender," interjected Clara, playing the role of peacemaker. "But just in one small place."

Sue Ellen went to retrieve her textbook, to justify her line of argument. As soon as she walked away, Marisela rolled her eyes dramatically. Clara whispered to me, "You'll have to learn to speak Spanish better, so we can tell you what we are thinking."

"I think I get the basic idea," I replied.

The mood in the group shifted only after Sue Ellen began talking about Marx's views on gender. "Basically, the wife is like another worker," Sue Ellen said. "The man, let's say he's called Bob, goes to the factory he owns. All the workers there do his bidding, then he comes home, and his wife is like another one of his workers."

"Yeah!" cried Marisela, in unity with her classmate at last.

Lisa Martínez called the class back together and asked for a list of Marx's key points. As the students called out suggestions, the professor wrote on the board:

Capitalism
Class conflict
Surplus value

"What would Marx say is the basis of inequality?" asked Martínez.

"Class," answered a blond athlete.

"That's right," confirmed Martínez.

Marisela looked unbowed. Then Martínez brought up the work of a contemporary Marxist theorist, Edna Bonacich. The professor asked the class to name Bonacich's major contribution to Marxist philosophy.

"Split labor market!" called out Marisela.

"Split labor market, good," said Martínez.

In *A Theory of Ethnic Antagonism,* Bonacich examines how societies can become stratified along racial lines when people of specific ethnicities typically perform certain jobs. "The central hypothesis is that ethnic antagonism first germinates in a labor market split along ethnic lines," writes Bonacich. "To be split, a labor market must contain at least two groups of workers whose price of labor differs for the same work, or would differ if they did the same work." Labor markets may split, according to Bonacich, when immigrants come from countries with a lower standard of living or when certain ethnic groups lack political resources or the ability to organize. Hostility appears to be racially motivated, but actually stems from the underlying class conflict, according to Bonacich. "If the labor market is split ethnically, the class antagonism takes the form of ethnic antagonism."

A blond student from Palo Alto, California, raised her hand. "It is so common now, it is hard to think about it as a theory," she offered. "It is so common that labor lines are drawn in certain ways. Like, different groups do certain kinds of work, and I'm just like, this is the way it is."

Marisela and Clara exchanged glances. It was often this way in Social Inequality. Marisela spoke up sometimes, and so did Deja, the president of the Black Student Alliance, but otherwise the students of color remained silent, allowing white students to dominate the conversation. When I asked why this was so, the girls from Roosevelt said they had grown weary of trying to educate other students about what it was like to be poor. "I used to bust out and speak a lot in my other classes," Marisela said. "It was so depressing. I got tired of doing that—having to share my own experiences so *they* could learn." She might spar with Sue Ellen occasionally, or call out an answer to a question, but if a student from Palo Alto expressed a worldview antithetical to her own, as often as not Marisela would allow it to go unchallenged. It seemed as though she felt she retained a kind of power by keeping her opinions to herself—as though she scored a victory by cheating the wealthier students out of what she had to offer.

In October, Lisa Martínez announced that she wanted to talk about class structure in the United States. Martínez had asked each student to identify what class they belonged to, and now she wrote the results on the whiteboard.

Upper—5
Upper-middle—4
Middle—8
Working-class—4
Poor—3

"What is the income of a middle-class household?" inquired Mar-tínez.

"I grew up in a part of California where if you make more than $150,000, you are still middle-class," volunteered the student from Palo Alto.

"I grew up in a neighborhood where if you made less than six digits, you were unusual," said Sue Ellen. "I have a friend who's very sheltered, and she would say that the poverty line is around $350,000 a year."

"I come from a working-class-to-poor family," announced Deja. "People talk about their families sitting around and discussing the news—well, we didn't have time for that. If we got to sit down and eat breakfast, that was special. It was usually breakfast on the bus, you know?"

Marisela and Zahra nodded.

Martínez drew a diamond on the whiteboard and labeled it "American class structure—popular view." Then she divided the diamond into three parts: a tiny triangle at the top, labeled "upper-class"; a large hexagon, "middle-class"; and a tiny triangle at the bottom, "lower-class." This was how America liked to think of itself, the professor told the students—almost entirely middle-class. Then Martínez drew a shape that looked more like an onion dome (it had a pointy top and a pronounced bulge in the middle), which she divided into six parts. The small triangle at the top represented upper-class families, who had annual incomes of more than $1 million. Under that, a sizable wedge of upper-middle families earned $75,000 to $1,000,000 a year. Families who earned $35,000 to $75,000 a year in wages occupied the next wedge, lower-middle. Third from the bottom, in the onion dome's bulge, working-class families earned $25,000 to $40,000 a year. "This is actually the largest group," observed the professor. Second from the bottom came the working poor, who earned $12,000 to $25,000 per year, and at the very bottom was the underclass, or families who earned less than $12,000 a year, mostly from public assistance. All three girls from Roosevelt had grown up working poor, one step from the bottom.

"By the way, what is the minimum wage right now?" Martínez asked.

"Five-fifteen an hour," responded Marisela.

"Right," said Martínez.

Sue Ellen offered that in wealthy communities, service workers often earned more than the minimum wage. "I have been going to Aspen for a long time, and the cost of living is so high here, I don't know anybody who makes less than nine dollars an hour," she said.

"Do you know any gas station workers?" asked a white working-class student in a voice laced with sarcasm.

"Yeah, and they make nine dollars an hour," Sue Ellen replied belligerently.

"People who make less than that probably can't afford to live in Aspen, and probably live in satellite communities," Martínez interjected.

"Well, the ski instructors are from South America and Australia, because we want the best of the best in Aspen," Sue Ellen responded. "And there is a lot of employee housing."

"I wonder, though, if that includes cooks and everything," said Martínez.

"Oh, yeah, it includes cooks," Sue Ellen said assuredly. "There are lofts on Aspen Mountain for cooks."

"Interesting," replied Martínez skeptically.

She told the students to read a chapter in Barbara Ehrenreich's book *Nickel and Dimed: On (Not) Getting By in America*. In the selection, Ehrenreich tells of her experiences working as a clerk at Walmart. She lives in a dingy motel, searches unsuccessfully for an apartment she can afford, survives on fast food, and develops a stress-related antipathy for the store's clients—whom the store managers call guests—because they perpetually mess up the displays that she organizes. "I even start hating the customers for extraneous reasons, such as, in the case of the native Caucasians, their size," writes Ehrenreich. "I don't mean just bellies and butts, but huge bulges in completely exotic locations, like the backs of the neck and the knees. This summer, Wendy's, where I often buy lunch, has introduced the verb *biggiesize*, as in 'Would you like to biggiesize that combo?' meaning double the fries and the pop, and something like biggiesizing seems to have happened to the female guest population." Martínez assigned the text because she knew most of her students would be unfamiliar with this side of American life. As bad as Ehrenreich's job may have been, however, she still had contact with guests, whereas Marisela's father spent his life cleaning places like Walmart after the doors had closed for the night. This was the challenge of social inequality: Most of the students had no personal experience of poverty, yet the handful who knew what it meant had experienced hardship beyond anything Ehrenreich had endured.

Lisa Martínez had grown up in the border town of El Paso, Texas, where her Chicano parents had raised her as an English speaker. El Paso was predominantly Latino, and when Martínez had moved to Austin to attend the mostly white University of Texas, she had experienced a radical sense of dislocation. Martínez wanted to remake the University of Denver into the kind of place that would not alienate minority students. At the moment, she was working with other Latino faculty to start a Latino center at DU. "We are trying to build a center that would do academic work, like a think tank, but would also interact with the community," Martínez told me. Several weeks into the fall quarter, the professor became concerned with her inability to induce the students of color to speak. She knew the girls from Roosevelt had compelling insights, because she had required every student to keep a journal. "Their journal entries were exuberant, lively, dynamic," Martínez said. "I thought, 'Oh my God, why won't you say this to the class?'" She decided to set up a meeting with all the students of color in her class to find out what was wrong. In the e-mail she sent to Marisela, Yadira, Clara, Zahra, Deja, and another Latino student from Denver named Gustavo, she asked if they would have coffee with her the following week. When the girls received this e-mail, they went into a tizzy: What did their professor want? Were they in trouble? Marisela fretted that Martínez might have stumbled onto the story of her immigration status. She wondered, "Do you think she *knows*?"

In fact, Lisa Martínez had heard a rumor about students on campus who lacked Social Security numbers, but that wasn't what she wanted to talk about. When they met, she told the black and Latino students that as far as she was concerned, they were on equal footing with the white students. Martínez did not harp on the idea that they had to educate others—she just thought they should not be silent. "You can tell some of your classmates don't know what the heck they're talking about, and they are still talking," Martínez pointed out. "Jump in there! It's *your* class, too."

The girls from Roosevelt wanted to please Martínez, and tried harder to participate, but in the end the subject was too personal. It cut to the heart of their differences with the rest of their classmates, and while all three girls felt closer to Martínez after her pep talk, none of them became outspoken in Social Inequality. Martínez had failed to transform the behavior of the students of color. She wanted to push for a closer relationship with Yadira—perhaps the most reticent of all—but decided it would be wiser to let Yadira come to her. None of the girls was ready to adopt her as a mentor yet, and all she could do was make clear she would welcome a chance to play that role in the future.

Several weeks later, Martínez began a discussion of poverty trends in the United States, using a PowerPoint presentation. The first slide asked three questions:

What is poverty?
How is poverty defined?
Who is more likely to be impoverished?

The next slide answered that 16.5 percent of the children in the United States were growing up in families whose incomes fell below the poverty line. "That's gone up a lot, actually," interjected Martínez. "It's probably 19 or 20 percent now." Martínez pointed out that the federal government defined the poverty level for a family of five as an income of less than $23,400.

"That's way too low," objected the student from Palo Alto. "A family of five? That is horribly unrealistic."

"What do you mean?" asked Martínez.

"I think the poverty level should be, like, a lot higher. I mean a family of five—even if you made around $30,000, you'd have a hard time getting by."

"Okay, let's define poverty," said Martínez.

She displayed another slide:

Absolute—what you can afford
Relative—compared to others
Official—government definition

Martínez explained that the federal government had been defining poverty for decades as roughly three times the amount of money required to provide a nutritionally beneficial diet, which was how the government had arrived at the figure of $23,400.

"Okay, the numbers make sense now—they are not considering housing costs, child care costs, etcetera," said a single mom.

"That's retarded," contributed a fellow classmate.

Martínez projected a new slide. It said: Who is most likely to be poor? She made new bullet points appear one by one.

Children under 18
Race, ethnic minorities

"I don't want you to take away the idea that I'm saying that all minorities are poor," Martínez paused to say. "It's just that they are disproportionately represented."

Then she clicked again:

Foreign-born

"Immigrants are often poor, right?"

"Well, I'm an immigrant, and we were never poor," said a student named Rebekah. "We were never dishwashers."

"Where is your family from?" asked Martínez.

"Hungary," replied Rebekah.

"European—that's different." Deja sneered. "It's not the same."

"Eastern Europe is different from the rest of Europe!" Rebekah shot back. "It's not like England or anything!"

Martínez interrupted to describe the work of Stanley Lieberson, a sociologist who had concluded that the ability of immigrants to assimilate varied greatly depending upon two key factors: numbers and visibility. Visibility was the extent to which immigrants stood out because of distinctive markers such as skin color or language. "The fact that there are not large numbers of people emigrating from Hungary means that there is not a great deal of hostility," said Martínez. "But the fact that large numbers of immigrants are now coming to the United States from Latin America and they are very visible means that there is a lot of hostility."

Martínez returned to the PowerPoint slide listing the characteristics of who was most likely to live in poverty.

Central cities

So far, the girls were four for four. When we first met, all of them had been under eighteen, foreign-born, members of an ethnic minority, and living in the inner city.

Martínez clicked her mouse again.

Single mothers—the feminization of poverty

Marisela and Clara had grown up in two-parent households, and met only four of the five characteristics that made a person likely to grow up in poverty, but Yadira had been five for five during those difficult years back in Los Angeles, when she had gone to all those different elementary schools. At the beginning of the quarter, I had imagined Yadira would find it empowering to chart her place in the socioeconomic waters with such academic precision—to find the proper sociological terms for what she had lived through—but she did not react this way to Social Inequality. Later Yadira said that listening to her classmates talk about poor people had made her uncomfortable because of the underlying assumption that most of the people in the room must be rich. "They talk about it like, 'Those people over there,'" Yadira said. "They talk about those people over there, when it's us."

12

THE CONCEPT OF CITIZENSHIP

Halfway through the fall quarter, Clara and Yadira spent hours papering the dorms and common areas with homemade signs announcing a *Noche Caliente* on Friday, October 21. By then, midterm exams would be over and students would be eager for a party. The girls had decided to organize a series of events that would make the campus a more engaging place for Latinos, and they wanted their first big event to have cross-cultural appeal. Student dance instructors were going to provide lessons in both salsa and hip-hop. By nine P.M., black, white, and Latino students were milling outside the ballroom, a cavernous space meagerly decorated with a few potted plants, strips of crepe paper, and randomly placed balloons. At the door, Yadira collected money; she wore a skimpy top with spaghetti straps that showed off her figure. Meanwhile, Clara had zipped up her black cardigan to her collarbone, exposing as little as possible of the black cocktail dress she wore underneath. Matías and Jaime strolled up together—after they began living together, they had become lovers—and an African American student named Tyrone arrived looking suave in a glow-in-the-dark necklace and a black baseball cap. The hip-hop instructor's sneakers squeaked on the floor as she did the lock, the pop, the jam—steps that involved a lot of heel-toe action. Most of the Latinas had worn high heels, which made it hard for them to jam but did not prevent them from doing the salsa. At first Clara would not dance, but eventually she relented and enjoyed four salsas in a row with a straitlaced *mexicano* from West High. Marisela arrived late and wound up dancing on top of a table with Jaime.

The university was a big place, however, and not everyone shared their worldview, as the girls were forcibly reminded the following afternoon, when another crowd congregated in a different part of the campus to attend a forum about illegal immigration. The list of people slated to speak included both Tom Tancredo and former governor Dick Lamm, and the primary organizers of the event were Fred Elbel and Mike McGarry, the codirectors of the Colorado Alliance for Immigration Reform. Elbel had also become involved with a new group, Defend Colorado Now, which was pushing for a statewide ballot initiative similar to Arizona's Proposition 200. Defend Colorado Now wanted to pass a constitutional amendment to deny nonemergency public services to immigrants without legal status in the state of Colorado. The measure was scheduled to come before voters in one year's time, during the same election cycle in which Colorado would pick a new governor, guaranteeing that one of the topics of debate was going to be the wedge issue of immigration.

A throng of protesters intercepted attendees on their way into Boettcher Hall, where the forum was being held. One carried a sign that read: "Tancredo—that's Italian, right?" Among the protesters, I recognized several members of the Mountain View Friends Meeting, the local Quaker Meeting to which I belong. In recent years, the subject of immigration had divided our congregation: Most of Mountain View had adopted a pro-immigrant stance, following the lead of the American Friends Service Committee, a Quaker political organization that was defending the rights of immigrants nationally, but a minority of Mountain View instead considered illegal immigrants a threat to low-skilled workers who had been born here. One person I knew from Mountain View Friends Meeting was a longtime friend of Mike McGarry's, and on several occasions, this woman had told me that I ought to get to know McGarry. While Quakers are supposed to try to see "that of God" in everyone, so far I had not been able to look past McGarry's interruption of my husband's State of the City address, though I did recognize this as a failing. At the same time, I disagreed with some of the local AFSC staffers, too. Once I had listened to a presentation in which an AFSC staffer mentioned there might be links between people who opposed illegal immigration and white supremacist organizations. I did not believe that racism was a primary motivation for most critics of current immigration patterns—the racism that existed seemed like a by-product of an underlying economic conflict—and such accusations struck me as counterproductive.

The crowd streaming into Boettcher Hall seemed invigorated by the baking-soda-and-vinegar experience of walking past pro-immigrant activists and then encountering a table full of CAIR literature. An older woman whose hair had been teased into a perfect 1950s bouffant remarked in a bright tone, "I don't know, I guess they are protesting us! They've got too much time on their hands!" Close to four hundred people, most of whom appeared to be Anglo retirees, filled the auditorium. Incongruously, the periodic table of elements hung over the stage, as though we had assembled for a chemistry lecture. Mike McGarry strode to the microphone wearing a tweed jacket and horn-rimmed glasses, his familiar thatch of white hair making him instantly recognizable. "Free speech is guaranteed by the United States Constitution," he told the crowd. "No one is barred from coming here, but essentially what we planned was for this to be a program of like-minded people. We have [police] lieutenants here who will enforce our right to free speech if the need comes up."

Then McGarry announced he was giving Gabriela Flora of the American Friends Service Committee six minutes to share her thoughts. I had not anticipated that McGarry would extend this courtesy to one of his detractors, and wondered for the first time if he might be a sensible human being.

"My organization's Christian roots are what bring me to the podium today, to talk about our concerns about how the discussion on immigration is framed here," Flora told the crowd. "We have a moral imperative to welcome the stranger. As Leviticus 19:33–34 says, 'And if a stranger dwells with you in your land, you shall not mistreat him. The stranger who dwells among you shall be to you as one born among you, and you shall love him as yourself; for you were strangers in the land of Egypt.'"

Flora asserted that immigrants contributed more to government budgets in taxes than they took out in services. Then she segued into a lengthy critique of how much CEOs were paid, in the hopes of realigning this working-class audience with the immigrants they viewed as their enemies. I was studying the crowd when I suddenly spotted Marisela, sitting with Zahra on the far side of the room, about one-third of the way back from the stage. Clara and Yadira had found seats behind Marisela and Zahra.

"We are all in the same boat, but we are blaming the immigrants," Flora told the crowd.

"*Illegal* immigrants!" yelled a heckler.

"Get it right!" hollered someone else.

"Six minutes is UP!"

Flora concluded with a passage from Matthew: "'What you do to the least of my brethren, you do unto me.'"

Protesters who had found seats in the back of the auditorium gave her a standing ovation, while CAIR supporters craned around to see who was clapping. Polarization bisected the room, and unfortunately the Roosevelt High girls had chosen seats in the wrong half of the auditorium. The four girls looked alarmed at their predicament, as they were huddled together whispering. Next, a man named Frosty Wooldridge took the podium. A former U.S. Army medical service officer, he now wrote pungent books about riding his bicycle (one was called *Salty Tights*). Wooldridge displayed a chart depicting the growth of the United States population in two colors: A green hump delineated the shape of U.S. population growth thanks to the procreation of those people who were living here in the year 1970, and then above that zoomed a red triangle that reached higher as time went on—the rate of growth due to immigration. Wooldridge pointed to a moment in the future when the total population of the United States would grow to half a billion people, and said that by then our living conditions would resemble those in Bangladesh. "Do we want that here?" he demanded intensely. "Can we afford to give our children that kind of crisis?"

Wooldridge hoisted up a new chart, a series of handwritten figures scrawled on poster board. It said:

$564.1 million ed. costs
$400 billion lost IRS tax
$2,700 per illegal in CO annually
$300 billion lost wages = US citizen
$7.4 trillion fed. debt
$10.2 billion cost CA = Illegals

Where did he get his numbers? And what did the federal debt have to do with illegal immigration? Wooldridge never explained. He called for Governor Owens to declare a state of emergency in Colorado, and the front of the room erupted in a huge cheer. When the back of the room started booing, a red-faced woman in front shook her fist at the infiltrators. Elbel ambled over to the mike.

"Folks, let's keep this civil," he said amiably. "Well, I guess it's been pretty civil so far."

"Except for all the hate being spewed!" yelled a protester.

"Hate?" repeated the man sitting next to me, in a puzzled tone. He turned around to stare at the protesters.

Evelyn Elstrom, a retired schoolteacher, took the microphone to argue that being raised without legal status led to character flaws. "How can a youngster cope when the only path to survival is to be devious?" she asked. "When the family has to be devious to enter the United States? How does a youngster handle a problem in school in a straightforward manner when he or she knows his family is here illegally—that his dad has a fake Social Security card?" I looked over at the girls. Yadira was leaning forward, with her chin cupped in her hand, but it was hard to see Marisela because she had slouched down so far in her seat. Later, Jim Spence, a former special agent with the Immigration and Naturalization Service, suggested stationing law enforcement officials at every type of public transportation in the country, so as to deny anybody who could not prove their legal right to be here any possibility of traveling, then taking away all job opportunities, medical services, and schooling.

"Fascist!" yelled a heckler.

"Cruel!" shouted another.

A young man dressed entirely in black walked over to a police officer and murmured something inaudible.

"So you want me to start throwing them out?" the cop replied.

"We have asked the safety police to tell anybody who is booing or making odd comments not to do that, or they will be asked to leave," Elbel announced. "And the more noise there is, the less time we have for the speakers, so please hold your applause.

"Now I'd like to introduce Congressman Tom Tancredo."

Tancredo strolled onto the stage wearing a mock turtleneck and a sports coat. The front half of the room jumped to their feet, whistling and hooting. "Don't listen to a thing he said about applause!" encouraged the congressman. "This is a tough issue. It is a controversial issue. It touches a lot of emotions, as evidenced by the folks here on both sides, frankly, but that is as it should be. It is something that we're going to have to deal with as a nation. We're going to have to talk about it, regardless of how controversial it may be." The police officers paced back and forth below the protesters, staring at them from behind mirrored sunglasses. None of the protesters said a word. Tancredo described arriving in Congress to discover that nobody wanted to touch the issue of immigration. He resorted to going onto the House floor late at night to court the C-Span camera crew. "It would be eleven o'clock, twelve o'clock at night and I'd be thinking, 'Is anybody out there?'" he said. "And I would get back to my office and all these faxes are coming in. I'm thinking, 'Somebody did watch! Somebody is out there, somebody who cares!'" The faxes sustained him during his lean years, until he started drawing crowds. "Now I'm traveling all over the country, and everywhere I go—it doesn't matter which state anymore. I mean, Iowa—Iowa, if you can imagine! It was like six o'clock in the afternoon and it was raining and there were five hundred people in parkas!"

Tancredo spoke in support of pending legislation that would make felons of every illegal alien in the country. He also advocated amending the U.S. Constitution to prevent American citizenship from being given to children who were born to parents without legal status, saying: "No more anchor baby!" The front half of the room roared, while the back maintained a stony silence. "We're actually starting to talk about the concept of citizenship, what it really means," he said in conclusion. "It's very difficult, it takes a lot of time, but it is enormously important. It really rivals in my mind the whole discussion of immigration. It is the discussion of who we are as a nation. What does citizenship really mean? Do we have all the rights that have been granted in the Constitution simply because we happen to reside here?"

"No!" shouted a supporter.

"No, absolutely not," agreed the congressman. "We are citizens of a unique place on this planet that all of us should be proud of, and anybody that comes here from anyplace else should be willing to say, 'I am willing to cut from the old, and I am willing to accept this idea of America.' Is that really too much to ask? Is it chauvinistic, xenophobic? Somebody who comes to this country and says, 'I want to be here, but I have absolutely no desire to attach myself to this idea called America—I come here for something else entirely, and as a matter of fact, I want to stay separate. I want to stay linguistically separate, and even politically separate.' Well, I suggest to you that you are in the wrong place."

The room erupted into sound. A series of other politicians followed Tancredo onto the stage, including a candidate for governor and two state representatives who had recently posed for press photos with gun-toting Minutemen at the border. But the emotional high point of the forum came when Mike McGarry introduced Carol Vizzi, the mother of a hit-and-run victim. Vizzi got out her reading glasses and a prepared statement. "Of course, my life turned on a dime on July 1, 2004 when my own innocent child, Justin Goodman, was tragically killed," she read. "Justin was only thirty-two years old when he was run down and killed by an illegal alien. He was knocked from his motorcycle in Thornton, Colorado. That motorcycle turned end over end, and when my child lay bleeding on a curb, dying, that illegal sped away." Six months later, the Thornton police arrested Roberto Martínez Ruíz—a thirty-three-year-old immigrant who had entered the country without permission, had used at least six different aliases, and had previously been arrested for driving under the influence, failure to appear in court, probation violation, careless driving, careless driving resulting in death, driving with a revoked license, and another hit and run. He was eventually convicted of leaving the scene of an accident and tampering with evidence, among other things, in connection with Goodman's dying. It was the scope of Martínez Ruíz's record that most incensed Carol Vizzi. "Despite his long rap sheet, his long histories of run-ins with the law, no official ever contacted the INS to have him deported, nor did he suffer any consequences as a result of his crimes," she said. Vizzi wanted to know how Mayor John Hickenlooper, Governor Bill Owens, and President George Bush would feel if it were their child who had been killed. She also wanted to know who was going to take care of her son's eleven-year-old daughter. "Who will feed her? Who will grant *her* a higher education? Who will take care of *her* health concerns?"

"Right on!" cried out an audience member. "That's right!"

John Vizzi followed his sister to the microphone to announce he wanted to boycott businesses that hired illegal aliens. "One of them—the first one—will be the company that hired Roberto Martínez Ruíz!"

"Yes! Yeah!" called out the crowd.

"And the mayor of Denver who hired the killer of Donnie Young!"

"Put them on the list!" yelled someone.

I glanced over and saw that the girls were gone. I decided it was time for me to leave, too. I had seen enough, and given the turn things were taking, it seemed prudent to go before I was recognized. Later, I told my husband about John Vizzi's plans to boycott the Wynkoop brewpub. "Somebody should tell him that the Wynkoop is probably the only restaurant in Colorado that *doesn't* hire illegal aliens," my husband replied dryly, referring to the new hiring procedures adopted by his business partners. But truth had played a subservient role at the forum, where emotions had trumped fact. For me, the most surprising aspect was who had spoken: Lamm never showed up, but the event had featured one congressman, two state legislators, and a candidate for governor. It was by their presence that I recognized the movement against illegal immigration had gone mainstream.

13

SORORITY GIRLS

On the following Monday, Marisela slipped into Social Inequality five minutes late, wearing a DU sweatshirt. The girls were clothing themselves in their identity as college students more and more frequently these days. Lisa Martínez analyzed poverty rates in different countries, then handed back their midterms. After class, Marisela and Zahra decided to have lunch at the Pub. The girls often ate meals there, as it was located on campus and they could pay for food using their student accounts. Clara was on her way to meet a prospective student who was hoping to win a scholarship from the Daniels Fund. "At the Daniels Fund meeting, I said, 'Anybody who wants a tour of DU, contact me.' Stupid me! I'll never say that again."

"You can bring her to see us," Marisela offered. "Our room is clean."

"Yeah, we just had a cleaning session," Zahra confirmed.

"Okay, I'll call you if I need to deposit her with you," said Clara.

Only a year had passed since the girls had crawled into the shrubs outside of Johnson-McFarlane, and already they were showing the new kids around. At the Pub, Zahra said that during the forum Marisela had alarmed the other girls by vociferously heckling the speakers. "You guys need to get educated!" she had yelled at Frosty Wooldridge. "Your figures aren't right!" People sitting nearby had turned around to stare in a threatening manner, frightening the other girls. *"Cálmate!"* Clara had hissed at Marisela, urging her to calm down. "Don't draw attention to yourself!" Afterward, they had stayed up late surfing the websites of anti-immigration groups and dissecting the experience. "We were talking afterward and saying it reminded us of Hitler," Marisela said. "All that data they gave? It's wrong. All their arguments were way off—and people believed it!"

"I knew there were a lot of bad sentiments toward immigrants, but

I didn't think it was that bad," Zahra said. "The speakers exaggerated everything. Undocumented or not—people kill, people drink. The deaths that they were talking about had nothing to do with anybody's immigration status."

"I went from being so mad to being sad to being freaked out," said Marisela. "We have to watch our backs now. I'm scared of walking down the street."

Marisela and Zahra moved on to discuss the social dynamics in their quad. The four roommates had agreed they would take turns cleaning the bathroom, but that was not happening. "Well, Alison is middle-class, and Beatriz is upper-class," observed Marisela. "So they will clean the sink, but they won't touch the toilet or the floor. Us working-class people, we know how to clean. I cleaned the toilet yesterday. They were like 'Wow! It's really clean!'"

Marisela's mind drifted.

"Oh, no!" she cried. "I've had my laundry in the basement of Nelson since yesterday morning!"

I went with her to retrieve her clothing. A dozen brand-new washing machines and dryers filled the laundry room at Nelson Hall. I remarked that I had vivid memories of the run-down facility where I had washed my clothes during college and there was no comparison. "It is really nice, isn't it," Marisela acknowledged. "Look at all these machines!" Glumly, she said she had received a 79 on the Social Inequality midterm—she had bombed the essay question. Martínez expected college students to demonstrate sophisticated writing skills, which Marisela still did not possess. "I'm not going to be a straight-A student anymore!" she griped.

To cheer herself up, Marisela pulled out a picture of Ramiro, the boyfriend who had invited her to the party at Salon Ocampo. He was holding his little sister in his arms and wearing the same kind of clothing favored by Marisela's father—Wrangler jeans, a Western shirt, *vaquero* boots, and a *Tejana* hat. They had broken up but were still seeing each other on again off again. Marisela said Ramiro was having a hard time: His father had been pulled over for driving without a seat belt, and when he was unable to produce the right type of identification, he had been taken into custody and deported. Meanwhile, Ramiro's mother had developed chronic kidney failure and required dialysis two or three times a week, which she obtained at no cost from various public hospitals in the metro area. Given that his mother was seriously ill and his father was missing, seventeen-year-old Ramiro had now become the sole breadwinner and caregiver for his three younger siblings. Marisela was helping out on the weekends. "It's really sad over there," she said. "They're all so sad."

Marisela never had enough time for Ramiro, never had enough time for her parents, never had enough time for her classes. She whirled from school to work, always in a hurry. On the weekends, she tried to find time to call her cousin Román. He was handling his prison time like a man, she said; he didn't whine about it. He told her little brothers to look at him, and make sure they never wound up in a jail cell. On top of everything else, Marisela had just agreed to help start a new chapter of a Latina sorority, Theta Theta Nu. A couple of seniors at DU had approached the girls to ask for help in bringing the sorority to campus—it had active chapters at several other colleges in the West, but nothing like it existed at the University of Denver—and the girls had just agreed to join an official interest group. Members had to attend study groups together, dine together, and perform volunteer work in the Latino community.

One week later, I found Clara and Yadira in Nelson Hall, getting ready to go to their first sorority study group. Yadira had just returned from delivering some money to her sisters. Down in Mexico, Alma had developed high blood pressure, forcing her to give up on the idea of returning before the baby's birth. Meanwhile, Jesús had announced he would no longer buy Zulema or Laura any new clothes, makeup, or hair products. He would pay for their rent and food, but no extraneous items. Consequently, Alma had asked Yadira to get a job so that she could supply her sisters with spending money. Yadira did not want to relinquish the work she had begun to enliven the campus, nor was she willing to miss out on the Latina sorority, so instead she was simply doling out some of her savings. She hoped to make her summer earnings stretch until the end of the fall quarter, and planned to work full-time over the winter break. She exhibited no resentment at her mother's request. "I wasn't surprised," Yadira said. "I would have felt that it was my responsibility anyway, even if nobody actually told me."

Outside of Nelson Hall, the two girls bumped into Jacinda, a pixie-faced freshman who had graduated from Roosevelt one year after they had. Recently she had dyed her hair an artificial shade of blond and now bore a striking resemblance to Madonna. The three girls set off together for Marcus Commons, a library over at the business school. "Geez, I am so hungry!" announced Jacinda. "They should have pizza at these things!"

"They're taking attendance; did you see that in the e-mail?" said Clara.

"I don't read my e-mails," replied Jacinda. "I just skim them."

Scores of students filled the polished wood tables of Marcus Commons. The girls slowed to a halt; nowhere could they see a concentration of young Latinas. Then Inés, one of the seniors, pointed them to a small study room nearby. As the girls headed in that direction, they spotted Luke. He waved to the girls and they waved back. "This is his building," Yadira observed. She meant that he was a business major, and often had classes here. Unfortunately, the appointed study room was already filled with other Latinas interested in the sorority, and Yadira, Clara, and Jacinda wheeled around to look for another place to sit. Back in the large common area, they finally found a vacant table. Clara pulled out her laptop and began doing calculations. "Oh my God!" she exclaimed. "My parents make so little money!"

"What?" queried Jacinda.

"Oh, it's for my Social Inequality class," Clara answered.

Inés and Petra, another senior, came over to brief the group. "Okay, you guys, sorry, I know you are studying, but I just need a few minutes," said Inés. "I talked with some of the sorority leaders, and they said we could become a colony, starting in spring, and be sisters. I don't envision remaining a colony for long—I think we'll become a full chapter before the year is over." Yadira wanted to know how much members had to pay in dues. "Well, dues don't begin until the pledge process starts," answered Petra. "If just five of us pledge, it could be, like, $100 apiece. If fifteen of us pledge, it could be under $50." Yadira said nothing. I knew that she would have a hard time parting with even $50; it would be money she could not give to her sisters.

A young woman with a round face and straight dark hair walked up. "Is this the sorority study group?" she asked in a near whisper.

"Yes," replied Inés firmly. "What's your name?"

"Catarina."

"Here, take my seat," Inés offered.

Catarina joined the interest group, and so did every other Latina that the girls knew. Zahra joined as well, even though she was originally African, because she identified closely with *mexicanas* who shared her immigrant experience. For the rest of the fall, the two pairs of roommates assiduously followed the sorority's rigorous schedule, logging the required number of dinners, study groups, and volunteer hours. In the process, the sorority enlarged their social circle. As the girls became absorbed by the sorority, Elissa faded out of their lives completely. When I asked Elissa why she no longer saw her old friends from Roosevelt, she replied, "Well, they got involved with the sorority, and that was where they made their friends."

That fall, Marisela's friend Alfonso signaled his interest in Clara by asking her to go to a movie. Then he became the first boy Clara ever kissed. "Are you dating him?" I asked in November. "We're just getting to know each other," she replied evasively. In fact their kiss had meant the world to Clara; she had hedged only because she was not certain of his affection. When Alfonso turned out not to be serious, Clara was devastated, but she kept her emotions well hidden. Nobody knew how badly she had been hurt except her roommate Yadira. Meanwhile, Yadira remained committed to Juan, even after they ran into problems. Juan had supported his girlfriend's decision to go to college; he had understood when her little sisters needed to be taken around town to buy shampoo and lip gloss. But when Yadira told Juan that she was joining Theta Theta Nu, Juan became incensed. He had heard about sororities and fraternities—flimsy excuses for college students to get drunk and have sex. After graduating from high school, Juan had begun working as a janitor and now cleaned office buildings for $8 an hour. He did not feel himself to be the equal of the privileged students who went to the University of Denver, and lived in fear that Yadira would find someone better. He had kept his anxiety in check for the most part, until learning about Yadira's plans with Theta Theta Nu. Juan viewed the time Yadira spent on the sorority as time she might have spent with him, and pressured her to forswear the group, but she would not. Instead, she dropped one of her courses—a required chemistry class. "It was going to bring my GPA way down," she explained. "I think I was going to get a D." Yadira said with pride, however, that she thought she was going to earn an A in Social Inequality. "Your essays are very clear and concise," Martínez had written on her midterm exam.

By the end of the quarter, the girls had achieved a new equilibrium in their friendship. With Elissa gone and the old pairings broken apart, Marisela had found her latest soul mate in Zahra. One weekend, Marisela and Zahra stayed up late, got drunk, and did a walk-through at McDonald's—they walked through the drive-through lane, giggling so hard they could barely order. Then they went back to the dorm and watched *Crash* for about the nineteenth time. The girls talked about the movie incessantly; it wasn't just about white people, and it wasn't just about blacks—finally, somebody had captured the triangular relationship between whites, browns, and blacks in all its complexity. There were always people in their dorm room, always a party. Meanwhile, over in Yadira's and Clara's room, serenity reigned. Yadira had enough drama in her life, and didn't need to manufacture any more. On the night that Marisela and Zahra did their walk-through at McDonald's, Yadira took her sisters to see *Chicken Little*. "I love that movie," she said afterward. Shortly before their final exams, both pairs of roommates walked out of Social Inequality together, and in the stairwell of Sturm Hall, they hesitated: Who was going where with whom? Clara announced she was going to her job at the Center for Multicultural Excellence, while Yadira said she wanted to go to the student center for coffee. Clara and Yadira began to descend the staircase; Marisela and Zahra turned to go up.

"Where are you going?" Clara called out.

"I'm going to see my adviser," Marisela answered.

"And I'm going with her!" announced Zahra.

"We go everywhere together! We are a pair!" Marisela yelled happily.

"You're a package now!" Clara acknowledged.

The girls had struck a new point of balance in the complicated mobile (each part slowly revolving around the others in an ever-changing pattern) of their interconnected relationships. In the process, Zahra had come to occupy the spot once held by Elissa. I didn't think it was a coincidence that Marisela's new best friend had black skin. Marisela had embraced the fact that she was a minority at the University of Denver. Meanwhile, Yadira and Clara alternated between being part of the dominant culture and seeking refuge in that alternative space where Marisela had become queen.

14

FRIENDLY BANTER

At the beginning of January 2006, while the girls were on winter break, John visited the University of Denver to participate in an electronic town hall about immigration hosted by *9NEWS*, a local television news program. John's political advisers had discouraged him from participating because they thought the issue was becoming radioactive, but John hoped to bring more reason into the discussion. For days on end, nervous staffers in the mayor's office had held briefing sessions with enormous notebooks containing every statistic and report on the topic. John thought their anxiety was misplaced; the other participants were Governor Bill Owens, former governor Dick Lamm, state representative Terrance Carroll (a preacher as well as an attorney and elected official), and U.S. Representative Tom Tancredo. John thought he would be lucky to get in a word or two.

On the night of the event, I waited with John in the so-called "green room," which was the size of a closet and contained a desk and a chair. I sat on the desk and gave John the chair. It was strange to return to the campus and find it devoid of students, but populated by political figures. John's staff had crammed him so full of details that I feared he might forget to be himself, so I made chitchat about anything except the immigration issue. Suddenly we heard a rap on the door, and John jumped out of his chair, thinking it was time to go. Instead, Governor Owens stuck his head in the door.

"Hello!" he said brightly. "I'm just coming to say good luck! I've just been to see Tom Tancredo!"

Although they came from different political parties, John and Governor Owens had struck up an unusually strong working relationship, which the press had hailed as a model of bipartisan cooperation.

"You're going to have fun this year," John told the governor now. "It's your last year, you can do anything you want!"

"That's right, John," said Owens. "I am going to be engaged, and I am going to have a good time."

Then he was off, chirruping, "Well, I better go say hello to Dick Lamm!"

As John headed for the stage, I found my way back to the auditorium. Under the spotlights, five politicians sat in a row, wearing identical dark suits. It was Congressman Tancredo, then John, Governor Owens, State Representative Carroll, and former governor Lamm. The first section of the audience had been reserved for people who were going to speak as well. None of the girls had come, but I recognized a teacher from their old high school, as well as Bob Copley, the head of the Colorado Minutemen, Mexican Consul General Juan Marcos Gutiérrez González, Fred Elbel of Defend Colorado Now (the group that wanted Colorado to ban nonemergency services to immigrants without legal status), and Estevan Flores, a prominent academic at the University of Colorado at Denver who had testified in *Plyler v. Doe* twenty-five years earlier. The evening started with a preliminary video. "Give me your tired, your poor, your huddled masses yearning to breathe free," began the narrator, reading from Emma Lazarus's poem "The New Colossus." But the only panelist who appeared in the video was Congressman Tancredo, and he said: "It is the policy of the United States government to allow illegal entrance into the United States in order to supply a cheap labor market." Moderator Adam Schrager, a veteran political reporter with *9NEWS,* credited Tancredo with thrusting this debate into the national spotlight and invited him to speak first.

"Why are they turning this into the Tancredo show?" I asked John's press secretary in a text message.

"TV ratings," she texted back.

Tancredo said: "I think it is important to place, at the top of the list of discussion topics on immigration reform, the issue of whether or not we are a nation of laws. Are we indeed what we say we are? That's supposed to be one of the basic tenets of the American experience: that we are a nation of laws. Almost all people will suggest, 'Of course we are.' 'Yes, absolutely we should be.' But then, depending on where you are on this issue, there's a tendency to have this sort of a pause, and at least the thought crosses someone's mind, 'Yeah, we're a nation of laws, but some of them really don't need to be enforced, especially if some of them prevent me from pursuing my economic desires and goals.'"

Tancredo glanced pointedly at John.

"I also think you've got to ask yourself whether borders matter anymore. Some people might think that's easily answered: 'Yes, they do.' But let me tell you, I serve with people in the United States Congress who feel—and sometimes I think even the president feels—that borders are anachronistic, that they are just a barrier to the free flow of goods and people."

John was up next.

"I see clearly that we have a system that is not working," he began. "You don't have to have a lot of insight to recognize that we have a problem. We can't have an open border. At a certain point—and that point isn't too far away—our public schools and our health care system become overwhelmed. But at the city, in the last two and a half years, one thing I've learned is that I spend an awful lot of my time fixing what are the unintended consequences of other people's solutions. And I think what we need is smart reform."

John advocated for securing the borders without closing them. Then he spoke about the contributions that immigrants have made to this nation, arguing that the sense of possibility the United States has represented to people around the world for two centuries has been at the core of its economic success. "I think ambition has always been a great thing for this country," he said. "People have risked their lives, whether crossing an ocean or coming across deserts, to seek a better life for themselves. And as each wave of immigrants has come to this country—when you go back through the Irish, the Germans, the Italians, the Poles—each time, they were greeted by fierce resistance. At one time in Baltimore, a third of the schools were predominantly German-speaking. All city council meetings were translated into German. And there was the same kind of resistance. But I ask now—looking back—which of those groups could we have done without? Which of those groups would this country have been better off without, if we'd just said, 'No, you can't come'?"

Governor Owens viewed illegal immigration as a burgeoning problem. He pointed out that the number of children in Colorado's public schools who did not speak English had doubled during his time in office. "John mentioned Baltimore," said Owens. "I was just reading Teddy Roosevelt's biography, and back when he was the police commissioner in New York, he would walk for miles and miles through the streets of that city, and he would pass through areas that were entirely

German. And yet there is a difference between those immigrants and the current wave that we are experiencing. Those waves came from other parts of the world, separated by an ocean. It was harder to stay in close contact with the home country. Today we have a different challenge, because of the proximity with many of the countries from which we are drawing immigrants."

Terrance Carroll said state legislators were besieged by questions about immigration from voters, and predicted that if the federal government proved incapable of resolving the matter, then state legislators would tackle it. He hoped they could manage to do so in a moral fashion. Dick Lamm approached the issue differently from the way the other panelists did. "For thirty years, I've been arguing that the whole world, particularly the developed world, has to move from growth to sustainability," he said. "I believe that global warming is a reality. I think the polar ice caps are melting, our oceans are warming, coral is dying, and that these are signs that the global ecosystem is in trouble. The last thing that the world needs is another half a billion or a billion consuming Americans."

Schrager turned to ask Bob Copley of the Minutemen for comment. Copley delivered a speech of his own about foreigners invading this country. He received thunderous applause, and I realized that CAIR had stacked the hall. Soon the panelists got into a debate over the merit of guest workers. "Friends, I don't know how we would get the peach crop in, here in Colorado, without people from other countries," said Governor Owens. "I understand that if the wages went up to $20 or $22 perhaps an hour, we might be able to. And I understand that there are all sorts of subsidies to us as consumers because so many producers use people who are here illegally. I would like to have a legal guest worker program that revolves around a background check, a noncounterfeitable ID. Then these workers would pay into our tax system, they would pay into our Social Security system, and we would take out of that to pay for their health care, their K through 12 education."

"Congressman, I saw you shaking your head," Schrager said to Tancredo.

"Well, I'm shaking my head only to the extent that we have such a program today," Tancredo replied. "People can come into the country with temporary work visas—it's the same exact process as the governor has described."

"The system for getting people here on work visas is actually broken," charged Terrance Carroll. "There are nowhere near enough visas to fulfill the labor demands that we actually have."

Lamm warned that guest worker programs were not a panacea. "I've looked at a number of European countries, and I know of no country that is happy with their guest worker program," he said. "I don't think it's working anyplace. They always run into the problem of: 'You're good enough to come to work, but you're not good enough to stay.' People get resentful about that, and I don't blame them. You have to really look at these programs and fill in the details. Are they going to be able to bring their families? Who is going to pay for the education of their kids? Who is going to pay for their health care? I mean, there are a thousand details that have to be worked out."

Tancredo interjected that he had just received a study showing that after adjustments for inflation, the median hourly wage for blue-collar manufacturing jobs and nonmanagerial service jobs—the kind of employment that many immigrants pursue—had remained essentially the same since 1973. "In a period of time when the economy grew by 100 percent and productivity grew by 80 percent, the typical man's earnings went nowhere!" objected Tancredo. "That's a moral issue, let's talk about it!"

Schrager asked for a response from the consul general of Mexico. Gutiérrez González was a member of the business-oriented, reform-minded PAN (National Action Party), and had been appointed to his post by Vicente Fox, the first opposition-party candidate to win the presidency of Mexico. He pointed out that the PAN was now trying to turn Mexico's economy around. "Five and a half million people just came out of poverty in Mexico, during this administration," said the consul general.

Fred Elbel of Defend Colorado Now brought up remittances. "They send back $20 billion to Mexico!" he protested. "It's a lot of money. Follow the dollars! I think we have something here that is undermining the sovereignty of the United States and is allowing Mexico as a corrupt foreign government to meddle in the affairs of the United States."

Consul General Gutiérrez González pointed out that throughout a five-year period, the United States had increased exports to its two closest neighbors, Canada and Mexico, by $100 billion. Now that NAFTA had transformed trading relations between the two countries,

70 percent of the goods that Mexico imported originated in the United States. Then the consul general took exception to the charge that Mexican workers were simply siphoning money out of the U.S. economy. "The gentleman said that we are taking $20 billion out of the country in remittances—perhaps that's the size. But it's also estimated that two times that amount remains to fill the economy here in the United States."

I glanced up to see how the panelists were reacting to the debate, and was taken aback to see John lean over to schmooze with Tancredo. At first the congressman did not reciprocate, but eventually they fell into what looked like friendly banter. I knew John believed in reaching out to his worst enemies—I just never imagined he would extend that philosophy to Tancredo. When the congressman had attacked the city's police department for having a sanctuary policy, I had viewed his remarks as personal attacks on my husband. Apparently, John had not taken his comments personally, however, and saw Tancredo's jabs as nothing more than a good game of hardball. Later that night, John said he wanted to invite Tancredo over for dinner.

"You have to be joking," I replied.

"You're as bad as he is, you know," John told me.

He meant that I let my emotions get in the way—that I held a grudge. Upon reflection I had to admit that John was probably right; we never did dine with Tancredo, but I saw that I had to get over my knee-jerk response to him if I was going to write about the immigration debate with anything approaching balance. I vowed to make a better effort to get to know the congressman from Littleton. Throughout the ensuing months, I spent most of my time with Marisela and Yadira, but I also tried to catch Tancredo's public appearances, and early that spring I found him at an immigration forum held by the Independence Institute, a conservative think tank based in Denver. In one of the panels, Tancredo squared off against Dan Griswold, the head of the Cato Institute, a Washington-based policy organization, in a hammer-and-tongs showdown, with Tancredo representing the socially conservative viewpoint and Griswold the fiscally conservative perspective. Griswold argued that the terrorist attacks of September 11, 2001, had nothing to do with illegal immigration, as all the terrorists had entered the country with legal documentation. On a typical day, one million people enter the United States with visas that classify them as students, tourists, or business travelers. "That is our security challenge," argued Griswold. "Not somebody who wants to come here and get a job and build a better life."

Griswold opposed the tough, sanctions-oriented immigration bill that Tancredo had just helped pass in the House of Representatives. "This House bill declares eleven million gardeners and retail clerks and drywall hangers as felons," he said. "Don't our county sheriffs, don't our homeland security people have enough to do chasing terrorists and rapists without taking up their time and jail space going after peaceful workers? The seven-hundred-mile wall that will cost more than $1 billion, all that will do is push the flow of people farther out into the desert. We will have even more bodies piling up in our morgues and the refrigerated trucks."

Tancredo came out swinging. "Dan still takes the position that is held by the *Wall Street Journal* editorial board and most libertarians—borders don't matter." He insisted they did, particularly when the country was at war. The original terrorists may have arrived with visas, but that did not guarantee the next group would follow suit. The congressman had heard unconfirmed reports of a link between Mara Salvatrucha and Al Qaeda—and members of Mara Salvatrucha, a violent gang that had originated in Los Angeles and then spread into Central America, had already been intercepted trying to smuggle all kinds of things across the country's southern border. "Let me point out that we have never been able to design a sieve that can actually separate out those people who are coming across the border just to do all those millions of jobs that no American wants to do, or those people who are coming here for other purposes," said Tancredo. "We just can't do it. We can say, 'Gee, this looks like somebody who wants to do my lawn—'"

"Or your basement!" shouted a heckler.

"—but on the other hand, it could be somebody a little more dangerous. We haven't got that sieve yet. We don't know how to do it. So we do need to secure the borders."

After the forum ended, I stopped to chat with Tancredo. To my surprise, he greeted me warmly. "Your husband just wrote me the nicest letter," he told me. "You know, my mother died—"

"Oh, John lost his mother during the mayoral campaign," I interjected.

"Yes, that's what he said. He wrote to me about that, when he sent his condolences."

Tancredo divided the world into friend or foe, and it seemed as though John's letter had moved us from one category into the other. The congressman said he would be happy to spend more time with me in August, after the House of Representatives went into recess. By now, I felt as though I understood the girls, but I still found him an enigma. Immigration meant such different things to different people, and it was not possible to grasp the entirety of the issue by considering only one point of view. I had already immersed myself in what things looked like from the girls' perspective. I hoped he could help me see another.

15

AUTO THEFT

Yadira took down a snapshot pinned to the bulletin board in her room and handed it to me. I beheld a black-haired newborn in a pink jumpsuit with a matching pink bow in her hair. "That's my new sister," she said proudly. It was early in the winter quarter of her sophomore year, and I hadn't seen the girls for several weeks. Recently Alma had called from the hospital in Durango to say that she had just named her new daughter Cristál. Now Alma was right back where she had started—mothering a child in Mexico, with the baby's father working for an American employer, twelve hundred miles away. At the moment, Yadira was working part-time to help support her siblings. Consequently, she was taking three courses instead of four—a math requirement, a sociology class, and a course on Spanish literature. Clara had signed up for the same Spanish course, a required science class about the evolution of life, a communications class, and an arts and humanities requirement. Both girls said their favorite class was Spanish, which was taught by Miriam Bornstein, one of a handful of tenured Latino professors at the university. Several other Latinos with tenure taught in various graduate schools at the university, but Miriam and her husband, Óscar Somoza, were the only tenured professors of Latino background who focused on teaching undergraduate students.

"Every day, I say to Yadira, 'I love Miriam. Don't you love Miriam?'" Clara announced. "The teacher is from Mexico, so we identify with her."

"Our first Spanish teacher was Argentinian, and she said our Spanish wasn't real Spanish."

"Miriam knows that even if we speak Spanglish, it's a means of communicating!"

Just then, Luke arrived with a bicycle messenger bag slung over his shoulder.

"You won't believe what happened last night," Yadira told him. "You know how Mercedes sometimes sleeps over? Well, last night we were like, why don't we steal Marisela's mattress—"

"Oh, my God!" Luke exclaimed. "I saw them! I saw them with the mattress!"

The girls often invited their friend Mercedes to stay overnight, because she lived in a dorm located in a remote corner of campus and hated walking home after dark. She usually slept on the floor, but this time Clara and Yadira thought it would be funny to play a trick on Marisela. Over winter break, she had started dating a construction worker named Omar, and they were now inseparable. While Marisela was out with Omar, the other girls snuck into her bedroom, giggling wildly, and stole her mattress. "We were just settling down to go to sleep, and then she started pounding on the door!" Yadira recounted. "We were, like, 'What do we do?' We thought maybe she would go away, but she kept pounding and pounding." Finally Yadira opened the door. "And she was scary, she was so mad!"

"I've never seen her so mad," confirmed Clara.

"Luke, she was seriously, seriously pissed."

"I know! I was watching *The Shawshank Redemption* in the lounge when Marisela and this guy came by with the mattress. They were cursing and yelling. I was, like, 'What's going on?' But I thought I better not ask. Hey—is that her new boyfriend? He looked so old."

"He's nice," said Clara, springing to Omar's defense. "I like him."

Luke still ate many meals with Clara and Yadira, although as the girls became consumed by the sorority, he objected that they didn't have enough time for him anymore. Recently he had started calling Clara "Granola" because she had abandoned her blue jeans and T-shirts for gypsy skirts and cotton blouses—what he referred to as "those peasant-y clothes." One evening, they had a conversation in which Luke envisioned Clara after college—he said she was going to marry a liberal academic and live a back-to-nature lifestyle, eschewing automobiles and energy-consuming household appliances. Then Luke pictured Yadira's future. "She's going to be one of those girls whose sheets match the towels, which match the walls, which match the tiles, and she'll have all matching silverware, and her kids will be very clean," he predicted. Yadira liked this tidy image, though thinking about the future always made her anxious. She did not tell this to Luke;

instead, she teased him back. "Luke is going to live in a huge house in a gated community and drive a big SUV," she said. "He's going to be a businessman, all about the money. He's going to marry a very Republican girl, very conservative, and he's just going to be very boring."

"That sounds about right," said Luke affably.

The winter quarter passed in a blur, as the girls were consumed with pledging Theta Theta Nu. When I inquired about the pledge process, however, they became evasive, because they weren't supposed to tell outsiders about the sorority's rules. Clara and Yadira even tried to deny that they were pledging at all, though they kept engaging in absurd rituals that they declined to discuss. Toward the middle of the winter quarter, I stopped by their dorm room and found they had written a list of important things about the sorority all over the ceiling in colored chalk, so they could lie down and memorize the information. When the two girls saw me notice their scribbles, they became distraught—I was spying on the sorority's private mysteries! They made me avert my eyes and told me I would have to leave the room if I did not abstain from reading their secrets. I changed the subject by asking about Alma.

"I don't think she's coming back," Yadira said in a flat tone. "We've kind of given up on that."

Once the baby had arrived, Alma had recognized that her dream of returning to the United States was not possible, at least for the moment. Now her older children were grappling with the idea that their mother might never come back. It was a possibility for which they had not prepared. "Like Zulema—my aunt and my grandpa are her legal guardians, but my aunt is busy with work all the time and my grandpa is often in Mexico," said Yadira. "So sometimes when she has an application or has to register for something like school, they aren't around to sign the papers. And no one has custody of Laura." This matter of legal guardianship had just come up because Zulema had been lounging outside of Abraham Lincoln High, where she was now a sophomore, when a friend drove up in a flashy car and asked if Zulema would like a ride. They had cruised the streets of Denver until a police car pulled them over, which was when Zulema supposedly learned that she had been taking a joy ride in a stolen car. The police assumed she had participated in its theft, however, and had considered the possibility of charging Zulema with multiple felonies. Usually Yadira did not have trouble holding her tongue, but when she accompanied her grandfather to police headquarters, it was hard for her to remain silent as she listened to the detective question her sister. "At one point, he said, 'You go to Lincoln, right?'" Yadira related. "'You know how many stolen cars we get from there?' And I was really angry. What difference should it make where she goes to school? But I chose not to say anything because I didn't want to make it worse for my sister. I just told myself, 'Breathe in and breathe out.'" In the end, Zulema pled guilty to a single misdemeanor.

For several months, both Laura and Zulema had been staying overnight with their older sister at Nelson Hall on the weekends. Early in March, I visited them one Saturday morning, after they had spent the night. The three sisters had stayed up late painting one another's fingernails and surfing the Internet for information about their favorite music stars. Now they were playing with a tiny Chihuahua puppy that Juan had given to Yadira on Valentine's Day. Pets were not allowed in the dorm, but Yadira had snuck Tiger inside for a visit. While the puppy gamboled around, I asked Laura about her journey to Mexico last summer. She said the bus ride had been boring; she spent most of the time listening to a new *reggaetón* CD that Yadira had made for her, while Raúl played on his Game Boy. The journey took thirty hours. In Durango, her grandmother's poverty-stricken neighborhood on the outskirts of the city had featured unpaved roads and primitive cinder-block houses. "It was ugly and it smelled bad," Laura related, wrinkling her face. "It smelled like dead dogs."

She whiled away the weeks watching *American Idol* in Spanish. The highlight of her time in Mexico was when her uncle took her to a fair. It was a hot day and she rode down a water chute and the water had been freezing. Her cousins had begged for shaved ice with sugary flavoring, but used a word Laura had never heard before. She often had trouble communicating. "At first, the plan was to stay there," she said. "Then my mom told me that we had a choice: I could come back here, or I could stay there. I didn't want to stay there—I didn't know that much Spanish. So I came back."

"Was it a hard choice to make, leaving your mother behind?" I asked.

Laura stared at me. "She said she was going to come, too!" she whispered. Her face crumpled, and she started crying. Then Zulema did, too. Aghast, I tried to steer the conversation back to neutral ground, but neither girl had much more to say. Later, Yadira asked that I refrain from bringing up the subject of their mother again with either of her sisters. They did not talk about emotional matters, she reminded me— the three sisters themselves had never had a direct conversation about their mother's absence. I agreed not to bring up the subject again. At the same time, I noticed that Yadira had issued the instruction with ease. Throughout the last year and a half, she had become more comfortable in the world. She had lost the scared look she used to wear in high school and acquired a new self-assurance. It suited her.

16

MACHISMO

I had thought of Kelly Young often in the days and weeks after her husband's funeral, but ten months passed before we spoke again. I wanted to know how she was faring, and wanted to tell her how the girls' stories intersected with her life's journey, but was reluctant to disturb her. Then in March 2006, John came back from the St. Patrick's Day parade wearing a ridiculous bright green blazer and half a dozen ropes of shiny green Mardi Gras beads and announced that he had spent most of the parade with Kelly. Detectives Jack Bishop and Donnie Young had been selected to serve as grand marshals this year, and Kelly had stood in for her fallen husband. John said admiringly that she was tough—she was going to be all right.

By this point, Raúl Gómez García had been incarcerated in Denver for three months, and the preliminary proceedings in his trial were scheduled to start in one week. Anticipating that we might see each other in the courtroom, I called Kelly to let her know why I would be there, and we talked for a long time. Crimes tear families apart, but they also stitch strangers together, and I had the sense of being bound to her by destiny. After asking about her children, I told Kelly about the girls from Roosevelt, explaining that one of them had a boyfriend who had attended the party at Salon Ocampo. I said I would be interested to hear her thoughts on illegal immigration, but would understand if she did not want to share them. "I'm sure lots of people would expect that I'd be the first one to say, 'Let's pack them up and deport them all,'" said Kelly. "And I'm not. To be honest, I'm not sure how I feel about it all. If I could change Mexico's laws so that when people commit a crime and flee to that country they could send them back immediately, I would. That part seems really unfair to me. But Raúl—he's just a kid. And now he's ruined his life, he's ruined the life of his girlfriend, and he's ruined the life of his child. I can't imagine what that child is going to go through, growing up thinking, 'My dad is a cop-killer.' I feel for them—I really do—even though he took my most precious thing. So, I have really mixed emotions about all of this."

Kelly said the murder had transformed her. Formerly she had been a proponent of the death penalty, but after her husband was killed, she felt relieved when the extradition treaty between the United States and Mexico prevented her from asking for that punishment. "I don't know if I could have lived with myself if I'd been the one who had to say, 'Put him to death.' So part of my personality has changed because of this."

Throughout the past year, people on both sides of the immigration issue had called to seek her blessing. Dick Lamm had called. "He wanted to know: 'Will you support our issue?'" Kelly recalled. "I said, 'I'm sorry, but I can't. I'm not strongly enough on one side or the other.'" A lot of reporters had called, too, and the police officer's widow had talked to each of them. She spent hours with the press because she wanted to fight for her husband's reputation. He may have used a little more force than was necessary to gain control of the situation with Gómez García, but it should not have cost him his life, and she would not let it tarnish his good name. Kelly thought that whatever had transpired between her husband and Gómez García outside Salon Ocampo had been an aberration. She knew what happened to a cop who was accused of police brutality—a label as encompassing as the tag "illegal alien"—and she refused to let a moment that she considered out of character define Donnie Young. He had been one of the good guys, in her opinion, and she listed all the times he had broken up bar fights, all the times he had stopped people from driving home drunk, all the times he had been, unsung, a hero.

She did not tell any of the news reporters, and only explained to me much later, that Donnie Young himself was half Latino. Kelly did not reveal her husband's ethnicity to the camera crews because it wasn't something her husband would have mentioned. He did not advertise his ethnic background, and maybe he had unusually complicated feelings about his parents. Donnie had inherited his Latina mother's coloring but his Anglo father's surname, and when they first started dating, back in Colorado Springs, Kelly had thought her new boyfriend might be Italian. It was not until Donnie introduced her to his Spanish-speaking grandmother that she realized his true heritage. Although his mother's family had emigrated from Mexico, they could trace back their roots to

Europe, and they did not refer to themselves as Chicano or Mexican—
they referred to themselves as Spanish. Kelly herself had grown up in
the United States with an American father and a British mother (who
never sought citizenship in this country, but preferred always to carry
a green card), which gave Kelly a familiarity with the issue of immigration that not everyone possessed. Donnie's parents had separated
when he was small, and for several years Donnie had lived with his
maternal grandmother in her Spanish-speaking household. Once his
mother remarried, however, Donnie moved back with her and her new
husband. Years later some of Donnie's nephews accused his stepfather
of molesting them, and his stepfather was subsequently convicted of
sexual assault upon a child from a position of trust. During the trial,
Donnie sided with the boys, but his mother, Loretta, refused to believe
them, and the ensuing conflict split the family in two. Donnie never saw
much of his mother again. He once tried to repair the relationship at a
family funeral, but Loretta was cold and he was cut to the quick. From
that point forward, he kept his distance. Donnie stayed in touch with
many people in his extended family, but some of his relatives were petty
criminals who bounced in and out of jail like it was community college,
according to Kelly. "Donnie hated that part of his heritage," she said.
"We would go to Cinco de Mayo and see the low rider cars—he really
didn't like it. He felt that those people had an opportunity to do better. He got himself out of a negative culture, and so he didn't feel that
anybody else could use excuses."

Donnie's most defining quality was his over-the-top gregarious-
ness. Kelly was an introvert, and she found it extraordinary that her
husband could befriend the entire world. They liked to vacation in
Mexico, where Donnie would speak Spanish with street vendors. At
the beginning of their relationship, Donnie was working as a sheriff in
Colorado Springs, escorting prisoners in and out of jail cells, and he
hated every minute of it. He had worked hard to distance himself from
relatives who could not tell right from wrong, and now here he was,
surrounded by the same types. The answer, Donnie thought, was a job
as a police officer—preferably in Denver. It wasn't easy to get into the
Denver Police Department, however; a lot of people viewed a police job
as the ticket to a better life. When he was filling out the application,
Kelly urged him to check the box marked Latino, because she thought
that would give him an advantage, but that was not Donnie's style. He

did not take shortcuts, and he did not think of himself as fitting neatly into a box. Sometimes he joked about being half Mexican, but he never referred to himself as Latino, and the last thing he wanted was to get a jump on another guy because of a label. The department could take him as he was—an outgoing person with a wicked sense of humor and an instinct to help people, as well as many other fine qualities and a few of the usual defects, who loved riding his Harley-Davidson motorcycle above everything except being with his redheaded wife, a guy who happened to have an Anglo dad as well as a Latina mother—or the department didn't have to take him at all.

The Denver Police Department hired Donnie Young in 1993. He worked in narcotics and with the bomb squad, and earned ten official commendations in the process. He also won the department's Medal of Honor and Distinguished Service Cross awards. In 2000, Donnie began working at Salon Ocampo to make some extra money. He quickly befriended the owners, Rubén Huizar Gonzáles and his wife, Gloria Huizar, and pretty soon he got to know Gloria's brother Carlos Ávila, a construction worker, and his wife, Anna Ordoñez, too. One night, Donnie saw a rum-looking guy with a long ponytail removing an abandoned car from a parking lot across the street, and of course Donnie walked over and struck up a conversation with the tow-truck driver, a man named Joseph Martínez. Later, he introduced Martínez to Rubén and Gloria, and soon the tow-truck driver had a steady job at Salon Ocampo, clearing out abandoned vehicles from their lot. Many of the people who came to Salon Ocampo for *quinceañeras* and other fiestas were immigrants, and he knew some of them didn't have legal status. Donnie didn't care—he chatted them up, too. You did not need a passport to talk to Donnie Young.

After the department changed its rules to allow police officers to move outside of the city limits, Donnie and Kelly bought a new home down in fast-growing Douglas County, in Tom Tancredo's congressional district. When Donnie needed work done on the house, he hired people he had met at Salon Ocampo. "Donnie met a guy at that place who spoke only Spanish, and I'm sure that he was illegal, but Donnie heard that he did great tile work, so we had him over here to lay some tiles for us," Kelly said. Donnie told her to address the man as Señor Borracho, and then hooted when she did—he had conned his wife into calling his friend Mr. Drunk. This was why Kelly Young could not take a stand one way or the other on the subject of illegal immigration. "Donnie was a part of that community," she said. "We had people over to our home all the time, and we didn't care if they were legal or not. Legal or illegal—we never spoke about that. When people came over here to work on the house, we never asked them for a Social Security number. That is the part that angers me the most. More than anything, I feel let down." Kelly had welcomed Mexicans into her home, and then one of them had ripped her family apart.

Now Kelly was raising two children on her own, children whom she had shepherded to school while the story of their father's murder blared over talk radio and television news shows. She knew too many Mexicans to mistake Gómez García for an example of his entire community. But she did wonder if machismo had caused her husband's life to seep away onto the floor of Salon Ocampo. "I feel like he maybe did what he did partly because of the culture he was brought up in—you know, 'men shouldn't be disgraced.' I think that Donnie probably embarrassed him in front of his group, when he grabbed his neck or whatever. And that probably influenced what happened—that culture thing, the man is not to be disgraced. I don't know."

On April 13, 2006, Raúl Gómez García would appear at a preliminary hearing to determine if there was sufficient evidence against him to warrant a trial, and Kelly planned to be in the courtroom. "I was out of town when he was extradited, so I didn't see him then," she said. "This is going to be the first time. I don't know what it will be like." Gómez García remained a blank spot in her heart, a person who had figured hugely in the unraveling of her life, yet remained obscure, unknown. "All the police officers, they are like, how can you not hate him? But I don't. Maybe that will change. Maybe if you talk to me after Thursday, I'll be like, 'Yeah, wring his neck.' I don't know. I don't know anything about him." I wondered if confronting her husband's killer was going to change her thoughts on immigration—whether, for her, the two matters would become intertwined. We agreed to talk again after the hearing.

17

LIBERACIÓN

After Kelly Young described what kind of man her husband had been, I decided that Donnie Young would have understood Marisela right away. He would have known where she was coming from and where she was going and why. He knew men like Fabián and he knew women like Josefa; he had cousins like Román. He even knew the specific clubs that Marisela frequented, for he had frequented them, too, albeit in his police uniform. I myself knew little about this other world that still preoccupied so much of Marisela's time and attention. No matter how engrossed she became in her classes or the sorority, Marisela always kept one foot in the world of *norteño* music and *reggaetón*—one foot in the world of Salon Ocampo. I did not fully understand why until one Saturday evening that spring, when I knocked on the door of her dorm room and found Marisela doing homework with Dulce, a Chicana who had gone to Manual High in Denver. Zahra lolled on the top bunk, while Marisela and Dulce sat on the floor. I made myself comfortable in the lower bunk.

Dulce informed me that she knew who I was. "I know the mayor," she announced in a breezy tone. "I've met him two or three times. I'm on the mayor's Youth Commission."

Dulce asked what Marisela and Omar had planned for the evening.

"I think we are going to go to Fantasía, because there's a group playing there that we love," said Marisela.

"Who's playing?" Dulce wanted to know.

"Liberación."

"Oh! I *love* them!" cried Dulce.

Belatedly, Marisela noticed that her cell phone was ringing. "Oh, fuck!" she said, upon noticing she had missed a call from Omar.

Marisela grabbed her student ID card, leapt onto the bed where I was lying, and hurled the card out of the window. Three minutes later, Omar walked into the room, having used the ID card to let himself into the building. He had thick dark hair, a full moustache, and an immense, goofy smile. His work boots were white with dust, because he had come straight from putting up plasterboard in a new assisted-living facility for the elderly retirees who kept moving into the state. He was making $650 a week. Omar sat down at Marisela's desk and began eating piñon nuts. Marisela chatted with him in Spanish while maintaining a separate conversation with Dulce in English. Omar offered me some of his nuts, and I ate them while lying on the lower bunk. Dulce looked over and said once her little sister had woken up with a piñon nut stuck in her ear after she rolled on top of it while sleeping. I promised not to leave stray nuts in Marisela's bed.

"Hey, can I come to hear Liberación with you?" I asked.

"Sure!" said Marisela.

Clara came by to ask what everybody was doing. When she heard I was going to Fantasía, she decided to come, too, as the idea of seeing me enter such a night spot struck her as comical. Zahra declined to join us. "The first time Marisela took me to a Mexican club, I came back with my jaw bruised," she said. "There was a fight and the security guard knocked me down."

"Marisela! Can I borrow something?" implored Clara. "I know what I want!"

She burrowed into Marisela's closet and pulled out a pair of black and gold trousers.

"Oh, I've got something that goes with that," said Marisela.

She dug out a black and gold top. It consisted of two diamond-shaped pieces of pleated fabric, from which strings trailed in a confusing tangle.

"I can't wear that!" yelped Clara. "How does it even work?"

"You could use some rubber cement to glue it to your boobs," offered Dulce.

Yadira and Juan arrived carrying Zahra's television set, which they had borrowed. "You're taking Helen to see Liberación?" asked Yadira in disbelief. They were going to see *The Da Vinci Code* instead. Mercedes showed up and declared she wanted to hear the band. Everybody left to get ready. At the other end of Nelson Hall, Yadira struggled to help Clara master the puzzling garment she had borrowed from Marisela as Juan played games on his cell phone while lying on Yadira's bed in a white T-shirt and baggy jeans with his huge sneakers unlaced. Clara tried on Marisela's top without taking off her own clothes. Yadira was tying the last of the strings together when Luke opened the door.

"That is a crazy shirt," Luke pronounced. "It looks like a fan."

One diamond hugged Clara's chest, while the other drooped.

"Wait, I think I didn't do it right," muttered Yadira.

"Are there instructions that come with it?" asked Luke.

Juan asked if Luke wanted to see *The Da Vinci Code,* but Luke had to write a paper. He mentioned that he was planning to study abroad next year, but nobody engaged him in a conversation about his travel plans. Then Luke asked Juan about the Honda CRX that he had just purchased. Luke sprawled on Clara's bed as they discussed what color Juan should paint his new Honda.

"Black would be awesome," suggested Luke.

"I don't know," said Juan.

"Did you sell the Camry?"

"No. It's still at home—it's boring, though."

Clara took a shower that went on for quite a long time.

"One day, Clara was in the shower for like forty-five minutes, and I was like, 'Clara! Are you okay?'" said Luke. "And she was like, 'Yes! I'm just starting to wash my hair!'"

Yadira giggled. "She does take really long showers."

"You would think she'd want to conserve water—Miss Nature," said Luke.

When Clara finally emerged in a bathrobe, Juan was showing Luke a photograph of Tiger on his cell phone.

"What is he eating?" Luke asked.

"It's a knee pad!" chortled Juan.

Luke announced that he wanted to catch the last episode of *Will & Grace* before doing his homework. Then he found an old brown banana in Clara's bed and started waving it around, demanding, "Clara! What's going on here!"

Clara giggled and pulled Yadira into the bathroom.

"Those two girls are joined at the hip," commented Luke.

"I know," confirmed Juan.

"I bet they'll be in there for like half an hour trying to figure out how to get that shirt on."

"Yep. And at the end they'll be like, 'I don't want to wear this shirt anymore.'"

Clara made the boys put their heads under the pillows as she opened up her underwear drawer to search for a bra.

"I can't breathe," complained Juan.

"Five bucks she doesn't wear the shirt," said Luke.

Clara pulled some documents out of the drawer and placed them carelessly on her bed. Luke examined one—it was Clara's green card. "Hey! You *are* legal!" he said. Clara had been joking about being illegal for so long that Luke had begun to wonder whether she really did lack documents, but now he had proof that she had been teasing. Apparently it never occurred to him to wonder about Yadira—Clara had served as a red herring. Just then, Marisela walked in wearing a strapless black minidress with big white stripes at the bust and hem. All of her thighs were exposed and it seemed miraculous we could not glimpse her underwear, assuming she had any on. She wore oceans of silvery eye shadow and stiletto heels, and a sweet smell like candy wafted in our direction. Omar hovered beside her in a navy dress shirt, extremely tight white Wranglers, pointy cowboy boots made of nubbly ostrich skin, and a *Tejana* cowboy hat, which had the sides pushed up close to the crown to form a *W,* in the trademark fashion favored by those who hailed from Durango. They might have stepped straight out of a red-light bar in Ciudad Juárez, and looked completely foreign in Nelson Hall.

"Ouch!" said Luke. "My feet hurt just looking at those shoes!"

"They're comfortable actually," maintained Marisela.

Marisela retied Clara's top so that it hugged her body and brusquely instructed her to change her earrings. Then she herded everybody out of the room. She wanted to get to Fantasía early—Liberación was popular, and she wanted to secure a table.

It was a fifteen-minute drive. Fantasía proved to be a nondescript cinder-block box on the west side of the metro area. To enter cost $20 for *mujeres,* $30 for *hombres.* Inside, the music was so loud it made my bones vibrate. Women wore anything sufficiently outrageous, while every man in the place was dressed exactly the same as Omar—Wranglers, boots, *Tejanas* that formed perfect Ws. Back in the dorm, Omar and Marisela had looked wildly out of place, but inside Fantasía they made complete sense. Marisela scanned the club with an expert eye.

"The tables down here are all full!" she bellowed over the music. "Let's go upstairs!"

We followed her up to the balcony, where we found a table with a view of the stage. A six-piece band dressed entirely in white was playing oompah-oompah polka music and wowing the crowd with James Brown spins and thrusts. Liberación would appear later, Marisela explained; this was only the warm-up band. Clara and Mercedes had large black Xs drawn on the backs of their hands and ordered only water, but Omar and Marisela ordered tequila with pineapple juice. Marisela had used her fake Mexican driver's license at the door, which said she was twenty-three, although she was only twenty. On the dance floor, couples shuffled to the music, looking like variations on the theme of Omar and Marisela. Guards moved constantly through the club, wearing black jumpsuits that said SECURITY, and carried radios, batons, and pepper spray. Although they were not necessarily police officers, they made me think of Donnie Young.

"There's a girl wearing the same shirt as me, only in blue!" Clara noted with surprise.

The impossible top looked much tackier in shiny aqua, I assured her. Marisela and Omar strolled downstairs to dance, and I leaned over the balcony to watch. Marisela threw her arms around Omar's neck while he fastened his big hands around her waist, and they sashayed easily around the floor. Other couples appeared stiff by comparison, as if they were uncertain about the propriety of touching, but Marisela and Omar moved like they were married. Pink and green spotlights lit the dance floor, and colored strobes blinked on and off. I saw a man who had shaved whorled patterns onto his face, and a young girl who looked maybe thirteen. This was the first time that Mercedes had set foot inside a nightclub, and Clara had gone clubbing only twice before, but Marisela had been coming to clubs like this for years. I understood immediately why she found the penetrating *norteño* music and the men in their *Tejanas* restorative. Here she could forget about the rejections and the slights she sometimes suffered in the white world—here there was no question about whether she belonged.

Omar spun Marisela around under the colored spotlights until humid curls escaped from the clips pinning up her hair. She made the saucy white stripes on her little dress jump up and down in time with the beat. Then she turned around and pressed herself to Omar backward. I thought: Omar better not get too excited, or he'll hurt himself in those Wranglers. Ten new musicians took the stage. Mercedes and I decided this must be Liberación, until Marisela came back and corrected us; it was merely the second warm-up band. They played *ranchera* songs—the Mexican equivalent of country—and a young man asked Clara to dance. The gold top was effective. Another suitor kept Clara on the dance floor for seven songs in a row, clutching his perspiring Corona against her bare back. By midnight, the serious dancers had arrived. One of them swooped down upon Mercedes and wordlessly extended his hand. She wore a startled expression on her face as he steered her masterfully through a series of intricate maneuvers.

"I was born to dance," announced Marisela, when she finally sat down.

"You've been leading a double life," I observed.

"Yes," she confirmed, delivering one of her incandescent smiles.

Not long ago, Marisela said, she had spotted Yadira's younger sister Zulema in this club. She thought Zulema was too young for Fantasía, even though she had been the same age when she first started coming here. The smattering of barely developed girls who were here tonight lent the seedy club a poignant sweetness. Fantasía was selling an intense combination of sleaze and innocence. I had expected the violent undertone, but not the purity.

"It's them!" shouted Marisela. "They're coming out now!"

She herded us over to the edge of the balcony just in time to secure a spot at the railing. The members of Liberación swaggered onto the stage with their hair slicked back in pompadours, sporting three-piece gray suits and black dress shirts and multiple gold chains and medallions. There were two lead singers, two drummers, a saxophonist, a guitar player, a bass player, a keyboardist, and an accordion player. As the two singers launched into a piercing a cappella duet, dancers froze and even the security guards ceased their prowling. One of them stood beside us on her tiptoes, craning to see the band. The crowd knew all the words to *"Enamorado de un Fantasma,"* and they belted out the words to *"Cómo Duele,"* too. Cigarette smoke stung our eyes as fans held up their cell phones in approval. At two A.M., Liberación left the crowd chanting: *"Otra! Otra! Otra!"*

The colored spots dimmed and the house lights came up, and in the sudden brightness Fantasía was revealed to be just a dingy box with cigarette butts littering the floor. Its allure had been a phantasm of music and desire. The crowd cleared out, leaving half-empty beer bottles in their wake. "Okay, little Clara, where are you?" wondered Marisela. We found her in the arms of José, the boy with whom she'd danced seven times in a row. Although Clara was half naked, she still managed to look chaste, as she had pinned the gaudy top closed safely above her cleavage with a gold rose. As Clara entered José's number into her cell phone, it occurred to me that he might have found one of the only virgins inside Fantasía.

The men in *norteño* costumes threw up gravel as they spun out of the parking lot in pickup trucks. I drove home slowly yet arrived at my apartment in fifteen minutes, even though it seemed as though the journey should have taken much longer, given the cultural distance I had to traverse. Marisela sent a text to ask if I had made it home safely, and I assured her that I had. "Thanks 4 letting us know—sweet dreams!" she wrote back. Our usual roles had become reversed; this evening, she was in charge. I could see how the authority that Marisela commanded inside clubs like Fantasía fed her self-confidence. Previously I had imagined that the world of the street only compromised Marisela, but now I recognized that her success on the dance floor enabled her success in the classroom.

18

PHYSICAL EVIDENCE

"Is this courtroom open to the public yet?" I asked. It was the second week of April, the girls were several weeks into the spring quarter of their sophomore year, and Gómez García's preliminary hearing was scheduled to start in ten minutes, on the third floor of the City and County Building. The prosecution would seek to prove they had amassed sufficient evidence to warrant a trial, while Gómez García's defense team would try to argue they had not.

"Are you a reporter?" the sheriff wanted to know. He had a ginger-colored crew cut and a rosy complexion.

"Yes," I answered.

That was still the role in which I remained most comfortable, anyway. I appeared in the local papers infrequently and was not surprised when the sheriff failed to recognize me, even though my husband's office was located just down the hall.

"We're putting all the reporters in the jury box," he said.

I had not anticipated being segregated with the rest of the press, and began to fear that I might inadvertently become part of the story. But when the two local court reporters finally showed up, neither of them appeared to know who I was, either. A few minutes later, Kelly Young arrived in blue jeans and a sleeveless blouse. She walked straight through the courtroom into a private waiting room, along with her sister and her niece, and the door closed behind them. Chief Whitman showed up, and then Donnie Young's best friend, Jeff Baran. He had a young face and silver hair, and wore an orange baseball cap; I recognized him from the funeral. When Kelly emerged from the waiting room, the chief gave her a bear hug. After a brief interlude, Gómez García shuffled into the room wearing leg irons, handcuffs, and a scarlet jumpsuit. For an instant his face betrayed a look of naked fear, but then he pasted on an expression of bravado, and seemed to smirk. Kelly

Young started practicing a deep-breathing routine that she had used when giving birth.

Prosecutors called Captain Michael Calo to the witness stand. The police captain was tall, handsome, and earnest—Gary Cooper in a uniform. Calo told the courtroom he had started out in the United States Air Force and later served as a police officer in the suburb of Arvada before joining the Denver Police Department. He had been with the Denver police force for twenty-one years. A deputy district attorney asked Calo to direct his attention to Saturday, May 7, 2005. On that particular weekend, Calo had been working off-duty at a bar called El Sagitario, directly across Mississippi Avenue from Salon Ocampo. He was still a lieutenant then. Working with him was another police officer, Alex Golston. At around one A.M., Calo said, he was standing outside of El Sagitario. The police captain paused and took a drink of water. He had a hard time continuing.

"I was talking to Alex Golston," he said finally. "He was standing down in the parking lot and I was up on the porch. And I heard four to five muffled gunshots."

"What did you do?" asked the prosecutor.

"I asked Alex, 'Did you hear those gunshots?' He said, 'Yeah, I think I did.'"

Kelly Young's sister reached for a tissue.

"I saw a man come out of the doorway backward, holding a gun in his right hand."

Silhouetted against the light spilling out of Salon Ocampo, the gunman leveled his gun at somebody in menacing fashion. "At that point, I tell Alex, 'Go,' or 'Let's go,' and I started to run." Calo and Golston sprinted across Mississippi Avenue, dodging traffic, but by the time they reached the other side, the gunman had vanished. Calo ran west and then north, going around one side of Salon Ocampo, as Golston ran east and then north to go around the other side of the building. Both officers pulled out their guns as they ran.

"At that point in time, did you know if anybody had been hurt?" asked the prosecutor.

"No," Calo replied.

"What happens after you lose sight of this guy?"

Calo explained that he met Golston at the back of the building. The gunman had simply disappeared. They could not fathom how—a high fence surrounded the parking lot, and they should have trapped the gunman between them. Then their radios came to life: officer down. In front of Salon Ocampo, they found Detective Jack Bishop, dazedly looking for the shooter. They all knew each other—when Bishop started out as a patrolman, Calo had been his lieutenant. Now Bishop worked in the child abuse unit, while Calo was dealing with internal affairs. Bishop said Donnie Young was down and it was bad. Together the three officers waded against the flow of people streaming out of the shattered party. "I remember as we went into the hallway, there was just a swarm of people," Calo said. "It was very chaotic. They were coming down this hallway, I don't know the actual measurements, it seemed like a mile. I'm sure it was more like fifteen, twenty feet. And it's just a sea of people coming out, and a lot of kids. I remember this one pretty little girl—I met eyes with her, and she was just crying and just horrified."

They found Young at the entrance to the dance hall. Calo testified that Young's feet were pointing north and his head was pointing south and that he radioed for an ambulance as soon as he saw Young's condition. "There was a lady holding Donnie's head off the floor and calling out his name. I told her to go get some towels because I didn't want his face and his head on that floor. And I started to talk to him and do everything we're trained to do and tell him he was going to be okay and try to keep him with us. It was just very bad. It was a very bad scene."

"Was he responsive to you?"

Calo struggled for composure.

"I want to believe he was."

Bishop kept telling Calo he didn't feel too good, and Calo suggested he look at the glittery disco balls and think about his family. When Bishop turned white, Calo finally realized that the police officer was going into shock. He must have been shot, too. Calo and Golston found bullet holes in Bishop's vest, and a vast bruise forming on his back. The vest had caught the bullets, but he had suffered blunt trauma. Calo and Golston kept Bishop talking as they radioed for a second ambulance. When the first one arrived, they carried Young out on a stretcher; a firefighter who had just arrived assisted. The navy fabric of Young's uniform did not show bloodstains, and Calo couldn't tell exactly where he had been shot, but there was an obvious exit wound on the right side of his face. It looked to Calo as though Young had been shot in the back of the head.

Lieutenant Jonathyn Priest took the witness stand. He was the commanding officer of the department's major crimes division, and he had interviewed Jack Bishop at noon on Sunday, May 8, 2005. When the lieutenant had asked if there had been any kind of problem at the party, Bishop had told him that a group of young men had been denied entry between ten and eleven P.M., and afterward one member of the group had grown belligerent. Young had escorted him outside. Bishop did not know what transpired, but apparently Young regretted his actions. When he returned, he said to Bishop: "I shouldn't have grabbed him by the neck."

The prosecution called Dr. Amy Martin, a forensic pathologist with the Office of the Medical Examiner in Denver. She had found three gunshot wounds in Detective Young's body: One bullet had entered his head at the corner of his left eye, passed behind his eye socket and through his sinuses, and then broken his jaw. A second bullet had penetrated his torso from the left and come to rest on the far side of his chest after grazing Young's diaphragm, damaging his spleen, puncturing his stomach twice, and injuring his liver. Martin had to perform an X-ray to locate the third bullet. It had entered Young's body on the left side, shattering a rib in the process, and had blasted through both pumping chambers of his heart, before lodging in another rib on the right side of his torso. It was this hidden wound, through the center of his being, that had caused the gravest injuries. "Even if he had been shot right in Denver Health Medical Center, that heart wound would have been very difficult to repair," said Martin.

As the reporters in the jury box craned to study the expression on Kelly Young's face, I had the urge to spirit her out of there—though of course she was the one who belonged, and we were the intruders. Her husband's best friend put his hand on her knee, in a gesture of comfort.

The prosecution called Martin Vigil, the lead detective on the case, who took the stand wearing one of his trademark bow ties. Several of the young men who had gone to Salon Ocampo with Gómez García had told the detective that after being denied entrance to the party, they had gone to a pool hall. While the young men were playing pool, one of them heard Gómez García state that he was going to go back and shoot the officer, according to the homicide detective. Later that night, one of the young men had asked Gómez García if he'd done something stupid. "He stated that he had shot the cop," Vigil told the courtroom.

A look of resignation came over Gómez García's face.

Vigil admitted that the police had never recovered the murder weapon. Apparently Gómez García had buried it in the desert somewhere between Denver and Los Angeles. The police did have a witness who said Gómez García had confessed to committing the crime—his girlfriend, Sandra Rivas. During the cross-examination, however, defense attorney Fernando Freyre pointed out that at first Rivas had maintained that her boyfriend was innocent, and suggested that perhaps the police had pressured her into changing her story by bringing up the question of whether she possessed legal status. Initially Vigil could not remember whether Sandra Rivas had told him that she had entered the country without authorization, but after Freyre allowed him to refresh his memory by reading a transcript of the interview, the homicide detective confirmed that she had done so.

"And then, by an amazing coincidence, right after the immigration topic comes up, she starts to say that Raúl did confess to her?" asked Freyre in a scornful tone.

"My recollection is not right after," said Vigil. "That was a long interview."

He conceded the police had no fingerprints, no hair, no fiber, no blood, no bodily fluids—no physical evidence of any kind that linked Gómez García to the murder. The testimony of key witnesses such as Sandra Rivas was pretty much all they had. Freyre's line of questioning made me wonder whether this case would have been solved if the Denver Police Department had been rounding up and deporting illegal aliens as advocated by Congressman Tom Tancredo. Would the Rivas family have cooperated with the police under those circumstances?

Judge Larry Naves decided the prosecutors had amassed sufficient evidence to warrant a trial. Later, at a separate hearing, the defense team argued that Judge Naves should suppress certain statements that Raúl Gómez García had made while he was in custody in Mexico. Freyre maintained that his client would never have made the remarks if he had been given a Miranda warning to let him know that anything he said could be used against him (Mexican law requires no such thing). At the hearing, United States Marshal José Chavarría testified that he was in a rental car with two Mexican federal agents immediately after Gómez García's arrest when the suspect started asking questions. "He was asking specifically which of the two police officers, which of the two had died, the thin one or the big one," said Chavarría. The big one had died, Chavarría had replied. "His response was that he hoped it was the one who was choking him." It was damning testimony, and the judge ruled that the jury would be allowed to hear it. The defendant had lost the second significant skirmish in the legal battle.

"Bad day for Gómez García," I observed to the chief of detectives after the proceedings had concluded.

"Good day for Kelly Young," he replied.

Television crews hovered at the door of the courtroom to catch the accused man as he left—cameras weren't allowed inside, making Gómez García's shuffling entrances and exits their only available footage. I waited until the commotion died down before walking out. It was jarring to leave behind the emotional universe of the courtroom and enter the grand marble hallway I knew so well from other occasions. Halfway down the hall, I stopped to chat with John's executive assistant, who was standing guard outside of the mayor's office.

"You just missed Gómez García," I told him. "Could have had a nice shot of Raúl and the mayor."

"I know," John's executive assistant replied. "That's what we're trying to avoid."

19

PORTRAIT OF A PARIAH

That spring, both Marisela and Yadira had signed up for a class called Latinas and Latinos in American Society, which was being taught by Lisa Martínez. Clara had not signed up to take the sociology course, but every other Latino student I knew was there—Rosalba, Matías, Jaime, Alfonso, Gustavo, and Dulce—as well as half a dozen Latinos I did not recognize, along with a handful of students who appeared to be Anglo. Not until I read their student biographies posted on the class website did I understand that many of these Anglo-looking students also had Latino relatives. The concentration of Latinos was unusual, and sometimes I felt as though I had walked into a class at Roosevelt High. It must have felt that way to the girls, too, because as the quarter unfolded they became increasingly like the students they had been when we first met—they shed their sullen silences and became outspoken again.

At the beginning of the spring quarter, Marisela had dashed into class wearing dress slacks and a nice blouse. It was short enough to reveal a tattoo of branching blue fire on her lower back—her street self, peeking out from beneath her business attire. Yadira, wearing a lime green sleeveless T-shirt, nursed an orange Gatorade nearby. "Today we are going to talk about the demographics of Latinos in the United States: birth rates, death rates, fertility rates, and migration," Martínez announced. "Those of you who have taken class with me before know that I love, love, *love* data." She wrote down a series of Web links on the whiteboard. "You can have your friends over some Saturday night, get a pizza, and some drinks, and look at U.S. Census data!"

The students laughed. All of a sudden, they had become topical. On the evening news, talking heads were dissecting the merits of the McCain-Kennedy immigration bill and the likelihood of comprehensive reform and the changing demographics of America. Martínez wanted the students to understand the sociology behind the politics. The slice of the U.S. population pie that was Latino had climbed from 9 to 12.5 percent in the last decade. Mexicans remained by far the largest group, in terms of foreign-born Latinos living in the United States, but in recent years the number of people coming from other countries in Central and South America had increased even more rapidly.

That was half of the demographic story—the story of *who* was coming. An even bigger shift had occurred in terms of *where* the newcomers were living. Martínez displayed a large map of the United States, similar to the color-coded map of the 2000 presidential election that defined states as red or blue. On Martínez's map, individual counties had been assigned certain colors according to how much their Latino populations had increased. Darker colors indicated greater gains, and counties that were dark purple had experienced gains of at least 200 percent in the last decade.

"What do you see?" Martínez asked.

"Well, the border states—it seems like they are not growing as fast," volunteered Marisela.

"Right," said Martínez. "Some counties in Texas even lost Latinos."

Dark purple appeared in unexpected places: Colorado, Georgia, the Carolinas, and throughout the Midwest. There were even two dark purple blotches in upstate New York.

"And look at Alaska!" said Rosalba.

"Yeah, even up there," said Martínez. "And you thought there were only polar bears in Alaska."

Martínez asked the students to think about why immigrants were moving to what she called "new destination" cities in the United States, such as Denver. The following week, she asked if anybody had figured out why immigrants were moving to the interior of the United States.

"I kind of looked into it," one student volunteered. "I think it's mostly low-wage jobs, like meat processing."

"Absolutely," confirmed Martínez. "In the Midwest, farms and meatpacking plants used to rely on working-class whites, and now they increasingly rely upon Latinos. In Arkansas, you've got Tyson chicken—and that's why you see what's happening there, in terms of the Latino population."

The class spent several weeks examining Latino representation in the labor market, then studied how educational achievement was distributed across ethnic groups. Nationally, only 11 percent of Anglos left school without attaining a high school degree, compared with 43 percent of Latinos. Of all foreign-born Latinos, Mexican immigrants had the least amount of education: Forty-nine percent of Mexicans left school with less than a complete high school education. Only 5.6 percent of them finished four years of college.

"In my family, my sister wanted to go to college in North Carolina, and my mom was like: Why go so far? What if you get sick?" said a *mexicana* student. "She changed her plans to stay in Colorado."

"Right," said Martínez. "The cultural dynamic of parents who don't want their children to go far away. You have to be at most a two-hour drive from mom and dad so they can bring you *tamales*. It's like: 'Oh, *mija*, what's going to happen to my baby!'"

And they studied theories of assimilation. Early sociologists such as Robert Park and Milton Gordon believed that immigrants had to surrender their cultural values and adopt the norms of the dominant society to become fully assimilated. Later sociologists dubbed these theories "the Anglo-conformity model," and pointed out the immigrants that Park and Gordon had studied came from Europe, just like the original colonists who had settled in America. It wasn't that hard for them to conform, given their shared European heritage. Cultural pluralists argued that non-European immigrants needed to retain elements of their own cultures. Instead of the melting pot, the pluralists argued for a salad bowl, in which ingredients could be tossed together without losing their integrity.

"I have a question," said Marisela. "So Park and Gordon—do they believe that we eventually lose all of our culture?"

"Not only did they say it *would* happen, they said that it *had* to happen," replied Martínez. "They thought it was a good thing. Pluralism models, on the other hand, say it's good to hold on to your ethnic identity—that doing so gives you support in a society where you are experiencing discrimination."

By Marisela's thunderous expression, I understood her to be a cultural pluralist.

Martínez asked what Alejandro Portes, a contemporary Cuban American sociologist, meant by the term *segmented assimilation*. A student said it had to do with skin color.

"Yes," said Martínez. "Why is identifiability huge?"

"Because the color line is always there," answered Dulce. "You can shed your culture or your language, but you can't shed your skin color."

"Right. It's harder to become fully assimilated with skin color difference. If you are distinct in some way, then the assimilation process is not as linear. Maybe you are a Latino person who speaks English, and maybe you put ketchup on your hot dog, but structural assimilation will still be hard, if you remain identifiable."

"We are in higher education, and that's where the color line becomes an issue for us," observed Dulce.

Over the next few weeks, Martínez assigned several readings on the subject of identity. This part of the course resonated in particular with Yadira, who harbored lingering questions about how society wanted to define her. Along with Matías and Jaime, she was taking another course that also dealt with this matter of how social interactions shaped individuals, called Portrait of a Pariah: The Politics of Exclusion. The professor had assigned a list of readings about individuals labeled as pariahs, and Yadira had just finished reading *Rahel Varnhagen: The Life of a Jewess,* by Hannah Arendt. Varnhagen was a nineteenth-century woman who escaped ostracism in her native Prussia by moving to France. When she changed countries, Varnhagen experienced an entirely new sense of self, as a result of being liberated from anti-Semitism. One day, several students began discussing Portrait of a Pariah during a break in Martínez's class.

"I'm thinking that immigrants are like pariahs," said Jaime.

"What's a pariah?" Marisela wanted to know.

"An outcast in society," Jaime told her. "And there's no way to move up."

"Welcome to America!" cried Marisela.

During the spring quarter, the national debate over immigration reached a crescendo as the U.S. House of Representatives and U.S. Senate battled over how best to reform the country's immigration laws. Basically, the House wanted to crack down and the Senate wanted to offer amnesty. Senators unwittingly teased Marisela and Yadira by suggesting they might create a path to citizenship in the near term; both girls desperately wanted to believe this type of reform might happen while they were still students, in time to solve the dilemma of what would occur after graduation. Marisela threw herself into her organizing job, recruiting Mexican immigrants to attend a series of rallies that were going to take place in Colorado through May. She imagined the rallies would persuade Washington politicians to fix all her problems, in the way hosts of Spanish-language television game shows provided miraculous answers to the impossible prayers of their contestants. Yadira was more cautious. While she wanted to believe in sweeping reform, she feared letting her hopes run away with her. What if the politicians accomplished nothing, or what if they passed the sort of bill that would make her life worse? The raging debate made Yadira uneasy. She preferred the status quo to an unknown future.

Meanwhile, immigration became the main subject of discussion over in the gold-domed capitol building, where state representatives were proposing and killing bills on the topic at an alarming pace. Immigration had zoomed to the top of public opinion polls, and state elected officials of every political bent were scrambling to take a stand on the issue. That session, legislators spent a day debating whether to require Colorado voters to present a passport or birth certificate before they could vote. The county clerks (who would have been forced to implement the new legislation) torpedoed that bill. The legislators also debated requiring public schools to ask students about their status, and that notion died, too. Then they considered prohibiting all illegal aliens who were arrested from posting bond, but the only problem was that the state reimbursed counties for holding inmates on a per diem basis, and one of the unintended consequences of such a bill would have been to blow up the state budget. Other bills sailed through the legislature: One required local police departments to report all foreign-born inmates to the federal authorities, while another required individuals purchasing a car in Colorado to prove they were a citizen or a legal resident before being given the title to their vehicle.

In the midst of the political turmoil, at a benefit dinner for Metro State University, where John was being honored as a Metro State Person of the Year, state representative Terrance Carroll, a fellow Democrat, walked over to tell us about another noteworthy bill.

"How are you?" John asked.

"I'm tired," Carroll confessed.

"Immigration is a big, nasty issue," replied John.

"Oh, yeah," acknowledged Carroll. "The Republicans in the state legislature were trying to pass this bill that some people were calling the Hickenlooper bill—"

"The Hickenlooper bill?" I repeated.

"Yeah," said Carroll. "It would have made employers responsible if an employee committed a crime. But we killed it in committee."

"See, you shouldn't have done that," John advised. "You should let them hang themselves. You should pick something that is completely anti-business, like that bill, find a few Democrats who would benefit from voting for it, and let it go through. Then the governor would have to veto it, and the Republicans would look like chumps."

In other words, John thought immigration was a wedge issue that could work for Democrats instead of against them. He thought the issue could divide the Republican party in two—pitting social conservatives against fiscal conservatives—and he wanted Democrats to use the issue to lure business into their camp.

"That's not a bad idea," said Carroll, grinning.

Not long afterward, immigration surfaced again at the annual fundraiser for the Denver Public Schools Foundation. Recently, Cole Middle School had received its fourth consecutive rating of unsatisfactory, and now the state board of education was in the middle of restructuring the school. Meanwhile, the school board had just selected John's former chief of staff, Michael Bennet, to serve as superintendent, in the hopes that he could manage to bring about a revolution. Ever since John had pledged to give scholarships to all the students at Cole, he had been trying to find enough money to extend the promise to every student in the district. He and Michael Bennet had just met with the man who would become the primary benefactor of the citywide scholarship program: oilman Tim Marquez, who had graduated from Denver's Abraham Lincoln High School. Marquez had told John privately that he and his wife would give a $50 million matching gift to establish the scholarship fund. They were still wrestling with the question of undocumented students. Marquez wanted to be scrupulous about observing the law, and his lawyers were telling him he should not fund students who lacked papers through a nonprofit that received federal tax breaks, but Marquez hated the idea of excluding anybody. He believed that his own grandfather might have entered the country illegally.

At the school foundation gala, Bryant-Webster K–8 School wowed the well-heeled crowd with its pint-sized mariachi band. Some of the

children were smaller than their instruments, yet they belted out mariachi ballads in ornate suits as if they already knew about heartbreak.
Then dancers from Skinner Middle School took over the stage to the
throb of hip-hop. I glanced up and locked eyes with Yadira's youngest
sister, Laura. The last time we saw each other, I had made her cry; now
she smiled at me in the middle of her dance routine. My two worlds col-
lided. Nobody else in the swanky hotel ballroom could see that Laura's
world was collapsing, nor could they see how we were all complicit. Her
mother was stuck in Mexico after buying a stolen identity to sort our
cast-off clothing, while her stepfather paid the rent by laying sewer pipe
to and from all the suburban homes that the developers in this room
kept building. And here was Laura, dancing for us while we drank our
cocktails. Soon afterward, I was driving along Speer Boulevard, a thor-
oughfare named for a bygone mayor of Denver, when I passed under
a sign offering traffic information. "Expect delays on Speer Boulevard
on May 1," the sign said in bright yellow lights, and it was not talking
about the weather.

20

Yo Pago Impuestos

Immigrant rights rallies were being planned for Monday, May 1, 2006, in major cities around the country. For weeks, Marisela had been stealing hours away from her schoolwork to attend planning meetings about the march that would take place in Denver. She had also been shooting text messages to other student leaders, and talking up the event on local Spanish-language radio stations. Now the organizers had asked Marisela to address the crowd at the conclusion of the march, and she was in the middle of preparing her remarks. Several days before the rally, Lisa Martínez was halfway through a lecture on affirmative action when she allowed her students to enjoy a five-minute break.

"Are you guys excited for Monday?" asked Alfonso.

"Yeah!" said Matías. "We're making posters. We've got glitter and sparkly stuff!"

"What are your posters about?" Martínez inquired.

"May first!" called out Marisela.

"I heard on the radio that the Minutemen are going to try to kill Mexicans!" said Rosalba excitedly. "You know what my dad says? He says he's an Hour Man!"

The class erupted into catcalls.

"How old is he?" asked Matías in a wondering tone.

On the night before the march, Theta Theta Nu hosted a poster-making session in the girls' old dorm, Johnson-McFarlane. I found Marisela and Omar in the common room, watching a Spanish-language game show called *Bailando por un Sueño* (Dancing for a Dream)— poor people were competing to fulfill expensive aspirations by dancing in a televised competition. Clara arrived in flip-flops and a spangled gypsy skirt, and Yadira showed up in a scarlet sleeveless T-shirt and jeans. Other sorority sisters appeared in matching white windbreakers bearing the Greek letters for Theta Theta Nu. Soon a dozen students sprawled on the floor of the lounge—eleven Latinos, one Anglo who was majoring in Spanish, and one punk with a Mohawk who thought that anything illegal was totally cool.

"Okay, you guys," said Marisela, turning down the television. "I went to an organizing meeting today. We need to bring American flags, and we need marshals."

"What do they do?" Matías asked.

"They scream things and stay in the middle of the street and stuff like that," said Marisela. "If you want to do that, wear a red T-shirt."

"We want to sit with you on the stage!" begged Jaime.

Marisela instructed them all to make signs with English on one side and Spanish on the other. She read suggested slogans from a list, and the students settled into work. Marisela scrawled SOMOS AMÉRICA! on one side of her poster and WE ARE AMERICA! on the other. Clara wrote YO PAGO IMPUESTOS and I PAY TAXES. Meanwhile, Yadira took forever to complete one word, as if the quality of her handwriting were directly correlated to the outcome of the march. Everyone stuck to the script except for Matías, who drew bubble letters that said: MINUTEMEN ARE NAZIS!

Jacinda tried to write NINGÚN SER HUMANO ES ILEGAL (NO HUMAN BEING IS ILLEGAL), but couldn't remember where the accent in *ningún* went. The others teased her.

"You don't understand," Jacinda replied. "Me and accents don't get along. It's like me and Tom Tancredo. He's stupid, that's what he is."

On the TV, a Latino couple dressed as 1950s greasers began a flamboyant interpretation of "Greased Lightning," the hit song from the film *Grease*. The man's brother was paralyzed from the waist down and they hoped to win money for an operation. Marisela regarded the pair critically. "I don't think they're doing so good," she pronounced.

"Do you watch this show regularly?" Jacinda inquired.

"I watch this every single Sunday night."

"Hey, I saw on CNN that they have these racist video games now, like one called *Border Patrol,* and you shoot Mexicans who are crossing the border!" Jaime announced.

"*What!*" exclaimed the Spanish major.

The conversation turned to the subject of housing. After sophomore year, students had to compete for rooms in a lottery. Marisela and

Zahra had secured a basement apartment in an older building euphe-
mistically misnamed La Chateau. Clara had also won a room in La
Chateau, which she was planning to share with Angela, the old friend
from middle school who had come to Marisela's *quinceañera*. Yadira
had not been able to select a room at all, however, and she was currently stuck on a waiting list. One of the sorority sisters asked what she
was planning to do next year.

"I'm going to live off campus with my boyfriend and my little sisters," Yadira announced. "We just started looking for apartments this
week."

Yadira's two younger sisters had recently moved out of the apartment they were sharing with Jesús and back into their aunt and uncle's
place, while their younger brother remained with his father; Yadira
refused to say what had precipitated the change in her sisters' living
arrangements. The idea of Yadira playing mother to her siblings—on
top of going to college and working part-time—seemed ambitious. I
wondered if she would be able to stay in school. As usual, though,
Yadira gave little outward indication of her internal stress, and kept
her voice light as she said, "I'm trying to get something close to the
campus."

"What price-range apartment are you looking for?" Jaime asked.

"I don't know," said Yadira. "I'm going to live with Juan because I
can't pay for everything by myself."

Jaime lowered his voice. "Can you put it under your name?"

"I don't know," said Yadira quietly. "That's a good question. Juan
doesn't have papers either."

She began meticulously outlining the words she had already written
on her sign. It said: HOY MARCHO, MAÑANA VOTO . . . AND YOU WON'T
STOP ME!!

Jaime pointed out that Yadira had put Spanish and English on the
same side.

"I know," said Yadira. "And on the other side, *el reverso*."

In the morning, they donned red T-shirts to mark their status as marshals and drove to Viking Park, a green patch of land located in Tancredo's childhood neighborhood. Everybody else had dressed in white.
It seemed as though every other person carried an American flag. Most
of the marchers clutched tiny flags, but I also saw a small boy who had
tied a large flag around his neck so that it streamed behind him like a

superhero's cape, and an older man who wore a Mexican flag draped over his shoulder like a serape. An American Indian strode by carrying no flag at all, wearing suede knee-high moccasins with shakers sewn onto them, so that he made a sound like maracas. One marcher carried a sign that said: "ANTI-IMMIGRANT? THEN SWIM BACK TO EUROPE!" Another woman had copied a familiar passage from the Bible onto her sign:

> The stranger who resides with you shall be as the native
> among you, and you shall love him as yourself, for you
> were aliens in the Land of Egypt.
>
> —*Leviticus*
> 19:34

Hundreds of marchers wielded identical sheets of aqua paper that had been handed out by organizers, which declared: I AM NOT A CRIMINAL. Across the country, similar crowds flooded the downtowns of Los Angeles, Chicago, Phoenix, and New York. An economic boom that seemed like it would never stop had been drawing immigrants to the United States for fifteen years now, but these workers had remained largely invisible, and the marches represented the first time that the rest of society saw the newcomers gather in such large numbers. When television stations broadcast aerial footage of the rallies, the American public was startled to see how many maids and janitors and roofers had taken to the streets. In Denver, the crowd spilled onto Speer Boulevard and flowed higgledy-piggledy toward the skyscrapers of downtown, paralyzing traffic along the way. The river of white grew so long that it took several hours to pass through the city's financial district. Office workers emerged from their glass towers to witness the spectacle and broke into applause when they apprehended the march's extraordinary size. Carried away by this warm reception, one of the marchers shouted: "*Viva Pancho Villa! Yo amo Colorado!* I love you!"

I found Yadira and Juan in Lower Downtown. We searched for Clara and Marisela, but it was impossible to locate them in the multitude. After streaming through the city's financial district, the marchers filled Civic Center Park, the sixteen-acre expanse of formal flower beds that lies between Denver's City and County Building and Colorado's gold-domed statehouse. Later, police would estimate the size of the crowd at more than one hundred thousand. Drawn by the noisy enormity of what was happening below, lawmakers on the third floor of the Capitol clambered to stand on the balcony and gawk at the sea of people. I recognized several members who had grappled with the question of in-state tuition. Over at the other end of Civic Center Park, my husband abandoned his desk in the City and County Building to walk among the demonstrators. When they saw him, people started calling out, *"El alcalde! El alcalde!"* (The mayor! The mayor!) Then somebody wrapped him in an American flag, which he wore like a robe as he meandered among the people.

Yadira and Juan threaded their way through the crowd, trying to secure a vantage point from which they could see Marisela. Suddenly Clara materialized beside them, grinning. The sun hammered down without mercy, and Clara pulled a jacket over her head to shield herself from its glare, while Yadira fanned herself with one of the fliers. Confusingly, most of the people on the grassy slope in front of the Capitol had their backs toward the makeshift stage set up on the steps of the building; it was like being at a rock concert with the crowd facing the wrong way. Finally, we turned around, too, and suddenly understood: It was breathtaking to look back at that ocean of white. There were so many people, and from this slope, you could see them all.

A middle-aged man wearing a white *guayabera* shirt pushed past, holding a framed map over his head, sun glinting off the glass. "This is from before the Treaty of Guadalupe Hidalgo!" he called out. "This is from 1847! It shows Colorado back when it was part of Mexico!" Turning around to face the stage, I spotted Omar on the steps of the statehouse, wearing a T-shirt with a picture of an American flag on it. He had found himself at the epicenter of a political movement, thanks to his love life. Marisela stood beside him, wearing a red marshal's T-shirt, with her hands in the back pockets of her blue jeans. She had curled her hair into cascading ringlets and had on large hoop earrings. Federico Peña stood nearby. After becoming the first Latino mayor of Denver, Peña had served as U.S. transportation secretary under President Bill Clinton. "I am here today to ask that we recognize the immigrant workers who come here to better their lives and send money back home," Peña told the crowd. "We should admire them for cleaning our buildings, building our homes, cooking our meals, cleaning our houses, producing our oil, digging our ditches, and fighting today in Iraq!"

Cheers drowned out his words, as the crowd began chanting, "USA, USA, USA!"

A series of other speakers followed, and then finally it was Marisela's turn. She bounded over to the microphone and hollered: *"Justicia para todos! Nosotros somos América!"* (Justice for all! We are America!)

Marisela stood with her left leg forward a bit, rocking back and forth as she spoke. Her right hand gripped the microphone stand, and I could see her many gold rings glinting in the bright sun.

"Hoy, este día, me recuerda al movimiento chicano, el movimiento de derechos civiles, el movimiento para los trabajadores migratorios! Hoy, este día, estámos pidiendo justicia, y libertad, y queremos amnistía! Es nuestra responsibilidad de seguir con este movimiento, para decirle a nuestros representantes del Congreso que no vamos a salir, y si nos hacen salir, vamos a regresar!" (Today I am reminded of the Chicano movement, the civil rights movement, the migrant farmworker movement! Today we are asking for justice and freedom and we want amnesty! It is everyone's responsibility to continue this movement, to tell our congressional representatives that we aren't going to leave, and if they make us leave, then we are going to come back!)

One hundred thousand marchers roared their approval. When we first met at Roosevelt High, I never imagined that one day I would see Marisela standing next to Federico Peña on the steps of the Capitol building, addressing such a crowd. Yet it seemed significant that we had arrived here—that Marisela wanted to have a say about what transpired inside the government buildings at either end of Civic Center Park. It was such an American hope for a Mexican girl to harbor.

Marisela flashed the crowd a huge grin, then scoured the crowd for her sorority sisters. Clara and Yadira stood on their tiptoes to wave. "Marisela!" they yelled. *"Aquí!"* Spotting them, Marisela grabbed Omar by the hand, and together they jumped off the side of the staircase. Everybody wanted to give Marisela a hug. She did not stay long, however; she had brought her brothers and her sister along, and at the moment they were unsupervised. Fabián was at home sleeping, and Josefa was cleaning houses. She had heard her daughter on the radio, urging *la gente* to put on *ropa blanca y marcharan,* and the only reason that she was not in Civic Center Park to hear Marisela speak was that her boss had threatened to fire her if she failed to show up for work.

I wandered over to the outdoor amphitheater where John had delivered his State of the City speech. This was where CAIR and the Minute-men had planned to stage a countergathering. I found Chief Whitman listening to a woman who was holding a sign that said, "I DON'T WANT TO LIVE IN THE UNITED STATES OF MEXICO." She was complaining that somebody had dumped a bottle of water on her head. I asked the chief how things were going.

"This woman says she was assaulted," he replied. "That's about the only thing that's happened."

Departing marchers were colliding with arriving counterdemonstrators, however, and it looked like things might escalate. Marshals fanned out to ward off the marchers, who were now chanting: "Mexican American, proud to be American!" A counterprotester yelled: "Go back to Mexico!" Television and radio reporters descended on the fracas.

"Hey, Walt?" Chief Whitman said into his radio. "Do you have another intervention team?"

Marshals valiantly broke up arguments, but there were too many protesters and counterprotesters and not enough marshals.

"You're a racist!" yelled one of the marchers.

"On what basis? On what basis are you calling me a racist?!" hurled back a woman dressed as Uncle Sam. "My parents came from Ireland and got their J-9s! Are you legal? It's all about abiding by the law! Go to the end of the line!"

"I took your job because I'm better at it!" yelled a marcher who was waving a Mexican flag.

"Oh, yeah?" taunted Uncle Sam. "Whose Social Security number did you use?"

Police officers filed into the fray. The intervention team formed a human barrier, dividing the combatants. Everybody was screaming except the police officers, who stood stony-faced in the hot sun.

"Looking good, guys, looking good," said the officer in charge.

It was Captain Mike Calo, whom I recognized from his appearance on the witness stand in the Gómez García hearing. He had been inside Salon Ocampo, and maybe that meant he understood the marchers; on the other hand, he had carried Donnie Young out of that place on a stretcher, so maybe he sided with Uncle Sam. It was impossible to tell as he wore a rigorously neutral expression. He had a job to do, and he was a professional. At Calo's instruction, a second row of officers moved alongside the first, and then the two rows of officers slowly stepped away from each other, pushing the two groups back and creating an empty zone between them. Calo walked up and down this zone of peace, talking quietly to the cops, making sure they stayed calm.

Chief Whitman called a total of sixty police officers to the scene, and they waited until even the most rabid demonstrators finally went home. That evening, news of the confrontation got equal time with footage of the rally, despite the fact that only several dozen had participated in the ugly face-off, while many tens of thousands had marched; 9NEWS cut away from a scene of the name-calling in the amphitheater to an interview with Congressman Tom Tancredo. He claimed that public opinion polls shifted in his favor every time illegal Mexicans took to the streets. "We hope they hold rallies like this in every city every week of the year," he said gleefully. On television, it looked like a draw, but that's not what it had felt like at the scene. Nobody had ever imagined that undocumented immigrants and their supporters would assemble in such numbers, and the sight of so many humble people marching with such pride had made an indelible impression on everyone who saw the march, including me.

21

LIVE FROM THE BORDER

Two weeks after the rallies, President Bush delivered a major address on the subject of immigration. It was the middle of May 2006, and the girls had only a couple of weeks left in the school year. After dinner, Luke tagged along with Clara and Yadira when the girls went upstairs to catch the news. Yadira found coverage of Bush on Univision, but Luke objected when she paused there.

"Find CNN," he urged.

Larry King sat in a folding chair in the desert, just outside of San Ysidro, California. A breeze lifted King's thinning hair, while behind him an endless series of immigrants snuck across the U.S.–Mexico border, obviously breaking the law.

"Tonight, the president in a prime-time address announces plans to send up to six thousand National Guard troops to the United States–Mexico border," said Larry King. "We come to you live from that border with immediate reaction from all sides of the immigration debate that's dividing America!"

CNN cut to a shot of Bill Richardson, the governor of New Mexico, in a television studio.

"It seems the president endorsed a legalization plan for the eleven million undocumented workers in America," Richardson observed. "That's encouraging. The fact that he also wants to see the law enforced—those that knowingly hire illegal workers should be punished and penalized—that's positive."

"*That* I agree with," commented Luke.

The camera cut away to a Latina woman in a close-fitting suit. "Look!" Yadira ordered. "It's María Elena Salinas!" Salinas worked as an anchor on *Noticiero Univision*, and the girls viewed her as a celebrity. Luke shrugged at their excitement and logged on to Yadira's laptop to check the BBC website. CNN ran a clip of Bush's speech. "We're a nation of laws, and we must enforce our laws," the president intoned. "We're also a nation of immigrants, and we must uphold that tradition, which has strengthened our country in so many ways. These are not contradictory goals. America can be a lawful society and a welcoming society at the same time."

"He's reading it," said Clara dismissively.

"They all read major speeches, Clara," chided Luke.

He turned up the volume on Yadira's laptop as the BBC site ran a story about a rancher whose property was invaded regularly by unwanted border traffic.

"This poor guy has, like, illegal Mexicans coming through his backyard!" he marveled.

"Then he should move!" retorted Yadira.

On CNN, U.S. Representative Dana Rohrabacher of Orange County, California, argued against legalization. "The fact is, if you normalize someone's status who is in this country illegally, and you make them here legally, that is an amnesty. Now whatever they call it, it is a normalization that will create a huge magnet to draw people into our country."

Luke nodded so furiously that he made Yadira's chair squeak, while Yadira pulled one of her fuzzy pink Costco pillows to her chest.

"I don't agree with giving them all citizenship," said Luke. "Why even have immigration laws if you just let everybody in!"

"They're not *all* getting citizenship," corrected Yadira. "Just people who have been here for a long time and have been working hard."

"They should do it the right way," argued Luke. "There are rules. They come here and get free medical care, and get on welfare!"

"Illegal immigrants don't get welfare!" Yadira disputed.

"They go to San Francisco General and they get free health care that *we* pay for!"

"But they also pay taxes, Luke," Clara pointed out.

"You know my stand," he responded. "Ship 'em out!"

I noticed that they were bickering like siblings—the running conflict had become familiar, even comfortable, and it did not stifle their mutual affection.

Lou Dobbs began bashing President Bush.

"Ah, CNN," Luke sighed. "It's time to change to Fox News."

"What channel?" asked Yadira.

"Up, up."

But Fox News was running a feel-good human-interest story, so they flipped back to CNN.

"What do you do with twelve million illegals?" King asked.

"What you do is create an earned legalization plan based on good behavior," answered Bill Richardson. "You set standards, benchmarks: If they speak English, if they pay back taxes, if they pay fines for coming in illegally, background checks, if they participate in civic activities. You put them to the back of the line, not ahead of those that are trying to get here legally."

As King asked María Elena Salinas to comment, Clara called out: "Look at the description of her!"

The tagline read: "Award-winning television journalist with *Noticiero Univision*. Father was illegal alien."

"I did not know that," said Yadira. Salinas had seemed so far above her—when all along they had this in common.

Dana Rohrabacher and Bill Richardson appeared side by side in a split screen.

"These fifteen to twenty million people, they should not be taking the jobs of Americans, and they should not be getting the education money, the health-care money, the housing subsidies, and all the other things that we provide American citizens," said Rohrabacher. "If we cut them off from that, from the benefits and the jobs, there will be a trend going in the right direction. They will start leaving."

"Well, I just looked at the bill that Dana sponsored and the House passed, and it's very clear," responded Richardson. "It makes felons out of the eleven million undocumented workers. And what about their kids? Two-thirds have children that are U.S. citizens."

"Why aren't you concerned about *our* children?" interjected Rohrabacher.

"That citizenship is revoked," continued Richardson. "And I think that's wrong. You put up a wall on the border. America—the country that tore down the Berlin Wall, that stands for freedom!"

"These are very good people who are coming to the United States," conceded Rohrabacher. "These are wonderful people, but we can't afford to give them our education dollars. Education in our state—I don't know about your state, Bill—is going to hell because of illegal immigration, as well as health care and criminal justice."

Eventually, the girls lost interest in the talking heads, and began doing their homework. Luke left to write a marketing plan for a business class, while Clara studied the shapes of various types of human skulls for her course on the evolution of life. Yadira read about the Spanish conquest of Latin America. Bush appeared on the TV over and over again, but the girls mostly ignored him; Clara glanced up only when CNN reported that approval ratings of Bush's immigration plan had jumped from 42 percent to 67 percent. Later Yadira stopped to listen to a discussion of guest worker plans. Then she said, "This issue is really big."

"What do you mean?" I asked.

"I don't know—there's just a lot to figure out."

There were no easy solutions, and the girls had become mature enough to recognize this.

Later that spring, Lisa Martínez announced to her class that they were going to hold a mock immigration forum. The students had to hash out the nation's immigration policy, after she assigned them certain roles. "I hope I get to be Tom Tancredo!" Jaime called out. Instead, Martínez asked him to play the role of a sociologist who provided data. Other students played a moderate Republican politician who wanted comprehensive immigration reform, a liberal Democrat whose constituents wanted illegal aliens rounded up, and a director of a human rights organization that served poor people on the border. Martínez asked the rest of the class to act as the media or the general public and ask questions. The mock forum quickly acquired the bite of satire.

"I represent the moderate Republican," announced Consuela, a Theta Theta Nu sister. "We think that sending illegal immigrants back home is unrealistic and difficult to enforce. Therefore we are proposing a guest worker program. We want guest workers to have special IDs, in addition to fingerprint cards, and small blood samples that they will have to carry with them. They need to have these on their person at all times."

A member of the press asked if guest workers could bring their entire families.

"No," said Consuela. "We only want workers here, we don't want families. We just want able-bodied people."

"Senator, since you feel only able-bodied people should come, are you planning to put restrictions on how much sex people can have?" asked Dulce.

Consuela suggested guest workers should abstain from sex for the duration of their time in the United States.

"I have a question for the moderate Republican!" called out Marisela. "With the ID cards, doesn't that remind you of the Nazis, where people had to wear yellow stars that identified them as different? And wouldn't that increase racism and lead to violence?"

"Violence is not our responsibility," replied the moderate Republican. "That's for the local police departments to handle."

Diana, a preppy-looking student who had grown up in the suburbs, raised her hand.

"My main concern is education," she said. "What about my kids? The more immigrants you let in, the less education funding there is for my kids. And what about financial aid for college—are undocumented students going to be eligible?"

Although he was supposed to be playing an objective sociologist, Jaime jumped in and said, "Once the DREAM Act passes, they won't be undocumented anymore."

"So then they are competing with my kids!" retorted Diana.

"They deserve aid too!" bellowed Jaime.

"My kids were born here!"

"You know what? The Republican party feels your pain!" interjected Consuela. "That's also one of our major concerns. This is why our program doesn't promote the idea of families coming here. Vote for me!"

Within a few weeks, the real-world debate ended in disarray, just like the mock immigration forum, when attempts at a compromise between the House of Representatives and the Senate fell apart. Every year, the girls dared to imagine that their problems might be resolved by national leaders, or by their local counterparts, but this never came to pass—the girls just got a little bit older and a little less naive. When Martínez asked her class to make their final presentations, she assigned Marisela to work with Dulce and Diana, the preppy-looking student from the suburbs. For the creative project that was supposed to accompany their oral presentation, the three students decided to make a board game about immigration called "Distance of a Dream." The board consisted of a map of the United States and Mexico, on which they pasted tiny dollar bills and an assortment of small plastic objects from World of Crafts—guitars, cowboy boots, automatic rifles. "Lib-

erty and Justice for All!" the board proclaimed. "Land of the Free!"
On the path leading north, they had drawn footprints. The basic idea
was to start in Mexico, enter the United States, and advance as far as
the White House. Players were subjected to the vagaries of fate in the
form of playing cards:

> You inherited land and sold it for $1 million. You can
> invest in an American company and get a business visa.
> Move to the United States.

> Lose a turn. You need twelve years of work experience
> in your trade to obtain a nonimmigrant work visa.

> You take classes to learn English. Move up one space.

> You commit a felony while in the United States. Go
> back to the beginning of the game.

When it was their turn to deliver an oral presentation, Marisela
plugged her laptop into a console and projected an image onto the front
wall of the classroom. Her classmates hooted at the digital photograph
that served as her laptop's wallpaper—a steamy shot of Marisela and
Omar in club mode.

"Who is *that*?" someone asked.

"Oh, that's just my cousin," Marisela replied evasively.

"Marisela!" objected Jaime. "No, it's not!"

At the moment, Marisela looked like a distant relation of the bombshell in the photo. In her striped silk blouse, black blazer, charcoal gray
slacks, and pointy-toed mules, she could have passed for a banking
executive. Along with Dulce and Diana, Marisela delivered a comprehensive lecture about the history of Latino political movements in the
United States and the current obstacles to political participation faced
by Latinos. Then the students explained their board game. "The whole
purpose of the game is to get your citizenship and be able to vote,"
Dulce said. "The point of making the game was to emphasize that
immigrants—they live by the roll of the dice, by chance."

Marisela interjected: "Me, Yadira, Clara, and a Republican friend
of ours were playing the game, and it's really interesting to play with

254

people like that, to help them understand the issue. It's more than just a philosophical debate—we're playing with people's lives here."

After class, Marisela confessed that in truth playing the game with Luke had been a catastrophe. "Luke got all the lucky cards," she recounted. "First he got the card that said, 'You've graduated from high school. Move forward three spaces.' And then he got another card that said, 'The committee has approved your citizenship. Go all the way to the White House.'" Meanwhile, Clara had gotten stuck with a series of bad-luck cards, such as the one that sent her to jail for five years because her car had a broken taillight. Marisela had tried to tell Luke that he was merely fortunate—not everybody could become a citizen so easily—but he had crowed about his victory and said it proved he was right. You got ahead when you played by the rules. What Luke had not been able to see was that everything had been at stake for Marisela; to him the game was only a game, but for her it was real life. The cards sounded like clever sayings to Luke, while for Marisela they represented the very twisting of fate, the reasons why things happened. She had hoped the game would teach American-born players what it felt like to be somebody whose parents had brought them over the border the wrong way—that it would teach Luke what it felt like to be her—but it had done nothing of the kind. Luke had won without questioning any of his beliefs.

22

CAUTION

S hortly after the girls finished their sophomore year of college, the Colorado state legislature held an extraordinary special session. As the federal government had failed to resolve the nation's immigration issue, state officials around the country had leaped into the void. That year, a total of 570 bills and resolutions would be introduced in the nation's fifty statehouses on the subject of immigration (and more than twice that number would be introduced the following year)—even though everybody agreed that it was a matter that would be better handled at the federal level. States that were ahead of the trend experienced problems: In Arizona, more than 5,000 people ran into issues when registering to vote, even though the vast majority were legal citizens who had recently moved there, according to the *Arizona Republic*. A total of two illegal aliens tried to sign up for welfare benefits. "We said it all along, undocumented immigrants don't get welfare benefits for themselves," Alfredo Gutierrez, a former state senator, told the *Republic*. "They don't use state services. The problem never existed." Yet the fact that making immigration law at the state level appeared to make little or no sense from a policy perspective did not deter elected officials from acting.

In Colorado, the legislature's special session on immigration took place in July 2006, while the girls were on summer break. It was two months before Gómez García was scheduled to return to the City and County Building to face murder charges, and it almost seemed as though the state's lawmakers wanted to put all immigrants on trial. The special session came about after a complicated series of chess moves: For months, Defend Colorado Now had been pushing for a ballot measure that would ban nonemergency services to immigrants who could not prove their legal status, similar to Arizona's Proposition 200. Then the Colorado Supreme Court unexpectedly declared the ballot measure invalid based on a legal technicality. Governor Owens blasted the decision as partisan, and threatened to call the special session to resurrect the moribund ballot measure. This placed Speaker of the House Andrew Romanoff and Senate President Joan Fitz-Gerald—the Democratic leaders newly in control of the state house and state senate—in an awkward position. Romanoff and Fitz-Gerald did not want to appear soft on immigration, which could cost them their majorities in the fall, and so they urged the governor to go ahead and call the special session. They even asked that he expand the scope to include employer sanctions. Romanoff argued that it was better to tackle the immigration issue by statute than by constitutional amendment, as that way the laws would be easier to alter if they produced unintended consequences. Perhaps the Democrats were also motivated to take care of the messy business of immigration in the middle of the summer, when few voters were paying attention, rather than in the fall, when Colorado would pick its next governor.

Governor Owens called legislators back into session at the beginning of July. On Wednesday, July 5, 2006, the day before the special session began, the Joint Budget Committee summoned all state agency heads to testify about what taxpayer dollars they spent on immigrants without legal status. Owens, with a keen sense of political theater, upstaged the Democrats by making a surprise appearance at the hearing. The phalanx of state legislators appeared flummoxed at finding themselves face-to-face with the highest elected official in Colorado. The lawmakers included Abel Tapia of Pueblo, who had argued for in-state tuition during earlier debates, as well as Nancy Spence, who had wondered whether high school dropouts lacked "pride," and Terrance Carroll, who had advocated taking a moral stance in the 9NEWS electronic town hall.

The governor said he thought the committee had framed their inquiry improperly, for the Joint Budget Committee had asked to hear from only seven departments, when additional monies were being spent in public schools and hospitals. Federal law mandated these expenditures, but Owens thought they should be tallied, too. "Let me say that I think that the people that are here illegally almost without exception are good people," said Owens. "I think that if I lived in Mexico and my children were hungry, I would do almost anything I could to feed them. The concern that I have as the representative of the people of

Colorado is how much can we afford. When some of our own people are going without, can we afford to have such an open-door policy to people who happen to make it to Colorado? I'm a moderate when it comes to immigration: I support President Bush's plan, I've debated Pat Buchanan on national TV, I've debated Lou Dobbs on national TV on the issue of illegal immigration. However, having said that, it has some huge costs in Colorado, and I don't think these costs are being properly recognized today." In terms of Medicaid expenditures, which were not being examined by the Joint Budget Committee, Owens said that the state had records of 8,542 births to parents who appeared not to have legal status, which had cost the state $30 million. "It comes down to about twenty-four children born a day, courtesy of the Colorado taxpayer," the governor observed. "That is about one per hour that we're paying for. That is a significant cost."

Owens proposed adopting a new law that would make it harder for immigrants without proof of valid status to work in Colorado. He suggested the legislature require employers to ask employees to show a state-issued ID. "Colorado could start to lead the way, as one state, without waiting for the federal government to fix the borders," Owens said. "We could simply say, 'To work in Colorado, you have to show us that you're a citizen—and one of the best ways to do that is through our driver's license.'"

"Governor, this is a unique idea I have not heard before, the idea of using the driver's license," observed Bernie Buescher, a first-term Democrat who represented a swing district on the Western Slope, on the other side of the Rocky Mountains. "How would you implement that in the agricultural world? In my area, when the peaches come in, the peaches need to be picked—you can't wait a couple of days. And if those peaches don't get picked, those farmers and agricultural folks lose their investment. The folks who pick the crops tend to move from state to state with the harvest. Have you thought about that issue?"

"Mr. Chairman, that's a very good question, and we have," replied Owens. "You could do a waiver. You could do a one-month waiver, you could do a six-month waiver. You could set up within the Department of Agriculture a very simple system for agricultural work, where they're not putting down roots. Where it's in fact labor that moves from state to state, you could set up a system to allow that, because you've raised a very good point. You have six days, eight days, three

weeks where you have to get the harvest in, and there wouldn't be time
for many of those people to get a Colorado driver's license or ID card,
even if they were eligible. So you could have that sort of waiver. Those
workers don't come with high social costs, because they in fact move
on to Wyoming to help with the next crop."

The Joint Budget Committee found that state tax dollars were
knowingly spent on immigrants without legal status primarily to jail
criminals and combat the spread of contagious diseases ("I can't even
fathom how to parse out the air an illegal alien breathes or the water
he drinks," testified Dennis Ellis, the executive director of the Colorado
Department of Public Health and the Environment). Also, the Department of Human Services spent about $460,000 per year on undocu-
mented children who lived in abusive homes. To their evident surprise,
the lawmakers learned it was possible to identify local employers who
hired people with names and Social Security numbers that did not
match.

"Can you identify employers that often have mismatches?" Buescher asked Rick Grice, the executive director of the state's Department
of Labor and Employment Standard Policy and Procedure.

"Yes sir," Grice answered.

"I'm trying to think where to go with that," Buescher hemmed.

The business lobby was the most powerful interest group in the
state, and elected officials crossed it at their peril. Buescher quickly
changed the subject. The following morning, Speaker Romanoff
announced a slew of bills, standing with his back to the great windows that looked onto the now-empty lawns of Civic Center Park.
Some forty bills were introduced, most of which had been drafted
hastily. Their sponsors were going to try to ram them through the legislative process with unusual speed, as the elected officials had given
themselves only several days to accomplish work that normally took
months. The scene inside of the gold-domed statehouse quickly degen-
erated into mayhem, as lobbyists scurried around trying to keep track
of what was happening, and individuals from pro-immigrant and anti-
immigrant groups made frantic phone calls to determine when and
where to testify. So many committee hearings were held simultaneously that elected officials jogged up and down staircases trying vainly
to be in two places at once. Meanwhile, construction workers who had
planned to repair the historic building during the normally sleepy sum-

mer months created additional confusion by walling off entire areas of the Capitol with yellow tape that said CAUTION, a warning that seemed apropos, under the circumstances.

Soon enough, most of the legislators got caught up in the strange, frenetic energy careening around the stately marble hallways. Occasionally, someone paused to note that there was something amiss—during one hearing, Terrance Carroll pointed out, "We are in an odd situation where 90 percent of the legal power is in federal hands, and 90 percent of the ramifications are at the local level"—but the legislators seemed incapable of slowing down the special session, which rollicked along with a momentum of its own. Meanwhile, outside of the statehouse, observers looked askance at the weird proceedings. Business leaders buttonholed John to complain that the state was going to pass laws that would place them at a competitive disadvantage. "They should do nothing at all!" railed one businessman. "If Colorado does something, then they'll just drive businesses into neighboring states. I've talked to the governor, I've been to see Andrew and Joan, and they all think that the public is clamoring for something to be done. They think that there is a political necessity that needs to be taken care of. There isn't! We'd all be better off if they just went home!"

Given the speed of the special session, the business community had no time to work out a united front. Dozens of different lobbyists represented various industries at the Capitol, and they were all lobbying for different outcomes, depending on the extent to which their clients depended on low-wage labor. Melanie Mills, an executive vice president for public policy with Colorado Ski Country USA, the trade group that handled marketing and public policy for twenty-five ski resorts in Colorado, told the House Business Affairs & Labor Committee that the governor's idea to require a Colorado ID had a number of flaws. It was a violation of federal labor law to require documents of an individual before they were hired, Mills pointed out; employers could not ask to see the documents until after the person was on the payroll. Mills also observed that international employees typically did not possess local IDs and could not easily obtain them, as local governments were prohibited from verifying visa documents. "Every year, Colorado Ski Country USA hires several thousand people in the months of September and October, and more than twenty thousand people in the month of November," Mills testified. "I question the ability of the government processes to function quickly enough to allow them to hire the number of people that they would need."

The elected officials appeared befuddled by Mills's assertions. The real world always proved so much more complicated than they imagined.

"When somebody comes to look for a job, what do you ask of them?" one state representative wanted to know.

"We can ask about their past employment, and we can tell them that when we hire them, they'll need to provide documents within three days," said Mills. "But we are not allowed to see the documents until they report for work."

"What is it that prevents you from asking?" another representative asked.

"Federal labor law," Mills reiterated patiently.

Out in the hallway, I found two members of the House hobnobbing about the special session. One was a Democrat, the other a Republican.

"It's impressive," the Republican was saying.

"You mean it's impressive that we actually came up with some legislation in a week?" the Democrat replied sarcastically.

"Yeah, it is," the Republican responded. "I think the governor's proposal is very interesting."

The Democrat said in a disgusted tone that the media had gone into a frenzy.

"Sometimes I worry that we're going to get swept up in the whole furor and get carried away and then look back on this with regret," the Republican responded.

"You mean like the Japanese American internment camps?" asked the Democrat.

The Republican nodded.

"Yeah," conceded the Democrat. "Well, it's not as bad as *that*."

Back in the committee hearing, I saw Justino Chávez escort a group of Latino high school students into the room. Chávez wanted them to see their local government in action. After several hours, he took the students out into the hallway, where they huddled around him as he explained the mysteries they had witnessed. Later, I bumped into Marisela, who had come to the statehouse on behalf of her nonprofit organization. She did not testify; instead, she roamed the marble hallways looking for camera crews, in the hopes of offering them a different perspective from what they might otherwise capture. She had streaked her hair blond for the summer and was wearing oversized sunglasses and a T-shirt that bore a political slogan.

The first day of the special session ended in an uproar, after Republicans hijacked a Democratic bill in the Senate that sought to cut services to illegal immigrants by statute. Republicans amended the bill to say the matter should go to the voters—effectively resurrecting the defunct ballot initiative. On the second day of the session, a crafty Democrat who had sided with the Republicans for tactical reasons successfully requested that the bill be laid over, setting in motion its demise. Meanwhile, over in the House, Speaker Romanoff introduced another bill to cut services via statute. It required anybody older than eighteen seeking public assistance to prove legal residency, and listed the federal benefits that those who could not offer such proof were already prohibited from receiving. Because the bill specifically exempted children younger than eighteen, it was supposed to preserve the state's ability to care for children who had the misfortune to be both undocumented and abused. Romanoff's bill answered the governor's call, but it did not change the world. If it passed, Democrats could tell voters they had addressed illegal immigration, yet still sleep soundly. Republicans immediately decried the bill as a do-nothing measure.

Around the statehouse, Republican bills started dying in committee, as Democrats introduced motion after motion to postpone indefinitely—a term used so often that elected officials just referred to it as PI. Generally, the Republicans took their drubbing without complaint, but after Terrance Carroll moved to PI a bill before the State, Veteran, & Military Affairs Committee, his colleague Larry Liston of Colorado Springs protested, saying, "Let's not play politics!"

"Representative Liston, in my opinion, this whole special session is about politics," shot back Paul Weissman of Louisville, Colorado. "It has more to do with robocalls and push polling than it does with making good public policy."

As I left the hearing, I bumped into Dulce, the Chicana student from the University of Denver. Dressed in a tan summer suit, she looked like an aspiring lawmaker herself. She said she had landed an internship at the National Conference of State Legislatures, and seemed poised to enter the middle class. I could not help thinking that Yadira's résumé would compare poorly to her classmate's, for Yadira was spending another summer working at the clothing boutique (the only place she could find employment given her status). It was drizzling and Dulce hurried inside. Justino Chávez walked up, and then a Latina state representative joined us. She asked how Chávez was feeling.

"Oh, kind of like a wetback," he quipped in Spanish, referring at once to the effects of the rain and the frantic debate.

That evening, rumors of a deal swept the statehouse. Supposedly Governor Owens had agreed not to put up a fight when the Democrats moved forward with their plans to kill the Senate bill that would have resurrected the ballot initiative, in exchange for their support of his plan to require employers to ask for a Colorado ID. Within hours, however, new rumors circulated, asserting the deal had fallen apart. Out on the front lawn of the statehouse, I saw Adam Schrager of *9NEWS* standing in the rain, with an assistant shining reflected light onto his face. The evening news shows were consumed by the shenanigans. At home, I watched Speaker Romanoff lobby for cutting off benefits by statute at this time, rather than putting the matter to the voters in the fall: "If taxpayer dollars are going to folks who are ineligible to receive the benefits, we ought to stop that now, we shouldn't wait months on end," he argued. "And this bill would require the state and every local government to verify the legal status of anyone over the age of eighteen applying for public assistance."

The news story cut to a shot of Bill Owens. The governor said he would prefer to have the issue go to the voters, but would support reform by statute as long as it was substantive.

Then Marisela appeared on the screen, as the reporter noted that some people believed undocumented workers contributed to the state's economy. "They still pay taxes," said Marisela. "They go to the store, buy like any citizen. And they also work and get taxes taken out of their paycheck."

The three of them had gotten equal time—the speaker of the House, the governor of Colorado, and an illegal immigrant.

On Saturday, the Republicans let loose. "When we were called into a special session, the people expected to get steak," railed Senator Jim Dyer of Centennial. "Now they're getting pablum!" In the House, Romanoff's bill to cut services by statute was called everything from ineffective to disastrous. Representative Ted Harvey, who had tried to ban in-state tuition for undocumented students, took exception to a phrase permitting local governments to opt out, saying it would allow a sanctuary city policy. Romanoff sat with his head in his hands, a pained look on his face; over at the press table, Schrager looked equally weary, and members of CAIR yawned up in the gallery. After an hour and a half of debate, Speaker Romanoff rose to argue that his bill would serve the state better than a constitutional amendment. "The alternative is subjecting services that we can't define to a ban that we can't enforce, and inviting everyone to sue," he pointed out.

The House voted to send the bill to the Senate. Meanwhile, various bills dealing with employer sanctions were scheduled for simultaneous public hearings on the third floor of the gold-domed Capitol building. Then one of the hearings was mysteriously canceled. Lobbyists milled in disarray, spreading gossip; according to the statehouse grapevine, the agriculture industry and the ski industry had worked out loopholes for their seasonal workers in back-channel meetings, but they had left out the state's oil and gas companies, and now those companies were complaining they would not be able to find enough workers to get oil and gas out of the ground. Supposedly, Owens was furious about the logjam. He wanted Colorado to become the first state in the nation to require a state-issued ID to work. Then he startled everyone by turning up unannounced at a committee hearing on Romanoff's bill, which he now wanted to sink. Lobbyists poured in to watch the showdown.

"Madam Chairman, thank you, and thanks to all of the members of the committee for your work during the special session," began the governor. "I want to tell you of concerns I have with House Bill 1023. The bill does nothing to ban state or local services. What it does do is list federal services that are banned already. We're not aware of any additional services that this bill would cut."

Owens objected that the bill required only an affidavit avowing legal status rather than proof of citizenship—fraud would be easy. He also pointed out that violations would result in a misdemeanor, which he thought was too lenient a penalty. He closed by reminding the room that he believed illegal immigrants cost the state a lot of money. "In K–12 education alone, children who are born to mothers here illegally, they cost us half a billion dollars," said the governor.

When it was her turn to speak, Senate President Joan Fitz-Gerald reminded everyone that children born here were American citizens "just like you and me," even if their parents had entered the country illegally. "I had hoped we would not have a debate about the value of children," she added later on.

"We are not having a debate on the value of children," the governor shot back.

Decorum continued to fray. On Sunday, a representative's toddler grabbed a gavel and gleefully banged it on every available hard surface in the House chambers. Over in the Senate, one lawmaker accused another of making "jejune remarks." Then everything ground to a halt. The Senate adjourned and the House adjourned, but nobody went home; elected officials huddled in knots or kept to corners, while reporters roamed around looking for action. "I guess there's a lot happening behind closed doors," muttered Ben Davis, the deputy communications director for Keep Colorado Safe, the pro-immigrant coalition.

Angry Republican legislators would later name the prominent business leader who spent the afternoon sequestered in the governor's office, trying to talk him out of the idea of requiring a state-issued ID to work. I knew this homebuilder slightly. He was the largest donor to the Republican party in the state of Colorado. His grandparents had emigrated from Poland and Russia, and he once told me that if they had been born in Mexico, they were the kind of people who would have walked across the desert in search of work. I never spoke to him about his conversation with the governor, but according to statehouse gossip, they held a ninety-minute meeting in which the mogul said the governor's plan was a bad idea. It would turn employers into immigration agents and it would put Colorado on unequal footing with other states in the region, sending business elsewhere. Supposedly Owens replied by saying he felt passionate about the bill, and then the homebuilder told him curtly to get passionate about something else.

Furious conservatives would later ascribe an almighty importance to the sitdown, as if the entire outcome of the special session pivoted around the conversation between the governor and the business leader. But people who were in the room when the two men spoke described things differently. They said the governor never backed away from his position, despite intense pressure. Yet as the conversation unfolded, it became clear to the governor that he did not have the votes to pass his proposal. The business lobby in Colorado was too strong, and they opposed his idea too intensely—he could not carry it out. After the meeting, exhausted lobbyists suddenly began counting votes. The governor's plan to require a state-issued ID to work was going to die, while Romanoff's bill to cut services was going to be altered. In the revised version, an individual seeking welfare benefits would have to present photo identification as well as an affidavit avowing legal status, and the acceptable forms of ID would be strictly limited. In the case of fraud, each misrepresentation would result in a separate count, upping the penalty. Finalizing the deal took another day. Late on Monday, the pro-immigrant coalition voiced last-minute objections. Senators got boxes of takeout food, while lobbyists stood around pontificating. "This is the Democrats' new abortion," opined one. "We don't know how to talk about it."

"I just want to go home and get some sleep," said another.

"I just want to go and get a drink," said a third.

Finally Speaker Romanoff emerged from his office and announced that the last-minute disputes had been ironed out. His revised bill would pass and the governor's idea would die. Romanoff stood at the shiny brass balustrade of the main staircase, looking down onto the ground floor of the statehouse. Nothing about the special session had been fun—later he would describe this week as the single worst experience of his entire legislative career—but he felt a certain sense of accomplishment. He believed he had averted a political and policy disaster by circumventing the ballot initiative. "I think we should be quietly happy about this," he said.

In the morning's papers, the state's Democrats claimed they had enacted the toughest immigration measures in the country. Republicans angrily dismissed this claim, but it took months to evaluate the true effects of the special session. In the end, the bill to cut services did not result in any measurable savings, as legislators learned when the Joint Budget Committee held another hearing to ask how much the new immigration bills had cost to enforce and how much they had saved. The *Denver Post* pithily summarized the main finding: "Colorado's new law banning state spending on illegal immigrants has cost more than $2 million to enforce—and has saved the state nothing."

As it turned out, homeless people were the main group who tried to access public benefits without adequate documentation, not illegal immigrants. The primary impact of the special session combined with other measures to tighten the security of documents was to disenfranchise legitimate citizens who led itinerant lifestyles. As the *Rocky Mountain News* wrote in an editorial, "Thousands of Colorado's most vulnerable citizens remain caught in 'identity hell,' unable to obtain a state-issued ID because they don't have a state-issued ID." At the county level, clerks who handled requests for public benefits began to report dramatically increased job aggravation. Unfortunately, the federal government had changed its regulations around receiving public assistance, too, and by coincidence, the federal and state reforms were implemented simultaneously. The two sets of laws prioritized different documents, and frustrated county officials had to consult complicated tables to decipher whether they should ask for a passport and a driver's license, or a driver's license and a birth certificate, or some other combination of papers, depending on the particular benefit being sought. Even the people who were supposed to train the county officials could not keep the new rules straight, which resulted in massive confusion.

Meanwhile, migrant workers began avoiding Colorado because of all the media hoopla. As a result, the fall harvest was plagued by labor shortages so acute that fruits and vegetables rotted in orchards and fields. The agricultural lobby vociferously demanded help, and soon the Colorado Department of Corrections started busing prison inmates in to take the place of the missing migrant farmworkers. Phil Prutch of Pueblo County told the *Denver Post*, "When you have a crop sitting in the field and you have no one to harvest it, you'll try anything."

Those immigrants who remained in Colorado found the new laws did not affect them much. The only statute that had any direct impact on Marisela was the one that prohibited illegal aliens from gaining title to a car, which had passed during the last regular legislative session. After her old clunker finally died, she tried to buy a used car and was turned away at the dealership when she could not provide a Social Security number. When I spoke with Marisela's father about the special session, Fabián shrugged his shoulders and said it was just something he had watched on TV. It did not affect him in real life. He still struggled to sleep during the day and still spent his nights waxing the floors at King Soopers.

PART III

Lo Que Pasó Pasó
(What Happened Happened)

I

HEADWATERS

During the summer between the girls' sophomore and junior years of college, I went to visit Alma in Mexico. Given my mediocre Spanish, I needed a translator, preferably someone who knew Alma, and Justino Chávez agreed to assist me if I paid his airfare and hotel bill. As our plane circled over the city of Durango, hard beside the dark green folds of the Sierra Madres, I could see why people from here felt at home in Denver, for I might as well have been looking down on my hometown from the air. Both cities spread out over the same high plains, under the same infinite sky, and both abutted tall mountains that belonged to one continuous series of ranges—although the peaks were called the Rockies back in the United States, and the Sierra Madres down here. The two areas depended upon the same industries of ranching and mining, and shared the same sere climate. In the summertime, identical purple thunderclouds mounted on the western horizon, hurling down the same blue forks of lightning. The only difference was that snow blanketed Colorado at regular intervals during the winter, but almost never fell in Durango. It seemed cruel that I could fly here when Yadira could not, and I arrived with the feeling that she should have been making this trip instead of me.

Alma, her sister, and their mother were now staying in a row house inside the city limits. As we drove to their neighborhood, we passed thousands of political posters fixed to lampposts and utility poles. Roberto Madrazo of the PRI, as well as his similarly suited rivals Manuel López Obrador of the PRD and Felipe Calderón of the PAN, smiled beneficently over and over again. The sheer number of placards was staggering, and I wondered what army had put them up. *"Vota el 2 de Julio!"* the posters urged. We had arrived at the height of the political season: In twenty-six days, Mexico would elect a new president. Most Mexicans had turned their attention away from the impending political showdown, however, as the World Cup had just begun, and the country was in the grip of soccer fever.

In Alma's lower-class neighborhood, we saw dozens of half-finished buildings, left unroofed with rebar pointing up to the heavens. To me, these empty buildings spoke of the future that never was, the Mexico that might have been—if only the peso hadn't tumbled in value, if only the country's wealth had been distributed fairly, if only the PRI had not held a century-long stranglehold on Mexican politics. We spotted Alma waiting for us by a tiny store that sold sundries. She was wearing blue jeans, a T-shirt, and running shoes, as well as pale pink lipstick and tiny gold earrings. She led us past houses painted mustard yellow, electric blue, rose. We turned onto a pedestrian street and threaded our way around planters filled with magenta bougainvillea, and followed Alma to a two-story cinder-block row house painted sky blue. The property belonged to her aunt, who was away tending to Alma's eighty-six-year-old grandmother. The current living arrangement was temporary—Alma would be moving back to her mother's house next week. Somebody had planted purple creeper by the front door, and inside the rooms had been painted peach. The lower level included one main living and dining room, a bedroom, and a small kitchen—it had a refrigerator but no dishwasher. The counter was made of plywood covered in oilcloth. Alma shared the downstairs bedroom with her mother Ramona, her sister Octavia, and her baby, while one of her brothers slept upstairs. We sat at a table covered with a pink lace tablecloth underneath a sheet of clear plastic. Ramona's hair had turned the color of pewter, and she wore a congenial, open look. Octavia seemed to be half absent, however, as if she were grappling with some internal distraction. Justino and I cooed over the chubby six-month-old baby, who wore a pretty green dress with matching bloomers. She had a thatch of black hair and gold studs in her ears.

"What is her name?" Justino asked in Spanish.

"She's named Maribel," said Alma in the same language.

"Oh, I thought you had named her Cristál," I said in English, and Justino translated this for me.

"Yes, but crystal breaks, so I changed her name," replied Alma.

Alma brought out *agua fresca*—it was *melón*. She had made it for us; she was delighted to have visitors. None of the women in the house was working, and boredom was their chief complaint. They paid their bills with money that Jesús wired, as well as money sent by Alma's other brothers and Octavia's sons who were working in the United States. They received additional help from Alma's father, who subsisted on a pension that he had set up in Mexico as a young man, and who also continued to work occasionally. Alma had tried looking for a job to supplement the family's income, but it had proved difficult—there were too many young people in Mexico, all eager to work. After weeks of searching, she had landed a job cleaning houses for the equivalent of $10 a day, but then Ramona had to leave to care for her mother (who was ill with diabetes) and could no longer watch Maribel, forcing Alma to quit. She had stopped working after that—the pay was so low, it hardly seemed worth it. Now Alma got up every day, cleaned the house, fed Maribel, and watched *telenovelas*. The soap operas in which she sought escape were full of improbable *giros*—twists of fate—that numbed the effects of the real-life setbacks she had endured. "When I first got here, I saw everything, and it was ugly for me," Alma told us. "Ugly, ugly, ugly. I couldn't get used to it."

"Why was it ugly?"

"I miss my children," Alma said. She began crying. "I'm sorry," she gasped.

We had been with her for only half an hour—we had stumbled into the heart of things too quickly. The breeze lifted an aqua-colored lace curtain hung over the back door, revealing a clothesline full of clothes. Maribel started fussing and Alma jiggled the stroller. "She's a handful," said Alma, pulling herself together. "She needs a lot of attention, and she wants to keep moving." Alma turned the baby around to face the billowing curtain that kept lifting and falling. Absorbed by the spectacle, Maribel quieted down. Justino began chatting with Alma's sister, Octavia, who slowly came to life. Like Alma, she spoke almost no English, and I relied heavily on Justino to translate. Six years ago, Octavia explained, she had returned to Durango after being apprehended by the Immigration and Naturalization Service while taking a Greyhound bus from Los Angeles to Denver. Octavia and her oldest son, who was traveling with her, were put into different holding cells; she had his birth certificate, proving that he was an American citizen, but she did not speak enough English to explain this to the authorities, and her son, who was sixteen at the time, chose not to reveal that he was a citizen because he didn't want to be separated from his mother.

They were both deported. Her son later returned to the United States, but Octavia remained in Durango, too terrified of being deported again to go back north. Her four children were now ages thirteen to twenty-two years old, and they lived with their father in Chicago, Illinois. The last time she had seen them was three years ago, when they had come to visit during school break.

We had arrived expecting to see one mother who was separated from her children, but instead we had found two. The absent children haunted them. Alma wanted to know if the political climate had gotten worse in the United States, and when Justino told her that it had, she looked crestfallen. "I'm not happy here, because all my children are back there," she said. "And if I bring the children here, it's like robbing them of their future. Their future is not here—it is in the United States." Alma said she no longer expected Jesús to pay for a *coyote*. "I'm having problems with Jesús. I'm done with him. We fight too much, and I don't want my kids to see that." Instead, she was hoping that her brother Martín—who was now caring for Laura and Zulema—might raise the money for her return. In the meantime, her son, Raúl, was coming to visit next week, and Alma's face lifted every time she spoke of his impending arrival. She had become anxious about her son's welfare after she heard that Jesús was leaving him in the care of the building manager for hours at a time, and it filled her with relief to think that Raúl would soon be with her again. Originally, Zulema had also planned to spend the summer in Mexico, but she had to cancel her trip after she was sentenced to perform twelve weeks of community service as punishment for her joy ride in the stolen car. Laura had opted to stay in Denver as well.

Later that day, we paid a visit to Alma's father, who had moved into his wife's house over in Valle Verde, a nearby *colonia*. Tomás and Ramona remained married but preferred to live apart, as they fought whenever they spent too much time together. Tomás was fixing up the small, olive-colored structure for Ramona while she stayed at her sister's place. The house consisted of one room, painted hot pink, which was divided in two by a curtain. On one side of the curtain was a kitchen with no sink (the only running water came from an outside faucet) and on the other side were two double beds. Tomás lay on one, his lean figure clothed in black jeans and a white T-shirt, in the grip of soccer fever. He was watching Germany trounce Costa Rica. Last summer, when Alma had arrived with Laura and Raúl, they had shared these two beds with Ramona and Octavia; Laura, a budding teenager, had made her displeasure obvious. Now the children were absent, but the walls remained covered with their photographs—there was Yadira, chin cupped in her hand, wearing a thoughtful expression, and Zulema, Laura, and Raúl, full of exuberance.

Tomás had been working outside and his skin had darkened to the color of teak, emphasizing the bright silver of his moustache. His tough palms and knotted knuckles spoke of a lifetime of manual labor. He had started working in the fields of Mexico at the age of ten, which was when he stopped going to school, and later he worked in the United States as a bracero. He had weeded sugar beets in Colorado, picked cotton in Texas, and harvested lettuce in Michigan. After three years of this migrant lifestyle, always moving with the crops, he settled down in California, where he tended yards. Later he washed dishes in Glendale, California, in the back of a restaurant called Barragan's. Periodically, he used to get deported, and that was when he saw his children. "When I was little, he would come and go, come and go," said Alma. "When we would least expect it, he would be back. He would just say, 'Oh, they caught me.'"

After Congress passed the Immigration Reform and Control Act, Tomás wrote to the ranch where he had weeded sugar beets, and the owner sent him a letter certifying that he was an agricultural worker, even though he was no longer doing that type of labor. Technically, he should not have been eligible for the amnesty, but the ranch owner's letter helped him obtain a green card. Afterward, Tomás had applied for legal residency for his wife and two of their sons who were living in the United States, but not for Alma. He had expected her to get a green card through her first husband. As Tomás spoke, I realized for the first time that Alma had once possessed another avenue to legal status—but now that she had acquired a police record, her father could no longer help. In the end, the application that Tomás had submitted for his wife and sons was denied anyway, because his birth certificate contained a clerical error, rendering the document invalid. At the moment, Alma was helping her father fill out a new application, as Tomás had never learned to read or write. She was also compiling the paperwork for her father to collect an additional pension from the Mexican government for the time he had spent as a bracero. Tomás had kept no papers to prove that he had weeded sugar beets, picked cotton, and harvested lettuce in America; all he had was a wrinkled identification card from the bracero program that he had hung on to for forty-seven years. They hoped it would be enough for the bureaucrats.

Talking about the past made Tomás nostalgic for the village where he had been born, which he described as a verdant place of abundant water and fertile soil. Tomás called this place Fábrica, though he was actually from an even smaller village, Tescalio.

"You should show them Fábrica," Tomás told Alma. "It's beautiful."

"I've never been there," she replied.

"*What?*" he exclaimed in disbelief. "You've never been there?"

"I don't think so," said Alma, uncertainly.

We agreed to make an excursion in two days.

As we pulled out of Valle Verde, we could feel the heat rising. Justino asked where we should eat lunch, and Alma said she had not been to a restaurant since returning to Durango. Did we want to go to McDonald's? No, we said, Mexican food. As we drove around, we spotted a Sam's Club, which Alma said was *"vale la pena."* She liked Sam's Club—it had good bargains. In the same shopping center, we also spied a restaurant called El Portón, and mistook it for a local establishment. In fact, the waitress who took our order wore a badge identifying herself as an employee of Walmart. Durango had been transformed during the years that Alma had been away, and sometimes she sounded like Rumpelstiltskin when she discussed these changes. Everybody she knew had vanished, gone elsewhere in search of work, and now the once familiar streets were lined with big-box retailers.

El Portón was decorated with paper cutouts of soccer balls, and the latest match was being piped over the restaurant's loudspeakers. Other customers congregated in front of a large-screen TV to watch Ecuador challenge Poland, while we tried to talk over the din. Alma said she had seen footage of immigrants demonstrating in the streets of Los Angeles and Chicago, and knew from Yadira that a similar march had taken place in Denver. Alma spoke to her children once a week from a pay phone outside of a Pemex gas station. The worst times were when the children were battling an illness or celebrating a birthday. So far, she had missed one birthday apiece in the case of Zulema, Raúl, and Yadira; Laura had marked her last birthday here, but Alma would miss the next one, this coming August.

"I talked to Yadira recently, and she said she was losing a lot of her hair," Alma fretted.

"Probably because of the stress," said Justino.

"Yadira told me that she used to pull back her hair a lot, but now she can't anymore, because you can see the bald patches. She said her exams were very hard."

"But she's doing very well, Alma," Justino soothed. "She's doing very, very well."

A tremendous roar erupted from the crowd. *"Goooooooal!"* boomed the television announcer.

After lunch, we drove to Dolores Hidalgo, the *ranchito* where Alma had been born. All of Alma's siblings had been born in the village, too, though none lived there now. We took a highway heading southeast, then turned onto a smaller road, and wove through fields of young corn. The cloud-dappled mountains secured the horizon, just like they did back in Denver. As we passed an orchard of Brazil-nut trees, Alma explained that all this farmland had once belonged to a great hacienda; her father had worked for the owners as a boy, after his family had moved here from Tescalio.

Dolores Hidalgo consisted of a dirt crossroads lined with eucalyptus and cottonwood trees. There were perhaps forty residences. The largest building in town was the elementary school—the only school that Alma had ever attended. A sober portrait of the town's namesake, Father Miguel Hidalgo, adorned the school's gate (he had led the movement to wrest independence from Spain). Alma pointed to an orange house and said it used to belong to her grandmother. The house she had grown up in used to stand farther down the street, but the previous year Alma's parents had sold the property for twenty thousand pesos (about two thousand dollars) to pay off the debt they owed to Jesús's brothers for Alma's bail, and the new owners had torn down the house. A woman walked by holding a large black umbrella, shading herself from the sun, and several mangy dogs patrolled the streets. At the center of town, we paused to examine a bust of Emiliano Zapata, the populist hero of the Mexican Revolution. In the evenings, after they had finished working in the fields, everybody used to gather here to talk. Occasionally, they held dances in the same location. Alma said she had met her first husband in this very spot, at one of those long-ago dances.

"What was he like?" I asked.

"Oh, he thought a lot of himself." Alma shrugged.

"Well, why did you like him?"

"He was tall. Tall and thin."

"So why did you want to marry him?" I persisted.

Alma made a face. "That's another story," she said. "My plan was not to get married until I was eighteen. Then I wanted a white wedding dress in a church." Instead, she had gotten a civil ceremony. When she was sixteen, Alma had spurned an offer of marriage from Mario Vargas, and he had broken off contact temporarily, then communicated through a friend that he wanted her to return some of his belongings. When she had appeared at this crossroads, he pointed a pistol at her and shoved her into a waiting taxi, took her to a hotel in Durango, and raped her. One month later, a justice of the peace had performed their wedding rite. "Those were different times then," said Alma, staring off into the distance. "Nobody would touch you after something like that. You were used goods."

A truck loaded down with feedbags drove by in a dusty clatter. Alma said she had heard through the grapevine that Mario had begun working as a *coyote*, ferrying people through the mountains by Tijuana, then graduated to transporting drugs. After multiple arrests, he had lost his status as a legal resident—that is, according to the gossip. Supposedly he, too, was back in Durango. "But I've never seen him," added Alma. "And in truth, I don't want to." The sound of children playing drifted over from the elementary school. I thought of Marisela's board game; it seemed as though Alma had been particularly unfortunate in terms of the cards she had drawn. She had made bad choices, too, but it all could have turned out so differently—if only she had married somebody else, if only her father had helped her obtain a green card, if only she hadn't bought a stolen identity.

"You must have felt very unlucky at times," I told her.

"I did," she said.

We bumped along the dirt roads out of Dolores Hidalgo, then lurched back onto the smooth blacktop that led to Durango. Despair lurked back at the dusty crossroads guarded by Emiliano Zapata, but why should we linger there, when the sun flared in the endless sky and crops flourished all around? We passed an old man in muddy boots riding on a bicycle alongside rows and rows of scarlet chili peppers. I wondered if I had exhausted Alma, but she seemed refreshed.

"The time passed so quickly!" she exclaimed. "At home, there's nothing to do, and it's so boring. The days are usually very long, but this day has been short."

My thoughts returned to the miasma of depression that filled the house where she was living.

"I have the sense that Octavia is very sad," I said.

"Yes," said Alma. "She is very sad, but also she suffers from nerves."

"What do you mean by nerves?"

"Like psychosis. She needs to take medicine."

Lately, Octavia had not been taking her pills, however, and had been hearing voices. Back at the house, we found Alma's sister sitting by herself, staring out the window, as Ramona watched an immensely popular *telenovela* called *Pasión* (passion), and Maribel slept in her stroller. It was the only baby gear I ever saw; Alma put the back up to make it function like a high chair, and put the back down to turn it into a bassinet. Justino picked up a framed picture of Yadira wearing an orange cap and gown, at her high school graduation. She was smiling shyly beside Irene Chávez. Alma was nowhere to be seen. She had gone to California and left Yadira behind so that she could have a shot at college. This was a portrait of what a mother would forfeit for her child.

The following day, Justino and I drove past an endless series of men watering flowers by hand in the medians of Durango's wide boulevards. In Mexico, it was cheaper to hire this army of laborers than it was to install automatic sprinklers. When we arrived at the house, Alma was busy feeding *frutas mixtas* to Maribel. I complimented Alma on her heart-shaped earrings with American stars and stripes, and she said that she had bought them at Goodwill. At first, Alma explained, she had worked there under her true name, using a made-up Social Security number. After three years, however, the manager of the store had told everybody on the six-person sorting crew that the Social Security Administration had sent letters announcing their Social Security numbers did not match their names. Unless they could provide legitimate Social Security numbers, they would have to leave. The following day, a coworker employed in the donations area volunteered that he could get documents for the entire crew. According to Alma, he discussed his idea with the manager of the sorting area and the manager of the store. None of the employees at the sorting table knew how the coworker described the matter to their superiors, but he told them he knew a man who worked in the records division of the Colorado Department of Motor Vehicles and sold real identities. For three hundred dollars apiece, they could purchase the name of a legal immigrant, as well as an actual alien registration number, Colorado driver's license number, and Social Security number. It had sounded like a good idea at the time. After being absent for twenty-two days, Alma had returned to her old job under a new name. She did the same tasks as before, and reported to the same supervisor, but now obtained her pay in checks made out to Isbel Morales. A spokeswoman for Goodwill declined to comment, saying the company would not discuss personnel matters.

When Alma resumed her old job, after returning from California, she was the only member left of the original sorting crew. The others had taken different jobs, moved away, or been terminated. The coworker who had helped Alma obtain her new identity had been fired, too, after a security camera taped him stealing. Alma feared staying at the same store for too long. She said that she confided this to the new manager of the sorting crew, telling him she was using someone else's identity. He pleaded with her to remain and gave her a substantial raise, according to Alma.

By this point, Maribel had finished eating her *frutas mixtas,* and Alma suggested it would be a good time to go to the market in the center of Durango. As we drove past wave upon wave of political posters, Alma said her family always voted for the PRI. "They seem to be the most honest," she said, with no trace of irony. As long as a significant portion of Mexico's population remained uneducated, I thought to myself, perhaps the PRI would continue to enjoy that rosy reputation. At the indoor market, we made our way through shady coolness, past packed stalls selling everything from dried herbs to souvenirs. We saw scorpions everywhere: burned onto leather purses, painted onto shot glasses, embalmed in plastic. The creature was ubiquitous in these parts, and had been adopted as the emblem of Durango. After Justino bought several colorful peasant blouses for Irene, we stopped for lunch at a place that advertised the tastiness of its *gorditas.*

"Are you still thinking about going back?" I asked Alma.

"Yes. I regret that I decided to return here."

"Well, it was a hard choice."

"I would have been better off staying there and finishing the case. But I was pregnant, that was the problem—I didn't want to have the baby in jail. I was afraid that the child would be taken away by the government."

Alma wanted to know everything about Yadira's life. Justino described how hard Yadira had studied and how well she had done in school. I described my visits to Nelson Hall, including the story of my trip to Fantasía. Alma wanted to know if Yadira had gone to the night-club, too. I told her Yadira had gone to see a movie.

"Oh, which movie?"

"The Da Vinci Code."

As we were driving home, Alma asked, "What was the name of that movie again?"

"El Código Da Vinci," Justino told her.

"Is that it?"

I glanced over and saw the name of the movie in huge letters outside of a theater.

"Sí, esa es la película."

It pleased Alma, this fortuitous connection to her daughter's life. She wanted so badly to immerse herself in the particulars of Yadira's daily existence. Back at the house, Alma told us about her time inside the county jail at Smith Road, after her arrest. She had been placed in a cellblock with thirty other women, where she had been assigned one of the top bunks. Alma had confided to a cell mate who spoke a little Spanish that she had just taken a pregnancy test, and was despondent that the result had been positive. Her new friend said she should not sleep in the top bunk if she was pregnant, and they switched beds. There was a Spanish-language Bible on the cellblock, and Alma passed the hours reading it; she did not often go to church, yet the Bible verses soothed her. When news of Donnie Young's murder appeared on the cellblock's communal television, it caused a terrific commotion. Alma heard cursing—"Oh, shit!" and other phrases she didn't understand—and then her friend cried: "It was a Latino, Alma! It was a Latino!"

Alma immediately worried for the couple who ran Salon Ocampo, where she used to go to buy Mexican remedies. Then she also wondered how an immigrant without legal status could dare to assault a police officer. She did not appreciate that Gómez García's crime might have any impact on her own fate—she found his actions unfathomable, and assumed they would have no bearing on her life. Not until she got out of jail did she recognize that his crime was like drawing one of those bad cards in Marisela's board game. It was an out-of-the-blue surprise that completely altered her position in life.

Later that evening, Alma suggested we buy a roast chicken for dinner, and we walked to a neighbor's home to purchase the *pollo rostizado*, pushing Maribel in her stroller along the bumpy sidewalks. A red station wagon with a loudspeaker affixed to its roof drove by, the driver's amplified voice echoing off the brightly colored houses: *"Paletas allí, aproveche!"* Popsicles, take advantage of it! Children came running, clutching pesos. *"Paletas, paletas!"* they sang. Alma stopped at a row house where an older woman was tending a rotisserie cooker full of chickens. Alma ordered one, and I paid for it. In search of lettuce, we drove to a Soriana supermarket, which was the size of a SuperTarget, and sold everything from appliances to meat. Alma picked up a can of peaches and observed that food was more expensive in Mexico, even though housing was much cheaper. In the produce section, we encountered a wiry man in blue jeans, cowboy boots, and a worn T-shirt that said: "Bob Beauprez for Congress." I stopped to stare. Back in Colorado, Congressman Beauprez was the Republican party's top contender to become the next governor of the state. I knew him personally—he'd come to our home for dinner. What was a man in a Durango supermarket doing in an old Beauprez for Congress T-shirt? Most likely, he'd bought the shirt while working in Colorado, probably secondhand. These two places were bound together, his T-shirt declared; they were symbiotic. Meanwhile, one thousand miles to the north, Beauprez was in the middle of adopting a hard-line stance on illegal immigration to secure the votes of Colorado's social conservatives.

We carried our groceries into the kitchen of Alma's aunt's home, where I could hear the sound of running water. When I looked out of the kitchen door, I saw Octavia using a hose and a washboard—she was doing laundry by hand out in the yard. She smiled at me wearily. The afternoon was losing its fierceness, the heat declining rapidly in the familiar way that it did back in Colorado. Alma made papaya *agua fresca* and gave Maribel a bath. Then she propped the baby up for dinner in her stroller with throw pillows. I went upstairs to use the bathroom and saw Alma's brother Salvador sprawled across a bare mattress, snoring away in his clothes with the television on. Alma said her brother was putting in six days a week on a construction project, and came home too tired to eat. I never saw him awake during our entire visit.

Maribel sat with us at the dinner table, shredding paper napkins.

"Have I ever been to Fábrica?" Alma asked her mother.

"No. Your relatives came to visit us, but you never went there."

After dinner we went outside. At night, neighbors sat by the bougainvillea, gossiping. This was their main source of entertainment, other than *telenovelas*. "Oh, it's so refreshing out here," Justino said with a sigh. Three teenage boys hid in the shadow of a cinder-block wall, drinking malt liquor. A gaggle of prepubescent girls waltzed by, pausing to flirt. Octavia disappeared into the night. Later, I spied her outside of a tiny store that sold cigarettes and candy, chatting up a crowd of men.

We departed for Fábrica the next morning. Alma dressed up like a soccer mom, while Maribel wore a flouncy pink dress trimmed with lace. She sat on Alma's lap, since they had no car seat. When we stopped to pick up Tomás, Justino pulled out a map, but Tomás waved it away, saying he knew the route by heart; Alma reminded us that her father could not read. We headed for the mountains. On the way, we passed an American-owned factory, and talking about the facility reminded Justino that he was curious about the name of Tomás's hometown. Why was it called Fábrica (the Spanish word for factory)? The full name of the town was actually Fábrica la Constancia, Tomás told us. "There was a big factory there once," he said. "They used to make carpets, textiles, clothing." Maps and signs referred to the town as La Constancia for short, but he just called it Fábrica.

A red pickup truck sped past with three girls standing up in the back, swaying. We left the plains and entered different terrain—rolling foothills of red rocks, populated by longhorns so skinny we could count their ribs. The highway rose and dipped. Tomás said it had been four years since he had last returned, and Alma asked if his older sister was still alive. "I don't know, but I haven't heard of her dying," he replied.

Justino wanted to turn off the highway when he saw a sign for La Constancia, but Tomás knew another way—it was unposted. "I don't want to get lost and end up in Jalisco," grumbled Justino. We turned down an unpromising byway instead. The land grew hellish-looking, as the rocks darkened to reddish black, and the vegetation grew sparse, prickly, and unforgiving. I was wondering why Tomás would revere such a godforsaken outpost when the road dipped again and we found ourselves driving through fields of the lushest green.

"It's beautiful," murmured Alma.

"There is a lot of water here," Tomás said proudly. "The water table is very, very high, and there's water just seeping up from the ground."

Indeed, puddles glistened in the fields and streams spilled out of the hills. We passed fields of corn and orchards of apricots. Tomás reminisced about growing beans on the *ejido* in Tescalio—communal farmland, shared by all the families in the area. Tomás's father had earned additional money hauling wood from the surrounding hills to be burned in the factory's voracious fires. Then one day there wasn't any more wood. In the center of Fábrica, Tomás pointed to a vast crumbling structure made of adobe. Vines roped up its walls and boards obscured its windows. "This was the factory," he said. "It's been abandoned." Various lovers had carved their names into the crumbling bricks: *Carmen y Ramón, Cesar y Christy, Luis y Nena.* Then there were young men with no lover to announce—*Felipe, Juan, Luis.* Tomás pointed to a stream that flowed out from under the vacant building. It ran through the center of the factory, and had once provided water for vats of dye and steam for the turbines. We walked the length of the factory, turned the corner, and confronted a river lined with giant trees that looked like cypresses, only bigger. Tomás called them *sabinos*—their Spanish name, after European *Juniperus sabina.* Later I learned that the Aztecs had called them *ahuehuete,* "old man of the water," in Nahuatl. They had roots like the ribs of cathedrals, and black butterflies flitted among their enormous trunks. Tomás said a spring fed the river, and it flowed day and night. He'd never been to the headwaters, but supposedly they were breathtaking.

"Here there is running water all day long, naturally," marveled Alma, "and back in Durango, there are neighborhoods where the water gets shut off, like in Valle Verde."

We made a loop around the vast factory, which occupied the town's heart. On the far side, we found a strip of stores. Six old men stood on the sidewalk, listening to a transistor radio—sounds of the World Cup. Nearby, I noticed a building with hand-lettered writing all over its walls. It advertised a bus service that went to the following destinations:

Colorado Springs, Colorado
Aurora, Colorado
Denver, Colorado
Longmont, Colorado
Pueblo, Colorado
Dallas, Texas
Chicago, Illinois
Phoenix, Arizona
Las Vegas, Nevada
Los Angeles, California
Albuquerque, New Mexico

No wonder Denver had become home to Marisela Benavídez and Yadira Vargas and Raúl Gómez García. Even in this forgotten backwater, the far-off towns and cities of Colorado beckoned to the impoverished people of Durango. Anybody with unfulfilled hopes, anybody with a restless soul could imagine they might find whatever they were missing at the end of a bus ride north.

We did not tarry, as Tomás was eager to see his sister. He took us down a narrow footpath that followed a rock wall. I picked up one of the rocks; it was porous and strangely light. Volcanic, Tomás explained. We walked in the shade of orange trees until we came to a white farmhouse. Tomás called out for his sister, whose given name was María del Refugio, though he just called her Cuca. An old woman emerged, leaning heavily on a walking stick, wearing an old cotton skirt with her slip showing. Cuca embraced her brother, then appraised the rest of us.

"And who are you? I don't remember you."

"I'm Alma."

"And the little one? Is she yours?"

Alma nodded.

"Oh, how beautiful! Come in! Come in!"

We crowded into a tiny room, sitting down on mismatched chairs. Birdsong filled the home, as Cuca kept canaries. On the walls hung an array of religious icons—sad, serene, bloody—the same Catholic imagery I knew from my own grandmother's farmhouse in County Cavan, Ireland. Cuca had lost her teeth but not her faculties, and she lambasted her younger brother mercilessly. It was scandalous that he had not been to visit her sooner!

"You have a line!" observed Tomás enthusiastically, attempting to distract her.

"Yes, I have a line," crowed Cuca, lifting up a piece of lace to reveal the black telephone hidden underneath. "I can use it with a card."

Cuca had been married already when their parents had moved away with Tomás. Now a spry eighty-two, she jabbed her walking stick toward pictures of her children and her grandchildren, recounting the diaspora. Three of her children had moved to other parts of Mexico, while one son remained behind. Her grandsons, Luis and Raimundo—whom she had raised as though they were her own—now lived in Tennessee, where they hung drywall. Just the other night, Luis had gotten drunk and called his grandmother at three o'clock in the morning to tell her that he was desperately lonely.

Flies buzzed around the baby and Alma waved a pillow at them. The heat swelled until the songbirds lapsed into silence. Alma bought some *gorditas* made by a woman who lived with Cuca's son, and as we ate our lunch, Tomás pushed back the baseball cap he always wore, revealing a much paler forehead. He asked his daughter if it was more *fresco* outside. Alma said no, it was more *caliente*.

"Oh, open the door behind you, and we will get a cross breeze," instructed Cuca.

A breeze ruffled through the room, as predicted. Cuca spun her walking stick between her palms. The old woman had all the time in the world, and made us feel as though we did, too. Childhood memories washed over her. Once, she had come across their father beating her little brother, and had thrown a rock to stop the violence. It hit her father squarely in the back, and he turned to chase her. "Run!" Cuca had yelled to Tomás. "Run! Don't just wait to get hit again!"

I asked Cuca if she could direct me to her bathroom.

"Oh, I don't have one. In the daytime, we just go outside."

Alma's face registered consternation. She asked if Cuca's son had a proper bathroom.

"Oh, no, it's okay," I said. "But where do I go?"

Cuca waved her hand airily. "Oh, outside somewhere."

"I'm sorry," Alma said in English.

"No hay problema," I told her.

The heat became thick as molasses and Cuca began telling stories about the local *curandera.* Supposedly she had cured one of Cuca's grandsons of a terrible ailment with only two eggs and a photograph. Alma thought maybe the *curandera* could silence the voices in Octavia's head. We were mired in torpor, pinned to our chairs by the lively old woman's endless stories, until at last Tomás broke the spell by saying that he wanted to see her garden. Geraniums and begonias and mint spilled from rusty old paint pails, and Cuca's son, Raimundo Sr., cut down oranges with a machete. Cuca sat down on a chipped toilet seat in the middle of her yard. "See! I do have one!" she cackled. "But if you use it, nothing happens!"

Tomás asked how her crops were faring, but Cuca had none. "Last year, we planted beans, but only got one peso for a kilo. That didn't even cover the cost of planting. You're losing money by planting."

"That's why people leave." Tomás nodded. "You just can't make enough money here."

The conversation turned to U.S. politics. Cuca had heard the federal government might grant an amnesty, but it seemed to depend on the higher-ups. Raimundo said he had watched the immigrant rallies on television. His girlfriend wondered if it wasn't dangerous for people without documents to congregate. Wouldn't the Border Patrol round them up?

"Ay, la migra," Cuca spat dismissively. "Eh!"

Justino said federal authorities typically raided workplaces, not political demonstrations. He blamed the growing anti-immigrant sentiment in America on politicians who wanted a safe enemy to bash.

"But what about that guy who killed a police officer?" said Tomás. "He was from Durango. Sometimes we bring these things down upon ourselves."

It was startling to hear somebody raise the subject of Donnie Young in Cuca's backyard. We had traveled so far; I thought we had left the story of his murder behind, but ties of kith and kin now bound

Durango and Colorado. Everybody had heard about the Mexican dishwasher who had killed an American police officer. Nobody had an answer for Tomás. Eventually, he said we should go to Tescalio while there was still light. When he squabbled with Cuca over the directions, she slapped him. They both burst out laughing, children once more.

The road to Tescalio was paved with stones, and we bumped along slowly, passing a boy on a burro and four girls dressed up for evening. Even in *el campo*, campaign posters proclaimed that smiling politicians were TODOS POR DURANGO. The house in which Tomás was born no longer existed, but he stood gazing at the field where it had once sheltered him. "We used to plant over here, on this side," he told us.

On our way home, we passed gleeful children shrieking and splashing in the river, while their parents waded nearby. Then the astonishing greenness of Fábrica vanished like an untold secret. Justino took us out of town by a different route, and soon we crossed over a high gorge. It opened up into an enormous canyon, filled with a silver lake. We parked the car and walked over to the edge of the canyon. It was so deep we found ourselves looking down onto the tops of giant *sabino* trees as they tossed about in the evening breeze. A huge waterfall thundered out of towering cliffs on the far side of the lake. "This is the headwaters!" exclaimed Tomás. "Here is the source! This is the first time in my life that I've ever been here."

Lovers embraced in a parked car, and *cumbia* music drifted over from their radio. We descended to the silver water by a concrete staircase adorned with graffiti. One tag simply declared: USA. At the bottom, gray river rocks carpeted the ground, and tree roots spilled over them like curly hair. Visitors had strewn trash among the stones—Carta Blanca bottles, Coke cans, gum wrappers. Nobody was taking care of this place.

Back up at the top of the gorge, we lingered to admire the spectacle. A talkative man emerged from his car carrying a can of beer.

"*Buenas tardes,*" he said.

"*Buenas tardes.*"

"*Qué hermoso lugar, verdad?*"

We agreed it was indeed a lovely place.

"Where are you from?"

"I live in Durango," Tomás replied.

"But where are you from?"

"Tescalio."

"Ah."

No more needed to be said. There was no work in Tescalio, but it was the kind of place you never really left behind. Tomás had a hard time tearing himself away from the silver lake, and the rest of us sat in the car as he strolled around, examining the view from every angle. We knew he was old and might never see this place again. Alma gave Maribel a bottle, and the blue gloom of twilight enveloped us, softening the forbidding red-black hills to purple.

"When you were using Isbel's identity, did you think about Isbel?" I asked her.

"Yes, I thought about her," Alma said. "I wondered if she was working and if it affected her taxes. And I wondered if she was not working and was receiving public assistance, if it would show that she was earning money and cause problems for her."

Tomás got back in the car and Justino started the engine. Maribel fussed until Alma wrapped her up in a small blanket and patted her bottom, whispering, *"Duérmete, duérmete."* The sun sank behind the mountains, streaking the sky scarlet, and the heat fled once more. I debated whether to tell Alma about my conversations with Isbel Morales. Eventually, as we rounded a pass and saw the lights of Durango spread over the high plains—just like coming down from the Rockies, and happening upon Denver—I told Alma about Isbel.

"Did she have to pay much in taxes?" Alma asked.

"She will have to document her case and provide a lot of paperwork, but she probably won't end up paying any additional taxes."

"And was she very angry?"

"She felt that her privacy had been violated, and she was shocked by the experience, but she was from Mexico originally, and her husband doesn't have papers. She thinks that he might be doing something similar. She kept saying, 'I can't judge.'"

"Oh. So she is a good person."

"I think so—though I was surprised that she pushed so hard for your arrest."

"Maybe she thought that I had used her name for something else."

"Did you? It would have been easy to get a credit card."

"I knew that some people used stolen identities to buy cars, or to

buy other things, but I never did that. I just used it to work. I thought
that to use her identity for other things would be wrong."

The car sped along in the dark.

"Wasn't it wrong to use her identity to work? You said it would
have been wrong to do those other things. What about using her identity to work?"

"It was wrong," conceded Alma. "I knew that if I was caught, I
would get in trouble."

Before we parted, Alma gave Justino shark oil capsules, full of
omega-3 fatty acids to help combat stress, for Yadira. Then she gave
us ceramic frogs for good luck. I thought she was the one who needed
a change in fortune, but thanked her profusely anyway, knowing she
didn't have money to spare on presents. On our way back to the
hotel, I observed to Justino that the punishment Alma had chosen for
herself—this painful exile, such a long distance from her children—
seemed far greater than her crime. We passed the familiar boulevards
full of fat cats wearing smiles that now appeared smug, oblivious.
Madrazo or Calderón—I couldn't tell the difference. If the future savior of this country appeared on one or another of the posters, it was
not apparent to me, for the politicians still looked indistinguishable in
their dark suits, and of a type with all those other power brokers who
had bled this country dry.

A car passed us going the opposite direction with the words *Viva
Mexico Cabrones* scrawled on the windshield. People honked and
waved sombreros. In the World Cup, Mexico had just defeated Iran.
The people of this country never seemed to win in the game of politics,
never in the game of life, but at least they found solace on the soccer
field. If Alma's version of events was true—and I believed her—then her
managers at Goodwill were as guilty as she was, yet they had paid no
penalty. American employers had been complicit in this thing we liked
to call illegal immigration (as if it had nothing to do with the rest of
us) for more than fifty years, even before Tomás began working in the
sugar beet fields of Colorado. I had always thought of Yadira as a first-
generation immigrant, and technically that was accurate, because she
had been born in Mexico—but she was actually the third generation
of her family to live and work in the United States. The headwaters of
her story began in the hills around Tescalio, more than half a century
ago, on that day when the slopes were finally shorn of lumber. This was

the significance of those hand-lettered place names covering the wall of the bus company in Fábrica. A list like that—so long and so specific—was born of generations of travel, generations of people leaving their humble paradise for the lure of jobs all over Colorado. And for every person who went north, there was an employer at the other end of the bus ride, willing to hire.

2

TANCREDOLAND

Eight weeks later, I found myself driving around his old neighborhood with Tom Tancredo. It was a hot Sunday afternoon in August, the girls were enjoying the last few weeks of their summer vacation, and Congress had just gone into recess. We cruised around in Tancredo's tan Chevrolet pickup. Again the congressman jokingly referred to this part of Denver as Tancredoland, although I had just visited Yadira at Irene and Justino Chávez's home—perhaps a dozen blocks away—to show her the pictures I had taken in Durango, which she had absorbed with a fierce wordlessness. Marisela had disappeared for the summer, too busy with boys and bars and lobbying to return my phone calls. I still thought of this part of town as her territory, however, for I had first gotten to know the area after her father had purchased a home here. Driving around the same streets with Tancredo gave me an entirely different perspective on the neighborhood. It was still half Italian, but becoming more and more Mexican every day. In the past I'd paid attention to the current immigrants, but not their predecessors. What I wanted to understand was how someone could grow up on these streets and hold Tancredo's opinions. Why would Tancredo and I—both of us from immigrant families—have opposite emotional reactions to the idea of more people coming? Why was my fundamental response one of sympathy, while his appeared to be one of antipathy?

The congressman's Chevrolet pickup was pristine and roomy. It had tan leather seats and Bose speakers and powerful air-conditioning. Tancredo pointed to a nondescript storefront on Tejon Street, beside Lechuga's Italian Restaurant & Lounge.

"This is where I took accordion lessons," he said, "from a man named Roxy DeCarlo."

"Isn't the accordion a German thing?" I asked, thinking of polka.

"Oh, no, no, no, no. It is *so* Italian."

Tancredo had hated the accordion, but his mother had insisted he learn to play. Now Roxy DeCarlo had passed away, and Mexican restaurants crowded the Italian landmarks. When we planned this tour, the congressman had suggested that we meet at a legendary Italian eatery called Gaetano's. Supposedly there used to be dozens of phone lines running into the establishment, and you didn't need that many phones if all you were serving was linguine and clam sauce. People said it had been a numbers joint back in the day. My husband's restaurant company had purchased the place after John was elected. "Ah, nothing has changed," Tancredo said with satisfaction, when he poked his head inside of Gaetano's to see if the photograph of Frank Sinatra still hung in the bar. "As long as Frank is still there—that's all I care about."

Ethnic rivalries had riddled North Denver when Tancredo was a boy. The Irish worshipped at St. Patrick's, the Mexicans at Our Lady of Guadalupe, and the Italians at Mount Carmel. There had been a lot of mixing in this neighborhood, and a lot of friction. Tancredo pointed out the modest brick house in which he had grown up; on a previous visit to the neighborhood, he had knocked on the door only to discover that a Spanish-speaking family lived there. "Tancredo—don't I know that name?" the new owner had said, with his son acting as his translator. Tancredo left quickly, without explaining why his name sounded familiar. Spoon-fed ethnic antagonism as a boy, and now Mexicans were living in his old house? It would be easy to dismiss his crusade against the latest immigrants as nothing more than an old-fashioned turf war. But that would be unfair; there was more to his worldview. I reminded the congressman that there were two dual-language schools within walking distance—the public school Academia Ana Marie Sandoval, and the private school Escuela Guadalupe—where students received instruction in both English and Spanish.

"I would assume that dual-language education in the public schools is something that you would not support?"

"No, absolutely not. Bilingualism for individuals is a wonderful thing, but for a country, it is a disaster."

Over in the parking lot of the Potenza Lodge, the congressman recognized several elderly Italian people who ran the Feast of St. Rocco. They were setting up booths for the celebration that would take place that evening. Patrons would play crazy dice and eat Italian sausages.

"It's called crazy dice, but it's a crap table!" said Tancredo. "I don't know, is there a special permit for that?" The Potenza Lodge had been a central gathering place for his family. The congressman's paternal grandfather, Joe Tancredo, had been born in the city of Potenza, in the Basilicata region of southern Italy, in the 1890s. Both of Joe's parents had died when he was young, and afterward, according to family lore, an aunt had put him on a boat headed for America with a tag pinned to his shirt saying he was to be delivered to a family in Iowa. The boat was called the *Sicilian Prince,* and it left Italy in 1903. During that period, Italians were coming to the United States in huge numbers—in proportion to the rest of the country's population, the influx was as large as the recent waves of immigration from Mexico. Joe was either nine or eleven when he sailed across the Atlantic Ocean—he always said nine, but when his grandson found the manifest of the *Sicilian Prince,* it recorded Joe's age as eleven. The ship's manifest records other passengers named Tancredo, but Joe always told the story of the voyage as though he'd made it alone. At any rate, when the ship docked at Ellis Island, supposedly there wasn't anybody there to meet him.

Joe worked at an Italian grocer in New York City for a while, and then began his westward trek. Two and a half years later, he arrived in Denver, Colorado. "I said, 'What happened to Iowa?'" Tancredo recounted. "And he said, 'I looked at the Rocky Mountains and said, if Iowa is past that, to hell with it.'" Tancredo chuckled at his grandfather's misbegotten sense of geography. Joe had not spent much time in school. In Denver, Joe found that immigrants from his hometown of Potenza had established a foothold on the city's north side, and he decided he was done traveling. He found work and sent for his bride. Although they had never met, Joe had been betrothed to Rena since they were children. Rena never fully adjusted to the United States, however, and spoke Italian for the rest of her life.

The congressman's maternal grandparents were also Italian immigrants. They came to the United States together as adults, after they had married. It was harder for them to learn English than it had been for Joe Tancredo, as they were older when they arrived, but they mastered the task, as they considered speaking English to be of paramount importance. When he was a boy, Tancredo's extended family went to mass together every Sunday, and afterward they would go out to lunch and take a drive. They liked to go to Westminster, where the grown-ups would marvel at the vast ocean of new houses springing up across the plains. It was the 1950s, and the suburbs were booming. On the drive back into Denver, his grandparents would sometimes begin to squabble, and if the argument grew heated enough, his grandfather would lapse into furious Italian. Then his grandmother would yell, "Speak American, damn it!" This was what Tancredo's maternal grandparents had taught him: If you moved to the United States, you spoke American, damn it. These grandparents never flew an Italian flag, only an American one, and they constantly talked about the importance of becoming Americanized.

"What did that mean?"

"It meant speaking English, perhaps not keeping your car out in the front yard. I had the feeling it meant they were quite reluctant to talk about Italy—and this is too bad; I'm not saying this is good. They never talked about it in a terribly positive way. They talked about it as poverty-stricken and essentially a bad place to live. America offered them this great opportunity, and they wanted to be Americanized."

Rena might have taught him other lessons, but Tancredo could not communicate with his paternal grandmother, as he never learned to speak Italian. Tancredo weaved his pickup truck up and down the side streets, pointing out the modest bungalows that held sentimental value. Here was where his best friend used to live, and here was the home of his first girlfriend. This was Aunt Marie's house; that was Aunt Rose's. He'd spent a lot of time at Aunt Rose's, since her home had served as a refuge from his own. These streets were dense with memories, and not all of them were pleasant—it was sweet to come back, but also bitter. "My dad was an alcoholic, and I don't look back at many of these days as very—with great—well, like a lot of people look back at their childhoods," Tancredo confessed. "Mine was not that."

Tancredo was no longer in regular contact with anybody in North Denver. His mother had passed away the previous year, and his father shortly before that. His siblings still lived here, but they had never been close. He had two brothers, both much older than he. "One is a retired teacher, and one is a retired postal employee. I can't say that I know them as my brothers." Tancredo did not point out their houses, but he drove past his two favorite movie theaters—the Federal and the Oriental. Besides Aunt Rose's, the movie theaters were where he had found his escape. "I remember going to see *Quo Vadis*," he mused. "Do you remember *Quo Vadis?*" (A Roman general falls in love with a Christian, and Nero throws both of them to the lions.) "Ah, it was great."

We parked beside an old circular gazebo, which was all that was left of the original Elitch's, a legendary amusement park that had moved to a new location. Tancredo had started out as a sweeper and worked his way up to summer park manager. He could still see it all the way it once was. "That was the merry-go-round. This was the midway; this was the confectionery," he said. But it was all gone. "Oh, man, this is so weird." He became lost in thought. Most of the good memories that Tancredo had of his childhood were buried here. "I was sick when this moved. It took so many kids off the streets, and I was one, I guarantee it. I was a punk." After about ten minutes, we got back into the pickup truck. The congressman's car phone rang.

"Hey, Tom, this is Dan," said a disembodied voice over a speaker.

"Dan, how you doing, buddy!" cried Tancredo. "Listen I've got an iPod thing and I'm supposed to have this microphone deal—well anyway, I can't explain it, I don't know the first thing about it, but I'm going to have to call you back."

"All right," said the voice.

"Thank you, buddy!

"I'm going to do this thing called podcasting," Tancredo explained. "I've got an iPod and a microphone thing that goes with it. I know how to record, but not how to get it out to others. They've got to show me how to do it."

"Podcasting! This is cutting edge!"

"Yeah, well, I've got great people working for me. I was the first member of Congress to actually blog."

I reminded the congressman of the memorable line he had written about the cow—how the federal government could find a single animal infected with mad cow disease, yet could not find twelve million human beings. He chortled. Tancredo had a pungent way with words, and knew how to exploit modern technology to make the most of his gift. We drove back to the Potenza Lodge, where preparations for the Feast of St. Rocco were now in full swing. "I remember thinking: There was a guy named Rocco who became a saint. What did he do, you know? A saint named Rocco? Was he the enforcer for the apostles?" Tancredo laughed out loud at his own joke. Actually, on a trip to Italy, he had discovered that St. Rocco had ministered to the ill during the plague.

We heard a band playing a march—it was the procession, they were carrying the statue. Every year, Italian residents of North Denver carry a plaster statue of St. Rocco to Mount Carmel for it to be blessed by a priest. Prominent members of the community then bid for the honor of carrying the statue around the neighborhood, in remembrance of someone who has died. Tancredo and I stood on a street corner, watching the procession go by. This year, it was only half a block long, but he could remember when it had stretched forever, with old women shuffling along on their knees.

Tancredo asked if I remembered the scene in the *Godfather* saga—real life often reminded him of the movies—when a youthful Vito Corleone (played by Robert De Niro) committed his first murder. As he crawls over the rooftops of Little Italy, a feast is taking place in the streets below. "There's the one part where it lights up, and the lights say, 'San Rocco,'" recalled Tancredo. "So it's the Feast of St. Rocco!" I wanted to walk over to Mount Carmel, where Tancredo's mother had been baptized and his brother had been wed, but the congressman begged off. He did not want to join the procession because he was no longer a Catholic. That was another part of his heritage that he'd left behind—he now belonged to an evangelical Christian church. "I don't want to betray myself. I would feel badly if people thought—I would not want them to think that I was a Catholic when I'm not." Plus, he had to figure out how to make a podcast. As the congressman left to learn another means of broadcasting his opinions, I thought of Joe Tancredo, coming over on a boat at the age of nine or eleven, orphaned and possibly traveling alone, and wondered if the congressman's black and white views on social issues had something to do with his grandfather's anarchic life. What did the absence of parents communicate to a child, combined with such a tremendous dislocation? If Joe had been nine when he had boarded the *Sicilian Prince,* then he had been only two years older than Marisela was when she had walked across the border and lain down in the back of that other pickup truck, wondering where her mother was. Who could say what kind of father parentless Joe had been to his own child—the immigrant's son who turned to drink on every special occasion. Clearly, Tancredo's alcoholic father had launched his son Tom on his particularly urgent trajectory out of North Denver, away from the past, into the safety and security of the suburbs. Now the congressman saw it as his mission to keep all threats at bay. It was another type of immigrant story—not the same as mine, not the same as Marisela's—but somehow Joe Tancredo's harrowing voyage had transmuted over the generations into this fervent need to defend America.

I walked over to Mount Carmel. Just as I arrived, the band broke into "The Star Spangled Banner." I couldn't listen to the National Anthem anymore without wondering where the latest immigrants fit into the land of the free. Several uniformed police officers stood around, watching over the ceremony, including Reuben Gomez, who had recently left John's security detail to return to the SWAT team. I stopped to chat. Soon people in the crowd wanted to shake my hand: The mayor's wife had come! She cared about the procession! "I'm known as the Italian fighter," said an older woman in a powder blue suit, pumping my arm enthusiastically. "It's wonderful to meet you!" The Italian fighter edged over to the podium to make sure the speaker announced my presence, and I found myself being applauded. Before I knew it, the statue had been blessed and bid upon and I had been drafted to join the procession. We were off down the streets of North Denver, and I was standing in for the mayor. Al Santangelo said his grandfather was from Potenza and had helped to found the lodge.

"Are you Mrs. Hickenlooper?" his brother Richard asked.

"I'm Helen Thorpe."

"I'm a third-generation member of the lodge!"

Their brother George, another active member of the lodge, explained that St. Rocco was the patron saint of all Italian immigrants. As it turned out, St. Rocco had been an immigrant himself—he was born in France, and had gone to Italy on a pilgrimage. "We adopted him as our patron saint because he watched over us when we arrived in this country," said George. The Santangelos were trying to put together a heritage center to celebrate the history of Italians in North Denver, and were also working to expand the lodge's membership. As we walked through the neighborhood, however, they pointed out the locations where Italian grocers had once sold their wares, but were no more. "I remember the sawdust on the floor at Cerroni's," said a woman beside us, "and the fish hanging from the ceiling." I wished the Santangelos well with their recruitment efforts, but wondered how many people in this neighborhood still felt an emotional connection to the city of Potenza. As we walked down Navajo Street, a group of perplexed Mexican laborers stared at us from their front porch. They did not know what all these gray-haired English speakers were doing on their street, but they recognized a religious event when they saw it, and removed their baseball caps. Tancredo said these workers didn't belong here—not if they lacked Social Security numbers, not if they had failed to learn English. I didn't disagree with his opinion, exactly—it's just that the workers *were* here. We wanted these guys around when it came time to remodel the basement, yet we also wanted to say they weren't proper Americans. We wanted to have it both ways.

3

GUILTY AS CHARGED

In September 2006, four days before their junior year began, Marisela, Yadira, and Clara helped organize a party to benefit Theta Theta Nu at a downtown club called Blue Ice. The ambience was cavelike. Clara showed up wearing a gauzy white blouse, while Yadira arrived in a tiny top covered in sequins that glistened when she moved. "I have a new crush!" bellowed Clara over the music. His name was Diego, and he worked in the customer service department at T-Mobile, she said. He was supposed to come that night, but hadn't shown up yet; Clara hovered anxiously by the door. Yadira announced happily that she had made it off the housing waiting list and had just secured a room in the same building as her friends, which she was going to share with her sorority sister Catarina. After spending the summer in Mexico, her brother Raúl had decided to stay there with Alma, while Laura and Zulema continued to live with their aunt and uncle. Yadira was not going to have to serve as mother to her siblings this year after all.

The girls had invited every student they knew at the University of Denver, and almost every Latino had come, yet the party was sparsely attended. There simply weren't enough of them for the sorority to break even. Through the club's large plate-glass windows, I saw Marisela and Omar outside on the sidewalk. Marisela had adopted a new look—her hair was dark, straight and sleek, and she had on rectangular glasses. You could no longer tell that she had grown up poor. Beside her, Omar was wearing baggy jeans and a white dress shirt. After he failed to produce adequate identification, the bouncer started hassling him. It looked like Omar might be shouting, though I couldn't hear anything through the heavy glass. Then Marisela turned on the charm and the bouncer let them enter. Omar sulked by Marisela's side as she socialized with her friends. Omar hated coming to Anglo clubs. They always made him feel illegitimate.

Usually I did not encounter anybody from my own social sphere when I was with the girls, so separate were our worlds, but tonight a gregarious woman with the Latina Circle of Leadership recognized me. "We have to get you on our board!" she sang. It did not occur to her that I could be there in any role other than as the mayor's wife, so I did not have to discuss my true purpose. Back when I first met Marisela and Yadira, I had thought we had much in common because our parents had brought all of us to this country at a young age, but now I knew how divergent their experiences were from mine. At the same time, I had come to feel connected to the girls for other reasons, one being that during the years we spent together, they were struggling with the question of their identity and so was I. All of us had acquired labels that were not of our own choosing, because of actions committed by people we loved. Their parents had decided to cross the border without the right documentation, and consequently the world labeled them illegal aliens. My husband had chosen to run for office, and now the public saw me as the mayor's wife. I still saw myself as a journalist, and could never accept that I would be defined by the actions of my spouse, just as the girls could never accept that they would be defined by the actions of their parents. The girls had to contend with a label that was toxic, while if anything the label I wore was insufferably positive. Yet both kinds of labels served to hide rather than reveal. After a few minutes, I escaped from the woman who wanted to make me her board member and sought refuge with the girls. They had migrated upstairs to a little lounge where they were taking group pictures with their cell phones. I crowded in beside Yadira.

Back downstairs, the sorority girls started dancing with one another, and I walked over to the bar for a beer. After placing my order, I glanced up at the television. There was Captain Michael Calo of the Denver Police Department, talking about what he had seen inside of Salon Ocampo. Then the camera cut away to a shot of Kelly Young. Today was the second day of testimony in Raúl Gómez García's murder trial, and I had spent the afternoon over at the City and County Building, watching various witnesses take the stand. The trial had begun yesterday with a bombshell. During his opening statement, one of Gómez García's public defenders had admitted that his client had shot the two police officers. "I'm not here to tell you that Raúl Gómez García did not shoot that gun, because he did shoot that gun," defense attorney

Michael Vallejos told the jury. "We are not here to tell you that he was acting in self-defense, because he was not." He said the prosecution had the right man, but the wrong charge. Vallejos maintained that his client did not intend to kill the two police officers, and therefore was guilty only of manslaughter. "It was a horrible thing that happened. It was bad. It was horrible. It was a stupid thing. But what he did was not murder. He didn't knowingly cause the death of Donnie Young."

The prosecutors began by calling Detective Jack Bishop, who testified that when Gómez García and his friends had tried to enter the club, sometime around ten P.M., he had been at the door by himself. Detective Donnie Young had moved off to another part of the club, leaving Bishop to confront the group of young Latino men on his own. "I asked for their invitations, in so many words," testified Bishop. "They didn't have one; they didn't produce one. I said, 'Sorry, guys. You're not welcome. You need to move on.'"

According to Bishop, Gómez García became belligerent and addressed him in Spanish, a language Bishop did not understand. By the time Young returned, the disagreement had turned ugly. Young relayed that Gómez García was making derogatory comments. "Donnie came walking up, and then he basically backed my decision up, that 'You're not welcome; it's time to leave,'" Bishop told the jury.

Then Young escorted the group outside. Although Young returned and said he should not have grabbed Gómez García by the neck, it was not clear to Bishop whether a physical encounter had actually taken place. "Knowing Donnie, I was like—well, I didn't know if he was telling me the truth or joking around with me like he sometimes would," said Bishop. "It was a statement he made. We didn't talk about it the rest of that night." After the band finished playing, the two officers were standing together at the top of the entrance hallway, looking into the dance hall. Bishop heard a series of loud pops and spun around. "I looked to my left and that's when I saw Detective Donnie Young. He grabbed his head as he was spinning toward me. I saw his face. He just grabbed his head and said, 'Oh, shit.' He instantly collapsed. There was no time for me to do anything."

Officer Alex Golston told the jury that when he made it to the top of the entrance hallway, he recognized Young from their time together at the police academy. He saw a woman cradling Young's head in her lap, and she looked like an angel. "Her voice was very soothing and

comforting to all of us at that time," Golston said. "It was very shocking to see."

Kelly Young sat in the front row, her strain visible in the way she
wound a gold necklace around and around in her hands. It was the
chain that her husband had always worn, and on it were a gold cross
and a medallion of St. Michael the Archangel, who had led God's army
into battle against Satan. He was the patron saint of police officers
and soldiers. Donnie had kept a second St. Michael's medal pinned to
the bulletproof vest that he had not worn on the night he confronted
Gómez García.

In the preceding weeks, Judge Larry Naves had tussled with the
media over how they would cover the trial. I had not attended those
hearings, assuming they pertained to broadcast journalists. I knew
the judge had restricted the number of cameras allowed inside of the
courtroom, but did not know he had also forbidden print reporters from making audiotapes. During the second day of testimony, I
blithely placed my tape recorder in plain view. After asking the jury
to leave the room, the judge demanded angrily that the journalist who
was tape-recording stand up. I did so gingerly, confused as to what I
might have done wrong. The following morning my hesitation became
the subject of two newspaper stories, and one made it sound as though
the mayor's wife had been trying to tape-record the proceedings sur-
reptitiously. Mortified, I slunk back into the courtroom, expecting to
be shunned. Instead, the sheriffs and police officers greeted me with
unusual warmth.

"Now you know how we feel all of the time," one police officer
said.

"*This* is how you feel?"

"Oh, yeah. We're always on, we're always in the spotlight. And
when we read about things that happen in the media later, it's like
another situation entirely."

The prosecution called its next witness, Rubén Huizar Gonzáles,
the proprietor of Salon Ocampo. He was a slim man in blue Wranglers
and a white golf shirt, who parted his straight dark hair in the middle,
like Raúl Julia. Huizar Gonzáles testified in Spanish that he had known
Donnie Young for five years. Young was his sole contact in the police
department—if the proprietor needed other officers, Young found them.
When Huizar Gonzáles heard the sound of gunshots, he was standing

inside the bar of Salon Ocampo, close to the doorway that led back to the main hallway. He looked through the door and found himself staring at the shooter. "He was holding the gun with both hands and the shots were ringing," testified Huizar Gonzáles.

He pursued the shooter outside, where the man ran straight into Joseph Martínez, the tow-truck driver. After leveling his gun at Martínez, the shooter kept running. The proprietor and the tow-truck driver both chased the suspect over to a hole in the chain-link fence, but then he lost them. They turned back to see if anybody was hurt.

"Do you see the man who did the shooting sitting in the courtroom today?" asked Levin.

"Yes," replied Huizar Gonzáles. He identified Gómez García.

"Can you describe the expression on his face when he pulled the trigger?"

"Objection!"

"Overruled."

"You want me to describe his face?"

"The expression on his face."

"He was angry."

After he finished testifying, Huizar Gonzáles gave Kelly Young a smile full of regret on his way out of the courtroom. She smiled sadly back and nodded at him a few times. They had met for the first time when Kelly went to see where her husband had died. Upon entering the dance hall at Salon Ocampo, she had seen all the presents for the baby still stacked in a corner of the room. The family had left the gifts behind. It had comforted Kelly—the sight of all those unopened gifts—because she felt as though the hosts of the baptismal party must have understood the enormity of what had happened. They did not take her suffering lightly. Later, Rubén and his wife, Gloria, had invited Kelly over to their home, and she saw they had pictures of Donnie everywhere.

Joseph Martínez took the witness stand in black jeans and a black T-shirt, with his hair in a scraggly ponytail. When a man had come flying out of the social hall and knocked Martínez against the balcony's railing, at first Martínez had assumed this must be the victim, but then he saw the gun. The area was brightly lit, and Martínez had gotten a good look at the man's face.

"Do you see him here in the courtroom?"

"Yes sir. He's over on this side."

"Your Honor, I ask that the record reflect that the witness has identified the defendant."

The prosecutor asked how Martínez knew Donnie Young. The truck
driver's chin started to wobble. "Matter of fact, it was through him that
I got that job there," he said in a shaky voice.

He wanted the jury to know that Young had been a good man. "I
was there a lot of times when he would bring peace between people and
nothing ever happened."

Carlos Ávila—Rubén Huizar Gonzáles's brother-in-law—testified
that he had been talking to the police officers when the shooting took
place. His wife and daughter were standing nearby, and at the sound of
gunshots, Ávila had told them not to worry; somebody was just firing
blanks. In the same instant that she heard her husband reassure her the
bullets were not real, Anna Ordoñez saw Donnie Young start to fall.
Maybe he was just ducking, she thought, but the police officer sprawled
facedown on the floor and did not get up. Ordoñez, a slim woman with
dyed blond hair, testified that she knelt down beside the police officer,
whom she knew well. When she turned him over, blood ran from his
temple. She yelled for her daughter to call 911, and lifted Young's head
into her lap. This was Golston's angel—an immigrant who worked a
second job as a waitress at Salon Ocampo on the weekends. Earlier in
the evening, Ordoñez had waited on a couple with a newborn baby. She
had asked if she could hold the infant. "I remember that the mother of
the baby was very, very young, and that the father of the baby had a lot
of tattoos on his hands," she told the jury. In one long night, Ordoñez
had held both Gómez García's newborn baby and the dying police officer he had assaulted—the life he had created, and the life he had taken.

The prosecutors called Leopoldo Rivas, Sandra Rivas's little brother,
a gangly seventeen-year-old in a pink dress shirt that he must have borrowed, as the cuffs came down over his hands. Rivas said he was no
longer in school—he worked at McDonald's. On the night of the murder, he had been hanging out with his older sister's boyfriend, as well
as a cousin, Samuel Rivas, and Gómez García's friend, Jaime Arana del
Ángel. After about an hour, the others dropped Gómez García off at the
Rivas family home, so that they could go to the baptismal celebration.
He drove himself and Sandra and their newly born child to the party.
The baby being honored was the child of Sandra's first cousin, and she
had received a formal invitation. Several hours later, Gómez García left

the party and picked up Leopoldo Rivas and the others and brought them back to Salon Ocampo. "Raúl was saying, Let us in, because I was already inside, and the party is for members of my family," testified Sandra's little brother. "The police officer said he didn't care. It required an invitation."

The prosecutor asked if Gómez García had gotten angry. Yes, Rivas said. He had argued heatedly with the second police officer, the one who took them outside.

"Did Raúl swear at the officer?"

"Yes. He told him, 'Fucking bitch.'"

Rivas said the police officer had grabbed Gómez García by the neck and shoved him against the balcony's iron railing. Back at the pool hall, Gómez García had fumed about this treatment. He said he wanted to shoot the officers, and convinced Rivas to return to the club with him. Gómez García left Rivas in the passenger seat of the white Neon with the engine running; Rivas moved over into the driver's seat. Five minutes later, Gómez García reappeared, running. "Drive, drive, drive!" he shouted.

Sandra Rivas walked into the courtroom wearing white jeans and a soft gray sweater. She had a rosebud mouth and pencil-thin eyebrows and the face of a gorgeous child. She told the jury that she was twenty, but she looked thirteen. Maybe she was the best thing that ever happened to Gómez García, for at the sight of her, he started blinking and wiping his nose on his hand. Finally his attorney handed him some tissues. The prosecutor asked Sandra Rivas how she knew the defendant, and the girl smiled broadly in a silly, embarrassed way.

"He is the father of my daughter."

The prosecutor asked when their relationship began.

The girl's silly smile dissolved. She whispered, "I cannot do it."

He said she had to.

On May 7, 2005, Sandra testified, she had gone to the baptism of her cousin's child with Gómez García and their one-month-old daughter. After about an hour, Gómez García had left to pick up her brother and cousin, saying he would be right back, but he never returned. Rivas was getting ready to leave the party when she heard gunshots; her father hustled her home. Maybe half an hour later, Gómez García came downstairs to the basement room where they shared a bed. When she asked why he had not come back to the party, he told her that he had tried, but the police officers would not let him enter. Rivas asked repeatedly if he had shot the two men. Gómez García denied doing so until Rivas asked him to swear on the life of their child. He would not swear, and then she knew that he was guilty.

"Did he finally tell you that it was him?"

"I cannot answer."

"You have to."

Silence.

"Yes."

Rivas looked down, and Gómez García looked down. Fate had assigned them the roles of antagonists, despite their feelings for each other, and the charge of their relationship hung over the room.

Fernando Freyre Jr. rose to cross-examine the witness. "When you were interviewed by the detective, he asked you if you are a citizen of this country," said the defense attorney. "Do you remember that?"

Freyre tried to suggest that Rivas had been intimidated—an undocumented immigrant who faced the charge of accessory to murder might have said anything to the police—but it was hard to undermine the stark power of her testimony. The attorney moved on to observe that Gómez García had asked for forgiveness.

"He wasn't bragging about it, was he?"

"No."

The defense attorney asked her to describe her boyfriend's emotional state.

Rivas said he had been *serio*—serious.

A house painter and a janitor placed Gómez García at the scene, and a construction worker identified his gun as a semiautomatic. Jaime Arana del Ángel had once worked as a roofer, but when he stepped into the witness box, he wore the gray uniform of a prison inmate. After pleading guilty to the charge of being an accessory to the crime, Arana del Ángel was serving twelve years in prison, and perhaps he disliked his new identity, for he was a spectacularly uncooperative witness. "What gun? I've never seen a gun," he scoffed. "That's what they told me to say!" Detective Teresa García took the stand to recount what Arana del Ángel had originally told the police. There was much discussion of Mexican slang. Someone said that Gómez García had committed a *tontería*, which Detective García translated as "he screwed up," but Freyre suggested that *tontería* meant rather a "stupid thing." Justice seemed difficult to achieve in two languages, when so much depended on what a person had said. The two agents of the Mexican federal police agency who had arrested Gómez García flew in to testify, and one of them made a rubber face of comic dismay, blowing out his cheeks like a chipmunk, while alluding to the politically sensitive nature of the case. "We were ordered to locate the subject because it was a delicate matter," he testified. Once they had Gómez García in custody, he would not stop talking, the Mexican agents said. The defendant wanted to know which of the two police officers had died, and expressed satisfaction upon learning that it was the big one. "He commented to us that he was the one that he wanted dead because he was the one who was choking [him], the one who assaulted him," said one of the agents.

The prosecution rested.

Judge Naves turned to address the defendant. "Mr. Gómez García, in every felony case, I am required at this phase to tell you that you have a right to testify," he said. "If you do, the prosecution can cross-examine you."

Gómez García asked if he could think about it overnight. The judge said no. After Freyre called back two witnesses, Judge Naves asked again if Gómez García wanted to testify.

"Your Honor, I call Mr. Gómez García to the stand," Freyre announced, to the amazement of everyone else in the courtroom.

Gómez García left the defense table and walked over to the witness box, broad-shouldered but short in stature.

"Can you tell your name to the jury?" his lawyer asked.

"Raúl Gómez García."

"Do you know how to spell your name?"

"No."

Gómez García said that after his parents had abandoned him to go and work in the United States, he had been raised by his grandmother, first in Durango and later in California. He had been given almost no formal schooling. In Los Angeles, his mother had worked at a clothing factory, and his father had sold drugs. Freyre asked what kind of work his father had done previously, back in Mexico.

"He used to be a judicial police officer," Gómez García replied.

This was the first I had heard about Raúl Gómez García being the son of a cop. At Salon Ocampo, Gómez García testified, he had recognized the security guards as police officers by the way they were dressed.

He claimed to believe that all police officers had to wear bulletproof vests because his father had told him it was required. Gómez García said he had purchased his gun at the age of thirteen, and once fired it at a bulletproof vest, just to see what would happen; the bullets had not even scratched the wall behind the vest. After Young had manhandled him, his friends had started making fun of him. "'Are you going to let them do that to you? Aren't you going to do something?'" He said he intended to shoot the two officers—but not fatally. "I never said I was going to kill them. I said that I wanted to scare them. And also I wanted to embarrass them, like they embarrassed me."

"Did you think if you shot bullets at them that you would kill them?" asked Freyre.

"No, because they were wearing bulletproof vests."

Judge Naves interrupted. It was late; the trial would continue tomorrow. The next morning, dozens of police officers in blue filled the courtroom. Freyre pushed through the swinging doors, caught sight of the rows of uniformed officers, and opened his mouth in a silent "Oh."

Gómez García resumed his testimony in a near whisper.

"Mr. Gómez García, no one can hear you, and I think people want to hear you," said the judge.

Freyre asked what Gómez García had seen when he reentered Salon Ocampo.

"Just the police officers."

"But you knew the salon was full of people, right?"

"Yes."

"Did you think there was a risk that someone would get hurt or killed if you started firing the gun?"

"Yes."

"Then why did you do it?"

"I don't know. I don't know why I did it. I wasn't thinking."

Freyre asked if he had aimed for the head of either officer. Gómez García said he had not—he had aimed "to the back."

"Is there anything else you want to say?"

"I'm sorry for what I did. I didn't mean to kill him. I didn't mean to hurt him or anything like that. I'm sorry very much."

Prosecutor Bruce Levin walked to the podium, laid down a legal pad, took off his glasses, put a photograph of Donnie Young on the overhead projector, and launched into a blistering cross-examination.

"Can you even look at this photograph?" asked the prosecutor. "That's the man you shot in the head."

"Yes."

"That's the man whose face you blew up."

"Yes."

"That's the man you shot in the heart."

"Yes."

A police officer put his hand on Kelly's shoulder.

"You're telling the members of this jury that because you were teased by a seventeen-year-old, you were willing to shoot six rounds into the backs of police officers?"

"It wasn't only him [Leopoldo]! It was Jaime, too!"

Levin pulled out the padded jacket that Young had been wearing. The prosecutor asked how Gómez García could tell whether the officer was wearing a bulletproof vest under such a jacket.

"Well, I wasn't 100 percent sure that they were wearing them, but I thought they were."

"Did you see a vest?"

"No."

Levin reminded Gómez García that he had fired in the direction of a dance hall filled with approximately one hundred families, including his own.

"I didn't think about that. I didn't think about my wife or my child."

"All you thought about was looking tough to your friends."

"Yes."

During closing arguments, Freyre suggested to members of the jury that they were dealing with a kid, not a murderer. "Raúl told you, 'I know that if you shoot a gun in the direction of people and in a room where people are, people could die. I didn't think it would happen. I didn't mean for it to happen.' That's reckless conduct, ladies and gentlemen. It's felony stupidity." Freyre harped on moments when witnesses might have mistranslated slang or made other errors, then returned to the theme of Gómez García's youth. "He's nineteen years old," the lawyer reminded the jury. "He can't read or write English. He can read and write a little bit of Spanish. He can't even follow a map and road signs to Las Vegas, Nevada, by himself. He's a real sophisticated guy we're dealing with here."

Bruce Levin delivered a stern rebuttal. He scoffed at the idea that the defendant had not meant to hurt the police officers because they were wearing bulletproof vests. "The fact of the matter is, ladies and gentlemen, that does not pass the straight face test." Levin said he understood the jurors might feel sorry for Gómez García—he had been given a lousy start in life, he had been dealt a bum hand. But they should consider the unalterable nature of his actions. "This is real life. This isn't a play. When this is all said and done, when it's all over with, Donnie Young isn't going to get up off the floor. He isn't going to step out of his grave, and stand up and take a bow, like something by Shakespeare. This is permanent. This is an eternity of a loss."

No verdict came that evening. I had to walk over to police headquarters, because I had lost my wallet and someone had turned it in to the police. I asked Detective Martin Vigil for directions to the property room.

"I'm on my way there right now," he said. "I'll show you."

Vigil was carrying a tan padded envelope labeled JACKET.

"Is that Donnie Young's jacket?"

"In here?" Vigil waved the envelope. "Yes."

Jack Bishop held open the door to police headquarters for us.

"Jack, you okay?" Vigil asked curtly.

"Yes," said Bishop, in a voice that did not sound okay at all.

I followed Vigil downstairs to the basement, where I retrieved my wallet and he returned Young's jacket. Back outside, I stopped at the monument to fallen officers that stood in the plaza. Sixty names were carved into a slab of granite, under the heading "Lest we forget." The last one on the list was Donald R. Young. I stood in the gathering chill, wondering what would have happened if Young had been at Bishop's side initially. Would it have mattered if the first police officer Gómez García had encountered had spoken Spanish? Would the evening have ended differently? I did not believe that Jack Bishop had done anything wrong, yet it had all ended so badly, and now he had to walk past this monument every day on his way to work. Perhaps he could not stop asking himself what might have been, perhaps he could not forgive himself for surviving. I wanted to tell him it was not his fault that he still walked across this plaza full of ghosts, while Young now lay in the ground.

On Friday morning, the foreman asked if the jury could see transcripts, and the court reporters grumbled it was going to be a while. They paced the marble hallways, trading war stories about bounty hunters. At 4:15 P.M., the jury buzzed to say they had a verdict. In the hallway outside of the courtroom, I crossed paths with Kelly Young. She was clenching tissues in her fists so tightly that her knuckles had turned white. Inside the courtroom, I found a seat beside the city's manager of public safety. The police chief and the district attorney had come to hear the verdict, too. The judge read it first to himself, then out loud. "In the case of the People of the State of Colorado versus Raúl Gómez García, count number one, charge of murder in the second degree, we, the jury, find the defendant, Raúl Gómez García, *guilty* of second-degree murder against Detective Donnie Young." Guilty as charged. On count number two, however, the shooting of Jack Bishop, the jury surprised everybody by finding Gómez García guilty of attempted murder in the second degree, rather than attempted murder in the first degree. It was not quite guilty as charged, but it wasn't manslaughter, either; the jury had split the difference.

When the sheriffs escorted Gómez García out of the courtroom, the frosted glass panels of the doors that closed behind them suddenly lit up with blue flashes. Out in the hallway, photographers jockeyed to get a shot of the guilty man—the media horde that Naves had held at bay. When Kelly Young left, the same blue flashes exploded around her, too. That evening, I watched coverage of the trial on television. The TV reporter closed with a monologue, standing outside of the City and County Building. She concluded that in the case of Bishop's shooting, the jury had gone down to second-degree attempted murder after being swayed by Gómez García's testimony. "That was the risk that his lawyer took, and it paid off," the reporter opined.

I switched off the TV. What seemed most noteworthy about the trial to me was not Freyre's bold defense, nor the strength of the prosecution's case. I could not forget the testimony of Rubén Huizar Gonzáles and Carlos Ávila and Anna Ordoñez. Before I knew the details of what had happened inside of Salon Ocampo, I had cast Gómez García in the role of being at home there, with the police officer playing the role of the intruder. I had thought each of them represented a different side of Denver, almost as if we were two cities. Yet the testimony of immigrants at the trial proved that the opposite was true: It was Young for whom these immigrants had felt affection, and the person they had viewed as a stranger was Gómez García. I recalled the rueful smile that the proprietor of Salon Ocampo had given to Kelly Young, and the way the tough-looking tow-truck driver had crumbled. When Donnie Young had lost his life, nothing was what it appeared to be at first glance. The killer was not a hardened assassin; he was an immature coward who thought the manhood he lacked could be supplied by a semiautomatic. The police officer was not a racist; he was someone who had forged strong alliances in the Mexican community. And the majority of immigrants who frequented Salon Ocampo could not be described as hostile to the uniformed representatives of official Denver; at the hour of his death, when a bullet had sped through both pumping chambers of his heart, Donnie Young had been surrounded by people who would have done anything to save his life. Yet somehow this side of the story never surfaced in the daily press, which left many longtime residents of the metro area thinking they must be at odds with the latest immigrants. If Marisela or Yadira had gotten equal time on the news with Raúl Gómez García, perhaps the rest of Denver would have been left with a more balanced view of the most recent arrivals, but the girls led quiet, unnoticed lives. And so the narrative of Gómez García perpetually threatened to hijack the collective understanding of who these newcomers were, even though nobody who was associated with Salon Ocampo would have considered him a fair representative of the people who congregated there. We were one city after all, I thought; the problem was that we just couldn't see it.

4

WELL-ORDERED SOCIETY

Entirely distracted by the start of their junior year, the girls from Roosevelt High paid little attention to the murder trial of Raúl Gómez García. Moving into La Chateau had been a semidisaster. The girls had to furnish their own rooms, and after Cynthia Poundstone sent out a mass e-mail, her friends had showered all three girls with used chairs and sofas. Juan borrowed his uncle's tortilla delivery truck to help Yadira transport her belongings, and at the last minute, Marisela begged for help, too. When Juan picked up Marisela, however, he discovered that she had bought a matching bedroom set from a neighbor—a bed, a dresser, an entertainment center, and a coffee table—all outlandishly oversized. By the time they finished loading the truck, Marisela's belongings took up three-quarters of the vehicle, leaving little room for Yadira's things. Then, at La Chateau, they got the entertainment center stuck in the stairwell and it fell apart.

Yadira and Catarina lived at one end of the basement, while Clara and Angela lived at the other. Omar practically moved into the room that Marisela shared with Zahra, across the hallway from Clara and Angela. Soon Zahra began spending most of her time in Yadira's room, as she felt like a third wheel in her own. At one point, Zahra and Yadira talked about living together during senior year, and listed the other women they would ask to join them. They included Marisela at first, but then crossed her name off the list, as they decided by then she would probably be married. Omar and Marisela seemed married already. Fabián and Josefa had made clear they would welcome this development. One evening, when Marisela and Omar went to Salon Ocampo to celebrate the *quinceañera* of the daughter of some family friends, I saw Fabián greet Omar by throwing his arm around the younger man's shoulders and asking if he would like a beer. Omar was the first boyfriend of whom Fabián had approved, and Marisela's father treated him as though he was part of the family. Omar dropped by to see Fabián and Josefa even when Marisela was not at their apartment. He had left all of his family members behind in Mexico, and adopted his girlfriend's relatives as their surrogates.

That fall, Marisela declared a double major in political science and sociology, with a minor in Spanish. She also hatched a new plan for the future: law school. It was the typical recourse for ambitious young people who were uncertain what to do with themselves, and perhaps I should have seen it coming, especially given the time she had spent inside of the gold-domed statehouse over the summer, but I had not anticipated that an illegal immigrant might pursue legal studies. I could see why the idea appealed to Marisela, though; she wanted to become a civil rights attorney and thought she could fight the system more effectively with a law degree. If she could find the money to go, law school would also solve her dilemma of how to handle adulthood without a Social Security number—at least by deferring the issue for another couple of years. Marisela began studying frequently over at the law library, where she soon grew close to one of the janitorial workers assigned to clean the place. This woman would cluck and fret over Marisela if she dozed off while reading her books.

Back at La Chateau, Yadira had a hard time adjusting to the changes in their living arrangements. Her new roommate was a Chicana who did not speak Spanish and did not listen to *reggaetón*. It was the first time that Yadira had shared a room with someone who had not also graduated from Roosevelt—someone who was not a *mexicana*. "It's kind of weird," she said. "I was so used to Clara." That fall, the two girls hardly had any time to see each other, as Yadira was working extra hours at the clothing boutique to assist her family, while Clara had been appointed by student government to oversee the social climate on campus and had a new work-study job as a student mentor. Later in the quarter, she also won a slot as vice president of Theta Theta Nu—beating out Yadira in the sorority's elections. Meanwhile, Clara was dating her summer crush. The other girls were rooting for Diego, a tall and handsome *mexicano* who possessed a sultry manner, but he exasperated Clara by showing up late for their dates. Once he brought her a dozen white roses to apologize for his tardiness, but by the time he arrived Clara was so angry that she hurled the flowers to the floor. "I think he really likes her," observed Yadira. "Clara has this attitude problem sometimes. She says, 'Come at 7:45,' and if he doesn't, then she calls back and says, 'Don't come!' We tell her to chill out. He is her first real boyfriend."

Halfway through the fall quarter, Clara received a phone call from her mother at three in the morning saying her grandmother had died. Clara had been particularly close to her grandmother, but could not travel to Mexico for the funeral because of her midterm exams. "Want to see a picture of my grandma?" she asked me afterward. She handed over a photograph of a fragile old woman wearing running shoes and a flowered dress, sitting in a wheelchair, in a room with paint peeling off the walls. Clara, young and vibrant, cradled the old woman from behind. "You must have been a wonderful granddaughter," I told Clara. "She was lucky to have a granddaughter who took such good care of her." At this, Clara became upset. "I didn't, though," she whimpered. "I didn't." Clara couldn't forgive herself for going to class, mentoring other students, attending meetings of the student senate, and dating Diego, while back in Zacatecas her grandmother took her final breaths. She broke up with Diego for the first time one week after her grandmother's death, and then again at the end of the quarter.

Over the summer, the girls had reunited with Elissa, but after they returned to school, nobody saw Elissa anymore. On top of her obligations at Regis, she was working as an intern on the gubernatorial campaign of Democratic candidate Bill Ritter that fall, which consumed all her free time. Meanwhile, many of their friends at DU were studying abroad that quarter, including Luke. He sent Yadira a message on Facebook that said, "Hi from England! It's really cool here!" She pressed for more details—maybe if he told her everything, she would know what it was like. When he wrote again, Yadira was disappointed to hear that he was living with another student from the University of Denver and spending a lot of time in pubs drinking beer. She told him he could drink beer anywhere, and should take better advantage of his time in England.

Starting in September, Laura and Zulema had begun spending several nights a week in Yadira's apartment at La Chateau. Typically, Juan dropped them off there on Sunday nights and they stayed until Wednesday. They slept in the living room, where they took turns on the couch and floor. Over the summer, their aunt and uncle had purchased a home in the nearby suburb of Aurora, using the tax-payer identification number that the IRS had given them to pay their federal taxes, since they didn't have a Social Security number. Laura and Zulema had moved with them to Aurora, but had continued to attend Abraham Lincoln High School in Denver. Alma had insisted upon this—she wanted the girls to have continuity in their schooling. Their aunt and uncle said they could not transport the two girls back and forth to Lincoln, however, and by public transportation it turned out to be a commute of more than an hour, involving several different buses. The girls stayed with Yadira as much as possible because it was far easier to get to their high school from the University of Denver. Technically, Yadira wasn't supposed to have half her family staying in her dorm room three nights a week, but Catarina said she didn't mind.

Hosting her sisters proved to be more trying than Yadira anticipated. Typically Laura showered at 4:30 A.M., and Zulema at 5:30 A.M., even though they did not catch the bus until seven. It was hard for anybody else to get into the bathroom for ages, and they regularly became histrionic over matters such as whether Yadira possessed the right brand of mousse. Zulema had inherited their father's rail-thin figure, but Laura was as curvy as Alma, and every morning the difference between her rounded body and the slender figures of her two sisters caused Laura to despair. "They fight a lot," sighed Yadira. "I can't control them, I guess. They're at that stage where if their hair isn't done right, or their clothes aren't perfect, they won't go outside."

Neither of the two teenagers had seen their mother in more than a year. At first, Yadira fretted about their welfare, but as the school year continued, the separation seemed to have an unexpected effect on her sisters: They threw themselves into high school. Lincoln became their shelter from the larger world, which had proved capricious. Zulema won a spot on the school's pep squad (Lincoln's equivalent of cheerleading) and joined the golf team, while Laura signed up for ROTC. Within a few months, Zulema began dating one of the high school's football stars. Yadira stopped worrying so much and assumed that everything would be fine.

Meanwhile, she remained devoted to Juan, who had a new job as an apprentice in an auto-body shop. His immediate boss did not have legal status either, so Juan felt comfortable confiding that he was using a made-up Social Security number. After a while, the owner of the auto-body shop began sending Juan to technical school for eight hours every Saturday, and Juan told Yadira it was better than college, as far as he was concerned—he was learning what he wanted to do most. It had been hard for Juan to watch Yadira immerse herself in college when he was cleaning office buildings, but now he did not feel so jealous.

At the end of her sophomore year, Yadira had asked Lisa Martínez to become her academic adviser. During the summer, Martínez had reached out by e-mail to ask if Yadira would like to work on a research project, but the position was a work-study job. "Oh, that's too bad, I don't qualify for work-study," Yadira wrote back, without explaining why. Yadira considered confiding in her professor about her immigration status, but decided it wasn't wise to communicate via e-mail. She thought maybe she would tell Martínez in person, but as her junior year unfolded, she never got around to volunteering the information. She had no doubt that Martínez would react sympathetically—it was a matter of getting up the nerve to tell her. Later, Yadira said that it just never seemed like the right time, but I thought perhaps the degree of shame she carried about growing up without valid status was so great, it required a large amount of courage to tell someone, and in the end she could not do it.

With Luke in England, Clara consumed by new commitments, and Marisela perpetually entwined with Omar, Yadira found herself at loose ends. Later, she would say that during the fall, everything had been "very fluid." Her relationship with Clara was cooling, and her relationship with Marisela was warming; in the meantime, lonely and in between friends, Yadira sought refuge with Zahra, Mercedes, and Rosalba. She and Rosalba were both taking a required science class that fall—a yearlong course that examined Earth's climate, hydrology, biosphere, and geosphere—and I sat with them through lectures on plate tectonics and volcanic activity in Boettcher Hall, where the girls had seen Tom Tancredo speak the previous year. Boettcher was located on the far side of campus, and Rosalba, who lived at home with her mother, usually stopped to pick Yadira up on her way, in a battered old Ford pickup. Rosalba was embarrassed by the state of the truck, which had been in her family for two decades and had lost most of its shine. Once she asked jokingly if she could borrow my nine-year-old Saturn wagon so that people would think she was rich. Another morning, after we clambered into her loudly rumbling vehicle, Rosalba said that two white students had just stopped to ask if she was an employee of the university. They wanted directions, and had mistaken her for a janitor. "Oh, well," said Rosalba. "It was probably this truck, it's so old and ugly. But whatever gets me to school, that's what I say."

That morning, the science professor showed slides of what wind and rain could do to stone. As they studied the pictures of rocks that had been carved into spires and turrets, it occurred to me that weathering was akin to what the girls were going through—they had put themselves into an environment where the elements were working on them fiercely, and now they were changing form. Marisela sported straight hair and glasses and was trying to get into law school, while Clara had become a presence in student politics, and Yadira was branching out socially. On Halloween, the sorority held a costume party, and everybody came. Omar made a particularly convincing pirate, with his large black moustache, while Marisela dressed like a man but confusingly wore her usual amount of makeup. Yadira went as a fairy, and Clara dressed as Athena, because of her love of Greek mythology. At the party, it seemed as though Marisela and Omar were as close as ever, but several weeks later, when I stopped by La Chateau on a rainy night, I found them fighting in the vestibule. It looked like a bad argument, so I stayed in my car and sent Marisela a text message to say I was there. We were supposed to go out for dinner. After a while, she broke away and ran over.

"Does he want to come, too?" I asked. "It would be fine with me."

"No, it's not that," she said. "We're in the middle of breaking up."

Marisela explained that Omar was eager to get married, and she had agreed to become engaged, but she wanted to delay their wedding until after she finished law school. Omar had been counting on the idea that Marisela would finish college at the end of the following year, and he could not believe that she wanted to continue her education for three more years. They had reached an impasse—he did not want to wait to start a family, and Marisela did not want to start one right away. The messy breakup dragged on for several more weeks—given the close ties that Omar had forged with her parents and her siblings, Marisela almost felt as though she were breaking up with her whole family—but in the end, she terminated the relationship. I had expected her to marry Omar, and the decision not to do so struck me as a critical turning point in her life: If she had wanted to pursue a traditional *mexicana* lifestyle, then he would have made an ideal husband. Now she had American goals, however, and she broke up with Omar to realize them.

That fall, Marisela was taking a political science course on immigration, along with Yadira's roommate, Catarina. The course was taught by Marc Smyrl, a lecturer in political science who spent half of his time in the United States and half of his time in France, the country of his birth. Smyrl had gray hair, wore wire-rimmed glasses, and had a cleft in his chin. "Laws on these matters are being passed or at least debated right now," Smyrl told his students. "The state of Colorado is ahead of the curve; the governor and the legislature here have chosen to take the lead, in a way, and we can look at what they did and decide what we think about it." But first he wanted the students to understand why nations categorized people as citizens and noncitizens.

Smyrl assigned a series of readings in political philosophy, starting with John Rawls. In a diverse society, members had to agree on the procedures by which they would make decisions, according to Rawls; they did not have to hold the same opinions, but they had to concur about how to determine whose opinion would prevail. "We need to agree on how to hold elections, we need to agree on how to hold trials," Smyrl said. "If we agree on these procedures, then it is okay to disagree on lots of other things." In Rawls's terminology, individuals who shared such a consensus belonged to "the well-ordered society." And the best test of whether a society was structured fairly, according to Rawls, was to ask a person to evaluate its rules without knowing which role he or she would play—wealthy restaurant owner or lowly dishwasher, uniformed police officer or jaded newspaper reporter, murderer or judge, elected official or immigrant's child.

Political theorist Michael Sandel had engaged in a long debate with John Rawls over this question of the ideal society. Sandel was a communitarian, as opposed to a libertarian. "The key to the debate between Rawls and Sandel is how big the area of overlapping consensus should be," said Smyrl. Sandel favored greater consensus and more homogeneity, even at the expense of personal liberty. Mentioning that he happened to live in the state's sixth congressional district, Smyrl pointed out that his congressman—Tom Tancredo—fell into the

Sandel camp. By contrast, Rawls believed the ideal society would have the smallest possible area of overlapping consensus and the greatest degree of personal liberty (the class did not discuss my husband, but it occurred to me that he belonged in Rawls's camp). Smyrl asked his class to debate whether personal liberty or overlapping consensus should be maximized. Were they libertarians or communitarians?

"John Rawls is machinelike," commented a young woman. "People have emotions. To form community, you need more than just rules."

"Community is dangerous," objected a male student.

"Why?" asked Smyrl.

"As soon as you have a community, you start to exclude other people."

The class became embroiled in a lengthy discussion of inclusion and exclusion. Smyrl interrupted to ask how much personal choice the students had in terms of their own identity, and a student whom I believed to be from India raised his hand.

"This whole question of national identity is interesting to me, because I was adopted," he said. "My mother is Norwegian, Swedish, Spanish, and Dutch, and my father is German and Irish. I grew up here. If I was going to choose an identity for myself, it wouldn't necessarily be East Indian."

"Right," said Smyrl. "Figuring out who belongs where can be a lot harder than we think it is."

Smyrl observed that the debate over the relative importance of liberty versus community divided each of the country's two major political parties. Both the Democratic party and the Republican party had one wing of voters who sought to maximize personal autonomy, and another wing who valued community more highly. When either party talked about immigration, an internal schism always developed along this philosophical crack. The class moved on to discuss the writings of political theorist Michael Walzer, who focused on the question of membership, and Smyrl asked the students what rules society should have regarding who could become a member—who could become a citizen. "Why shouldn't membership be universal?" asked Smyrl. "Why not include all of humanity?"

A student answered it was possible to create a system of justice only if one established boundaries, so that it was clear to whom the rules applied.

"Yes. Ultimately, this is a story about obligation. We can make claims on one another, if we are part of some group, that we cannot make if we are all just human beings."

The professor noted that Walzer posed the question of whether nation-states should resemble neighborhoods, clubs, or families. A state that resembled a neighborhood would have boundaries that were purely geographic—anybody could become a member, simply by virtue of crossing a geographic line. Walzer concluded this was a bad model, and predicted that any country adopting such a model would see smaller subdivisions of itself begin to assume functions normally ascribed to federal entities. "If nation-states become big neighborhoods, then neighborhoods will become little nation-states," summarized Smyrl. "If nation-states become too open, in other words, then neighborhoods will try to have something that looks like immigration policy." This was what had happened in Colorado over the previous summer, he said. Alternatively, states could resemble families. "How might the family analogy apply to a state?" asked the professor.

"When you're born here!" called out a student.

"Right. But that's the easy one. What else?"

"Refugees."

"All refugees from anywhere?"

Silence.

"Who has automatic citizenship in Israel?"

"Jews."

"Yes. The analogy to family is perhaps most clearly observed in Israel. You also see it in Germany, particularly right after World War Two. These are examples of nation-states acting like family."

Countries such as Germany and Israel have historically granted citizenship based on the concept of *jus sanguinis* (right of blood) or ancestry. Other countries, including the United States and France, have instead relied upon the principle of *jus soli* (right of the soil), and have granted citizenship to those individuals born within the country's boundaries. In rough terms, *jus sanguinis* corresponded with Walzer's idea of family, while *jus soli* corresponded with his concept of neighborhood. Instead, Walzer recommended acting like a club. Nation-states that acted like clubs functioned better than those that operated like neighborhoods or families, Walzer argued, because they chose their members based on shared values, not ancestry or geography.

"How many of you are a member of a sorority or a fraternity?" asked Smyrl.

About half of the class raised their hands, including both Catarina and Marisela. Smyrl asked why a nation-state should be modeled on a club like a sorority.

"I have a question," said Marisela. "Who is making the decision about who gets to belong?"

"Good question. What do you think?"

"It says here that the founders get to decide, and then whoever the members are get to recruit new members."

"Right."

"But it's extremely hard for somebody who doesn't have a connection to gain membership," she objected.

"And is that a good thing or a bad thing?" asked Smyrl.

Marisela had no answer. Somebody else brought up the Augusta National Golf Club, perhaps the most prestigious golf course in the United States, which had attracted intense controversy because of its tradition of excluding women, and asserted that clubs were prone to barring types of people based on prejudice. Smyrl played devil's advocate: "Walzer argues that clubs like to pick their own members, and this is a good thing. If my club is an athletic team, then I'm going to select people with skills who can contribute something." Nation-states that acted like clubs could run into difficulties, however, if they permitted nonmembers to live alongside of members. "What do you do if you have people within your society who are not citizens?" asked Smyrl.

"Walzer argues that you need to make them citizens," volunteered a student. "He talked about Athens, and how they had slaves—people who couldn't become citizens. He said it was unfair."

Athens had claimed to be a club, but had functioned more like a family. There was a fatal hypocrisy between the rhetoric that Athenians used to describe themselves and the manner in which they behaved. "Of all the questions that are dealt with in this chapter, this is the one Walzer answers most clearly," said Smyrl. "He says the one thing that is never fair to do is to keep a population within your territory to whom citizenship is denied. You can call them guest workers, you can call them slaves, you can call them whatever you want, but if you put on them the obligations of citizenship—'you need to follow the rules; you need to pay taxes'—but you don't give them the advantages of citizenship, then that is clearly unfair. He says boundaries are good and you can exclude people, but once you let them in, you cannot deny them membership." After getting to know the girls from Roosevelt, I had come to agree. Society expected all four of the girls to shine, yet had given only two of them the means to do so. Walzer was right—there was nothing fair about this situation.

5

Blessing

At the beginning of spring, I said to Yadira it was hard to imagine that the girls were almost seniors—they had just one more quarter left in their junior year. "Don't put it like that!" she cried. Every day that brought them closer to graduation also brought them closer to the moment when they would have to confront their dilemma again, and both Yadira and Marisela were dreading the end of college. Recently, Cynthia Poundstone had called an immigration attorney to see if there were any steps the two undocumented girls should be taking to prepare themselves for life after graduation, but the phone conversation had been discouraging. "Their situation is not unique," the attorney had said, according to Poundstone. "There are thousands of young people in the same situation, and there just aren't any options for them." The attorney focused on clients who had been abused or were seeking political asylum. She was performing triage, and did not want to be bothered about a couple of college students who were warm and safe in their dormitories. The girls lacked legal entry visas—there was no way she could help them gain citizenship.

"What about pending legislation on immigration reform, how does it affect people like the girls?" asked Poundstone. "Should they be applying for citizenship in order to be eligible?"

"You can't count on anything being passed, and you don't know what form it will take until it's written," said the attorney dismissively.

"Well, I'm a 'be prepared' kind of gal. Isn't there some type of documentation that we want to assemble now? Couldn't one anticipate what might be needed to build a portfolio?"

"We can't really anticipate anything and I'm too busy to talk to you about this."

"I'll pay you for your time," said Poundstone.

"There's no point," said the attorney.

It did not seem as though the girls could fix the essential problem. They would just have to continue managing their impediment. In the middle of April, Yadira sat through a lecture in her environmental science class about daughter elements and parent material, and it seemed to me as though Alma's spirit hovered over us in the lecture hall. It was only a matter of weeks until Mother's Day, a holiday that now made me think of both Kelly Young and Alma Vargas, even though in Mexico they celebrate it on a different date. Rosalba had not made it to school that morning, and Yadira and I had walked over to Boettcher Hall. On our way we had passed a crew of men in blue jeans and sweatshirts, turning over the soil in a flower bed. They were all speaking Spanish.

"How was your weekend?" I asked Yadira.

"Oh—it was stressful," she answered. "My sister Laura wears glasses and she can't see without them at all. She just broke her last pair, so I tried to take her to get new glasses, but they needed a parent signature to give her the eye exam. So she's probably missing school today because she can't see."

By this point, Laura and Zulema had stopped sleeping over at La Chateau. Their aunt and uncle had not been able to afford the mortgage payments on the home they had purchased in Aurora, and they had also decided to get a divorce; Laura and Zulema had just moved back into their old apartment building in Denver, along with their two cousins and their aunt. Although they were related by blood to their uncle, it was their aunt who had legal custody of Zulema. "In my family, the women run everything," explained Yadira. Her sisters soon had to move again, however, after one of Yadira's sisters brought home a dog, which wasn't permitted, and then a neighbor called the police to complain of loud laughter. The police officer who came to their door instructed the cousins to please laugh quietly, which became a family joke. The cousins started telling one another to please laugh quietly all of the time, which only made them shriek more hysterically. After the building manager kicked them out, Yadira's beleaguered aunt found a new place for them to live. She worked all the time, pulling double shifts as a waitress, and Laura and Zulema hated feeling like a burden. If they had to go to the doctor or they outgrew their bras, they turned to their older sister first, because it was easier to ask her for help. Zulema now began sleeping over at her boyfriend's house on a regular basis—often without asking permission. Yadira tried to warn Zulema about sexually transmitted diseases and pregnancy, but she wasn't sure if her sister had listened. What Zulema needed was somebody to keep an eye on her around the clock, and Yadira couldn't be there for her sister in that twenty-four-hour kind of way, not while she was going to college.

That spring, Yadira was taking five classes ("You know what class I'm doing really good in? Statistics! Like, I really get it!"), and the girls were now running the sorority. After the most recent elections, Yadira had become the organization's secretary, Marisela had become vice president, and Clara president. Sorority meetings were almost the only time the three girls found themselves in the same room anymore. Yadira consoled herself by saying that no matter what happened, they would always be the Brownies, but Clara seemed less nostalgic. These days, she often came to class with her curly hair ironed straight, wearing business attire. Clara's status on campus had clearly changed, too. During a break in one of her classes, an Anglo student who was running for president of the senate made small talk, and then brought up his candidacy. "I'm going to be counting on your sorority," he told her meaningfully.

Clara was now dating her second serious boyfriend, a good-looking twenty-seven-year-old graduate student from Ecuador. Confusingly, he had the same first name as her last boyfriend, although the new Diego was quite different from the old one. Clara's last boyfriend had never gone to college, while her new boyfriend had already obtained his bachelor's degree and was now studying for his master's—in composition on the piano. Recently, he had invited her to come to Ecuador to hear one of his piano recitals. "I want to go," she said. "I *really* want to go, but—my parents." They would never grant her permission to travel with a boyfriend.

By now, Yadira had warmed to Catarina, but still had not confided about her immigration status. This often created complications, such as when Yadira turned twenty-one, and Catarina suggested they celebrate by going to a bar. Yadira kept postponing the drink (she didn't feel well, she had another commitment, she had too much homework) until finally Catarina stopped asking. "I feel like she thinks I don't want to go out with her, or I don't want to spend time with her," said Yadira. The truth was, she just didn't want Catarina to see that she could not get served for lack of an ID.

Luke had returned from England in the middle of winter, but he no longer lived on campus, as his parents had bought him a condominium. One evening, Luke invited Clara and Yadira over for dinner and gave each of them souvenirs that he had picked up in London, and later they went to an ice hockey game, but after that the two girls stopped spending time with Luke on a regular basis. By spring quarter, he had learned not to drop by La Chateau, for the girls' new roommates clearly didn't get his acerbic sense of humor—Clara's roommate Angela was so offended by one of his offhand comments, she had kicked him out of their room. Luke tried making other plans with Clara and Yadira, but the two girls were hardly ever free, and Luke, who was not as active on campus, did not understand how they could be so booked. He took their unavailability personally and became uncommunicative. "He dumped me," joked Clara. They never had become romantically involved—Luke seemed young and not yet able to say what, if anything, a girl like Clara could do for him. Now they went their separate ways.

Yadira got a new job that spring. This occurred after Marisela recommended Yadira for an opening at the nonprofit where she worked, and the director hired Yadira as an office assistant. She worked ten hours a week, reorganizing the group's databases, and made $11 an hour. Working with Marisela brought things full circle: While Yadira and Clara hardly saw each other, Marisela and Yadira spent hours together once more. "Before, Marisela wouldn't tell me everyday things," Yadira said. "Now it's like that with Marisela again."

One night that spring, despite their busy calendars, the two girls without legal status wound up in Clara's room, along with Catarina, Mercedes, and Zahra, to watch a movie. (Elissa was studying abroad in Argentina that spring, and nobody had heard from her since she had left for Buenos Aires.) The girls had gathered to see *El crimen del Padre Amaro,* starring Gael García Bernal. Clara said she found the movie star devastatingly handsome. "Have you guys seen *La mala educación?*" asked Marisela. "He plays a transvestite—and he looks as good as a woman, too!" The others giggled. Marisela sat on the floor eating ramen noodles, while everyone else squeezed onto Clara's two sofas. As they watched the movie, the girls wrote text messages on their cell phones and surfed the Internet, but still managed to follow the plot of the film. At one point, a crazy old woman pilfered a communion wafer and fed it to her cat. "Calm down, Clara!" teased Yadira.

"Breathe in, breathe out!" Then, in a scene about catechism, a small child asked the meaning of the word *fornicate,* and his teacher said it meant you don't eat meat on Fridays. Marisela consulted an online dictionary. "Oh!" she hooted. "I didn't know what *fornicate* meant! I just looked it up!"

Clara found a photograph on her cell phone of herself embracing Diego (the Ecuadoran) and passed it around. "You guys know who I'm in love with?" announced Marisela. "Manuel Landeta! He's like a forty-year-old guy. I don't know why, I had a dream about him." Landeta was a *telenovela* mega-star widely known in the Mexican community, but some of the other girls had never heard of him, so Marisela found a photo on her laptop. Landeta's shiny leather pants clung to his muscular thighs, as he held open his white dress shirt to reveal a well-oiled torso. Yadira flapped her hands in the air. *"Marisela!"* she remonstrated. "That is simply *unacceptable*!"

"He's a gentleman," Marisela replied with equanimity. "I like him."

"I don't know any gentlemen who oil their bodies," I remarked.

Several weeks later, Marisela announced that she was moving off campus. I was surprised that she wanted to separate herself from the cozy world of La Chateau, but none of the girls in the dormitory was taken aback. The evening they had spent together in Clara's room— eating ramen noodles and watching *Padre Amaro*—had been the exception, not the rule.

"It's like she's already living off campus," said Yadira. "We never see her."

"Yeah," confirmed Zahra. "I don't even see her, and I'm her roommate."

Eventually I realized that Marisela always lived several steps ahead of her peers. She had been the first to get a job, the first to lose her virginity, the first to become engaged, the first to break off an engagement. Now she had become the first to sign a lease. It had not been easy to find the apartment. Thanks to all the publicity around illegal immigration—a result of the legislature's special session and Gómez García's murder trial—every landlord Marisela had approached had asked to see a government-issued photo ID. She told the landlords that she possessed a Social Security card and a student ID, but when she could not produce a U.S. driver's license or a passport, they turned her away. One woman said she did not want any "illegals."

Finally, Marisela discovered a one-bedroom apartment for $575 per month in a complex called Park Avenue Apartments, where the manager accepted her story about being an international student. Marisela had been paying $610 per month to live at La Chateau, so she was actually saving $35 per month by moving. And her new place was only an eight-minute drive from campus. I found her there one afternoon, slouched on a maroon sofa, watching the news on Univision. She had painted the place red and furnished it with the same stuff she had carried into La Chateau back at the beginning of the school year. The apartment complex had a twenty-four-hour gym, which she used sporadically—these days Marisela was struggling to keep her weight down—but she spent most of her time squirreled away in cafés. "I live at coffee shops now," she said. "If I study here, I fall asleep." The other night, she had stayed at one establishment that offered free wireless until two A.M. On her way home, a police officer had pulled her over after he noticed that one of her headlights wasn't working. Marisela had chosen not to fix the problem because it was electrical in nature and was going to cost $200. When the officer approached the car, Marisela accidentally locked her windows and couldn't roll them down. In a muddle, she opened the car door. The officer immediately drew his gun, which terrified Marisela. Then he saw her sorority sweatshirt.

"Don't be nervous," said the cop, putting his gun back into the holster. "You're a student, huh? I just need to see your driver's license and your insurance."

"Well, I'm an international student," said Marisela gamely, handing over her fake Mexican driver's license.

"Okay, this is the best one I've seen so far," said the police officer dryly.

Marisela felt busted and wasn't sure what to say, so she just gave him one of her high-wattage smiles. As the officer returned to his car to run a check on the vehicle, she called her mother. "I'm going to put you on speaker phone, and you're going to hear if I get arrested!" Marisela told Josefa. But the police officer found nothing else amiss. "Okay, it's fine to go," he told her. "Just make sure you fix your headlight."

Once again, Marisela had gotten by. Whenever she didn't have the right documents, she just turned up the brightness of her smile and usually people were charmed. Fabián and Josefa might have explained their daughter's good fortune differently, for they viewed everything through the prism of their faith. Shortly after Marisela moved into her new apartment, Fabián insisted on bringing over a priest to perform a blessing. "I don't even think priests are good people!" grumbled Marisela. Fabián called his daughter on a Friday evening and informed her that the entire family as well as the priest would arrive for dinner in twenty-four hours. Marisela had to cancel her Saturday night plans. "My dad is very religious," she said, rolling her eyes. "And he had good intentions, so I didn't say anything. But he, like, totally ruined my whole weekend!"

Josefa arrived early to help Marisela make homemade salsa and *carne asada*. Fabián and the boys arrived a few hours later, along with Marisela's aunt and uncle and their baby. Marisela's uncle brought an entire case of beer, upsetting Josefa, who believed this would make a bad impression. As the men lugged the beer into Marisela's bedroom, one of the boys yelled that he could see the priest approaching. "He looks like an Indian!" Nestor called out irreverently. Indeed, Padre Sergio had dark skin and long black hair that he had pulled back into a ponytail. He had on blue jeans and was nothing like what Marisela had expected. Fabián offered him a cash donation, but the priest would not take money; when Fabián offered him a beer, however, Padre Sergio gladly accepted *una cerveza*. "See!" Marisela's uncle crowed. "And you guys made me hide the beer!"

Challenging the priest, Marisela told him that she objected to the teachings of the Bible—a book she confessed she had never actually read—because it condemned women as sinful. "You need to understand that people were very naive and very ignorant about certain things back then," Padre Sergio replied gently. He did not even flinch when Marisela brought up menstruation; although Marisela expected the priest to say that her monthly cycle was God's punishment for being female, he did not, leaving her flummoxed. "I have this thing toward priests because of all the scandals and I think they're very oppressive toward women," she told me. "But actually, he was different. He was very open-minded."

"How did he bless the apartment?"

"Oh, he just said stuff and threw holy water all over the place."

"What did he say?"

"Prayers—like, to make sure there was always peace in this house, no violence, always love, always bread on the table."

Part of Marisela's interest in finding her own apartment stemmed from a desire to live alone. Earlier that year, Marisela had left a note for Zahra in which she mentioned their cleaning agreement and asked Zahra to wash the dirty dishes in the sink. This had prompted her roommate to complain to the other girls in La Chateau about Marisela's high-handedness, which had gotten back to Marisela. By the time they had watched *Padre Amaro* together, the two roommates had smoothed out the wrinkles in their relationship, but Marisela was weary of living with other students. "I like it so much better here," she said. "I had problems with Zahra—I really liked living with her, and I do miss the girls, but at same time, I can focus more. And I don't have so much drama in my life. Living with girls can be too much drama."

The main reason for her move, however, had nothing to do with anyone at La Chateau. Recently, Josefa and Fabián had decided to return to Mexico. They were tired of always working, tired of just scraping by; Marisela might achieve the American dream, but they had concluded they never would. They wanted to return to Durango, and were planning on bringing Rosalinda with them. They thought they would leave the two boys in Colorado; Rafael was twelve years old, and Nestor fifteen, and their parents believed that Marisela was now capable of caring for her siblings. At one point, Fabián had even told Marisela he could safely leave Rosalinda behind, too. "No you can't, *Papi*!" Marisela had replied. "Think about how I was at that age!" Marisela had rented the apartment so that she could be prepared to receive her brothers. Also, she wanted to have a place to live during the summer if her parents went to Durango. They said they were going as soon as they saved up enough money.

I did not understand that Fabián and Josefa were under the mistaken impression that Marisela was now married until I went to visit them in Thornton, Colorado. Marisela had downplayed the current situation in her love life to me, and explained what was really going on only after I talked with her parents. After breaking up with Omar, Marisela had found herself unable to go out to Mexican clubs for several months, for fear of what might happen if they bumped into each other. By spring, she was ready to go dancing again, but none of the sorority girls wanted to go with her—the scene was too *charro*, they said. Ultimately, Marisela returned to her old haunts with friends from Roosevelt. One night at Fantasía, she bumped into Omar, and he came home with her. This initiated a confusing period during which Omar spent the night on a semiregular basis, although, according to Marisela, they were not together again. Once Fabián and Josefa learned that Omar was spending the night, however, they concluded that he and Marisela were man and wife. It was common in the Mexican community to forgo the expense of a formal ceremony, and as far as Marisela's parents were concerned, two adults who cohabitated were by definition married. They had no other way of thinking about such a situation. Marisela allowed Fabián and Josefa to hold on to this illusion, rather than go through the discomfort of telling them the truth. After I mentioned her parents' understanding of things, Marisela looked sheepish. "I can't explain it to them," she said. "They're too old-fashioned!"

Marisela was in the middle of trying to organize another immigrants' rights march, to take place on the anniversary of last year's triumph. Since the original May 1 rally, however, the Immigration and Customs Enforcement agency had conducted a series of raids across Colorado, sending a chill through the state's immigrant community. Over the previous year, ICE had arrested thirty-eight workers at a palette recycling facility in Commerce City, and then the agency had arrested 120 workers at a military housing project next to Buckley Air Force Base. Two weeks before Christmas, ICE had raided meatpacking plants in six states owned by Swift & Company, arresting 260 workers at their flagship operation in Greeley, Colorado. For weeks, newspaper stories had talked about the families that had been broken apart and the children who had been left behind. In February, ICE had arrested a dozen janitorial workers at three major chain restaurants in the metro area. As a result, Marisela was gloomy about the march's prospects. "I don't know if it's going to work," she said. "Lots of people are scared. I think there is a split in the immigrant community now—half of them are really mad because of the raids and will do anything, and half of them think that we are having all of these raids because of the marches. They are for being quiet and minding our own business. The mood has really changed."

One night that spring, Omar told Marisela that he thought it was their fault the raids were happening. He said it was because of the big march, the one where she had spoken—if only unauthorized immigrants had not turned out in such numbers, if only she had held her tongue, maybe people wouldn't be getting deported. Marisela was so upset by what he said that she decided never to speak to Omar about politics again. Ten days before the anniversary march, ICE conducted another raid, this time arresting twenty-two employees at a potato processing plant in the San Luis Valley, in southern Colorado. "Farm groups said the raid by U.S. Immigration and Customs Enforcement was believed to be the first in recent memory on a Colorado agricultural operation tied to a field crop," reported the *Rocky Mountain News*. On May 1, the march drew perhaps one-tenth as many people as the year before. Marisela herself missed much of the event, because she was taking a midterm exam in a course on civil rights. "I think the raids suppressed turnout," she said afterward. "I think people are worn out."

Certainly Marisela was worn out. She had grown tired of her job—she loved her boss, but the work was grueling. She said she was eager to do different work, but did not think she could find an alternative, due to her lack of a Social Security number. She felt trapped. Marisela still hoped to go to law school, but never seemed to find time to study for the LSATs. In the end, she postponed studying for the exam until the summer, saying: "It will be my number one priority then!" Something more than mere logistics seemed to deter her—she appeared to have a psychological block. "I'm scared of law school," she admitted. "I'm scared of the test, and I don't know if they'll accept me, because of my status. I'm scared of lots of things—but I'm more scared of the LSATs than anything else." She said that if she did poorly, she would see it as a personal failure, one she could not blame on her immigration status. "Especially if people say they will help with money and then I don't pass—that would be really horrible."

Several days after the immigrants' rights march, the girls met at the Pub to plan the sorority's final event of the year. It was a warm spring evening in May, and a rock band was playing out on the campus green, where fraternity brothers whipped Frisbees through the fading light. I found Clara, Marisela, Yadira, Mercedes, and Nevara—a sophomore who had also grown up in Denver—crammed into a single booth, looking bleary. Several of them had taken midterms earlier that day, and all of them still had papers to write. Coincidentally, the girls had chosen to sit directly under a sepia-toned photograph of their counterparts from an earlier era—white-gowned Anglo students with demure bobs from the Colorado Women's College. Clara might have been able to pass for one of those women, but it would have been a stretch for Yadira, and impossible for Marisela. Tonight her hair had new bronze streaks, and the gold contact lenses were back, as was the dramatic blue eye shadow. Meanwhile, Clara wore a gypsy skirt and a peasant blouse and had wound her hair into a bun. "You look like a hippie!" Marisela told her.

For its last event of the year, the sorority was planning to show a documentary film about the passage of an in-state tuition bill in Texas. They needed to pick a date. Marisela dug around in her backpack without success. "Oh, no!" she cried. "I lost my calendar!" The rest of the girls settled on the last Wednesday of the month. Clara volunteered to handle the logistics of renting an auditorium, while Marisela agreed to take care of publicity. She suggested that if they raised enough money, perhaps they could give a $1,000 scholarship to an undocumented student. "It could mean a lot—for somebody who does not have all the money they need, one thousand dollars could be the line between being able to go or not."

Nevara lobbied for the sorority to start a scholarship fund that could give away even more money. The other girls agreed in principle; they just weren't sure that they had time to start a nonprofit organization before the end of the school year. "Can I just say my opinion on this?" said Marisela. "If we want to start a scholarship fund, it is, like, a lot of work. And we could actually make a difference in one person's life by giving money to one student."

"And a scholarship fund wouldn't do that?" asked Nevara.

"It would—I just think maybe it's beyond our capacity," replied Marisela. "I think we need to focus on this event for right now."

"I'm, like, right in the middle," said Yadira. "I would like to start something like what Nevara is arguing for before we graduate. I feel like this event could be the beginning of it."

The girls decided Nevara should try to set up the scholarship fund, while the rest of them focused on the upcoming event. Marisela began reapplying her makeup, and then Nevara leaned over to grab the last chicken wing, sprawling over Clara's lap in the process. "Clara! I told you not to cheat on me!" objected Marisela, waving her lip gloss wand at the pair of them.

"What are we going to call the event?" asked Yadira.

"College is a right, not a privilege!" answered Marisela.

Nobody said anything.

"We have a dream," suggested Nevara.

That worked. Out on the campus green, the rock band was in full swing, but the busy sorority girls did not stop to listen. Clara had to get up at six for her work-study job, and announced that she liked to see the sun rise. "Oh, what a nerd!" cried Marisela. As they walked back to La Chateau, they gossiped about the upcoming sorority elections. Because she possessed a green card, Clara was going to be able to study abroad in Italy during the fall of their senior year, which meant that the sorority would need a new president. Several sorority sisters had nominated Marisela, but she was not sure she wanted to run. "I don't really want the presidency," she said. "I don't want people bitching at me all of the time."

"That is what the presidency comes down to," confirmed Clara.

"Clara, why do you have to leave?" Marisela lamented. "Don't study abroad! Stay with us!"

It was clear she was not serious. Neither Marisela nor Yadira had exhibited much jealousy toward Clara for planning to study abroad. It was not like when they were in high school, and they had realized for the first time that their lives were going to be different. By now, the two girls without legal status had grown accustomed to their liability.

Several weeks later, I walked into the auditorium the sorority had rented for the documentary showing, and saw only two people seated in the audience. "Where is everybody?" I asked. Clara replied tartly, "You're supposed to be supportive—especially when we fail!" At last people began filing into the room. Perhaps thirty people showed up. After the documentary film, a series of speakers urged the audience to support the DREAM Act, and then Marisela took the microphone. "Okay, who paid money to get in? The money you gave us is going to go to Becas del Pueblo, a nonprofit fund for undocumented students to go to college." They had done it—they had roped a Latina graduate student into setting up the fund. The only problem was, they hadn't drawn enough of a crowd. Outside in the lobby, Mercedes handed Clara a large wad of cash, but when Clara riffled through it she observed that most of the bills were singles. "There's probably only about $100 here," she said. "It's not enough to cover our costs."

"What costs?" asked Marisela.

"It cost $400 to rent the media equipment," replied Clara.

Crestfallen, the girls scattered to complete their homework assignments. After their finals, Marisela learned she had received low marks that quarter, and would not even tell me her grades. Yadira earned a D in Environmental Science—her first ever—but scored A's in all her other classes. She had particularly impressed an anthropology professor who specialized in globalization and poverty. This professor had written a note on Yadira's final paper, saying it was a phenomenal piece of writing. "You are destined to do big things!" wrote the professor. "You're going great places!" Yadira cherished the compliment, even though it also touched the doubt at her core. The anthropology professor did not know her shame, her sin—for growing up without papers carried the weight of sin, even if she had not been guilty of making the decision to cross the border. Was she really destined to accomplish big things? Or was she just another illegal alien with a fake Social Security card, about to marry an auto mechanic? The world told her one thing, and then it said another. Nobody seemed to recognize that it might be possible to be multiple things at once—a person with limited prospects and a promising writer, an illegal immigrant and a star student.

6

SURPRISE APPEARANCE

Shortly before the girls finished their junior year, I met Kelly Young for lunch at a restaurant in south Denver, a part of the city where she and Donnie had once lived. They had raised Kourtney in a house nearby. It had been a small place, with barely enough room for the three of them. "We took off the garage, we added on, we redid the kitchen, and just when we had everything done, we learned that I was having Kelsey," said Kelly. "The house just wasn't big enough. And when we looked for another house, you know, everything that we could afford had orange tile and blue bathtubs, and I mean, I just could not go through that again. I didn't want to remodel. So we found a new place in Douglas County." Her eyes filled up. She had arrived early for our lunch, she explained, and on the spur of the moment she had driven down her old street. "I'm sorry," she said. "I just drove past the house. Usually I'm okay now. I'm okay for weeks at a time. But I just drove past the house."

One week earlier, Kelly had gone over to police headquarters to pick up a box of her husband's personal belongings. "I just got the last of Donnie's things," she said. "They had a bunch of his stuff—his gun, his holster. It was the final thing that I had to do." The belongings had been waiting for her in the property room all this time; it had taken her two years to pick them up. Kelly said perhaps she might start dating. "Which completely sucks, by the way." But she feared that moving forward with her life would mean severing her ties with the police department. The other cops had become her second family, and she was loath to let them go. "Some of the guys in the department came over and helped finish off my basement. They brought over all this stuff—all these tiles, all this material. I probably have about a $60,000 basement, and it cost me around $5,000." Last Saturday night, she had held a party to celebrate the renovations, and realized in the process that she feared stepping outside of this circle. What if she became involved with a civilian? "One of the officers, his wife said something about how cops stick together. 'We don't let other people in.' And I was like, Damn it, I'm never going to be part of that again. I'm not on the inside anymore."

I said I thought everyone in the police department would consider Kelly Young part of the family forever.

"No," she corrected me firmly. "My relationship to them was through Donnie, and he's gone now. And my life is going to become my own."

Kelly said she might pursue a career in victim advocacy, once the girls were older. Right now, she needed to stay at home. The trial had been easier than she had anticipated—she had been relieved when the defense team had not launched a full-out assault on her husband's character—yet the sentencing had been harder. That had taken place last fall, at the end of October, and had included two unwelcome surprises. First of all, Kelly had thought she was going to have an opportunity to communicate directly with Gómez García about what he had done to her family, but instead defense attorney Fernando Freyre Jr., wearing a grim expression, had said to the judge: "With all due respect, I have spoken to Mr. Gómez García this morning, and he asked that I request on his behalf that the court waive his presence for this sentencing hearing. He does not wish to be present."

"Why not?" asked Judge Naves, perplexed. He'd never had this happen before.

"For a variety of reasons, Your Honor. It would be his request that he not be required to be present."

Naves turned to his computer to look for precedent. He wanted to compel Gómez García to appear at his sentencing, but did not want to trigger a mistrial. The judge struggled in silence. Finally he pronounced that Gómez García could skip the sentencing, but had to make the request in person. Freyre appeared frustrated with this outcome. After his client arrived, I could see why, for Gómez García had shaved the number thirteen on the back of his head. A photographer began snapping away, while the Young family whispered. The conclusion they drew, with the assistance of several police officers, was that they were looking at a gang sign. Supposedly the number stood for the letter *M*—the thirteenth letter in the alphabet—used by the Sureños branch of the Mexican Mafia gang to stand for *Mexican* and for *murder*.

Judge Naves advised Gómez García of the rights he would forfeit, and asked if he wished to skip his own sentencing.

"Yes," said Gómez García.

Naves let him go.

Jack Bishop was the first victim to address the court, and his voice shook with anger. "Look at him today, he has the number thirteen etched in the back of his head in big, bold letters," railed Bishop. "Oh, poor kid. He has no gang affiliations, no gang ties—the defense covers it up the entire time and then he comes in with the number thirteen on the back of his head! Give me a break."

Kelly Young spoke next. "First of all, I, too, judge, have to say how disappointed I am that he didn't have to stay here. This was our day, I thought, to make him listen to what his actions that night did to myself and my family. He was a coward the night he took Donnie's life, and he's a coward now, because he can't sit there and listen." Kelly told the judge that on the day when one of her daughters earned a driver's license, on the day when one of them graduated from high school, on the day they walked down the aisle to be wed—all of these were supposed to be happy occasions, but instead they were going to be sorrowful. Even the girls' soccer games were sad affairs, because they missed their dad. "And why? Why did this even happen? It happened because he got his ego hurt that night. For a split second, Gómez García's ego was hurt. He was embarrassed in front of his friends. You know what? That's life. We all go through embarrassing moments. You don't shoot and kill someone because of a hurt ego."

Judge Naves read out loud from a letter written by Kelly's older daughter, Kourtney. "If I could ask the man that killed my dad one thing, it would be to ask him why," he read. "Why did he take my dad away from me? Why did he pull the trigger? Why didn't my dad come home that night? The way I see it is that Gómez García had no self-control, no feeling. He couldn't handle the fact that my dad was the bigger man and maybe embarrassed him in front of his friends." Kourtney expressed scorn at the idea that Gómez García had intended only to frighten her father and his colleague. "[W]hen you think about it, if he grew up in L.A., I guarantee you he knows for a fact what a gun does." Her father was the person she had turned to for validation.

"He was that one person I just wanted to be proud of me, and now that he's gone, I'll never truly know for sure. Or I'll never actually get to hear him tell me that. One bad decision made by some guy I don't even know forced me to grow up at fourteen."

Judge Naves found it mitigating that the defendant had no significant criminal history, but noted that his actions had endangered the lives of many. He also believed the defendant had blatantly lied when he testified that he was only trying to scare the police officers. "What the evidence showed is that defendant Gómez García has a low threshold of perceived aggravation before he will resort to deadly force," pronounced the judge. "The evidence showed that the passage of time does not cause him to cool down and that the so-called voice of reason and humanity that most of us hear does not speak to him." Naves sentenced Gómez García to serve a total of eighty years, the maximum time allowed given the verdict.

The second surprise of the proceeding had been the appearance of Donnie Young's mother. Loretta had not attended the trial, but shortly before Freyre told the judge of Gómez García's desire to be absent at the sentencing, she had walked into the courtroom and sat down on a bench immediately behind Kelly Young. One of the sheriffs had approached the unfamiliar Latina woman, who appeared to be in her mid-fifties. "I'm sorry, you're going to need to move back," the sheriff said. "The first two rows are reserved for family."

"I am family," Loretta replied. "I'm Donnie's mother."

What did Loretta want to achieve now that she had not been able to accomplish while her son lived? This was not the confrontation for which Kelly had prepared, and when she turned to face her mother-in-law, she said only, "I'm not sure what you are doing here. You have a right to be here, but just don't talk to me." Then she focused on the speech that she needed to make to the judge. In it, she said nothing about Loretta, nothing about her husband's heritage. She had not played that card with any of the court reporters, nor at any point during the proceedings. Judge Naves was African American, and the jury had been racially diverse; Kelly might have imagined that the story of Donnie's parentage would win the sympathy of the judge or the jury, but she could not tell that story without betraying her husband, because he would never have traded on his mother's identity. And so Loretta's surprise appearance went entirely unremarked.

When we had first spoken, Kelly Young had not yet made up her mind about Raúl Gómez García. He had been a blank spot in her heart, someone she was not so willing to condemn. Now she considered him a punk. "I had done so much work to get emotionally prepared to face him," she said. "I'd stayed up all night. I felt like I was sucker punched. I felt like, once again, he was winning." Despite Gómez García's parting shot, however, Kelly was able to say she did not believe her husband's killer to be a completely bad person. She understood he had not been provided with the best of upbringings. Neither had her husband, though, and he had made mostly good choices in life. Kelly believed that people did not always get lucky breaks—the point was to make the best hand out of the cards you were dealt. In the end, she felt a sense of equanimity about Gómez García's fate, because she believed he had chosen it of his own free will.

"And how do you feel now about illegal immigrants in general?" I asked.

"You would think I would be prejudiced toward them, but I'm not. I struggle with myself sometimes because of it: Why don't I take a stand? But it's just that I've met so many people—so many different people— and I can't lump them all into one category." Some people wanted to see Gómez García's crime as iconic—to use his actions to rally others to their point of view—but she resisted this impulse. The puzzle was vast and confusing, and she had only laid her hands on a few of the pieces. She judged Gómez García as an individual, and did not extrapolate from his story. It was unique, and one of twelve million. Who could say, while these twelve million different lives were still unfolding, what they might signify in the aggregate? She did not dare to assume that she knew.

7

Gun Show

Two weeks after I had lunch with Kelly Young, I flew to Iowa to catch up with Congressman Tom Tancredo. It was spring 2007 and he had not yet officially declared that he was running for president in the 2008 election (he would do that the following month on talk radio), but he was already spending a lot of time in New Hampshire and in Iowa. On this particular evening, Tancredo was delivering the keynote address at the Johnson County Republicans spaghetti dinner, just outside of Cedar Rapids, Iowa. The no-frills facility on the Johnson County Fairgrounds had walls made of aluminum siding and a floor of concrete, and the din of many voices debating politics ricocheted off these hard surfaces. Red, white, and blue posters that said "Tom Tancredo for a Secure America" covered the podium, and several guests arrived bearing copies of Tancredo's book *In Mortal Danger*. Longtime party regulars mixed uneasily with these devotees. "Well, my mother-in-law is a big fan of his," one of the organizers told me. "She thinks we should build a Berlin Wall around the whole country. I don't know—I guess it will be interesting to listen to him speak."

Outside, a soft gray day darkened imperceptibly into evening. Trees were in bud but had not yet leafed out, which was about where things stood in the presidential campaign: It was more than a year before voters would choose the country's next leader, and on the Republican side, eleven candidates were jousting for dollars and attention. Iowa would play an important role in narrowing down the field. Tancredo hoped to upset the status quo by making a surprisingly strong showing in the caucuses to be held here next January, but at the moment he was stuck in Chicago, where his plane had not yet left the ground. Party functionaries took turns stalling for time.

I sat down next to Steve Jennerjohn, a mild-mannered mechanical engineer of Scandinavian descent who had never before participated in a political event. After checking out Tancredo's website, however, Jennerjohn had made his first political contribution—for $25—because he liked the congressman's opinions on immigration. "If there's a flood in the basement, you need to fix it," Jennerjohn advised me.

I ate my spaghetti, basking in the anonymity I enjoyed outside of Colorado. If this event had been held in Denver, the organizers would have been coming over to say hello. Here, nobody knew who I was— bliss. As one speaker succeeded another, an older gentleman nearby began drumming his fingers on the table. After they consumed their spaghetti, a few people left.

"Well, our candidate is wheels down!" announced the cochair of the Johnson County Republicans.

Jennerjohn, appreciating for the first time the challenges of scheduling a public life, said: "It would kind of suck to be a politician, wouldn't it?"

"I am quite certain it would," I told him.

At last, Tancredo jogged into Building C, smiling broadly. "You have got to be the diehards!" he cried. Then he delivered a civics lesson. "As you probably know we had a vote on the House floor," he said. "The vote was on the supplementals, the Iraq supplementals. Now a supplemental—it's not part of the regular budget, it's something extra that you need. In this case it is for the war—or at least that's what it was *supposed* to be for." After the Democrats had attached conditions to the Iraq supplementals, however, the bill had foundered, and to get it passed, they had loaded it up with pork. "How do the Democrats end up with the votes to actually pass this supplemental that included all these provisions that I just described? On what moral issues did this turn? Peanuts! Literally! *Peanuts!* There were millions of dollars included for some kind of drying process for *peanuts!*"

Tancredo moved on to his favorite topic. Illegal immigration cost American taxpayers in all kinds of ways, he told the Iowans—they were paying for the education of children whose parents were here illegally, and they were paying for the health care of these families, too. Even more important, the latest immigrants were attacking our culture. "If you come here, all we ask is that you do what my grandparents did. Because I understand: You come here for the same reasons, you come here for the economic opportunity. It is totally understandable—you are doing the same thing, right? But I ask you this: When you come here, you cut the ties that bind you to your country of origin, political and otherwise, and you connect to America."

The audience burst into a furious storm of applause. Last year, Tancredo had helped torpedo the Comprehensive Immigration Reform Act. The immigration caucus he had helped start had swelled to 110 members, and these lawmakers had objected to the inclusion of a path to citizenship for undocumented immigrants in the legislation. Yesterday, Senator Harry Reid of Nevada had introduced the Comprehensive Immigration Reform Act of 2007—a second major attempt to tackle the issue. "Here we go again," said Tancredo to the Iowans. "*Amnesty.*" He vowed to oppose any law that offered illegal aliens a path to citizenship. "It is lousy public policy. Citizenship should *never* be given to people who came here illegally. When you have broken the law? The one thing we should never consider in a million years is handing over something so valuable as citizenship papers, if somebody came under those circumstances." He thought the very fate of the country was at stake. "We are in a clash of civilizations. We are at war with radical Islam. And I'm telling you, my friend, they know exactly who they are, and why they hate us, and why they fight. I worry that we don't know who we are. If we don't, we can't win any battles."

The Johnson County Republicans rose in unison to deliver a standing ovation.

"What did you think?" I asked Jennerjohn.

"I'm impressed," he said.

Reluctantly, I was, too. It had been a masterful speech. Tancredo had cloaked his conservative ideas in the language of moderation, delivering his comments about the country's most recent immigrants in an almost mournful tone. I even found myself wondering whether he had become more moderate—perhaps the change was more than rhetorical. The following day, however, Tancredo sounded more like his old self over at Hawkeye Downs, a popular stock car racetrack outside of Cedar Rapids. More than one hundred gun dealers had taken over a vast hangarlike building to display their wares. A steady stream of men, many wearing camouflage, entered to peruse the rifles, pistols, and semiautomatics laid out on tables like items at a flea market. The gun show drew more than three thousand visitors daily, and the majority were conservative white men who looked as though they might lack college degrees—Tancredo's base. The congressman strolled up and down the aisles, admiring guns, shaking hands, talking politics. Today he drew no analogies between illegal immigrants and his own kin. "We've got twelve million of them here, and [people say,] 'We can't just deport them,'" he said to a knot of followers. "Stop! *Stop!* Now wait a minute. Yes we can! We *can*. We can stop giving them jobs, and then millions of them will go home. And if they don't go home, then we *can* deport them."

A bevy of Minutemen strode up. Craig Halverson, the director of the Iowa Minuteman Civil Defense Corps, wore a Tancredo for President T-shirt. The Minutemen stuck close to Tancredo, scrutinizing the crowd intently as if they were his security detail. One of them asked me, "Are you friend or foe?" I replied that when I first met Tancredo, I had disagreed with almost everything he said, but that I had just heard him give a speech with which I found it hard to disagree at all. This seemed to satisfy my questioner. At the Minuteman booth, I saw Tancredo posters and Tancredo bumper stickers and copies of Tancredo's book on display. Halverson maintained that his organization did not take sides in political contests, although I couldn't see literature supporting any other candidate. Then Tancredo walked around the table to stand behind it, as if it were his turn to man the booth. "This is a terrific group," he said. "Great patriots."

He told an anecdote about the Mexican military crossing over into U.S. territory during what the border patrol deemed to be an accidental incursion. "People don't want to call this an invasion, but I don't know what else to call it, if you've got foreign troops actually in your country, firing weapons!"

He tapped the cover of *In Mortal Danger,* lying on the table at the Minuteman booth. "In my book, I talk about this."

In the months that followed, Tancredo returned to Iowa frequently. One survey predicted that he would place second in the straw poll that took place every four years in Ames, Iowa, but surprisingly few people turned out, and two other social conservatives—former governor of Arkansas Mike Huckabee and United States Senator Sam Brownback of Kansas—surged at the last minute. Former Massachusetts governor Mitt Romney won, and Huckabee came in second (after his rock band wowed the Iowans with a spectacular cover of "Free Bird"), while Brownback placed third. The pundits ignored Tancredo's fourth-place finish. The following year, after he failed to make a strong showing in the Iowa caucuses, he dropped out of the race. Tancredo decided not to seek reelection to Congress, and everybody wondered what he would do next. Some people began saying he might run for governor of Colorado in 2010, when Bill Ritter would seek reelection.

At any rate, by the time he dropped out of the presidential election, Tancredo had already accomplished his primary goal—he had changed the way the country's leaders spoke about critical issues. Back while Tancredo was still in the running, all the Republican candidates had appeared in a debate sponsored by CNN in St. Petersburg, Florida. It began with a twenty-minute verbal brawl over immigration. Questions came from ordinary people over YouTube, and the first was directed to Rudy Giuliani. "Under your administration as well as others, New York City was operated as a sanctuary city, aiding and abetting illegal aliens," said Ernie Nardi (apparently the Mike McGarry of Brooklyn). "I would like to know if you become president of the United States, will you continue to aid and abet the flight of illegal immigrants into this country?"

Giuliani declared that New York was not a sanctuary city. Then he described policies, such as allowing immigrants to report crimes without fear of deportation regardless of their legal status, which led Mitt Romney to argue the city did deserve that label. Giuliani shot back that Romney used to live in a sanctuary mansion, because illegal immigrants from Guatemala had tended the lawn of the Massachusetts governor's residence while he resided there. The only candidate who appeared to regret the tenor of the argument was Senator John McCain. He promised to address the immigration problem without "demagoguing." Overall, Tancredo could not have been more pleased. "Well, I'll tell you, this has been wonderful," he said. "Senator McCain may not be happy with this debate, but for a guy [like me] who typically stands here on the bookends and just listens, so far it's been wonderful. All I've heard is people trying to out-Tancredo Tancredo!"

8

LAUGH NOW, CRY LATER

After my trip to Iowa, while the girls were still finishing their junior year of college, the U.S. Congress failed for the second time in as many years to reform the nation's immigration system. This time around, Marisela and Yadira hardly paid attention. When I brought up the latest deal's collapse, at the beginning of their summer break, Marisela simply shrugged. "I was kind of expecting it to fall apart," she said. "The bill was already messed up. They wanted to build more deportation centers and then start legalization. Our analysis was therefore there would be a lot of raids before anybody was legalized." Marisela gave up on the idea of comprehensive reform, and focused instead on passing the DREAM Act. She no longer held any illusions about the likelihood of such legislation coming to fruition in time to help her gain a path to citizenship while she was still an undergraduate—she did not think Congress would act before her graduation ceremony, which was less than one year away—but she did hope that a bill would pass at some point, perhaps in time to make life easier for her younger sister.

Rosalinda was now fourteen years old, and living with her parents in Thornton, Colorado, on the far north side of the metro area. I saw her there on a sweltering Sunday in July, when I drove up to visit Fabián and Josefa. They were living in an inexpensive apartment complex perched beside a busy road. When I arrived it was midmorning, and an older man in a straw hat was pushing a blue cart full of *paletas* around the parking lot, suggesting that a lot of Mexican families lived there. Marisela's parents were supposed to be expecting me, but when Rosalinda opened the door of their apartment, she said that her parents were still sleeping. I asked her not to disturb them, since I knew how hard it was for Fabián to get sufficient rest, but she went to rouse them anyway. The apartment was crammed full of photographs, including one that depicted Marisela at fifteen, celebrating her *quinceañera* in a white gown and a serious expression. She had already seen a lot of life by then, yet her face looked so young.

Josefa emerged wearing a blue nightshirt, yawning. Fabián followed in blue jeans and a T-shirt that said NATIONAL MAINTENANCE. These days he was cleaning supermarkets for a different janitorial service, making $1,000 every two weeks—close to the same salary he'd been earning before National Maintenance had slashed his pay, four years prior. Marisela's parents told me that they had decided to postpone their plans to go to Mexico. "We're tired of being here, we're ready to go, but the kids don't want to leave," said Josefa. "We're tired of working, working, working." Her husband added, "We're just going to wait for the children to grow up a little more. Maybe we'll go home in two or three years. Then Marisela and Omar can take care of the children together."

Nestor emerged from the bedroom that he shared with Rafael, looking confused at finding a visitor in his living room. He had grown tall and rangy, and was almost a man. In the fall, he would start his junior year of high school. Nestor said he was planning to go to college like his older sister, but he seemed more excited about his job at Carl's Jr.—"Home of the Six Dollar Burger"—where he earned $7.25 an hour. He had just helped Rosalinda score a job there, too. When Fabián and Josefa took her to buy a fake green card and a fake Social Security card, Rosalinda had added two years to her age, claiming that she was sixteen. I had a sense of déjà vu. Years had passed, and nothing had changed—now Rosalinda was about to learn what it was like to come of age without a driver's license, without a checking account, without the ability to rent a movie from Blockbuster. She was going to have to learn how to hustle and lie, how to get by with a smile and fake documents. The country had endured four years of political strife over the subject of immigration, yet in every essential way, Rosalinda's prospects remained exactly the same as Marisela's had been when we met. The same story was beginning all over again.

For Marisela, the highlight of the summer came in July, when she and Yadira took a road trip to Atlanta, Georgia, to attend a national conference on social justice. Coworkers at the nonprofit where they were employed arranged for the two girls to ride as passengers in a vehicle driven by other people. Aside from Marisela's trip to visit her parents in Arizona, this was the first time that either of the two girls without documents had traveled outside of the state of Colorado in the time that I knew them. The girls were thrilled—finally, they were going to see the rest of America! I loaned them my camcorder so they could memorialize the experience, and they brought back extensive footage of a road game that involved yelling "BOOTY!" a lot. On the first day of their journey, Marisela wore a black sundress and immense sunglasses that looked like Chanel knockoffs with her hair up in a messy ponytail, while Yadira looked neat and tidy in a tiny sleeveless T-shirt and her favorite hip-hugger blue jeans. After several hours, the car fell silent, and they drove through endless flatness. "This is all we've been seeing for the past seven hours," said Yadira wearily.

At last, a cityscape appeared on the horizon.

"St. Louis! St. Louis, baby!" sang out a coworker. "The St. Louis arch!"

"What is it?" asked Marisela.

"It's just an arch," replied Yadira.

"Where? I don't see it!" cried Marisela. "Oh! There it is! It's pretty! Wow—it's big."

Day two, the girls blasted Daddy Yankee's *"Lo Que Pasó Pasó"* and Elvis Crespo's *"Suavemente,"* as rain pelted the vehicle. Marisela took over the camcorder, amid verdant greenery. "It looks Kentucky-ish!" she said. "Doesn't it look Kentucky-ish?" When they got to Tennessee, the urgent chords of Juanes singing *"La Camisa Negra"* filled the car, now littered with candy wrappers, empty soda bottles, and abandoned shoes. "There's a lot of trees," narrated Marisela. "We've been looking at trees for like ten hours." "And there's no brown people," added Yadira. "A couple of black people here and there, but no brown." Celia Cruz belted out *"Rie y Llora."* The song's title refers to a famous Spanish-language maxim that says laugh now, cry later—a saying so popular among Mexican immigrants that they sometimes tattoo it onto their bodies, alongside the happy mask of comedy and the sad mask of tragedy. The juxtaposition of the scenery and the music on the car stereo captured the ongoing enigma of the girls' lives: They were taking the quintessential American road trip, with a Latin soundtrack. Everybody in the car was punch-drunk by the time they reached Georgia. "Hey! Somebody stinks!" yelled Marisela. "Smell your armpits, everybody!"

They reached their hotel after twenty-two hours of driving. In Atlanta, they discovered humidity and attended a series of workshops, including one that linked immigration to the International Monetary Fund and the war in Iraq. "It was cool because they presented the three topics individually and then connected them all," said Yadira afterward. "It just clicked how immigration wasn't only people coming here to the United States, but was happening all over the world. It was, like, *deep*."

The girls started their final year of college in the fall of 2007. By that point, the presidential election was in full swing, even though there was a year to go before the nation would vote. Almost a dozen Republican contenders were still jockeying for position, but on the Democratic side it had come down to Senators Barack Obama, Hillary Clinton, and John Edwards. Clara left for Italy in September. Nobody heard from her for weeks, and then she sent an e-mail saying that for the first time she had seen the sea. "The ocean seemed like a big quilt to me," she wrote. "I can't swim so I was afraid to go in. So I just walked along the beach with the waves hitting my legs." Clara saw all the sights in Rome, took trips to several islands, and flew to Germany, where she took a tour of Dachau. Italy reminded Clara of Mexico—it had many of the same flowers and similar-looking brown-eyed people and a culture that placed emphasis on the extended family structure—yet she wasn't able to speak the language. She had three roommates, all Anglo, who came from various parts of the United States. Clara liked the other girls, but they did not understand her background. Once, her mother called to wish her happy birthday, and one of her roommates answered the phone. Clara's mother lapsed into silence because of the language barrier, and her roommate laughed when she reported this. Clara had watched her mother try and fail to learn English at night school, and her roommate's callousness filled her with fury. How could the girl laugh, when she was here in Rome, struggling because she didn't know how to speak Italian? Clara tried to point this out, but did so gently, because her roommates had just prepared a birthday dinner for her. "It was the first time that I was just a student, with nothing else attached to it, and I wanted to fit in, I wanted to be part of the crowd," Clara said later on. "So I didn't say much, even though I was just boiling inside. I'm not outspoken like that."

Back at the University of Denver, Marisela and Yadira took several classes together that fall. One was an upper-level Spanish class about the conquest of Latin America, taught by Miriam Bornstein. The students began by reading the famous letter penned by Cristóbal Colón (also known as Christopher Columbus) in which he described the inhabitants of the New World as naked, unarmed, and "naturally timid and fearful." Colón painted a picture of the New World as a virgin land, practically without a civilization, which became widely accepted in Europe. Then the students read what Hernán Cortés had to say about an Aztec city in his *Segunda Carta*:

> There is in this city a market, in which every day thirty
> thousand people are engaged in buying and selling, beside
> many other merchants who are scattered about the city.
> The market contains a great variety of articles both of food
> and clothing, and all kinds of shoes for the feet; jewels of
> both gold and silver, and precious stones, and ornaments of
> feathers, all as well arranged as they can possibly be found
> in any public squares or markets in the world. There is
> much earthenware of every style and a good quality, equal
> to the best of Spanish manufacture. Wood, coal, edible and
> medicinal plants, are sold in great quantities. There are
> houses where they wash and shave the head as barbers, and
> also for baths. Finally, there is found among them a well
> regulated police. . . .

Perhaps no European dispatch from the New World was quite so startling, however, as the strange account of Álvar Núñez Cabeza de Vaca. (His ancestors had acquired the curious surname, which means "head of cow," after they helped a Christian army recognize a mountain pass by marking it with a cow's head.) Cabeza de Vaca spent eight years in the company of various Native American tribes after being shipwrecked off the coast of modern-day Florida. He became a slave and later a *curandera,* or folk healer, as he walked across the expanse we now know as the Gulf States. He met up with Spaniards again near the present-day location of Culiacán, Sinaloa (where, centuries later, the Mexican federal police would arrest Raúl Gómez García). By the time he returned to living among Europeans, so many years had elapsed that Cabeza de Vaca had a hard time wearing clothes and could not abide the softness of a bed, having grown accustomed to sleeping on the hard ground. In the annals of conquest literature, Cabeza de Vaca's perspective is unique because of his detailed observations about the customs of the different tribes he came to know, and because, most of the time, he was not in charge. Unlike other conquistadors who lived to write about their experiences, Cabeza de Vaca found himself at the mercy of cultures he had expected to dominate, a total inversion of typical relations in the New World. Bornstein tried to get her students to imagine what it must have been like for a person of Cabeza de Vaca's stature to find himself enslaved, with his worldview turned upside down.

"What happened inside of him?" Bornstein asked the class in Spanish. "What happens to a person who is bought and sold?"

"He was depressed," offered one co-ed.

"Yes, depression, certainly," said the professor. "What else?"

"Fear?" asked Yadira.

"Yes, and what is even stronger than fear?"

"Terror," said Marisela.

"Terror, yes—a kind of trauma. And a conflict of identity."

On that particular day, Yadira happened to be wearing a shirt that said LUCHA Y RESISTA—fight and resist. Given the subject of conversation, this seemed appropriate, as when it came to identity conflicts, she always seemed to experience the most hand-to-hand combat. During the time that I knew her, she was always searching for an explanation for why this was so, and I thought Bornstein's class supplied part of the answer. People of Anglo descent who are born in the United States often think of their country as being two hundred and fifty years old, but the literature that the girls were reading described a drama that began more than five centuries ago. As the girls read Colón, Cortés, and Cabeza de Vaca, the question of why some students spoke Spanish at home and others spoke English took on a whole new light. In October, the streets of Denver filled with demonstrators on Columbus Day, with proud Italian Americans who favored the holiday sparring with Chicanos, *mexicanos,* and Native Americans who opposed it. Of course Marisela was there, shouting that the city's leaders should abolish Columbus Day; Yadira did not go, as she had too many other commitments. Yet I thought her life story and the questions she kept asking herself could best be understood within this larger context, within this history of countries in conflict and countries locked in eternal embrace. It seemed the conquest had never really ended, for we were still living out its legacy.

Marisela never did get around to taking the LSATs ("I keep putting it off!"), but she clung to the idea of law school. That fall, Yadira decided she might pursue a law degree, too, instead of becoming a teacher. "The educational system disturbs me too much," she said. "And I don't want to fight the system from inside—I would be a teacher saying I don't want the teachers' union, and that would be weird." To me, Yadira's notion of following Marisela's lead did not seem like a genuine calling, but rather a means of dealing with her uncertainty. Still, both girls seized the opportunity to introduce themselves to José Roberto Juárez Jr., the new dean of the university's law school, when he appeared as the featured guest speaker at an event held by the university's fledgling Latino Center, halfway through the fall quarter. Marisela and Yadira dashed in at the last minute, looking smart. Yadira wore jeans and a long rose-colored top, while Marisela had on a black blouse with silver stripes and black trousers. She had toned down her makeup, and wore sophisticated-looking gray eye shadow, instead of the startling blue color she sometimes favored.

The dean of the law school was a distinguished man with silver hair and a banker's sober suit. At heart, however, he remained a rabble-rouser. Juárez delivered an impassioned speech about the need for all Latinos—particularly those with an education—to identify with the country's most recent immigrants. He pointed out that white and black people frequently looked at him and assumed incorrectly that he was foreign-born or had foreign-born parents. "Let me tell you a scary secret," he told his mostly Latino audience. "Other people take one look at you, and they are not only going to assume that you are an immigrant, but they may also assume that you are an illegal alien, and some of them may even assume that you are coming to murder and rape." He called upon everyone in the room to join the struggle for immigrants' rights.

"I'm going to go up and talk to him!" Marisela announced, as soon as the speech was over.

She corralled Yadira into joining her, and they lined up with other students who wanted to meet the popular dean.

"We are undergraduates here, we're in our senior year, and we are interested in applying to law school," Yadira told Juárez, when it was their turn to speak.

"I would be happy to talk to you about law school," he replied. "You want to apply to a variety of schools—you don't want to put all your eggs in one basket. Now, what are your majors?"

"I'm majoring in political science and sociology with a minor in Spanish," volunteered Marisela.

"Fantastic!"

"Sociology and Spanish double major," said Yadira.

"Great!"

"And also we are the cofounders of the Latina sorority here on campus," added Marisela.

"Excellent!" said Juárez. "So, you're troublemakers, huh?"

"That's right," Marisela confirmed, flashing him a grin.

Juárez told them both to contact his office. He wanted to help them figure out the next phase of their lives. Back at the table, Yadira held up his card with both hands before putting it carefully into her wallet. "This is very, very important!" she said.

As the crowd began to disperse, a cleaning crew arrived wearing maroon uniforms. Marisela approached a woman who was emptying a trash can while wearing rubber gloves.

"*Cómo estás?*" How are you?

"*Muy bien, y tú?*" Very well, and you?

"*Ay, estoy cansada!*" Oh, I'm tired!

I assumed she already knew the cleaning woman, but as we walked out Marisela said she had never met this crew before. The two college seniors spanned such a great social divide—in one half hour, they had related to a powerful law school dean and also the woman who emptied his trash. Clearly Yadira and Marisela had matured into enterprising young women. I did not know exactly how they would manage their lives after college, but it seemed likely they would always find work, for they had been working as long as I had known them. Marisela felt trapped in her current job, however, and it seemed probable that this would be a chronic issue for both young women—they would have a tendency to get stuck. They would not be able to compete fairly with their peers for opportunities, and it would always be harder for them to find a new job. Yet the encounter with the dean also suggested they were equipped to handle whatever was coming, and afterward I felt a sense of optimism about their future. Life would hand them many puzzles, but if they couldn't arrive at the answers on their own, at least they knew how to charm someone like Juárez.

The girls did not share my equanimity, however, and as the fall quarter sped by, they became increasingly anxious about their impending graduation. Compounding matters, Bush Administration officials now announced their opposition to the DREAM Act, saying it would allow individuals who had broken the law to obtain citizenship before those who had been waiting to enter the United States the right way. When the legislation came to the floor of the U.S. Senate, Republicans blocked its progress by filibustering. It takes sixty votes to overcome a filibuster, and the bill's supporters were able to amass only fifty-two. The headline over the editorial in the *New York Times* decrying the impasse said: CONGRESS TO IMMIGRANTS: DREAM ON. By November, Yadira was a wreck. She had final exams *and* papers due in each of her classes, spread throughout a three-week period, during which time she became physically sick, as well as emotionally overwrought. So low did she sink, her boss at the nonprofit organization told her to stop coming to work until she pulled herself together. Yadira didn't answer calls or e-mails during this phase, and I didn't see her again until December. "I had, like, a breakdown," she said during winter break. "I was just thinking about graduation and what to do afterward and all this stuff. It just seems like it's so near the end, and nothing has changed. Before, when I graduated from high school, I was, like, we have four years. But now four years have gone by, and nothing has changed. Time is running out, and I'm so tired of fighting."

In the middle of her breakdown, Yadira had not been able to go to sleep one night, and cried for several hours. Toward dawn, she had an epiphany. "I was thinking about the future, graduation, and how it's going by so fast. And while I was lying there awake, I thought of going to see my mom. It just kind of came to me. I never really considered it before." She had been trying so hard to make it in America, she had never given herself permission to think of going back to Mexico. The thought of seeing her mother again brought Yadira immense relief. The only people she told about her idea were Juan and Marisela; she feared telling Irene Chávez, for she thought Irene might criticize the idea and she didn't want to be talked out of being reunited with Alma. Yadira thought she might find a decent job in Mexico, given her education—maybe she could even figure out how to return to the United States with legal documents. Graduate school would offer only an interim solution, when what she longed for was true resolution, and now she imagined this might be found in Mexico. Juan said he would go with her, but cautioned that Yadira's command of Spanish was not fluent, and predicted she would feel like an outsider in her country of origin. Marisela urged Yadira to stay in Colorado and marry somebody with papers, even if it wasn't easy to get a green card that way. She offered Nestor as a prospect, but Yadira didn't want to marry Marisela's little brother.

Yadira clung to her vision of going to live with her mother until the start of winter quarter, when she learned that Alma opposed the plan. I heard about this development one evening when I joined Yadira at an ice hockey game. She was standing outside of the Magness Arena with a group of friends, while burly Caucasian guys sporting mullets and hockey shirts streamed past. Marisela wasn't coming to the game—she was going to spend the evening dancing instead—but Zahra was. Clara arrived late with Diego Number One, who was dressed entirely in black and looked like a ladies' man. I raised my eyebrows—I knew she had broken up with Diego Number Two (the graduate student from Ecuador), but did not know she had reinitiated contact with Diego Number One (the communications worker from Mexico). Clara just shrugged and smiled like Mona Lisa.

Yadira examined her ice hockey ticket carefully. "Oh, no!" she said. "They want to see IDs!" Juan had nothing to show the security guards. The guards asked only to see their tickets, though, and Juan made it inside without a problem. As we sat down in the cheap seats, Juan reported that his apprenticeship at the body shop was going well. Yadira was book smart, while Juan possessed mechanical genius; he could hack anything digital, fix anything electronic. At the hockey game, he borrowed my iPhone and made it do several things I didn't even know were possible. I told him that he must be appreciated at the body shop, but perhaps he would have an even brighter future at a technology company. "Yeah, maybe," he replied in an offhand tone. I knew what he was thinking: How could he get a job like that without a real Social Security number?

DU scored and the arena erupted. Down in front, rabid fans cheered and heckled assiduously, but the girls were more laid-back about their approach to hockey. In the middle of the game, Yadira sent Clara a text inviting her to see a movie later, and Clara texted back to ask what movie. Yadira said which one and Clara said she didn't like going to scary movies because she lived alone and Yadira said why don't you ask Diego to stay overnight and Clara said she was a bad influence. Clara crackled with energy in the company of Diego Number One, yet kept him at arm's length. "Is it a thing?" I asked of their reunion, when we had a private moment. She replied, "No, I don't want a thing right now."

Toward the end of the game, Yadira volunteered that her mother had made new friends in Mexico. "Call me on my cell phone, because I'm never home," Alma had told her recently. Yadira believed her mother might even have *un pretendiente* (a suitor), because her mother had asked casually, "Would you mind if I had a new boyfriend?" Alma sounded happy. Yadira said her mother had moved into her own place at the center of the city, where she had found a job making *paletas* for the equivalent of five dollars a day. When Yadira had explored the possibility of joining her in Mexico, however, Alma had made clear that she didn't like this idea. Mexico was not a land of opportunity, in Alma's estimation, and she had suffered extensively to make sure Yadira could live in the United States. She could not imagine Yadira turning around and coming back to a place where everybody worked so hard for so little money. Alma pointed out that Zulema was almost eighteen, and said perhaps Yadira would be able to apply for citizenship through her American-born sister once Zulema reached maturity. "Hold on," Alma told her. "One more year, *mija,* just one more year."

Meanwhile, Yadira was fretting about her sisters. Over the summer, Laura and Zulema had gone to see their mother in Mexico, then returned to live with their aunt and cousins again. Nobody thought Laura and Zulema should live with their uncle, as he was sharing an apartment with a relative who drank a lot, but their aunt was providing only minimal supervision. "They're just going crazy," said Yadira. "They're very—how would you say it?—in Spanish the word is *rebelde.* They're very rebellious. I don't know what to do with them. I don't have time to go see them, and they don't want to come visit me—they say I'm boring." Zulema was now a senior in high school, and was expecting to graduate in the spring, but her grades had dropped significantly. She stayed over at her boyfriend's house a lot, and wouldn't answer anybody's phone calls. Meanwhile, their aunt had come home from work one day to find Laura alone with a boy. Everyone in the family thought of Laura as naive, and who knew what favors the boy had requested.

"How old is Laura now?"

"She's sixteen."

"Oh. I got into plenty of trouble at sixteen."

"Yeah."

"So have you talked to your sisters about sex? Or is that your mom's job?"

"No, it's mine. I mean, my mom talked to them, too, but she asked me to speak with them because she is, like, old and everything, and they might not listen to her. I did have a conversation with them, but we didn't get into a lot of details. Maybe it's time to talk to them again."

Meanwhile, Marisela's love life had grown complicated. Shortly before the winter break, she had begun a torrid love affair with her old friend Julio. Since their time together at Roosevelt, Julio had matured into a burly young man with a goatee, and he now worked as an organizer in the labor movement. Back when Marisela had encountered difficulties with Omar, she had begun relying on Julio for support, and later they had started going to movies together. At some point during the fall, Julio had proposed they get married, ostensibly so that Marisela could stop worrying about her invalid immigration status, but then one night Julio confessed to Marisela he was actually in love with her. They fell into bed. Over the ensuing weeks, Julio gave Marisela so many hickies that her boss warned her love life was proving a distraction for her coworkers.

Julio was kind and supportive and loving, which confused Marisela. "I'm not used to getting treated so good," she said to Clara one day. "So nicely," Clara replied. "Hey, I haven't corrected your grammar in such a long time!" Another issue was that Julio did not know how to dance. Marisela was trying to teach him, but he wasn't really interested in clubs, and they spent most of their time elsewhere. This left Marisela feeling cut off from an important aspect of her life. And whenever she thought about the possibility of getting married, Marisela grew anxious. "If we do, it wouldn't be like an actual marriage, it would be kind of like pretend," she told me. "I mean, that's what we planned before, but now—what if it's more real? I don't want to—I'm not ready for that yet. I'm scared of that big a commitment. I'm scared of divorce, and I'm scared of making the wrong choice."

In the end, the relationship simply unfolded too quickly. Marisela wanted to take it slow, but Julio couldn't remain casual. In January 2008, Marisela broke up with him not once but twice—first on the telephone and then again in person. "I confused friendship with boyfriend," she said afterward. "He was really serious about the relationship and I didn't have the same feelings. I was really honest and explained why—which probably hurt him the most. But he took it well, we're still good friends. We still talk a lot. Sometimes I feel like nothing ever happened, but I know he still likes me and wants to get back together with me." It wasn't a clean break, however, and sometimes they still fell into bed. Throughout the winter quarter, nobody could keep track of when Marisela and Julio were in a platonic phase or a romantic phase, as they kept slipping out of one mode and into another.

That winter, the girls rearranged their alliances yet again. When Clara had first returned from Italy, she had moved into Yadira's apartment temporarily, and the two girls had stayed up all night talking. Within a few weeks, however, Clara began spending much more time with Marisela, who was often free, while Yadira was always busy with Juan. The point of equilibrium shifted and the mobile of their relationships revolved into a new configuration. One snowy Saturday morning, I dropped by to see Clara's new place at the absurdly named Brittany Manor, a low-rent apartment complex near campus. "I love how everywhere you live has a superfancy name," I told her when she opened the door. "I know," she said. "And they look really crappy." Marisela was there, too. It was ten in the morning and they were both swigging Coronas.

"Clara! You're drinking beer!" I said in surprise.

"I'm twenty-one now," she replied archly.

The two girls were listening to *ranchera* songs and preparing for a secret sorority ritual that they declined to explain. After a while, the girls decided to do shots of tequila. They asked me to join them, and I decided one shot wouldn't hurt. Vicente Fernández began singing one of Marisela's favorite songs and she turned up the volume. Fernández had recorded more than fifty albums and was known as *El Rey de las Rancheras* (the King of Mexican Country Music).

"When he dies, people are going to be so sad!" said Marisela emotionally.

"He's old already—don't even say that!" Clara chastised.

Lately, Marisela's neighbors had been complaining about the volume at which she played her music over at her apartment. The manager of the building had just told her that if he heard more complaints, he would evict her. The girls laughed about this and did another shot. I asked Marisela about law school, and she said she had decided to postpone it for the time being. "I don't want to go to law school right now. To go, you have to be emotionally stable and financially stable, and I am not either one of those things. So I don't want to go right away. I want to wait a year." Clara started doing laundry. Her studio had a double bed pushed into one corner, and sun poured through the windows. In her bathroom, where she would see it every day, Clara kept a dog-eared photograph of herself at age seven, taken right before she left Mexico. It was the annual pilgrimage in honor of Our Lady of Guadalupe, and she was an angel in the desert. The small child wears a white dress, a silver crown, and large wings made out of plaster. She stands alone, surrounded by cactus—unprotected innocence loosed in a harsh world. What a distance she had traveled, that angel child.

Clara returned with her empty laundry basket.

"Hey, Marisela!" she said. "You've got another beer! I'm going to get another beer. Let's toast. To our new beers! Oh, our toasts are getting really crappy. You two need to drink more—I'm more buzzed than anybody else."

"I'm an alcoholic, okay, so I'm more tolerant of alcohol than you are," Marisela joked.

"Marisela, do another shot! Wait—what are you going to be like when you're drunk?"

"I'll just go to sleep."

"Okay, we can take a nap together then."

At the end of January 2008, former Senator John Edwards dropped out of the presidential election, and on the very same day Senator Barack Obama spoke at the University of Denver. He packed the Magness Arena, generating even more enthusiasm than the Pioneers had during their hockey games. Lines to enter the stadium snaked up and down nearby side streets. My husband's security detail whisked him into the Magness Arena for a private greeting with Senator Obama, while I stood outside in one of the mammoth lines. To my surprise, none of the girls was particularly engaged by Obama, who had failed to make a strong connection with the Latino community, but Julio loved the idea that a man of color might become the next president of the United States, and had dragged his on-again-off-again girlfriend to the political event. Now Marisela sent a text to say that she and Julio had snuck into the arena through a side door with help from Zahra. I finally made it inside as well, and Marisela stood up to wave at me from across the arena. Caroline Kennedy dazzled the crowd with her thoughtful glamor and then Obama strolled up with his lanky, rolling grace. He gave a speech just like he walked—with a concentrated ease. After he finished, I shot Marisela another text. I had found the candidate's speech inspiring, and wanted to hear her reaction. Had he captured her attention at last? She didn't reply immediately, however, because she had left halfway through Obama's speech to go to a class. She remained unmoved.

That spring, the girls began the final quarter of their senior year. Both Marisela and Clara signed up to take a sociology course called Family and the Law. Their professor, Jennifer Reich, was smart and sarcastic, and the course she taught examined laws about marriage, adoption, and surrogacy, as well as the question of when the state should remove children from their parents. Reich delivered her lectures with a wry appreciation for the soap opera quality of family law, and a lot of dry asides. "Many people think of marriage as the culmination of romance," she said one day. "The culmination—the end, right?" Marisela listened to Reich's lecture on the legal rights of married people while surfing the Internet on her laptop, in search of a venue for the next sorority event. She still managed to pay attention, however, for when Reich asked if anyone knew when it was legal to marry in Colorado, Marisela raised her hand and said: "Eighteen, or younger with parental consent." She knew the answer because she had friends who had married before eighteen. Later, when the class debated the merits of mothers staying at home with their children, Marisela grew agitated at the presumption that everybody was free to make such a choice. "I think it depends on the socioeconomic status of the couple," she interjected. "Because in low-income families both parents have to work, but then the woman comes home and has to clean the house and cook and everything, too."

"There's a word for that," said another student. "What is it?"

"The second shift," replied Reich.

Both Marisela and Clara now decided that starting a family was something for which they were not ready. "I'm never getting married," Clara announced at the end of one class.

"Me neither," said Marisela.

I observed that only Clara had been able to find a Latino boyfriend with a college education, and he had been Ecuadoran. It seemed hard to find Mexican men with bachelor's degrees.

"I know," said Marisela. "That's why all my romances don't work out. So I can't get married unless I marry a white guy, and I'll never do that."

"Could you imagine marrying a black man?"

"I might do that."

Clara said she wouldn't have a problem marrying a white guy, although the idea of marrying a black man seemed to give her pause. It was that stark, the difference their own skin color made: The one who was *más blanca* could imagine marrying into the white world, while the one who was *más morena* could not. In any event, both preferred the idea of finding a Latino who could understand them, but at twenty-one, Marisela thought she might be too old. "My parents think I'm past the age to get married now," she said. "They think it's too late for me." We walked back to Clara's apartment, where both of the girls lay down on the floor. I said that Marisela's breakup with Omar seemed pivotal. "If you had wanted to live a traditional Mexican lifestyle—to settle down and have kids when you were young—you could have, but you chose an American life instead." Clara rolled over to hug Marisela. "I'm so proud of you!" she said. Marisela just closed her eyes and covered her face with her hands.

"I'm sorry," I said. "I know it was hard."

"It still is," she said in a low voice.

In March, Marisela moved back in to live with her parents, after the manager of her apartment complex raised her rent. The six members of her family were now sharing a two-bedroom apartment. For several weeks in a row, Marisela listened to Reich's lectures while scrolling through pictures of rental homes on craigslist, searching for a new place for her family to live. After one class, I asked how it was going at her parents' place. "It's so crowded there," she said, with a grimace. "I'm sleeping in the living room. I don't have the privacy that I'm used to."

Yet somehow, at the end of April, Marisela found time to help the sorority throw its first wildly successful event. To celebrate the induction of new members, Marisela persuaded the sorority to host a dance party at a Mexican nightclub called Revolución. Revolución turned out to be a seedy-looking place on the edge of the city, covered with signs in Spanish advertising Latin music and cheap drinks. Black lights made my notebook glow in the dark, while disco balls twinkled overhead. I sat down under a black velvet poster of Pancho Villa. Two DJs played a cross-cultural mixture of *cumbia, reggaetón,* and hip-hop. They were blasting *"Lo Que Pasó Pasó"* by Daddy Yankee when Yadira and Mercedes arrived—they were sharing a room this year (to Yadira's relief, her sorority sister Mercedes understood her situation completely, for she shared Yadira's Mexican background, even though she possessed legal status). Yadira looked like a supermodel, tall and slender in bell-bottom slacks and a boxy red wool jacket. "This is one of Marisela's favorite hangouts," reported Mercedes. "She told us that she's danced on the bar!"

Marisela arrived about an hour later, wearing the shortest skirt and the highest heels I'd ever seen. Zahra arrived with her, in heels that were kelly green. Julio showed up, and a friend asked when he was going to dance with his girlfriend, but they were back in platonic mode, and Julio said sadly, "Not right now." The girls had invited students from the Community College of Denver and Metro State, and by eleven P.M., the dance floor was jammed. At midnight, a group of young Latinas walked onto the dance floor wearing silver tinsel crowns, as Elvis Crespo's *"Suavemente"* blasted throughout the club like an anthem. It was the sound of their lives, the song they had been listening to over and over again. Even I knew all the lyrics by heart. Crespo sang that he wanted someone to kiss him gently, to kiss him again, to kiss him a little more, to kiss him softly and without hurry, that someone should *"Dame un beso bien profundo que me llegue al alma"*—give him a kiss so deep that it would reach his soul. The new girls did a line dance, following one behind the other, moving their hips in unison, turning around at the same time, shaking their hands in the air. Marisela and Yadira and Clara would graduate in one month's time, and then they were going to leave the sorority they had helped to build in the hands of these new members.

Eventually, I joined the girls out on the dance floor.

"I have to keep dancing or I'll fall asleep," I told Zahra. "This is past my bedtime."

"How long are you staying?" she asked.

"I don't know. I want to see Marisela dance on the bar."

"Oh, she's planning on it!"

Actually, Marisela became embroiled in a complicated emotional drama, and left the club around one A.M. to see a friend who was having an unexplained crisis, leaving Julio behind wearing a glum expression. Meanwhile, Matías and Jaime turned up the heat on the dance floor, sandwiching various women between them. White students showed up, and black students, and dozens more Latinos. Suddenly Revolución was the hip place to be. The music got loud and the dancing got dirty. Matías pushed Yadira's former roommate Catarina up against a pole, stuck out his tongue, and pantomimed licking her body. Earlier in the evening, I had introduced myself to the off-duty police officer working security, and now I stopped to say good night on my way out. I figured he would be fine—these were college kids—but the combination of alcohol, police, and social inequality always seemed so combustible. "Good luck," I told him. It was two A.M., and the party was still going strong. Later, the girls would tell me they had raised $1,400.

That spring, Yadira was taking a sociology course called Schooling and Society, along with Zahra and Matías. Their professor, Hava Gordon, was a warm and perspicacious woman who worked hard to create an atmosphere in which all students would feel comfortable speaking, yet the class discussions were riddled with tension due to the vast differences in the backgrounds of her students. As they tried to debate the history of segregation, the merits of tracking, and the reasons why some minority students might rebel against the very idea of succeeding to secure their identity in a society with which they were at odds, it became clear that the subjects being discussed were deeply personal and divisive. Yadira said nothing for the entire quarter, and Zahra was almost as silent. Weird energy caromed around the classroom. They read *Savage Inequalities* by Jonathan Kozol, written almost two decades earlier, but since then the inequalities between students had grown only more savage. The rich kids were defensive about their privileges, and the poor kids took offense at everything.

After a heated debate over school uniforms, I walked with Yadira back to La Chateau. She and Mercedes were now living in an apartment on the second floor, and recently Yadira's sister Laura had moved in, too. We found Laura in the apartment, watching a game show called *Beauty and the Geek,* eating a peanut butter and jelly sandwich for dinner. I had not seen her since she was in middle school. Now she was a sophomore at Lincoln, and had transformed into an emerging beauty.

"How's high school going?" I asked.

"It's okay," she said.

"How's the new principal?"

"He's interesting—we have to wear uniforms now."

"Do you like wearing them?"

"It's good."

"What do you like about it? Not having to worry about what to wear?"

"No. It's good because you know that everybody is supposed to be there. It makes it easy to identify somebody who doesn't belong in the school."

Laura was living the reality that Yadira's classmates were so busy debating—yet Yadira had never volunteered anything about her sister's experience in class. Yadira had so much to offer her wealthier peers, but they never made her feel safe enough to tell them. At any rate, these days, Laura was in a tailspin. Earlier in the year, their aunt had become involved in a new relationship and had kicked both of Yadira's sisters out of her apartment; they had moved in with their uncle briefly, but then he was evicted. Now Zulema had moved in with her boyfriend and his family, while Laura was sleeping on the floor of Yadira's bedroom. With their mother gone and their makeshift lives falling apart, both of Yadira's sisters had begun failing at school. Zulema had not managed to complete the FAFSA, nor had she applied to a single college. And Laura's grade point average had plummeted. (Meanwhile, Clara's younger sister had just been offered a full scholarship to Stanford University.) Here was the tragedy of Alma's absence: All those moves had made Laura think she was the kind of girl who didn't deserve a real home, and her mother wasn't around to tell her that she was actually magnificent. I didn't know how many afternoons Laura had been spending unsupervised in the company of high school boys, but I hoped she wasn't turning to them for solace.

The derailment of her sisters blindsided Yadira. She had always imagined they would go through life effortlessly, because they had been born with American citizenship. "It's so weird," Yadira said of Zulema's failure to apply for college. "I thought she was going to have no obstacles. I thought everything was going to fall into place for her. She started off in AP classes, so I just thought she was going to be in the group of students that the teachers and counselors would automatically help. I don't know what happened." She did not blame Zulema. "All the moving around, my mom being gone—it's not her fault." Instead, she blamed herself. She thought she had not watched over her sisters closely enough. She said she should have made sure that Zulema had filled out the college forms, applied for scholarships, kept up her grades. "I feel guilty for not doing that for her. But I was just too busy. Part of it was that I didn't make the effort to reach out to her, and the other part was me thinking that because she had papers, it was going to happen for her on its own."

Elissa was the first of the four girls from Roosevelt High to graduate from college. Regis held its ceremony at the beginning of May, several weeks before the University of Denver. Elissa did not invite Marisela, Yadira, or Clara to her commencement, for she had not talked to her old friends for ages. Elissa and Yadira had never been particularly close. Elissa and Clara had stopped speaking to each other after a series of miscommunications in which each left messages for the other on the wrong cell phones. "Oh, we got a divorce," Clara said airily. "I never talk to her anymore." And Marisela had severed ties with Elissa, too, after she returned from studying abroad with an attitude. "We used to go to Mexican clubs together all the time," said Marisela. "And then when she came back from Argentina, I saw her at a party and asked her if she wanted to go to the clubs, and she said, 'No, after you've been to other places, it's hard to go back there.' It kind of hurt my feelings."

I went to her graduation, though. At first I wasn't sure how to find Elissa in the sea of students wearing identical black gowns and mortarboards, but suddenly there she was. She leaned out over the black velvet rope separating the crowd from the graduates to give me a fierce hug. "I'm so happy you're here! You made it! I was afraid maybe you wouldn't come!" Several police officers stood by the stage, as imperfect as the rest of us, sweltering in the sun so that these kids could graduate without any kind of disturbance. In his commencement address, Father Michael Sheeran told the graduates that traditionally a Catholic education has been for people who are on the economic margins, and he pleaded that the graduates not lose their focus on those of greatest need. "As you leave us today, remember the poor, and remember your obligations to them are not a matter of choice, for every human being has claims on you."

Shortly after Elissa's graduation ceremony, the first children who had attended the pep rally at Cole Middle School completed their high school degrees. Out of the 542 schoolchildren enrolled at Cole when John gave his promise of aid, only thirty-eight had made it through high school in Denver. The others had moved away, dropped out, vanished. Of the thirty-eight who had finished high school in Denver, ten identified themselves as having grown up here without legal status. Lawyers had advised philanthropists Tim and Bernie Marquez that they should not fund undocumented students through their new scholarship foundation, for fear of creating legal problems, and none of the undocumented students was given money by that organization. John had decided to keep his promise anyway, and had raised enough additional private funds to provide the students who lacked legal status with exactly the same subsidy being given to their legal counterparts. That sum was not enough to meet the needs of the undocumented students, however, because they were not eligible for public subsidies and had to pay out-of-state rates. "We acknowledge the fact that the mayor is giving us partial help, but that is not what he promised," one student told the *Los Angeles Times*. John's senior policy adviser, Katherine Archuleta, responded by saying, "The decision by the state legislature [to charge out-of-state rates] was not in his control. He's doing everything he can."

After their final exams were over, the girls from DU threw another party at Revolución. Clara arrived with her hair straightened, while Yadira and Zahra sat together in the ticket booth, looking relaxed for the first time in ages. "Hava's class—oh my God, it was so hard!" said Yadira. "We had to do an anthology with twelve sources." She was wearing a pink top with spaghetti straps and a lot of lip gloss. Throughout the course of the night, Marisela did so many shots I feared she might get alcohol poisoning, and Yadira and Clara kept up with her as best they could, with interesting results. "Don't write about anything I do tonight," ordered Clara as she made a haphazard beeline for the dance floor. Everybody had finished their schoolwork except for Marisela. "I have one more paper to write," she groaned. "I can't get it done because we're moving right now."

"You've been moving during finals?"

"Yeah. We finally found a house."

I asked Marisela if she and Julio were together again, and she said no, but she was thinking about it. "I'm so drunk!" she shouted happily. *"Suavemente"* filled the dance floor, and so did *"Lo Que Pasó Pasó."* When the lights came up, Marisela wasn't ready for the night to end, and threw her arms around me in a wobbly embrace. "Go tell them to play a Vicente Fernández song, would you?" she yelled loudly into my ear. "Tell them you're the mayor's wife! They'll do what you say!"

Two days later, I found Yadira in her cap and gown, walking out of La Chateau on a perfectly cloudless spring morning. If the weather portended anything, her life was going to be much brighter and clearer than I had ever imagined. At the moment, however, she was frazzled—nobody could find Zulema. She had promised to come to La Chateau so that Yadira could give her a ticket to the commencement exercises, which were going to take place in half an hour, but she hadn't shown up. Juan was there, even though he was under house arrest—he had been caught speeding for the umpteenth time and was now wearing an ankle bracelet. His boss had agreed to pretend that he was spending the day at work, so that he could sneak out to see Yadira obtain her diploma. Cynthia Poundstone, who no longer lived in Colorado, had flown in for the ceremony. The graduation was being held in the Magness Arena, where the girls had watched all those hockey games. Outside the entrance, we found Clara huddled with Zahra and Alison, her freshman year roommate, who was wearing a lei of fresh orchids. The flowers were magenta on the edges with tender white centers. "Look what I got for being Hawaiian!" she said excitedly. Nobody had seen Marisela. Zahra muttered, "That girl is always late."

As the students began filing into the sports arena, I found a seat high up in the stadium with Irene and Justino Chávez. Yadira's younger sister Laura sat down beside us. She had given herself the inverse of a French manicure—her nails were painted black at the tips instead of white—and wore red costume jewelry. I asked if she was going to do this, meaning college, and she looked stricken and said shyly with no certainty in her voice that she would. Irene reeled to discover how badly Laura had been doing academically, and suggested firmly and gently that she should think about repeating this year over again. I was relieved that at last someone was paying the right kind of attention to this girl, and thought for the first time maybe she would be all right. Irene and Cynthia walked down to photograph Yadira as she filed into the arena. She didn't have her mother or her father here, but she had us. Then Zulema came running up, wearing an aqua sundress. She had snuck in without a ticket, she announced proudly, with a wide grin at her own daring. Julio walked over to say hello.

Marisela waved enthusiastically.

"You made it!" I called. "We were worried!"

"Where's my mom?" she cried in an urgent tone of voice.

"She's up there, right behind Justino," Julio assured her.

Robert Coombe, the chancellor of the university, told the students that the university had wrought great changes in them, and that they had wrought great changes in their alma mater. Then he introduced the commencement speaker—his predecessor, Dan Ritchie, who had overseen an era of tremendous construction. "Fifteen new buildings built in a single decade, beautiful gardens, an amazing landscape, turning this into one of the most beautiful campuses in America," said Coombe, listing Ritchie's accomplishments. I couldn't help but remember that Jesús had done some of the actual labor. And who else? Who had dug the foundations, who had laid the bricks, who had painted the walls, tarred the roofs, laid the sod on the campus green? In his commencement address, Ritchie spoke of Enron, peak oil, and the subprime mortgage disaster, which was just beginning to spiral out of control. He remembered a day when corporate leaders had been heroes, and asked these students to bring that day back again. "A corrupt organization will fail," advised Ritchie. "A corrupt society will fail."

Ritchie thought the problems were monumental but that this institution had bred leaders. "I hope that you lead in the spirit not of finding fault, but finding solutions," he advised. Finding fault or finding solutions—for me, that was the defining difference between Tom Tancredo and John Hickenlooper. I was proud to have John as my husband, and hoped that at least a couple of students understood the importance of what Ritchie was saying. During the interminable roll call, I watched for Marisela and Yadira and Clara to receive their diplomas, and then glanced around to see two police officers conferring on the other side of the arena. Donnie Young's ghost was here, too—it seemed to me as though he was everywhere, watching over everybody.

Cynthia Poundstone asked whatever happened to Luke. None of the girls had spoken to him at all during their final days of college, I told her. He just hadn't really known who they were, because they hadn't been brave enough to tell him. Now he was planning to go into the hospitality business, where presumably he would learn valuable firsthand lessons about the intersection of American business and undocumented labor. The roll call finished at last. "Congratulations and godspeed," said the chancellor.

Irene Chávez shook hands with Cynthia Poundstone.

"It's been nice traveling these four years together with you," said Cynthia.

"And with you," said Irene.

We found Yadira outside. Under her black robe, she was wearing a wild purple and yellow minidress. Justino gave her a big hug and Irene gave her a big hug and Yadira started crying. In all the years I'd known her, it was the first time I ever saw her lose her composure. Nearby, Marisela introduced Poundstone to her siblings. "I threw my cap up in the air and then I couldn't find it and I got this one instead and it's too big!" cried Marisela. "It won't stay on my head!" On my way home, I drove past La Chateau and saw a Mexican laborer using a hammer to tamp down the metal siding on a flower bed. That afternoon, Irene and Justino threw a party in their backyard for Yadira. A friend made *carne* on the grill and they bought *pollo rostizado* and made guacamole and beans. Yadira arranged every award she had earned in her lifetime around the couple's fireplace, turning it into a kind of altar. Looking at this display, I thought that her education had given her something ineffable, the kind of gift that is hard to quantify. It had given her a shield—a shield against the future, a shield against a world that would judge her harshly. College had given her a sense of dignity.

"Have you talked to your mom today?" I asked Yadira without thinking.

"Not yet," she said stiffly.

Juan rescued me by announcing that he had hacked into his new iPhone to make the camera zoom. Soon Marisela's mother called to say that guests were arriving at their house, for the party being held in her honor. As Marisela left, she invited everyone to her party, and called out her new address. It was unfamiliar to Irene. "MapQuest it!" Marisela told her breezily.

The Benavídez family had landed in a nondescript ranch house on the outer edges of the metro area, in one of those hidden neighborhoods where poor people live, and as I pulled up I could see the party going on in the driveway. Josefa and Fabián had set up several folding tables there, and one featured a large cake and the word CONGRATULATIONS in big blue letters. In the garage, a DJ was playing Marisela's favorite songs. Fabián had put on his ostrich skin boots and his *Tejana* hat, which always made me think of Omar. At this party, the guests had darker skin and more tattoos, and the music was much, much louder. A small child tried unsuccessfully to ride a tricycle down the concrete stairs that led to the backyard, and a little girl carefully distributed gold tinsel one piece at a time to party guests. Rosalinda held court in the basement, where half a dozen teenagers were making out. ("Did you see what's going on in the basement?" Marisela asked her mother in Spanish. "It's like a whole other party down there!") These days Rosalinda looked a lot like Marisela did in high school, and Marisela looked a lot like Josefa. All the sorority sisters arrived in their party finery, and then professors Lisa Martínez and Miriam Bornstein and her husband, Óscar Somoza, showed up, too.

"This is how Mexicans like to party!" Marisela yelled to her professors.

"I'm getting emotional," Lisa Martínez said, welling up.

"Do you think we'll ever have students like these again?" Bornstein asked.

"I don't know," Somoza answered. "There were so many great ones this year."

Once again, the students had charmed their professors into becoming their friends. The girls from Roosevelt had earned mediocre marks during their last year of college, and this morning not one of them had graduated cum laude, which seemed like a terrible shame, as I believed they all had the capacity to do so. Yet when I thought of what they had accomplished—staying in school despite the intense upheavals in their families, holding down jobs the entire time, lending financial support to their relatives, creating a Latina sorority, mentoring younger students, transforming the campus, forging strong emotional alliances with their professors—it seemed miraculous. Now they would have to figure out how to make their way in the real world, which tested people in such a different fashion. Yet again, as had been true when we met, their possibilities looked vastly dissimilar. Tonight Clara had an easiness to her manner—she wasn't too worried about the future, because she knew her prospects were bright—that her friends without legal status did not possess. Fate had decreed they would struggle more in their lives, but who knew what riches tomorrow might hold. Already, Yadira had learned that a Social Security number was not a panacea, for those nine digits alone had not been enough to guarantee her sisters success.

A cold front blew in and the men carried the folding tables into the garage. Marisela poured shots until she ran out of tequila, then dispatched her uncle to buy more. Cynthia Poundstone sat down beside me. "Of all the things I've done in my life, if I were to get hit by a bus tomorrow, this would rank as the most important thing of all," she said.

Josefa coached Julio on his dance steps. To everyone's surprise, he dragged Marisela onto the dance floor, instead of the other way around. Marisela said her spike heels were killing her and a sorority sister told her to put on lower heels. "Oh, these are the lowest ones I have!" laughed Marisela. "You know me!" The DJ put on *"Suavemente"* and she kicked off her shoes to dance barefoot with Julio. It looked like they were about to become lovers again. Sure enough, a few weeks later, Julio decided to take Marisela on a road trip to Los Angeles. He told her that he wanted to treat her to sushi, bring her to the beach, show her Disneyland.

"Is this a platonic road trip or a romantic road trip?" I asked.

"I don't know!" Marisela giggled. "Maybe both!"

Before they left town, Julio pestered Marisela until she finished her final paper, and as a result, several weeks after the rest of her classmates, Marisela received her diploma from the University of Denver.

Her graduation party had lasted all night long. Even the arrival of the police, who had turned up around one A.M., had not brought about an end to the celebration. Fabián tried to deal with the officers, but did not speak enough English, and ultimately Marisela intervened. In her skimpy black minidress, the vivacious young woman flashed a brilliant smile at the cop standing in the driveway of her new home.

"Guess what!" she told him. "I just graduated from college!"

"Oh, yeah?" said the police officer, cracking a grin. "Where did you go?"

"The University of Denver!"

The officer was clearly impressed.

"Well, all right! Congratulations. Listen, no problem. Just turn the music down, okay? People are trying to sleep."

And Marisela complied, *por un ratito*—for a little while.

EPILOGUE

After four years at the University of Denver, Yadira and Marisela still had not resolved the question of whether they considered themselves to be Mexican or American. Once, I had imagined that by now the two undocumented girls would have been able to say whether they were *"Mi Gente"* or *"American Women,"* but when I asked them which of these categories they would assign to themselves, they could not answer the question. They were living in a state of irresolution. This made a certain amount of sense, given that during their formative years, America had been debating vociferously whether people like them should be welcome. I figured it would probably take another decade or two for the girls to reach clarity, for people often did not discover who they really were until they reached their thirties or forties, and in terms of what kind of relationship the girls would eventually forge with this country, a lot depended on what would happen in Washington. The girls weren't going to make up their minds about America until America made up its mind about them.

Senator Barack Obama returned to Denver to accept his party's nomination for the presidency at the National Democratic Convention on August 28, 2008, three months after the girls had graduated from college. Thanks to her connections in the labor movement, Marisela obtained several of the coveted passes to hear Obama speak inside Invesco Field at Mile High. After she stood in a security line that did not budge for several hours, however, she gave up. "Oh, I'll just watch him on TV," she said as she left. Yadira persisted and made it into the stadium. After much searching, I found her in the uppermost bleachers, in a seat that had a spectacular view of the sunset, even though she could barely see the podium. Why wasn't Marisela there, too? Important people had been calling the mayor's office all week in search of a ticket, yet Marisela had given hers away. She had always seemed engaged by politics, and I couldn't understand why she shrugged at Obama. Finally it occurred to me that Marisela could not vote, which went a long way toward explaining why she did not feel personally invested in the election's outcome. Also, it was immigration politics, not politics per se, that absorbed her—and at the moment, both Barack Obama and John McCain were studiously avoiding the controversial subject of immigration. It split each of their parties in two, and neither of the candidates could address the issue without running the risk of alienating approximately half of his supporters.

I did not spot Clara at Invesco Field, although she also made it into the football stadium. She had spent most of the summer visiting relatives in Zacatecas, and shortly after she had returned from Mexico, she had completed all of the paperwork necessary to become a naturalized citizen of the United States. At the end of October 2008—eleven days too late to register to vote in the upcoming presidential contest—Clara acquired her certificate of citizenship.

"You're American now!" I said, when she told me the news.

"Oh, Helen," she replied, with laughter in her voice, "I was American before."

Having become naturalized at exactly the same age myself, I thought I knew what she meant. Becoming a citizen changed everything and it changed nothing at all—at least for somebody who had come of age with a green card. Clara could now register to vote, and could even hold public office, but she was still the same person she had always been. And while she felt more at home in this country than she did anywhere else, she would never become *unequivocally* American, for there was no erasing the matter of her birth. Inside of her there would always reside a seven-year-old girl with heavy plaster wings on her shoulders, standing alone in a Mexican desert. No government could ever take that away from her, nor give her anything so precious.

By the time her proof of citizenship arrived, Clara had secured a part-time job with a local foundation that provided college scholarships. Clara was making $16 an hour advising poor students how to amass the funds they needed to continue their education. That fall, she discovered that two of her charges lacked legal status, and over the course of the school year she watched the pair of undocumented students grow closer to each other and more distant from their legal peers. "It's funny to hear their conversations," she said. "They are the exact same ones that we had." Clara was planning to go to graduate school in a year or two, to fulfill her ambition of becoming a social worker. She now possessed a college degree, citizenship, and good job credentials, and was biliterate as well as bilingual. The only remaining question I had about her future was to what extent she would maintain ties with her *mexicana* friends from high school, after she began to achieve professional success.

When Yadira had finished college, she and her sister Laura had moved in to live with Irene and Justino Chávez for the summer. In the fall, however, Yadira found an apartment of her own, and moved out of the Chávez house—which had served as a refuge during some of the hardest years of her life—taking Laura with her. As the two sisters settled into their new home, Yadira shone with pride at having accomplished her heart's goal: creating a stable household of her own. She remained faithful to Juan, her boyfriend of six years, but she did not invite him to live with her. Yadira was discovering her independence. For the moment, working full-time and paying rent on her own place seemed to satisfy her, but I could see that she would soon outgrow her current job, and wondered what would happen next.

The professors who taught at the University of Denver had reserved a special warmth for Yadira, who had charmed them with the striking combination of her shyness in person and her boldness on paper. She had chosen never to reveal her absence of legal status to any faculty member, but had confided in both Hava Gordon and Lisa Martínez about the dissolution of her nuclear family. The story had rendered both professors even more personally invested in Yadira's future. On separate occasions, each of them asked me with evident concern if I thought that Yadira would make it into graduate school, mentioning the quality of her intelligence. "I hope so," I told them, without giving away her secret. Of course, Yadira would be able to go only if she could find enough private dollars to cover her tuition or if legislators created a viable path for her to move forward—she was facing precisely the same dilemma as she had when we first met.

By the time Barack Obama defeated John McCain in November of 2008, the subprime mortgage crisis had exploded into a global financial disaster. For the first time in decades, as the American economy foundered, the numbers of immigrants who were entering the United States started to drop. Given the seriousness of the economic crisis, and the impact it was having on American voters, the debate over immigration was temporarily tabled. Still, as 2008 drew to a close, outgoing federal officials made clear that in their minds, the immigration quandary was one of the most important policy riddles they had failed to solve, suggesting that it would inevitably return to the top of the national agenda. And once the economy righted, the flow of immigrants would presumably increase again. Meanwhile, President-elect Obama tapped Senator Ken Salazar (whom Clara, Yadira, and Marisela had helped to elect by registering new voters) to join his cabinet as secretary of the interior.

With the economy contracting, unemployment soared, making it a particularly miserable time to enter the job market. All three of the girls who had attended the University of Denver already had jobs—Yadira and Marisela were still employed by the same nonprofit organization where they had been working for several years, and Clara obtained her position right before the worst news hit—but their former friend Elissa could not find a job of any kind. After assiduously circulating her résumé and getting no response, she sank into a depressed state while sharing a one-bedroom apartment with her mother. "I've applied to so many jobs that I have somewhat given up on myself," Elissa wrote in an e-mail. "I'm doing whatever I can, but am struggling financially. Slowly, I am regaining my positive energy, and my motivation, but it has been so hard, especially knowing that I have a degree yet remain in this situation. It has been six months since I graduated. I have felt impotent."

Elissa had been born a citizen of the United States, and possessed a go-get-'em personality. I had always thought that out of the four girls, she would have the easiest time starting a career. The fact that she suffered the most after the economy seized up came as a reminder that legal status did not guarantee work. I sympathized with Elissa's distress, but suspected it would prove short-lived—while it was hard for her to keep the matter in perspective, to me it seemed obvious that she was on the verge of entering the middle class, and was equipped with everything necessary for the journey, including gumption and drive.

Indeed, it soon occurred to Elissa to check whether her Gates scholarship could be extended, and she learned that it could, for certain types of degrees. She immediately applied to a graduate program that would allow her to become an English as a Second Language teacher.

This career choice surprised me—I had expected Elissa to become an executive in the business world, with a lucrative salary and snazzy suits—but then I remembered how she had once hectored Marisela and Yadira into staying in high school, back when they had wanted to quit. Teaching would suit Elissa. She liked to root for people, and she had the capacity to believe in others even when they doubted themselves.

Marisela did not apply to graduate school in fall 2008, as she had planned to do. Instead, she broke up with Julio, returned to the Mexican nightclubs that she loved to frequent, briefly dated one or two other men, and then returned to Julio's arms again. Shortly afterward, I met Marisela for dinner. "Guess what?" she said. "I have some big news: I'm going to be a mom!" Marisela was evidently excited by this turn of events, and I did not want to hurt her feelings by revealing my own acute disappointment, based on an immediate concern for her ability to achieve a meaningful career, now that she was going to have a child. This would be considered an appropriate reaction in my own Anglo social circles, and not at all appropriate in the Mexican community from which she came. I stared at her from across this cultural gulf, and noticed that she looked happy.

"Wow!" I finally managed to say. "Well, the timing is good—you waited until you finished college."

"I know!" she said. "That's why I've decided to keep the baby!"

Marisela believed that abortion was an acceptable option, but had not seriously considered having one. Rather, she felt an immediate and deep conviction to succor the life that was growing inside of her. It wasn't something that she needed to think about, it was something that she simply acknowledged. Marisela told Julio that he was free to do as he pleased (she always thought she could do it all alone), but I was relieved when Julio told Marisela that whatever she needed—friendship, love, support—he would provide. As her pregnancy continued, they became inseparable once more, and Marisela developed a newfound appreciation for Julio's many admirable qualities, such as his dependability. Meanwhile, Fabián and Josefa were ecstatic over Marisela's news, for they believed that a new life was sacred, and always to be celebrated. Her parents immediately pledged to help with the baby. Josefa went to Target to buy yarn for a baby blanket, and teased Marisela by saying that if she ever moved out of their house again, she would have to leave her infant behind, because of the degree of excitement Josefa felt at the prospect of raising another child. Clearly, Marisela was going to have as much assistance from her family as any new mother has ever had.

When I asked what this development meant for her future, Marisela said firmly that she was still going to law school—after the baby. I realized then that I had misunderstood the basic trajectory of her life. All this time, I had been expecting that she would someday reject her Mexican heritage, or at least loosen its hold upon her identity, and that if this did not happen, then she would surrender her American goals and her Mexican side would triumph. But she was never going to stop being a *mexicana* or an American. She was going to remain a hybrid creature. Sometimes she would excel in school and make political speeches and charm the deans of law schools, and sometimes she would celebrate an unwed pregnancy at the age of twenty-two. Growing up without a legal home in the country where she lived had taught Marisela how to hold two ideas about herself—about everything—in her mind at once. America had been telling her for years that she was both a legitimate and an illegitimate member of society, and this basic bifurcation of meaning now shaped the way she thought. Marisela considered herself a girl of the street, yet believed she could earn a law degree; she thought of Julio as a close friend, but took him as a lover; she said she was a *mexicana* first, then declared in the very next breath that she was just as American as me or you. And Marisela could tolerate this degree of ambiguity about essential issues because she had grown up immersed in ambiguity all the time.

Of course, this meant that she had chosen the hardest way. She had decided to pursue her American dreams and her Mexican ambitions, despite the fact that they coexisted in tension. She was going to attempt to fulfill both sets of aspirations at once. I worried for her, because I thought that she might suffer immensely in the process—raising a child as a single mother while putting herself through law school, for example, struck me as a recipe for constant stress—but I admired her, all the same. And I suspected that she might even have the capacity to pull off such an extraordinary feat, given that she was the girl whom friends had once nicknamed Superwoman. It also comforted me to think that in the years ahead, if life brought Marisela to her knees, and forced her to relinquish her prized career goals, at least she had already succeeded during the first phase of adulthood in fulfilling both sets of ambitions. Against all odds, she had managed to acquire an American college education while still holding on to her Mexican self, and as a result I thought she was going to raise the child that she was now carrying quite differently from the way she would have otherwise. The single most reliable indicator of whether a child will succeed in the United States is the level of education possessed by his or her mother, and Marisela had put herself in a position to make certain that her son or daughter had the greatest possible shot at prosperity.

At first, Marisela's chances of obtaining money for law school looked entirely bleak, but in spring 2009, almost one year after the girls had graduated from the University of Denver, immigration advocates reintroduced the DREAM Act in Congress. The latest version of the bill created a path to citizenship for immigrants who had been brought to the United States before age sixteen, if they enrolled in college or the military. This time, the bill's sponsors raised the age limit for eligibility to thirty-five, meaning that if the bill passed, then Marisela and Yadira would be able to apply for citizenship at last, thanks to the years they had spent at DU. Marisela had just begun her final trimester when the bill was introduced, and it looked as though she would give birth before the next set of political arguments.

Her baby was due in June 2009. Barring unforeseen developments, by the time this book is published, I expect Marisela will have given birth to an infant who entered the world in Denver, Colorado. Because it was not going to be possible for her to secure legal status before she became a mother, the fact of the baby was going to raise again, in an entirely new manner, the very same question that the lives of Marisela and her friends had raised earlier. It had to do with this intersection between the terrible mystery of our being and the inevitably flawed fashion in which we govern ourselves. In all the time that I had known the girls, no adequate solution had been provided by elected officials to the perplexity of Marisela's existence. Now here was the enigma of her child. With any luck, Marisela's son or daughter would be born with an American birth certificate, and would grow up in the United States without worrying quite as much as Marisela had about whether he or she belonged. As long as Marisela herself lacked legal status, however, her child was going to have to worry about whether his or her mother might someday be deported.

In other words, unless she acquired a viable means of applying for residency, in some future chapter of Marisela's life, there was the awful possibility of her becoming the next Alma (winding up in Mexico after getting deported or being arrested for some crime related to her invalid status), and her child becoming the next Laura (left without a mother). This was the essence of what it meant to be categorized as an illegal immigrant—one lived with the possibility of salvation or despair close by, all the time. And so, neatly encapsulated in the developing form that lived inside of Marisela was this query: What was the weight of one human soul, and where did the measure of a soul fit into the enormous drama of nation abutting nation on this globe? As soon as I considered this question, I began to wonder whether the political drama was really quite so big. We typically think of politics as something that occurs on a grand scale, but the more I watched politics unfold, the more I wondered why. Did the idea of a country—an abstract concept, really—truly matter more than the sum happiness of all the individuals living within its boundaries? No, I thought. People mattered more than governments. In fact, this country was founded on that very idea.

Afterword to
the Hardcover Edition

O nce the four girls graduated from college and this book went to press, I ceased to follow their lives so assiduously, but we stayed in touch. Turns that I hadn't foreseen kept surprising me, as their destinies continued to unfold. In the summer of 2009, Marisela showed signs of preeclampsia during the final month of her pregnancy, and doctors hastily induced her baby's arrival (two weeks early), fearing that otherwise Marisela's blood pressure might skyrocket, putting her in danger. I wasn't aware of these developments until she sent the following text message: "Emilio is here. If u want to meet our baby boy I'm at Good Samaritan Hospital." I hurried over. It had been a tough delivery; after hours of labor, the baby's heart rate had plummeted, and doctors had rushed to perform an emergency C-section. Now the baby seemed fine—he was a wrinkled little peanut with a thatch of dark hair—while Marisela looked weary. She flinched when she moved, and said she was still trying to get the hang of breastfeeding. Julio sat nearby, reading *What to Expect When You're Expecting*.

Marisela and Julio married at the beginning of 2010. The ceremony took place in the living room of a friend's house, and during the event Josefa and Fabián took turns minding Emilio, who was dressed in a miniature black suit. He had become a chortling toddler with shiny black eyes, determined to get the hang of walking. Marisela's two brothers moved furniture and arranged chairs and suggested that guests standing near the front door should step inside. "The bride will be coming through here," one of them announced importantly. Five years earlier, the boys had hazed Marisela before her senior prom, but tonight they weren't joking. This was serious, and they wanted to get it right.

Colorado law allows any individual to marry a couple, and, surprisingly, Clara, in a pale green wrap, performed the service. Somehow Marisela and Julio had known that Clara would possess the gravity of a minister. Yadira served as maid of honor, looking glamorous in a brown sheath with turquoise jewelry. Elissa had not been invited, however, which spoke volumes about how far from the other three she had drifted.

When he walked his oldest daughter down the aisle, Fabián wore his Tejana hat, that trademark symbol of Durango, along with a dark suit. Marisela's white gown was sleeveless, leaving her shoulders bare, and on her head she had placed a silver tiara. She seemed perfectly at ease until the middle of her vows, when she suddenly broke into loud, convulsive sobs. The rest of us were confused by this abrupt transition in mood, until we noticed that two elderly individuals in humble clothes had just entered the room. Marisela's grandparents had driven all the way from Durango, in a total surprise to the bride. It was the sight of their worn faces filled with love that had undone her.

At the end of the service, Marisela led Julio over to the marriage certificate. "It's not official until we sign," she said.

"This is a big landmark for all of us," Yadira observed, when we met in the crush of guests.

"I don't know why, but I was nervous, too!" said her boyfriend, Juan.

When the groom's little sister saw me, she exclaimed, "I read your book! I loved it!"

"How old are you?" I asked in wonder.

"Twelve!" she said. "But I'm a good reader!"

This kind of thing had been happening a lot: I thought I'd written a book for grown-ups (especially those who didn't have any experience with immigration), but the book kept reaching a younger audience, too (many of whom were living this story). For months, I'd been getting e-mails from young Latinas across the country. My favorite arrived one morning shortly before the sun came up, about a month after Marisela's wedding. "It is now 4:50 am, I just finished your book," the young woman wrote. "I have so much to say, but the only thing I can tell you is thank you. From the first page I read, it felt like I was reading not only my story but my family's story. I have never related so much to a book. If you are still in touch with the girls, tell them that I admire all of them, but mostly Marisela and Yadira." Of course I passed her admiration along.

Marisela and Julio found an apartment of their own, and the two of them worked full-time to pay the rent. Marisela cobbled together a patchwork of child care involving her extended family and a woman who lived down the street. Meanwhile, both Marisela and Yadira continued to work in the immigrant rights movement, as only in that sphere did employers seem to comprehend their predicament as well as their attributes. Yadira continued to date Juan but did not appear to be moving toward marriage. She stayed in close touch with her sister Zulema, who kept talking about going to college, though she had yet to apply. For a while, her sister Laura moved into the tiny basement apartment that Yadira had secured, a place they kept spectacularly tidy. Then Laura and Yadira had a bad fight, and Laura vanished. Months passed before Yadira eventually learned that her youngest sister had abruptly moved to Chicago, where she was now living with a boyfriend and his family. Laura had struck out on her own, and nobody in Denver knew much about her current circumstances.

Clara was accepted into a program to study social work at the University of Denver, but deferred enrollment. She was still dating Diego, who had turned out to be more reliable than anybody had anticipated. It was harder and harder to find time for Marisela and Yadira. "You're like a mythical creature," Clara said to Yadira at one point, after they tried and failed to have dinner. "I hear about you sometimes but never actually see you." Meanwhile, Elissa found a new job as a counselor to at-risk youth, and simultaneously began her first year of graduate school.

Yadira and Marisela felt lucky to have good jobs and college degrees, but their hopes of attending graduate school had dimmed—law school just wasn't happening. The possibility of finding enough private funding seemed far-fetched, and once they left the safe haven of college, perhaps they also began to doubt again whether they were the type of individual meant to take such an esteemed path. Marisela and Yadira felt blocked by their lack of legal status from becoming full-fledged professionals.

The extent to which other undocumented students shared this predicament (and how lucky Marisela and Yadira were simply to have found work that was meaningful) became apparent at Emilio's baptismal celebration, which took place on the occasion of his first birthday, at an Elks Hall in North Denver late in the spring of 2010. JUSTICE, CHARITY, BROTHERLY LOVE, proclaimed the stained-glass windows. Yadira arrived late in an electric blue minidress. "There was a mess at home, so I had a cleaning attack," she said, explaining her tardiness. It was hot, and Clara persuaded Diego to fan her with a piece of paper. *"La reina!"* cracked Irene Chávez. The queen! Marisela dashed about in four-inch heels and a psychedelic muumuu, a hot pink cell phone stuck in her bra cup. She organized a series of party games—I had to sing *"Suavemente"* using a karaoke machine—and cajoled little ones into bashing a store-bought piñata. Six years earlier, she'd been the one wielding the stick, and now I watched as she handed it to her first born.

Half a dozen college graduates who also lacked legal papers attended the party, and after a while the main subject of conversation became the dispiriting state of their careers. One had just lost a job at a real estate company because of his immigration status and was selling tamales. Another had accepted a miserable job doing debt collection, the only place he could find work. A third had just decided to return to Mexico. Nobody thought that was a great plan, but a few wondered if they'd be forced to do the same. "I'm so frustrated," one of them said wearily. Then the DJ cranked up the volume on a fast-moving *reggaetón* song and the party moved onto the dance floor. Emilio fell asleep as his parents and their friends forgot their troubles to the sound of Daddy Yankee.

After the DREAM Act failed to make it through Congress yet again, Marisela did grapple once more with the question of whether she could change her status by other means. She was now the mother of an American citizen, the wife of an American citizen, and the sibling of several American citizens. Yet when she consulted another attorney, she discovered she still had no legal path to citizenship herself, as long as she remained on American soil. There was no form she could fill out nor any process she could set in motion that would allow her to acquire residency from this side of the border, given that her parents had once brought her across that boundary illegally. Even her marriage did not alter the fact that she would have to leave the country to apply for documents. Marisela thought maybe someday she would travel to Mexico and plead her case to the American officials stationed there, and hope for the best, but not right now—not with a son to raise and a marriage to begin. Then Cynthia Poundstone (her former benefactor) urged action, and Marisela did authorize her attorney to file documents that ultimately would require an extended trip to Juarez. Poundstone said the idea of sending Marisela off to such a place in the hopes of coming back with legal status "scared the bejeezus" out of her, but neither of them could see another way forward.

This was the illegal immigrants' dilemma: One had to risk everything in order to rectify the original transgression. Millions of workers chose to hold on to the certainty of current jobs rather than giving up those wages to pursue uncertain legal redemption. Meanwhile, American voters by definition remained personally untouched by the country's immigration laws, and had only a hazy sense of the pertinent statutes (and of all the reasons why so many individuals remained mired in the limbo of illegality). This collective ignorance became increasingly clear to me as I traveled around the country to speak about this book. At almost every event, someone in the audience would ask why Marisela and Yadira didn't go ahead and "apply for citizenship," as if the whole problem was simply that they had neglected to complete some form. People with legal status seemed genuinely surprised to hear that the young women would have to surrender the lives they had built in the United States and return to Mexico before they could become eligible for citizenship here. And so the need for reform—felt so acutely by immigrants—was not nearly as apparent to the voters who would have to support it. This skewed distribution of awareness put elected officials in the awkward position of benefiting from looking the other way.

As the lives of the four young women continued to unveil, figures in national politics turned away from and then returned to the subject of their existence. During his first year in office, President Obama pledged to tackle immigration, but other priorities kept taking precedence. First Obama struggled to pass what grew into a voluminous bill on health care. Then a deep-sea oil well owned by British Petroleum blew up and started spewing millions of barrels of crude oil into the Gulf of Mexico, and Obama turned his attention to energy. Advocates for immigrants pushed for progress, but the president's team stalled, supposedly because pragmatists believed that taking action on immigration would cause the Democratic Party to lose seats in the midterm elections that would take place in the fall of 2010.

In April 2010, however, state legislators in Arizona passed their own type of immigration reform, adopting a controversial law that made it a crime to be in Arizona without proper documentation. The law required immigrants to carry their documents at all times, and charged local police with enforcing the new policy. Police officers were authorized to question anybody they suspected of being an immigrant. Civil rights leaders immediately objected, pointing out the law was bound to cause racial profiling. Police chiefs in Arizona rebelled, too, fearing the law would compromise their ability to solve violent crimes in low-income communities and shred their budgets by forcing them to lock up nonviolent offenders. But the law was popular with voters. Politicians across the country took notice of the bill's power to electrify audiences, and within a short time legislators in more than a dozen other states announced plans to copy the legislation. At the same time, various entities including the Department of Justice sued the state of Arizona, arguing that the new law was unconstitutional, and a federal judge blocked the implementation of key portions of it.

Meanwhile, in Colorado, a series of political supernovas turned the state upside down. First, Governor Bill Ritter, a Democrat, abandoned his bid for reelection, smack in the middle of an ongoing race, unexpectedly creating an open seat. My husband, John Hickenlooper, jumped in to fill the void, and we found ourselves in a statewide competition, alongside Republican opponents Scott McInnis (the establishment favorite) and Dan Maes (a Tea Party type). Then McInnis was caught plagiarizing from a state supreme court justice, and Maes was snagged in a campaign finance scandal. At the eleventh hour, saying neither McInnis nor Maes looked fit for office, former congressman Tom Tancredo tossed his hat into the busy ring (securing a spot on the ballot under the Constitutional Party, as it was too late to run as a Republican). McInnis promptly lost the Republican primary, sending a damaged Maes into the general election, alongside Tancredo, to the dismay of virtually the entire Republican establishment. Reporters in Colorado demanded to know whether the candidates would support Arizona-type legislation here. Tancredo and Maes both declared their enthusiasm for a similar approach, while John opposed following Arizona's example. The law attracted strong support among the state's voters, however, 60 percent of whom favored a similar measure. Immigration served as a wedge issue that the other candidates used to drive voters away from John. Nevertheless, John ran an entirely positive campaign, earning praise from many quarters, and won 50.3 percent of the vote. He took office on January 11, 2011.

Finally, with various states erupting into immigration-related arguments, Barack Obama gave a speech announcing that he would tackle immigration at the federal level—after the midterm elections, when the political stakes would be lower. Demonstrations swelled in size, and undocumented students escalated their protests. In Chicago, several students publicly announced their illegal status to show their impatience with the status quo. In Tucson, undocumented students sat down in Senator John McCain's office and refused to leave—protesting his support of the controversial state law. And four undocumented students walked from Florida to Washington, D.C., to call for passage of the DREAM Act. That legislation had been sidelined while elected officials debated new versions of comprehensive reform, but as the nation's mood remained sour on the subject of offering citizenship to illegal immigrants, some observers began to wonder if it might not be wise to abandon hope of inclusive reform and just pass the DREAM Act. This idea divided the immigrant rights lobby. Some advocates didn't want to choose between children or parents, while others felt it was immoral to pass up a chance to help children when the likelihood of helping parents remained so small. Marisela, who had once been so outspoken, now let others speak for her. She worried about what would happen to Emilio if she put herself at risk, and eschewed a leadership role in the ongoing protests. She did lobby for the bill furiously behind the scenes. At the end of 2010, however, the DREAM Act failed to pass once more.

During all the political back and forth, my attention was drawn to a curiously candid moment that took place inside of a school. One month after Arizona adopted its new law, the president of Mexico visited the president of the United States at the White House, and at that point the immigration debate swerved in an unexpectedly innocent direction. While Felipe Calderón discussed border policy with Barack Obama, their wives went to visit a nearby school in Maryland. The school visit was intended to highlight Michelle Obama's efforts to improve the physical health of schoolchildren, but the elementary school happened to serve large numbers of immigrant families, and when the First Lady took questions, a small girl who had other things on her mind spoke up.

"My mom, she says that Barack Obama is taking everybody away that doesn't have papers," said the girl.

"Yeah, well, that's something that we have to work on, right?" replied Michelle Obama. "To make sure that people can be here with the right kind of papers, right?"

"But my mom doesn't have any papers," said the girl.

It was just the simple truth, spoken by a child, but we as a nation had become used to not talking about such things. I was struck by the child's trusting assumption that it would be safe to voice her deepest fears to a woman of great stature and authority. I also felt for Michelle Obama, who couldn't possibly have anticipated such a confession. She was the first First Lady of color, the first First Lady whose ancestors had been slaves, and that put her in such a curious position, symbolically. On the one hand, she represented the full authority of the federal government. On the other hand, she also stood for the complicated history of a country that has repeatedly obtained labor from people that it has refused to honor with full rights. I couldn't help but notice that the elementary school child was just a few years older than Marisela's son, Emilio. If reform did not pass, that would be his fate—to go to school in a country where the textbooks claimed we fought for liberty and justice, while his mother somehow didn't fit into the phrase "for all," and he had to worry about whether the police might take her away. It was refreshing to hear an elementary school child speak a truth the rest of us were afraid to name. Marisela and Yadira had now lost that childhood innocence—they knew they couldn't speak up without risking deportation. But they found it such hard work, keeping quiet about so large a secret, and they longed for a time when they could finally say who they really were.

ACKNOWLEDGMENTS

My son has had to share his mother with this project for the entirety of his life thus far. So first, thank you, Teddy Hickenlooper! I also want to say how much I appreciate my parents, Marie and Larry Thorpe, for showing me that nobody is a stranger.

Working on a project of this scope with an editor as intelligent as Colin Harrison was pure joy, and made me as happy as I can imagine being as a writer. I am deeply grateful to have had the opportunity to write my first book with an editor of his talent and experience. He was able to say what was missing, and key passages in this book exist only because of his wisdom. Plus, every conversation we had was fun. Thank you, Colin, for giving this book the time that it required.

All thanks go to literary agent Denise Shannon for steering me toward Colin in the first place. Denise expertly shepherded this project from inception to publication, and I am glad for her thoughtful advice at every turn. I am also thankful for all of the support, guidance, and warmth that she provided before this idea came along.

Kat Jones set this project in motion by asking what I wanted to accomplish as a writer and steering me toward the answer. It took five years to report and write this book, and many other people helped along the way. At the very beginning, Ricardo Ainslie gave indispensable encouragement, and also conducted interviews with Spanish speakers. Lisa Pollak was an early believer, and made it possible to air a radio story about the girls on *This American Life*. Many other radio journalists provided assistance as I went on to produce a half hour radio documentary, and I am particularly grateful to Sam Fuqua, Max Wycisk, Ed Trudeau, Mark Coulter, and Eric Whitney. Special thanks to Sam Fuqua for airing the radio documentary on KGNU, and for suggesting that I sell the project to Soundprint for national distribution.

The radio documentary grew into a book project after Malcolm

Gladwell paid us a visit in Denver just as this story was darkening. At the time, Yadira's mother had been charged with felony impersonation, and Raúl Gómez García had been charged with murder. Unnerved by these developments, I had become uncertain about whether to press forward. Malcolm convinced me that I should not let the awfulness of what had happened scare me away. Later, Chip McGrath reminded me that I had been a writer before I became a political spouse, and would always be a writer first. His endorsement gave me the courage I needed to go on.

I am indebted to Texas writers Lawrence Wright, Pamela Colloff, and Karen Olsson for their counsel and enthusiasm as I was pulling together the book proposal. Mark Eddy and Ted Conover gave sound advice at several key junctures, and Karen Rosica loaned me inspiring books. During my early years as a journalist, I was lucky to stumble across good teachers, and remain especially thankful for the lessons of Ken Paul, Paul Burka, Laurence Gonzales, and Chip McGrath; their words came back to me as I wrote this book. I could never have tackled such a long journey without the close companionship of my fellow Colorado writers David Grinspoon, Janis Hallowell, Peter Heller, Lisa Jones, Tory Read, Rebecca Rowe, and Juan Thompson. In addition to their excellent company, these writers provided invaluable comments on drafts, and moral support all along the way. Special thanks to Peter Heller for coffee dates and to Tory Read for long walks in the mountains. My sister-in-law Betsy Hollins painstakingly edited a very rough first draft, and taught me all kinds of things about English grammar. Nell London, Andrea Dukakis, Suzanne Myers, and José Mercado offered valuable improvements. Jay Heinrichs assisted mightily by suggesting how better to shape the book. I also admire his skill in a canoe, and am glad we got to talk in one while suspended on Squam Lake.

Muchas gracias to Lilia Selenke, who taught me Spanish, translated material, and assisted in interviews. Former consul general Juan Marcos Gutiérrez González, as well as his formidable staff—especially Mariana Díaz and Marcela de la Mar—helped me get to know the Mexican community in Denver and assisted in planning my trip to Mexico.

At Denver Public Schools, I am grateful to former superintendents Jerry Wartgow and Michael Bennet, former press secretaries Mark Stevens and Alejandra Garza, and all of the principals and teachers who welcomed me into their schools. At the University of Denver, I would like to thank former chancellor Dan Ritchie, Chancellor Robert Coombe, and Provost Gregg Kvistad, as well as all of the professors who shared their time and their classrooms. And I would like to acknowledge my copyeditor, Vivian Gomez, for her fluency in both English and Spanish.

The young women that I call Marisela, Yadira, Clara, and Elissa were brave to allow a writer to tag along during some of the most vulnerable moments of their lives. I appreciate the immense trust they placed in me. I feel similarly beholden to Kelly Young, who allowed me to come into her home when she need not have been so welcoming. Thanks to all the members of the Denver Police Department who provided guidance and information. Attorney Richard García spent hours answering my questions about immigration law, and attorney Andrew Fair read a draft and provided further education on the subject. Irene and Justino Chávez were incredibly generous with their time and their insights, and I am particularly indebted to Justino for days of help while we traveled together in Mexico. I also want to thank Tom Tancredo for sharing his views, even though he must have known that we were not of like mind.

A great irony—not lost on me—is that this book could not have been written without the help of two Mexican-born immigrants in my own household. During the years that I spent on this project, Ariceli Cabral and Lidia Casas performed most of our domestic tasks, and I want to thank them for giving me the freedom to write. (Needless to say, both are legal.) Meanwhile, PJ Orazen kept us organized, Vicki Novak expertly helped care for my child, and Karina Hamalainen assisted in so many ways: babysitting, Internet research, tracking down documents, filing notes, and videotaping public events, among other things. Brad Goeddel used his formidable skills as a librarian to nail down stray facts. Much appreciation to all the parents of young boys who supervised hastily arranged play dates when I had to scramble to meet a deadline. To Gillian Silverman, Mary Caulkins, Niamh Mesch, Annie Brown, Jane Ginsberg, and Chantal and Doug Unfug, thank you for the hours you spent listening to me talk about this project.

Most important, I am grateful to my husband, John Hickenlooper, for I could not have written this book without his wholehearted blessing. Most politicians of his standing have a spouse who serves as a full-time helpmeet, but he never asked that of me. Instead, when I decided to continue writing, he urged me on; when I said I wanted to write about illegal immigrants, he endorsed the idea; and when I concluded that I had to write about Gómez García, he never flinched. Then he read a rough draft of this book and crossed out only one word. In truth, writers and politicians should never marry, so at odds are the two endeavors, and our farfetched partnership probably would not work at all except for the fact that John is so funny and fair-minded. I also admire him for being, above all else, a man of ideas. Oh, and I'm glad we spent our honeymoon in Oaxaca, *estudiando español*. John, *muchas, muchas gracias y mil besos.*

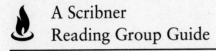

JUST LIKE US

HELEN THORPE

In *Just Like Us* journalist Helen Thorpe chronicles the true coming-of-age story of four Colorado teenage girls: Marisela, Yadira, Elissa, and Clara. All four girls have grown up in the United States, but only two have documents. As the girls attempt to make it into college, they discover that only the pair who have legal status can see a clear path forward.

When another immigrant without legal status kills a Denver police officer, the political climate shifts dramatically. Politicians begin a fierce debate about illegal immigration. The growing debate coupled with increasing familial difficulties and tensions over the girls' differences threaten to drive a wedge between the four girls, who have promised to stick together through thick and thin.

Just Like Us is a vivid account of adolescence, friendship, and identity. It also explores the realities of immigration, one of our country's most complicated social issues. It challenges readers to question what makes us American, who gets to live here, and most important, what happens when we don't agree.

1. Being born in London, but later immigrating to the United States at a young age, Helen Thorpe admits to feeling a sense of dual identity that the girls in *Just Like Us* also felt. How is her experience similar to that of the girls? How is it different? What does she mean when she says that she and the girls had "something in common and . . . nothing in common" (p. 2)?

2. While at Theodore Roosevelt High School, Marisela, Yadira, Elissa, and Clara face all the same "growing pains" that any other teenage girl would. How are their problems compounded by Marisela's and Yadira's lack of legal status?

3. Marisela pays state and federal taxes during her employment at a local supermarket, despite the fact that she is not a legal resident or a citizen. Thorpe writes, "even though she [Marisela] would never collect Social Security payments—she was padding the fund for America's legal retirees" (p. 39). Why do you think Thorpe chooses to mention this fact? How did you react to this statement?

4. Discuss the differences between "Chicanos" and *"mexicanos"* at Theodore Roosevelt High School. Were you surprised to learn that there are divisions within the Latino community? Where do the girls fit in? What tensions does this division cause?

5. The author does not shy away from the tough issues that her husband, John Hickenlooper, faced during her writing of *Just Like Us*. Why do you think she chose to make mention of his difficulties? Do you think he ever made questionable decisions related to immigration? How about other business owners who employ the students and their family members?

6. The girls bond over their common struggles. However, when Yadira, Clara, and Elissa obtain financial aid, they avoid telling Marisela. Yadira comments, "Now I've got money, and she

doesn't, and I'm almost sure I'm going to make it—and that built a wall right there" (p. 63). Do you think that the girls were destined to have these conflicts because of their difference in status? How is the financial aid experience a metaphor for the struggles that immigrants without legal status continue to experience?

7. How does the dance showcase at Theodore Roosevelt parallel Yadira and Marisela's relationship? How does it speak to the lives they lead in contrast to the lives they want?

8. How does the shooting of Denver police officer Donnie Young cast an unfavorable spotlight on the immigrant community? How did the events surrounding the investigation of his death affect the girls? The author? Were you surprised to learn about Donnie Young's heritage and fluency in Spanish? How did that affect your understanding of what happened inside Salon Ocampo?

9. Irene Chávez speculates that race caused conflict for the girls in college. Do you believe her assessment that Yadira and Clara were trying to fit in with white students? How does their friendship with Luke exacerbate the problem? Why do they hide certain things from him? Is the conflict really that Yadira and Clara are trying to assimilate while Marisela cannot (p. 134)?

10. Do you agree with the author when she theorizes that opportunities for immigrants were "curtailed by their lack of documents—their inability to obtain legal status perpetually threatened to stunt their potential" (p. 149)? Do you think Marisela and Yadira rise to these challenges? *Just Like Us* was originally published in 2009. Discuss how the political climate surrounding immigration has changed. If the girls were applying to college in the present day, do you think they would have had a different experience?

11. In the introduction the author writes, "immigration is . . . inherently messy. The issue bleeds. And we are all implicated" (p. 2). Do you agree? After reading *Just Like Us,* what steps do you believe still need to be taken?

12. It is obvious that the author comes from a much different background from the girls she writes about. At the conclusion of the book Thorpe comments that she was looking at Marisela from "across this cultural gulf" (p. 379). Is Thorpe's comment one of disappointment or acceptance? Will that gulf ever close?

13. *Just Like Us* begs the question, What makes us an American? Is the answer any more clear to you after reading the book? What do you think makes someone "American"?

ENHANCE YOUR BOOK CLUB

1. Readers are first introduced to Marisela, Yadira, Elissa, and Clara on the eve of their senior prom. Have everyone in your book group share a story from their own experience at prom. Compare your prom memories and experiences to what prom was like for the girls in *Just Like Us*.

2. Trace your family origins: Where do you come from? Who were some of your ancestors? When did your family arrive in the United States? Share your ancestry findings with members in your book club.

3. Illegal immigration was the political hot topic during the course of *Just Like Us* and continues to be headline news. Go online and research current events relating to the ongoing immigration debate. Bring an interesting discovery or related news article to share with your group.

ABOUT THE AUTHOR

Helen Thorpe was born in London, England, in 1965. One year later, her family immigrated to the United States. She now lives in Denver, Colorado, with her husband and son. Her magazine work has appeared in *The New York Times Magazine*, *The New Yorker*, *New York* magazine, and *Texas Monthly*. This is her first book.